to all clients net on or before

Marketing
in a
Multicultural
World

To my parents, Dave and Teddy,
who taught me what it means to be a part of,
and apart from,
an ethnic group.
JAC

To my parents, Alan and Sherlene,
who loved me enough to let me establish my identity
in another culture, on another continent.
GJB

Marketing in a Multicultural World

Ethnicity, Nationalism, and Cultural Identity

Janeen Arnold Costa
Gary J. Bamossy
Editors

SAGE Publications
International Educational and Professional Publisher
Thousand Oaks London New Delhi

For information address:

SAGE Publications, Inc.
2455 Teller Road
Thousand Oaks, California 91320

SAGE Publications Ltd.
6 Bonhill Street
London EC2A 4PU
United Kingdom

SAGE Publications India Pvt. Ltd.
M-32 Market
Greater Kailash I
New Delhi 110 048 India

Printed in the United States of America

Library of Congress Cataloging-in-Publication Data

Main entry under title:

Marketing in a multicultural world : Ethnicity, nationalism, and
    cultural identity / edited by Janeen Arnold Costa, Gary J. Bamossy
        p. cm.
    Includes bibliographical references and index.
    ISBN 0-8039-5327-5 (acid-free paper). — ISBN 0-8039-5328-3 (pbk.:
    acid-free paper)
    1. Marketing—Social aspects. 2. Communication in marketing—
Social aspects. 3. Intercultural communication. 4. Consumer
behavior—Cross-cultural studies. 5. Ethnicity—Cross-cultural
studies. I. Costa, Janeen Arnold. II. Bamossy, Gary J., 1949-
HF5415.122.M424   1995
658.8'348—dc20   95-3036

This book is printed on acid-free paper.

95 96 97 98 99 10 9 8 7 6 5 4 3 2 1

Production Editor: Tricia K. Bennett   Typesetter: Christina Hill

Contents

Part II: Case Studies and Applications

Preface

The general objective of this book is to explore cultural identity and its impact on various aspects of marketing. Although some research has been conducted in this area, it has not been extensive, and the global trends in ethnicity, nationalism, and other expressions of cultural identity make it a particularly important topic at this point in time.

Two dramatic and opposing forces are at work in the world today. On the one hand, sophisticated and complex communication and transportation systems move us toward a homogenized existence and identity. Evolving political, economic, and social interdependencies on a global scale enhance this trend toward similarity and uniculturalism. As a powerful countertendency to this homogenization process, however, self- or group identity on the basis of cultural background is on the rise, expressed as ethnicity, nationalism, or supranationalism, for example. World media report daily on issues relating to this resurgence in cultural identity, sometimes manifest in violent and poignant forms. *Tribalism* and *ethnic cleansing* are familiar terms; bloodshed in the name of cultural identity and fervor has occurred in the former Yugoslavia,

Haiti, Somalia, Rwanda, and elsewhere. Other global developments that make this subject particularly relevant at this time include:

- The development of the triad trading blocs in Europe, Asia, and North America, perhaps as a prelude to a rise in nationalism
- The loosening of political and economic constraints on ethnic groups in Central and Eastern Europe and the former Soviet Union
- The liberalization of the flow of labor and the increase of human movements throughout Europe and in other parts of the world, leading to increased ethnic tensions
- The growing size of ethnic groups by virtue of their elevated birth rates relative to "dominant" populations in various countries
- The rise of cultural borders and barriers within the European Union, even as the economic borders begin to fall

Within the academic discipline of marketing, all international marketing texts and even some of the introductory principles texts devote a chapter to stressing the importance of understanding the cultural dimension to marketing. Despite this acknowledgment, the body of knowledge in the discipline does not seem to have favored culture as a focus of research efforts. This is in part because of the elusive nature of culture itself. There is in every culture a tacit dimension, a set of beliefs that are subconscious because the members of that culture take these so for granted that they fall below the threshold of awareness. Because of the methods and approaches adopted by marketers in their research, assessing the underlying, seemingly invisible influence of culture has been difficult.

Borrowing first and most heavily from economics, marketers used concepts and methods to study transactions—how people used money in a rational, decision-oriented framework. Developing taxonomies, describing institutional frameworks, and working with aggregated data, investigators ignored a dimension that is at the heart of all enterprises and that makes all economic activity possible: human relationships. Seldom did early research try to investigate why people did things the way they did, what their motives might be, or what meanings could be given regarding behaviors, relationships, and objects. As the field developed and academics in the marketing discipline became more dissatisfied with economic concepts that were value empty, other theories were applied and extended from different social science disciplines that did look at psychological and social aspects of consumption and marketing behaviors. Although this broadened and enriched the body of knowledge, much of the research produced followed a constructivist view of scientific knowledge, in which "the truth" is basically the result of cumulative confirmations of studies following a logical positivist paradigm and conventional methods. This perspective does not favor doing research in which culture is the main focus. Clearly specified relationships between independent and dependent variables are not easy to hypothesize and test when culture is the study's focus and when cultural dimensions are difficult to measure or even define in the first place.

The contributions in this book move the discipline in the direction of a more full and complete understanding of the cultural processes involved in marketing and consumer behavior. The authors break new ground, synthesizing materials, analyzing trends, assessing data, and defining and describing culture and cultural identity in its various manifestations. In the first part of the book, the topic of culture and cultural identity in marketing is laid out in all of its complexity, examined in five chapters. The second part of the book provides specific examples of the interactions among marketing, consumer behavior, and cultural identity.

The book is thus timely both from a scholarly perspective and in terms of the political, economic, and social realities that grip the world today. Although we cannot claim to solve the world's ethnic-based problems, we can shed some light on the more benign if still ardent expressions of cultural identity found in the context of marketing and consumer behavior.

Our research and editorial efforts in producing this book were supported by our colleagues at the Vrije Universiteit in Amsterdam, the Netherlands, and at the David Eccles School of Business, University of Utah. We also wish to express our appreciation to the authors whose dedication and efforts find expression here.

Janeen Arnold Costa
Gary J. Bamossy

PART I

General Issues of Cultural Identity and Marketing

1

Perspectives on Ethnicity, Nationalism, and Cultural Identity

JANEEN ARNOLD COSTA

GARY J. BAMOSSY

We live in confusing times. More than a hundred new countries have come into existence since the end of the two great ground wars and the cold war of the 20th century. Still, the proliferation of new nations is overshadowed by the emergence of a new world order in which the conventional barriers of nation-states become less meaningful under the weight of global economic forces. This new world order involves social, political, and economic processes intent on both building up and breaking down. On the one hand, the triad blocs of Asia, North America, and Europe are consolidating their global positions through strategic trade alliances. On the other, the collapse of Marxist ideology and Soviet imperialism and the increasing transnational nature of the global economy are fostering a borderless future in which the traditional sovereign powers of nations are fading as the century draws to a close.

While the triad bloc consolidates, hundreds of political subdivisions are forming regions, both large and small, that will cut across geographic boundaries and render countries less relevant as economic

3

units. Regions such as "Greater South China" (Taiwan, Hong Kong, and Guangzhou), "Mexamerica" (labor and consumers south of the Rio Grande combining with technology and capital from California, Texas, and the American Southwest), and "Eastcentraleurope" will all flourish and function beyond the confines of national borders (see Bergsten, 1993). Powerful forces will continue to shape these regional alliances: The continuation of huge income disparities among regions of the world, the aging of industrial regions with their attendant needs to import labor, and the continual democratic pressures for openness have already stimulated the largest migration of peoples since the Middle Ages. Tensions and conflicts arise out of these movements as nations continue to find ways to realize globalist economics and national politics.

As the new world order rapidly evolves, the process of breaking down and building up also has its impact on groups and individuals. The tremendous advances in global travel, communication, and media reach have led to suggestions that cultures are converging and that the globalizing of markets will create, or at least lead to, a common culture worldwide. Being able to listen to Walkmans while eating Big Macs in Prague, filling up on *döner kebap* in Berlin, and drinking Coca-Cola in Beijing may be evidence of increasingly "common" activities, but these observed commonalities in behavior remain superficial. However common or uniform these behaviors appear, there continue to be clear differences in what these behaviors *mean* to the individuals and groups of different cultures. The global resurgence in ethnic identity and pride suggests that as superficial aspects of behavior converge, people tend to cling more to their own sense of cultural identity. The chapters in this book embrace this "groups and individual" perspective, which, although not exhaustive, addresses the range of relevant behaviors within the context of marketing and ethnicity.

Part I of the book deals with general issues of cultural identity and marketing. In this chapter we begin with a consideration of the multiple manifestations of cultural identity in and through marketing, summarizing the relevant literature in marketing and the social sciences and providing a framework for discussions throughout the rest of the book. In Chapter 2, further developing the notion of multiple manifestations of culture, Venkatesh moves forward the ongoing debate in comparative cultural studies regarding the use of a single theoretical framework for studying different cultures (Arnould, 1989; Sherry, 1987). He proposes a new conceptual framework to study consumer behavior using the theoretical categories originating within a given culture. Chapter 3 explores national identity and ethnicity in light of their increased importance in the world today. Here, Bouchet looks at such topics as the emergence of lifestyles, supranational institutions, and world marketing with specific reference to identity in a unifying Europe. Chapter 4 examines globalization as a social and economic phenomenon that has a critical impact on culture and meaning. Using the tourism industry for illustrative purposes, Firat argues that culture in this context is maintained primarily through commodification and simulation. This marketization of cultural identity raises the income and the means to participate in the global market for those groups able to respond appropriately, while condemning cultures that do not market themselves well to cultural anonymity and eventual destruction. In Chapter 5, Roosens frames the topic of ethnicity as "a question of being." Setting out clear conceptual boundaries regarding cultural and ethnic identity, he elaborates on the various strategies that have developed and have been used by ethnic groups in Europe and North America to establish their place in dominant cultures and in economic systems.

Part II of the book is composed of case studies and applications. Chapters 6 and 7 focus on cultural identity and consumer behavior. Joy, Hui, Kim, and Laroche use an ethnographic approach to advance our understanding of the way in which the cultural organization of space and objects in the Italian Canadian home creates an atmosphere that both reflects the past and shapes the future in an ethnic context. Belk and Paun employ historical and cultural perspectives to describe the way in which internal and external ethnic identities affect current Romanian consumption patterns. They focus specifically on Romanian consumption behaviors that serve to separate Romanians from "lower social status" groups, on the one hand, and those that, conversely, are part of a process of emulation of foreigners, on the other hand.

In business, group cultural identity is emphasized as part of a political, social, and economic strategy, often in the context of minority status within a dominant society. Thus, entrepreneurs exploit the goods and services associated with their identity to succeed. Examples of such enterprises include Greek and Italian restaurants throughout the world, Chinese laundering services, and Jewish domination of midlevel distribution in the diamond industry. In Chapter 8, Caglar describes and analyzes the evolution of Turkish-Germans' success in establishing a niche in Berlin's fast-food market. This chapter offers a discourse on the many political, social, and economic meanings of *döner kebap* to Turkish-Germans and German nationals in Berlin and the Federal Republic of Germany.

Chapter 9 presents a case study of cross-border shopping in Northern Ireland, providing information both on retailing strategies and on consumer behaviors that express cultural identity as affected by changing border policies in this part of Europe. Wilson concludes that economic strategies may, in the long run, be more powerful and persistent than are ethnic identity processes in accounting for the observed behaviors. Chapter 10 focuses on issues of individual artistry versus ethnic group identity. Drawing on his research in India and Mexico, Basu explores the impact of individual identity on the marketing and consumption of traditional ethnic crafts. He argues that although the work of the individual artist is well-known, easily recognized, and a source of prestige to the artist within the craft-producing community itself, such individualism is antithetical to the marketing of ethnic identity to the external consumer. Thus, the individual identity of the artist must be suppressed for the purposes of selling the product to the consumer who resides outside the local community; this "external consumer" wishes to purchase an "ethnic product," rather than the signature work of a specific individual. In Chapter 11, we focus on marketing and tourism. Drawing on site visitations in numerous parts of the world, we consider the interaction of national culture and the marketing of cultural products in museum retail shops.

Literature Review

The social science literature of relevance to our concerns here is vast. We have chosen to focus on anthropological and sociological studies that deal explicitly with ethnicity as a phenomenon. The studies presented in the chapters of this book explore issues of group formation and of individual and group identification along ethnic lines. Nevertheless, the theoretical issues raised are relevant not only to the topic of ethnicity but also to the broader topics of cultural identity in such arenas as nationalism and supranational regionalism. Thus, it is appropriate to begin with a brief consideration of the definitions of ethnicity and nationalism.

Ethnicity is a concept of individual and group identity that "embraces differences identified by color, language, religion, or some other attribute of common origin" (Horowitz, 1985, p. 41). Although this definition may seem overly broad, our intent in citing it is to allow sufficient definitional room to encompass those many manifestations and variations of ethnicity and other forms of cultural identity that are, in fact, found in the real world. Thus, individuals choose to identify themselves and are identified by others, either on an individual or group basis, according to one or more of these attributes of common origin.

Nationalism is a specific form of cultural identity that deserves further consideration here. Horowitz (1985) has maintained that the concept of ethnicity, as applied to various social and spatial dimensions, embraces "tribes," "races," "nationalities," and "castes" (p. 53). For many social theorists, then, nationalism is a form of group and ethnic identity, in which there is "a coincidence of . . . common culture and territory of residence" (Parsons, 1975, p. 53). According to Patterson (1977), for example, "nation-state" refers to a social entity that "is based on, and identified with, a single ethnic group" (p. 79). As such, nationalism is the expression of belonging to, or identification with, that single, politically and spatially bounded ethnic group. It is in this sense that nationalism is explored by contributors to this book.

Every decade since the 1960s has witnessed the publication of at least one major social scientific treatment of the subject of ethnicity, each proclaiming that ethnicity is "becoming" a topic of major concern. In the 1960s, Glazer and Moynihan (1963) discussed the American melting pot, and Barth's (1969) work on ethnic groups and boundaries was a key publication that gave a new perspective to much of the research on ethnic groups undertaken by anthropologists and sociologists. The 1970s witnessed the publication of Glazer and Moynihan's (1975) expanded study of ethnicity in America, as well as the exploration of ethnic identity in the individual and group by De Vos and Romanucci-Ross (1975) and Epstein (1978). Concern with ethnic tension brought about Horowitz's (1985) study, followed in the late 1980s by Roosens's (1989) work on ethnogenesis dealing with ethnicity as a political and economic strategy, and in the early 1990s by various treatments of ethnic influences in business, including *Tribes* (Kotkin, 1993) and *Ethnic Entrepreneurs* (Waldinger, Aldrich, Ward, & Associates, 1990). Yinger's (1994) treatment of ethnicity is the most recent seminal work in this area, summarizing developments in theory and in ethnic manifestations and concluding with a consideration of ethnicity both in terms of social strength and social conflict.

GLAZER AND MOYNIHAN:
ETHNICITY VERSUS ASSIMILATION

Glazer and Moynihan's (1963) early discussion of ethnic groups brought scholarly attention to the fact that unlike what had been popularly accepted as the likely course of social history, distinct cultural groups had *not* disappeared in the vast American metropolis of New York City. Rather, the groups had taken on new meaning, new vitality, and new identity:

> As the groups were transformed by influences in American society, stripped of their original attributes, they were recreated as something new, but still as identifiable groups. Concretely, persons think of themselves as members of that group, with that name; they are thought of by others as members of that group, with that name; and most significantly, they are linked to other members of the group by new attributes that the original immigrants would never have recognized as identifying their group, but which nevertheless serve to mark them off, by more than simply name and association, in the third generation and even beyond. (p. 13)

Thus, Glazer and Moynihan summarily demolished the concept of the American melting pot and transformed societal expectations. Assimilation, increasing homogenization, and uniformity would not be realized to the extent previously anticipated. Their research suggested, instead, that the American social landscape would be characterized by a growing, dynamic ethnicity and a mosaic of groups and individuals with distinct identities recognized by both themselves and others.

Glazer and Moynihan (1963) went on to suggest that this process, whereby virtual absorption of immigrant groups would not—could not—occur, perhaps was not merely a feature of American society but a result of *"the nature of human society in general"* (p. 14; italics added). The implication was that provincialism throughout the world would be challenged by the influx of foreigners, and an emphasis on separation, multiculturalism, ethnicity, even racism, would be a likely response. Thus, Glazer and Moynihan claimed that full integration or assimilation was not to be expected. We have seen in the 30 years since the publication of their 1963 work that it is, indeed, the *differences* among groups rather than the similarities that often govern both social interaction and personal identification.

BARTH: GROUP BOUNDARIES AND INTERACTIVE PROCESSES

Later in the 1960s, Fredrik Barth's (1969) book, *Ethnic Groups and Boundaries: The Social Organization of Culture Difference*, represented an important new development in ethnic studies. Barth claimed that ethnicity is best understood in the context of ethnic group boundary formation and maintenance, particularly in situations of social interactions between or among members of different groups. In emphasizing ethnicity as a process, Barth rejected the previously dominant view that groups were best understood as constellations of cultural traits. Instead, according to Barth, the cultural traits should be seen as a *result* of ethnic group formation and interaction with other groups and individuals, rather than as a list of cultural characteristics that *defined* and *isolated* the group from other groups in a complex society. This meant that our understanding of ethnicity would be enhanced by looking at situations in which groups or group members present themselves to, and interact with, other groups and the outside society. This approach is of particular relevance for our consideration, because it is often precisely at the point of *interaction* that ethnicity is expressed through marketing practices and in consumer behavior.

In considering the ethnicity of Greek Americans, for example, a traditional cultural trait approach would list the role of the Greek Orthodox church in community formation and a matrifocal family organization with strong indications of overt patriarchy as cultural characteristics. The use of the Greek language in specific contexts, obvious Greek overtones in ritual celebrations of Christmas and Easter, (the latter of which differs temporally from that of "American" Easter), the teaching of Greek dance to some members of the family, certain types of foods consumed during special occasions, and the tendency for Greek Americans to engage in small-scale entrepreneurship might all form part of this cultural trait list.

Although such a list would be interesting, it would fail to place due emphasis on the social *processes* that have contributed to the salience of these cultural traits. It would not, for example, provide adequate insight into the way in which Greek Americans *interact* with the larger society through their foods, which are made available through Greek restaurants, Greek ethnic festivals, and Greek celebrations open to non-Greeks and which serve as an identifying focal point for Greeks and non-Greeks alike. It would not describe the way in which young Greek women (and men) learn special Greek recipes that continue the tradition of ethnic identity regardless of their marriages to non-Greek individuals. It would not assess the impact of traditional notions of marriage and the importance of the family on shopping and consumption behaviors.

Although the cultural trait approach provides information about content, it does not describe process; it does not describe the way in which groups are formed and maintained. Of particular interest is the fact that the cultural trait approach does not adequately assess the functioning of ethnic groups in the marketplace, the way in which individuals ascribe to ethnic group membership through marketing or consumer behaviors, and the maintenance or crossing of group boundaries as groups and group members interact in specific contexts directly or indirectly related to marketing. Barth's approach emphasizing these interactive processes, rather than a cultural trait list perspective, is more appropriate for the purposes of this book.

Barth's (1969) emphasis on the formation and persistence of ethnic boundaries through interaction rather than through isolation is coupled with his suggestion that ethnic-based forms of behavior increase in intensity and number in the face of constant interaction. In the last decades, it may well be that mass communication through global media has served to intensify interactions with out-groups and that personal communication using the fax, telephone, and computers allows for global networks that facilitate behaviors within the ethnic group. Thus, ethnic dichotomization, the distinctions between one's own group and those outside the group, may intensify as social contact with nongroup members expands. Reminiscent of Glazer and Moynihan's (1963) prediction, Barth's perspective also presaged the fact that in the 1990s, rather than confronting a world of growing homogenization, a blurring of ethnic boundaries, and a melting pot phenomenon, ethnic differences are becoming more visible, tangible, and important.

Another point of interest from Barth's (1969) work is emphasis on the use of assets in ethnic identity. Although self-ascription in an ethnic group "rests on criteria of origin and commitment," according to Barth, and therefore does not necessarily involve the use of specific assets, the actual *performance* of ethnic status "in many systems *does* require such assets" (p. 28; italics added). Thus, the use of assets in the marketplace, in production, distribution, or consumption, may be and often is affected by ethnic identity. When a Jewish entrepreneur chooses to engage in the wholesale level of the diamond trade, committing his time, energy, and resources—his assets—to this traditional Jewish enterprise, he may be enacting an ethnic status. When a Hispanic American refuses to use promotional coupons in the purchasing act because of the social stigma associated with coupon use, ethnic identity is affecting the use of his or her assets.

Finally, Barth (1969) explores the importance of ethnic interdependence. The interaction of ethnic groups is often positive: "The positive bond that connects several ethnic groups in an encompassing social system depends on the complementarity of the groups with respect to some of their characteristic cultural features. Such complementarity can give rise to interdependence or symbiosis" (p. 18). In marketing, for instance, when certain ethnic groups control the middle level of distribution of a given product and when other ethnic groups function primarily in retailing of the product, each group occupies a niche, often to the mutual benefit of both. Some suggest that this is the case with Muslim distribution and Senegalese retailing of gems in Sri Lanka, for example.

ISSUES OF THE 1970s:
EXPRESSING ETHNIC IDENTITY

We turn now to an expanded discussion of the role of identity in ethnicity. In a work appearing nearly 10 years after Barth's, Epstein (1978) correctly suggested that the process of ethnic identification *underlies* Barth's emphasis on group boundaries. Epstein claimed that it is this powerful sense of identity, the cognitive and affective nature of ethnicity, that makes it such a potent force in human behavior. Ethnic identification is important both to the individual, in which "a strong identification with the ethnic group becomes, as it were, an extension of the self" (pp. xiv-xv), and as a social identity perceived by others. Isaacs (1975) argued at approximately the same time that indeed the affective, emotional sense of identity is a critical aspect of ethnicity, drawing on the deepest human needs:

> An individual belongs to his basic group in the deepest and most literal sense that here he is not alone, which is what all but a very few human beings most fear to be. He is not only not alone, but here, as long as he chooses to remain in and of it, he cannot be denied or rejected. It is an identity he might want to abandon, but it is the identity that no one can take away from him. (p. 35)

This potent sense of ethnic identity is dramatically demonstrated by overseas Chinese, who are responsible for some 80% of the total foreign investments in mainland China. Speaking to a conference of overseas Chinese entrepreneurs in Hong Kong, Lee Kuan Yew, former prime minister of Singapore, identified a key rallying point of Chinese ethnic identity:

> After Tiananmen on June 4th, 1989, Japan and the West stopped their tourists and investors from going into China. During this critical period, ethnic Chinese from Hong Kong, Macau, and Taiwan seized the opportunity and increased their trade and investments, profiting from China's

increasingly free-market economy. After they succeeded, ethnic Chinese from South-East Asia joined in. Three years later, in 1992, the results startled the world. China's growth went up to 12% per annum. This has revived American, European and Japanese interest in China. ("China's Diaspora Turns Homeward," 1993, p. 65)

In the context of marketing and consumer behavior, the identification of self as belonging to an ethnic group can precipitate certain behaviors. For example, an individual consuming a cup of Turkish coffee with other Turkish immigrants is expressing ethnicity. When a retailing entrepreneur chooses a particular product assortment as representative of his or her cultural background, ethnic self-identification is coming into play. In the latter example, customers visiting such a shop ascribe ethnic identity to the entrepreneur on the basis of the product assortment. As such, the identification process takes place both within the individual and in the community, on the part of others reflecting on the marketing practices of the individual.

Epstein (1978) went on to say that the "various facets and dimensions" of ethnic identity remain largely unexplored and that we must pursue "such questions as how the sense of collective identity is generated, transmitted, and perpetuated; how new social identities come to be formed and their interaction with pre-existing ones; and the circumstances in which established identities are abandoned or simply disappear" (p. 5). Epstein's questions about the generation, transmission, perpetuation, evolution, and disappearance of ethnic identities are relevant in the marketing context, in which business practices reflect and reinforce ethnic identity, as well as serve as agents of change in the ethnic process.

Ethnic identity is adaptive and is based on affiliations to the past as well as on adjustment to present circumstances. According to Epstein (1978), "Identity formation, then, is intimately bound up with the social context within which the person grows up and matures" (p. 144). But as political, economic, or social situations change, the identifying attributes of ethnicity also change. This "capacity to redefine the new situation in terms of established meanings and values" (p. 144) is a characteristic of the ethnic identification process, maintaining the continuity of ethnic identity itself, although the specific content of that identification varies. Horowitz (1975) pointed out that ethnic groups themselves do not remain static in terms of size, composition, and affiliation; he referred to "processes of ethnic fusion and fission" (p. 117), countervailing forces of assimilation and differentiation, which continually define and redefine ethnic identity and group boundaries.

De Vos and Romanucci-Ross (1975) suggested that as an identification process, ethnicity differs from citizenship or "professional, occupational, or class loyalties" (p. 364). Focusing on ethnicity as a symbolic activity, they indicated that language, customs, representations of the past, religious beliefs, a sense of common origin, rules of comportment, behaviors that contrast with those of outsiders, a sense of inclusion and exclusion, levels and modes of belonging, leadership, and tension in identity are all issues in the process of ethnic identity. In 1979, Gans similarly emphasized symbolism in identity and provided concrete examples of American consumption activities related to food choice and trends in the media and entertainment, which he interpreted as expressions of ethnicity.

De Vos and Romanucci-Ross (1975) concluded their book with a discussion of "instrumental and expressive uses of ethnicity" (p. 378). The instrumental concern of achievement may be seen in "the exclusion-inclusion process in trades and professions" along ethnic lines, for example. Competition and cooperation, forms of the instrumental concern of mutuality, are also affected by ethnicity, whereby, for example, "competitive activity may be de-emphasized within the group at the same time that competition with individuals outside the group is encouraged" (p. 384). The expressive use of ethnicity in harmony or its antithesis, discord, can also be manifest in business- and consumer-related activities. The refusal to patronize businesses run by members of a particular ethnic group is an example. Nurturance, another expressive use of ethnicity, may be practiced within an ethnic group or may become part of the identity of an ethnic group within the society at large, as in the case of American Jewry pioneering practices in professional welfare agencies in the United States. Clearly, De Vos and Romanucci-Ross's analyses are applicable to the context of marketing and business in general.

ETHNICITY: CONFLICT, INTEREST, AND POWER

Presaging important treatments characteristic of the 1980s and early 1990s, Glazer and Moynihan published their second book in 1975, in which they expanded on their earlier suggestion that ethnicity rather than assimilation and integration would come to dominate social history. In this important edited work, Glazer and Moynihan concentrated on ethnicity as a strategy and process; their attention turned to conflict, power, and interest (see also Bell, 1975). Assessing the societal landscape of the 1970s, they suggested that focus on conflict and strategy had to do with two social conditions. First, ethnicity could be used effectively to make political and economic claims on the modern state system, a point that later would be expanded on cogently by Roosens (1989). Second, Glazer and Moynihan argued, ranking and stratification—in a word, inequality—characterized human social structure throughout much of the world. They claimed that socially established values and a condition of differences in norms from one ethnic group to the next, as well as differential access to resources, generated conflict.

A concern with conflict and the politicization of ethnicity characterized approaches to ethnicity in the 1980s and early 1990s in general. This is attributable both to the continuing flare-ups of ethnic conflicts throughout the world and to the overt political machinations of ethnic groups within the United States. Horowitz (1985) suggested that "ethnicity is at the center of politics in country after country, a potent source of challenges to the cohesion of states and of international tension. . . . Ethnicity has fought and bled and burned its way into public and scholarly consciousness" (p. xi). Yinger (1994), claiming that we now live in the "ethnic era" (p. viii), is concerned with the need to balance the potent social force of ethnicity with humane interests; the failure to attain balance has resulted in ethnic conflicts in Bosnia, Somalia, South Africa, India, the European Community, and the United States—indeed, throughout the world.

Both Patterson (1977) and Horowitz (1985) focused on the power of economic interests as they influence ethnic identity and activity. According to Patterson (1977), economic interests presuppose ethnicity, and ethnicity is enacted only when it provides economic advantage, essentially:

> The primacy of economic factors over all others has been demonstrated . . . people never make economic decisions on the basis of ethnic allegiance, but on the contrary, . . . the strength, scope, viability, and bases of ethnic identity are determined by and are used to serve the economic and general class interests of individuals. (p. 145)

Horowitz (1985) suggested that this interaction of economic interests and ethnicity takes place throughout the economic processes of production, distribution, and consumption. The use of resources in an ethnic context could increase interethnic conflict, however. This is the case both when "employers use the labor of one ethnic group to undercut the price of labor of another group" (p. 106) and when ethnic groups control parts of the channel, using ethnic-based resources to exercise such control:

Conflict occurs, not merely because of ordinary business rivalries, but because immigrant minorities are able to undercut their rivals by the use of their own credit institutions, their guild techniques of restraining competition among themselves, and their use of cheap, usually family, labor. Their interests also collide with the interests of those with whom they transact business: consumers, tenants, clients. Finally, because trading minorities have the ability to obtain their own cheap labor, they depress the prospects for labor in the host society. . . . Eventually, workers in host society firms come to identify immigrant businesses and the low wages they pay as the source of the low wages paid in the economy generally. (p. 107)

ETHNICITY AND BUSINESS

Clearly, many societies are characterized by ethnic specialization in various economic sectors and in occupations within sectors (Horowitz, 1985). Recruitment of ethnic group members into particular economic specializations has often been accompanied by or resulted in ethnic stereotyping characterizing a particular ethnic group as composed of individuals with characteristics uniquely suited to the sector in which the specialization occurs. So, for example,

in Guyana and Trinidad, Indians had the right combination of thrift, industriousness, and docility for field work at low wages. . . . In Bombay textile mills, Pathans and Punjabis were most suitable for heavy labor, Sikhs were the most outstanding artisans, and Muslims were the most accomplished weavers. These assessments of special ethnic aptitudes have survived. (Horowitz, 1985, p. 110)

It is also the case that policies and practices related to "credit, savings, land tenure, education, and bureaucratic recruitment" reinforce ethnic occupational or sectorial concentration (Horowitz, 1985, p. 110). The latter phenomenon, involving bureaucratic recruitment, has resulted in ethnic control of various parts of the civil service in many countries; examples include the Tamils in Sri Lanka and the Chinese and Indians in Malaysia.

Glazer and Moynihan (1963) realized early on that ethnicity would influence business practices. For example, they described ethnic hiring practices and ethnic control of the channel of distribution:

The network of Jewish businesses meant jobs for Jewish young men and women. . . . In addition, the small businessman had patronage—for salesmen, truck drivers, other businessmen. In most cases the patronage stayed within the ethnic group. The Chinese restaurant uses Chinese laundries, gets its provisions from Chinese food suppliers, provides orders for Chinese noodle makers. The Jewish store owner gives a break to his relative. (p. 31)

Glazer and Moynihan (1963) also recognized the propensity for ethnic groups to concentrate control within certain businesses, which varied from one ethnic group to another. So, in New York City in the 1960s, Glazer and Moynihan found that Black Americans (then referred to as Negroes) had "beauty parlors, barber shops, the preparation of special cosmetics, and undertaking parlors" (p. 32). The Jewish population in that same time and space was prominent in real estate development and in education and continued to have numerous workers in the garment industry, painting, and carpentry and as waiters, barbers, and taxi drivers. Jewish entrepreneurial activity was evident in Jewish neighborhoods, as well as in the diamond and jewelry sectors of the city. The Italian focus on small business in the 1930s in the form of "many thousands of stores, restaurants, wholesale food concerns, produce-handling firms, small contracting businesses, trucking and moving concerns . . . clothes manufacturing factories, and the like" (p. 206) had given way by the 1960s to a diffusion of the working force in a pattern whose outlines and eventual outcome were as yet unclear, according to Glazer and Moynihan.

Many ethnic group members start their careers as immigrants, arriving as strangers in a new country, and in time develop an entrepreneurial niche in the market. Boissevain et al. (1990) suggested that ethnic entrepreneurs use ethnic resources as their approach to resolving business problems and that these outsider strategies and resources distinguish ethnic entrepreneurs from mainstream entrepreneurs (see also Wilken, 1979). Furthermore, they argued that the employment of these resources is highly similar across disparate ethnic groups in diverse national settings. The ethnic resources go beyond whatever wealth and human capital the ethnic entrepreneurs may bring to the market, and these resources characterize a *group*, not just isolated members: "Typical ethnic resources include *predisposing factors*—cultural endowments, relative work satisfaction arising from nonacculturation to prevailing labor standards, and a sojourning orientation—and modes of *resource mobilization*—ethnic social networks and access to a pool of under-employed co-ethnic labor" (Boissevain et al., 1990, p. 132).

Ethnic business strategies can be characterized as conscious and centralized at the level of the individual owner in the sense that the strategies reflect the effective disposition of each ethnic group's social, cultural, and economic resources. Ethnic strategies, however, are also collective in two other senses:

> First, ethnic trade associations are sometimes in a position to channel ethnic commerce in one direction rather than another. This direct influence can affect how ethnic minorities perceive niches and then open them for their own commercial exploitation. Second, because the resources most available to individual entrepreneurs are those common to the whole ethnic group, individual entrepreneurs independently adopt similar strategies. . . . Although no coordinated master plan exists, parallel decisions of the ethnic entrepreneurs push the ethnic group into selected niches. In this sense, a collective ethnic strategy develops without conscious, centralized coordination as long as ethnic entrepreneurs have access to sociocultural resources that are different from those of the mainstream entrepreneurs. (Boissevain et al., 1990, p. 133)

In sum, sociological and anthropological theorists have produced a plethora of studies and approaches to the subject of ethnicity/cultural identity and its various manifestations. They have addressed the issues of absorption versus differentiation, the formation and maintenance of group boundaries, the symbolic and affective aspects of individual and group identity, the political and economic strategies involved in ethnicity, and the social cohesion and conflict that characterize the social climate of the world today. In the following section we assess the marketing and consumer behavior literature as it relates to cross-cultural studies. Compared with the wealth of theory, analysis, and empirical work in the other social sciences, we find that the marketing and consumer behavior discipline is sorely lacking. Furthermore, the few cultural analyses that have taken place typically suffer from a narrow perspective that places the researcher's own culture at the center of any endeavor, comparative or otherwise. To enrich their intellectual treatment of ethnicity, nationalism, and cultural identity as they affect marketing and consumer behavior, we suggest that marketing scholars draw to a much greater extent on the extant literature of the other social sciences.

The Evolving Literature in
Cross-Cultural Consumer Research

Within the marketing discipline, publications of empirical studies examining cross-cultural consumer research first emerged in the 1970s, most often with studies that extended themes of interest to U.S. researchers by replicating those studies abroad. Given the growing interest in international marketing, these studies were a logical extension to the literature. These studies were also a natural extension of the heretofore dominant research paradigm within consumer behavior (i.e., logical positivism). Extending theories borrowed from other social sciences (primarily psychology and sociology) by testing them in "market" settings, consumer behavior studies were implicitly or explicitly comparative studies, examining differences between experimental and control groups, differing social classes, heavy versus light users, and so forth. The unique aspect of the cross-cultural studies that examined such topics as working and nonworking wives (Douglas, 1976), innovators versus noninnovators (Green & Langeard, 1975), different types of information seekers (Anderson & Engledow, 1977), and differing lifestyles (Plummer, 1977) was that these studies compared U.S. data with those of other cultural settings.

Early marketing studies that examined subgroups often used the conceptual category of *subculture* as an independent variable and typically were comparative studies between the mainstream White market and the growing Black market in America (Akers, 1968; Bauer & Cunningham, 1970). Subsequent published studies that examined how Blacks or Hispanics responded to differing marketing tactics regarding elements of the marketing mix were almost exclusively empirical and made use of survey data (Choudbury & Schmid, 1974; Gould, Sigband, & Zoerner, 1970; Krugman, 1966; Muse, 1971; O'Guinn & Meyer, 1984). In these studies, the focus was generally to examine these subcultural groups concerning their potential as new market segments in the U.S. market. As such, the basic criteria for assessing market segments, such as measurability, substantiality (segment size or growth potential), accessibility, and variation in response to marketing efforts, often determined the direction of the study and the type of knowledge generated.

Marketing studies that deal with ethnicity as a complex social structure wherein the distinct ethnic values of a group are linked to consumer behavior have appeared only recently. Here again, the majority of the studies involve ethnic groups living in developed country markets and often deal with processes of consumer acculturation (Albonetti & Dominguez, 1989; Delener & Neelankavil, 1990; Desphande, Hoyer, & Donthu, 1986; Hirschman, 1981, 1983; Imperia, O'Guinn, & MacAdams, 1985; O'Guinn & Faber, 1985; Penaloza, 1989, 1994; Saegert & Hoover, 1985; Tan & McCullough, 1985; Valencia, 1985; Wallendorf & Reilly, 1983).

Within the stream of cross-cultural consumer behavior literature, studies vary in the theoretical and management issues that they address, in their assumptions about universality, in the approaches used to deal with similarities and differences, and therefore in the methodological problems that they must confront. The social science literature has produced a number of useful publications addressing theoretical and methodological issues in cross-cultural research (Berry, 1969, 1980; Irvine & Carroll, 1980; Stanfield & Dennis, 1993; Strauss, 1969; Triandis, 1972; Triandis, Malpass, & Davidson, 1973), as well as analysis of the cross-cultural consumer behavior literature in the past two decades (Boddewyn, 1981; Douglas, Morrin, & Craig, 1994; Green & White, 1976; van Raaij, 1978; see also Chapter 2 by Venkatesh in this volume).

In spite of the instructional value that these publications offer with respect to negotiating the theoretical issues and methodological problems that are encountered in conducting cross-cultural research, much of the cross-cultural marketing and consumer behavior literature published to date can be characterized as *parochial* or *ethnocentric* and (still) methodologically flawed. In part, this is because of the nature of the dominant scientific paradigm followed in marketing and in consumer behavior. Stanfield (1994) has suggested that when it comes to critiquing the knowledge contents of social science disciplines, there are two levels of analysis. The first of these is the paradigmatic critique, which is an attempt to critique and perhaps revise the "cognitive map" of a particular discipline or clusters of disciplines. The second level of analysis is the knowledge production critique, which involves examination of formal epistemologies, theories, methods, data interpretation styles, and patterns of knowledge dissemination. Within the cross-cultural consumer behavior literature, the "instructional" publications most often cited that address issues of theory and methodology tend to focus on topics that are central to the logical-positivist paradigm. Issues such as sampling and construct equivalence are presented in detail to allow researchers some degree of confidence regarding their use of cross-cultural measures and testing of hypotheses. (See Durvasula, Andrews, Lysonski, & Netemeyer, 1993, for an excellent example of assessing constructs for cross-cultural equivalency.) In surveying what "passes for knowledge" in the field of cross-cultural consumer research, the methodology of the research is not particularly problematic (although flaws sometimes remain undetected in the review process). Rather, the difficulty lies with the underlying assumptions of the research, which often are uninformed, and the weak a priori or inappropriately applied conceptual frameworks, which go unchallenged. Within the marketing discipline, literature, training, and paradigms focus to a much lesser degree on learning to assess what is, in fact, culturally relevant outside the researcher's own culture. As a result, much of the literature tends to be parochial and/or ethnocentric in its perspective.

Parochial studies are research efforts that are originally designed and conducted in one culture by researchers from that culture. By ignoring other cultures, parochial studies tend to assume similarity across the world's industrialized countries. As such, the knowledge generated and presented has the implicit message that the results of the domestic study are universal. Very seldom is culture mentioned as a factor in domestic studies, either as a dependent or independent variable or as a limitation to the study's results. This type of research is constrained, in terms of both theory construction and practical applications. In the majority of marketing and consumer behavior studies published in North America and Europe, culture is implicitly considered to be a constant, and the interpretation and discussion of the studies' results tend to reflect the dominant norms, values, and processes of the researchers' origin.

Avoiding the parochial research perspective of those assuming universality are ethnocentric research publications, which question the universality of the results and the universality of theories in a particular but nevertheless problematic way. Here, researchers are interested in asking whether a theory or construct is culturally dependent or universal. The goals underlying this type of research are to test theories relevant to their own culture in other cultures to expand the power of the theory, search for similarities and differences across cultural conditions, and extend the range of independent variables and their effects on the dependent variables of interest. Although these studies take specific efforts to avoid the constraints inherent in parochial research, they open themselves to new challenges and problems.

Quite often these studies have a pseudoetic perspective (Douglas et al., 1994; Triandis, 1972), which focuses on the values that are characteristic of (usually) industrialized and North American values. Here, researchers tend to choose topics and measures that have been studied, operationalized, and validated in one country and to replicate the study in another cultural context. Replication has its own methodological issues (Douglas et al., 1994; van Raaij, 1978), but the main difficulty with these studies is the presumption often made regarding the relevance or centrality of the construct or theory in another cultural context (see Venkatesh's discussion in Chapter 2 of this volume). Frequently, researchers look at behaviors of individuals and decision-making processes that reflect the norms and values of the researchers' culture instead of attempting to understand these values and processes in the context of the societal framework or cultural system in which the data are being gathered. (See Lynn, Zinkhan, & Harris, 1993, for an example of the ethnocentric application of theory that attempts to explain tipping behavior cross-culturally.) This ethnocentric perspective has implications for the interpretation of findings as well. Similar findings are most often interpreted as confirmation that the theory being tested is, in fact, universal and that the research results are not culturally dependent. A more appropriate conclusion would be either that the particular results are not *solely* dependent on cultural factors in the first culture or that the results appear to be applicable to the second culture. It is too simplistic to conclude that statistically nonsignificant differences in data between two cultures is evidence of similarity.

Finally, ethnocentric research tends to have a pejorative flavor in two respects: First, the superiority of the home country or culture over the other country or culture is often implicitly communicated in the reporting of results (i.e., higher scale values in the home country compared to the other country on measures such as "satisfaction," "efficiency," or "innovativeness"). Second, it is assumed that important learning will come from extending home country research to another culture; seldom is it acknowledged that a reverse flow of knowledge through learning *from* the other culture can occur.

Beginning with theories and methods primarily from psychology and sociology, cross-cultural consumer research has made a number of advances in the past two decades. Recent publications appearing in the literature that employ ethnographic perspectives have also greatly enhanced our understanding of the need to become more critically thoughtful before imposing theoretical frameworks and constructs from one culture on another. Developing a body of literature that is based in informed theory and using culturally appropriate categories for data collection, analysis, and interpretations will move the discipline toward truly *comparative* research programs that are designed to identify an emergent universality.

In contrast to ethnocentric perspectives in which one culture's "universal" theories are imposed on another culture, comparative studies develop evidence of universality through attempting to define patterns of behaviors that emerge from all cultures studied. Comparative studies search for both similarities and differences, labeling the emergent similarity (in all its diverse manifestations) as universality and the emergent differences as cultural specificity. An important and potentially difficult mind shift for Western and North American researchers who are exposed almost exclusively to English-language publications is to recognize that in comparative studies, one must be willing to assume that there is no dominant culture.

The recent call for a more general theory of cross-cultural consumer behavior research suggests that researchers must better explicate the constructs used, better relate them to one another, and address a wider range of phenomena in our models (Douglas et al., 1994). The next era of cross-cultural consumer research can meet these challenges in a variety of ways: At the most simple level, we can improve on our efforts in developing sampling frames and gathering data. Supranational granting agencies responsible for gathering data for policy-making bodies and commercial research and advertising agencies with clients serving global or multicultural markets avoid the use of small, convenience samples that are typically found in academic research. Cooperation through these channels will enhance the quality of data, regardless of whether the methods are surveys or ethnographic case studies. A much more formidable challenge is to become more exposed to and accepting of other cultures to reduce the likelihood of imposing an inappropriate framework on our topics of study in different cultures. Becoming comfortable with diverse and rigorous methods and applying them with a sensitivity and appreciation for other cultures will improve the quality of our knowledge and ultimately broaden our sense of what constitutes good scholarship.

References

Akers, F. C. (1968). Negro and White automobile buying behavior: New evidence. *Journal of Marketing Research, 5,* 283-290.

Albonetti, J. C., & Dominguez, L. V. (1989). Major influences on consumer goods marketers' decision to target to Hispanics. *Journal of Advertising Research, 29*(1), 9-21.

Anderson, R., & Engledow, J. (1977). A factor analytical comparison of U.S. and German information seekers. *Journal of Consumer Research, 3,* 185-196.

Arnould, E. J. (1989). Toward a broadened theory of preference formation and the diffusion of innovations: Cases from Zinder Province, Niger Republic. *Journal of Consumer Research, 16,* 239-267.

Barth, F. (Ed.). (1969). *Ethnic groups and boundaries: The social organization of culture difference.* Boston: Little, Brown.

Bauer, R. A., & Cunningham, S. M. (1970). The Negro market. *Journal of Advertising Research, 10*(2), 3-13.

Bell, D. (1975). Ethnicity and social change. In N. Glazer & D. P. Moynihan (Eds.), *Ethnicity: Theory and experience* (pp. 141-174). Cambridge, MA: Harvard University Press.

Bergsten, C. F. (1993, September 11). The rationale for a rosy view. *The Economist,* pp. 59-62.

Berry, J. W. (1969). On cross-cultural comparability. *International Journal of Psychology, 4,* 119-128.

Berry, J. W. (1980). Introduction to methodology. In H. C. Triandis & J. W. Berry (Eds.), *The handbook of cross-cultural psychology* (Vol. 2, pp. 1-29). Boston: Allyn & Bacon.

Boddewyn, J. J. (1981). Comparative marketing: The first 25 years. *Journal of International Business Studies, 12*(1), 61-79.

Boissevain, J., Blaschke, J., Grotenberg, H., Joseph, I., Light, I., Sway, M., Waldinger, R., & Werbner, P. (1990). Ethnic entrepreneurs and ethnic strategies. In R. Waldinger, H. Aldrich, R. Ward, & Associates (Eds.), *Ethnic entrepreneurs* (pp. 131-156). Newbury Park, CA: Sage.

China's diaspora turns homeward. (1993, November 27). *The Economist,* p. 65.

Choudbury, P. K., & Schmid, L. S. (1974). Black models in advertising to Blacks. *Journal of Advertising Research, 14*(3), 19-22.

Delener, N., & Neelankavil, J. P. (1990). Informational sources and media usage: A comparison between Asian and Hispanic subcultures. *Journal of Advertising Research, 30*(3), 45-52.

Desphande, R., Hoyer, W. D., & Donthu, N. (1986). The intensity of ethnic affiliation: A study of the sociology of Hispanic consumption. *Journal of Consumer Research, 13,* 214-220.

De Vos, G., & Romanucci-Ross, L. (Eds.). (1975). *Ethnic identity: Cultural continuities and change.* Palo Alto, CA: Mayfield.

Douglas, S. P. (1976). Cross-national comparisons and consumer stereotypes: A case study of working and non-working wives in the U.S. and France. *Journal of Consumer Research, 3,* 12-20.

Douglas, S. P., Morrin, M. A., & Craig, C. S. (1994). Cross-national consumer research traditions. In G. Laurent, G. Lillien, & B. Pras (Eds.), *Research traditions in marketing* (pp. 289-306). Boston: Kluwer Academic.

Durvasula, S., Andrews, J. C., Lysonski, S., & Netemeyer, R. G. (1993). Assessing the cross-national applicability in consumer behavior models: A model of attitude toward advertising in general. *Journal of Consumer Research, 19,* 626-636.

Epstein, A. L. (1978). *Ethos and identity.* Chicago: Aldine.

Gans, H. J. (1979). Symbolic ethnicity in America. *Ethnic and Racial Studies, 2*(1), 1-20.

Glazer, N., & Moynihan, D. P. (1963). *Beyond the melting pot.* Cambridge: MIT Press & Harvard University Press.

Glazer, N., & Moynihan, D. P. (Eds.). (1975). *Ethnicity: Theory and experience.* Cambridge, MA: Harvard University Press.

Gould, J. W., Sigband, N. B., & Zoerner, C. E. (1970). Black consumer reactions to integrated advertising: An exploratory study. *Journal of Marketing, 34,* 20-26.

Green, R. T., & Langeard, E. (1975). A cross-national comparison of consumer habits and innovator characteristics. *Journal of Marketing, 39,* 34-41.

Green, R. T., & White, P. D. (1976). Methodological considerations in cross-national consumer research. *Journal of International Business Studies, 7* (Fall-Winter), 81-87.

Hirschman, E. C. (1981). American Jewish ethnicity: Its relationship to some selected aspects of consumer behavior. *Journal of Marketing, 45,* 102-110.

Hirschman, E. C. (1983). Cognitive structure across consumer ethnic subcultures: A comparative analysis. In R. P. Bagozzi & A. M. Tybout (Eds.), *Advances in consumer research* (Vol. 10, pp. 197-202). Provo, UT: Association for Consumer Research.

Horowitz, D. L. (1975). Ethnic identity. In N. Glazer & D. P. Moynihan (Eds.), *Ethnicity: Theory and experience* (pp. 109-140). Cambridge, MA: Harvard University Press.

Horowitz, D. L. (1985). *Ethnic groups in conflict.* Berkeley: University of California Press.

Imperia, G., O'Guinn, T. C., & MacAdams, E. (1985). Family decision-making role perceptions among Mexican-American and Anglo wives: A cross-cultural comparison. In E. C. Hirschman & M. B. Holbrook (Eds.), *Advances in consumer research* (Vol. 12, pp. 71-74). Provo, UT: Association for Consumer Research.

Irvine, S. H., & Carroll, W. K. (1980). Testing and assessment across cultures: Issues in methodology and theory. In H. C. Triandis & J. W. Berry (Eds.), *The handbook of cross-cultural psychology* (Vol. 2, pp. 127-180). Boston: Allyn & Bacon.

Isaacs, H. R. (1975). Basic group identity: The idols of the tribe. In N. Glazer & D. P. Moynihan (Eds.), *Ethnicity: Theory and experience* (pp. 29-52). Cambridge, MA: Harvard University Press. (Material expanded to book length in Isaacs, H. R. [1975]. *Idols of the tribe, group identity and political change.* New York: Harper & Row.)

Kotkin, J. (1993). *Tribes.* New York: Random House.

Krugman, H. E. (1966). White and Negro responses to package designs. *Journal of Marketing Research, 3,* 199-200.

Lynn, M., Zinkhan, G. M., & Harris, J. (1993). Consumer tipping: A cross-country study. *Journal of Consumer Research, 20,* 478-488.

Muse, W. V. (1971). Product related response to use of Black models in advertising. *Journal of Marketing Research, 8,* 107-109.

O'Guinn, T. C., & Faber, R. J. (1985). New perspectives on acculturation: The relationship of general and role specific acculturation with Hispanics' consumer attitudes. In E. C. Hirschman & M. B. Holbrook (Eds.), *Advances in consumer research* (Vol. 12, pp. 113-117). Provo, UT: Association for Consumer Research.

O'Guinn, T. C., & Meyer, T. P. (1984). Segmenting the Hispanic market: The use of Spanish language radio. *Journal of Advertising Research, 23*(6), 9-15.

Parsons, T. (1975). Some theoretical considerations on the nature and trends of change of ethnicity. In N. Glazer & D. P. Moynihan (Eds.), *Ethnicity: Theory and experience* (pp. 53-83). Cambridge, MA: Harvard University Press.

Patterson, O. (1977). *Ethnic chauvinism: The reactionary impulse.* New York: Stein & Day.

Penaloza, L. N. (1989). Immigrant consumer acculturation. In T. K. Srull (Ed.), *Advances in consumer research* (Vol. 16, pp. 110-118). Provo, UT: Association for Consumer Research.

Penaloza, L. N. (1994). Atravesando fronteras/Border crossings: A critical ethnographic exploration of the consumer acculturation of Mexican immigrants. *Journal of Consumer Research, 21,* 32-54.

Plummer, J. (1977). Consumer focus in cross-national research. *Journal of Advertising, 6*(2), 5-15.

Roosens, E. (1989). *Creating ethnicity.* Newbury Park, CA: Sage.

Saegert, J., & Hoover, R. J. (1985). A catalog of hypotheses about Hispanic consumers. *Proceedings of the Division of Consumer Psychology, 23,* 56-61.

Sherry, J. (1987). Cultural propriety in the global market place. In A. F. Firat, N. Dholakia, & R. Bagozzi (Eds.), *Philosophical and radical thought in marketing* (pp. 179-192). Lexington, MA: D. C. Heath.

Stanfield, J. H., II. (1994). Ethnic modeling in qualitative research. In N. K. Denzin & Y. S. Lincoln (Eds.), *Handbook of qualitative research* (pp. 175-188). Thousand Oaks, CA: Sage.

Stanfield, J. H., II, & Dennis, R. M. (1993). *Race and ethnicity in research methods.* Newbury Park, CA: Sage.

Strauss, M. A. (1969). Phenomenal identity and conceptual equivalence of measurement in cross-national comparative research. *Journal of Marriage and the Family, 31,* 233-241.

Tan, C. T., & McCullough, J. (1985). Relating ethnic attitudes and consumption values in an Asian context. In E. C. Hirschman & M. B. Holbrook (Eds.), *Advances in consumer research* (Vol. 12, pp. 122-125). Provo, UT: Association for Consumer Research.

Triandis, H. C. (1972). *The analysis of subjective culture.* New York: John Wiley.

Triandis, H. C., Malpass, R. S., & Davidson, A. R. (1973). Psychology and culture. *Annual Review of Psychology, 23,* 355-378.

Valencia, H. (1985). Developing an index to measure "Hispanicness." In E. C. Hirschman & M. B. Holbrook (Eds.), *Advances in consumer research* (Vol. 12, pp. 118-121). Provo, UT: Association for Consumer Research.

van Raaij, F. W. (1978). Cross-cultural research methodology as a case of construct validity. In H. K. Hunt (Ed.), *Advances in consumer research* (Vol. 5, pp. 693-701). Ann Arbor, MI: Association for Consumer Research.

Waldinger, R., Aldrich, H., Ward, R., & Associates. (Eds.). (1990). *Ethnic entrepreneurs.* Newbury Park, CA: Sage.

Wallendorf, M., & Reilly, M. D. (1983). Distinguishing culture of origin from culture of residence. In R. P. Bagozzi & A. M. Tybout (Eds.), *Advances in consumer research* (Vol. 10, pp. 699-701). Provo, UT: Association for Consumer Research.

Wilken, P. (1979). *Entrepreneurship: A comparative historical study.* Norwood, NJ: Ablex.

Yinger, J. M. (1994). *Ethnicity: Source of strength? Source of conflict?* New York: State University of New York Press.

2

Ethnoconsumerism: A New Paradigm to Study Cultural and Cross-Cultural Consumer Behavior

ALLADI VENKATESH

In order to follow a baseball game one must understand what bat, hit, an inning, a left-fielder, a squeeze play, a hanging curve, and a tightened infield are.
Clifford Geertz (1983, p. 69)

What happens to understanding when empathy disappears?
Clifford Geertz (1983, p. 56)

The story about the death of positivism is highly exaggerated.
Anonymous

In a seminal work, Geertz (1983) raised the important issue of the "native's point of view."[1] As he himself admitted, this is not a new but a recurrent theme; it has, however, assumed certain epistemological significance in the postmodern and poststructuralist era.

AUTHOR'S NOTE: This research was supported by a Senior Fellowship Grant from the American Institute of Indian Studies.

The purpose of this chapter is to examine a new paradigm in consumer behavior that I have labeled *ethnoconsumerism,* which is a conceptual framework to study consumer behavior using the theoretical categories originating within a given culture. The motivation for this chapter is twofold. The primary reason is the ongoing argument in comparative cultural studies regarding the use of a single theoretical framework for studying different cultures. The second reason has its origin in certain insights or intuitions that I have gained during my own introspection about my role as a researcher (see the appendix in this chapter).

The general tendency in the social sciences has been to use the same theoretical categories across cultural settings, with supposedly appropriate modifications to suit the conditions of the particular cultural group being studied. Ethnoconsumerism is the study of consumption from the point of the cultural order in question, using the categories of behavior and thought that are native to the culture—*ethnos* means nation or people, and *consumerism* is used here in the classical sense of consumption as a set of cultural practices, as discussed in the works of cultural theorists and social historians to represent the tendencies of consumer orientation (as an example, see Campbell, 1987). *Consumerism* in this chapter is not to be mistaken for concepts such as consumer activism, consumer rights, and so forth.

This chapter is at the intersection of three areas: consumer behavior as a cultural phenomenon, ethnic studies, and comparative and cross-cultural research. I shall first give a brief introduction to ethnoconsumerism and follow this with a discussion of the three areas. The discussion will serve as a lead into a more elaborate development of ethnoconsumerism with illustrations in the second half of the chapter.

What Is Ethnoconsumerism?

Ethnoconsumerism is the study of consumption from the point of view of the social group or cultural group that is the subject of study. It examines behavior on the basis of the cultural realities of that group. Ethnoconsumerism follows the intellectual traditions of comparative methods and cross-cultural studies, but it differs from existing versions of comparative or cross-cultural studies in several ways. First, ethnoconsumerism is not a method, as the others tend to be, although cross-cultural comparisons can and must be made. Ethnoconsumerism begins with basic cultural categories of a given culture. It studies actions, practices, words, thoughts, language, institutions, and the interconnections between these categories. In general, cross-cultural comparisons are easier at the level of actions and become increasingly problematic at deeper levels of analysis. Seemingly similar practices across cultures may contain deep cultural meanings that differentiate cross-cultural practices in fundamental ways. Hence, one must carefully analyze cultural underpinnings of various events and actions. An example of this can be found in the following quote describing Geertz's Balinese cockfight:

> The intelligibility of any action requires reference to its larger context, a cultural world. So, to take a powerfully developed example, when Clifford Geertz describes the Balinese cockfight, a text analogue, he progressively incorporates other essential Balinese symbols, institutions, and practices that are necessary to an understanding of the seemingly localized cockfight. The Balinese cultural and social world is not incorporated into the cockfight, but must be brought into analysis in order to understand the event. . . . *The aim is not to uncover universals or laws but rather to explicate context and world.* (Rabinow & Sullivan, 1987, p. 14; italics added)

The idea of studying a culture from the point of view of the researched group is not new and generally is known as the emic perspective. There is a superficial resemblance between emic perspective and ethnoconsumerism, but they are not equivalent. *Emic* is a loose term that refers to the subject's point of view, is limited to strategies of data collection, and rarely leads into a discussion of any deeper interpretive issues. Ethnoconsumerism advocates not only the so-called native's point of view but goes deeper into the development of knowledge constructed from the culture's point of view. From a philosophy of science perspective, ethnoconsumerism is an example of an ethnoscience that views all social sciences as ethnosciences that lay no claim to the universality of social science. Before developing ethnoconsumerism in fuller detail, I will examine some related topics that provide the theoretical context to my later elaboration.

Consumerism as a Cultural Phenomenon

CONSUMERISM AS AN ETHNOCULTURAL PHENOMENON

After pursuing my cross-cultural fieldwork in different settings—India, Denmark, and the United States—and reading varied forms of cultural and textual material, I am left with no choice but to consider all consumer behaviors as primarily sociocultural phenomena that must, therefore, be discussed in sociocultural terms.[2] There is a confusion in our field (consumer behavior or, more generally, marketing) that results from observing behavior at the individual level and subsequently regarding the phenomenon itself as individualistic. The argument is less than convincing, because we, as researchers, are the ones who have chosen to study consumer behavior at the individual level. The behavior is not primarily individualistic simply because we have chosen to study it that way for epistemological convenience. There is ample evidence to show that all individual identities are derived from interaction within a sociocultural environment (Douglas & Isherwood, 1979; McCracken, 1988; Sahlins, 1976). In fact, quite often, when we describe consumer behavior, we use the cultural group, explicitly or implicitly, as the level of analysis—Americans, Californians, Indians, Hispanics, and so forth. The reason we do it is because only at that level does consumer behavior seem to make intuitive sense. Seldom are we interested in what Mr. Smith as a single American or Mrs. Singh as a single Indian does. We are more interested in what Americans or Indians collectively do. Of course, we collect data from many individual Smiths and Singhs, but our ultimate aim is to say something meaningful about the collectivities to which they belong. Individuals are products of their culture and their social groupings; therefore, they are conditioned by their sociocultural environment to act in certain manners (Douglas & Isherwood, 1979; McCracken, 1988). Only derivatively can their behavior be called psychological. I am not denying that psychology has something to say about individual behavior, but before psychology come culture, family, and group norms. Psychological approaches to consumer behavior are a curious blend of reductionism, mentalism, and naive empiricism.

In this chapter, culture includes various aspects of social life—from religion to everyday practices, from mundane to profound, from institutions to ideologies, from ideas to activities, and from social formations to meaning systems (McCracken, 1988; Williams, 1981). In fact, many aspects of cultural life have developed historically, either through internal evolution or by external imposition. Dealing with such varied topics requires a rich framework that can be obtained only by a deeper examination of the cultures in question and their practices, value systems, and behavioral norms as they relate to consumption.

The ability to understand consumer behavior in its many-sidedness has been hampered by academic specializations and the division of labor into subdisciplines such as psychology, sociology, and anthropology. These specializations have caused researchers to put on blinders, with psychologists appropriating the study of the human mind, soci-ologists the social order, and anthropologists the culture.

For the typical researcher, these distinctions have become rather cumbersome because reality is not partitioned that way, even though university departments are (Goody, 1993). As mentioned earlier, sev-eral cultural theorists adopt the view that individuals are products of their cultures and that as their cultures change, so do they. Similarly, the social institutions and their organizational philosophies reflect the cultural values and norms of a given culture. Consequently, a rea-sonable position to take is that culture is what defines a human com-munity, its individuals, and social organizations, along with other economic and political systems. Thus, the individual and the social are but part of their culture, and culture is the overall system within which other systems are organized. The modernist perspective regards cul-ture and economy as two separate spheres of activity (as is usually the approach taken in the traditional discourse on capitalism and Marx-ism), but this position is not tenable if culture is to be viewed realisti-cally, that is, as a more encompassing system. See Firat and Venkatesh (1994) for elaboration of this idea under modernism and postmod-ernism. Figure 2.1 contrasts the two views of culture, the modernist view and the proposed view.

CONSUMERISM AS A GLOBAL CULTURAL PHENOMENON

No culture stands still. There is no such thing as a pure culture except in the minds of people. By both definition and historical circumstance, cultural phenomena are subject to change. Cultures evolve constantly, because of either their own internal dynamics or external (global) influ-ences. About the only thing that can be said in regard to cultural change or constancy is that some cultures change more rapidly than other cul-tures, and some cultures may experience more rapid changes at some points in their history than at other times. History is full of examples of how cultures have changed because of external influences. The rise of Buddhism in China and Japan and other Eastern countries in ancient times and the spread of Christianity and Islam during the first millen-nium are good examples of how cultural changes were brought about globally. Similarly, the expansion of colonial regimes to Africa, Asia, and South America in more recent periods has had major cultural im-pact on local communities and nations. In the contemporary world, lo-cal cultures are changing quite rapidly because of the rising tide of consumerism. A new form of industrial and market culture is develop-

I. Premodern

No distinction between Culture and Economy. One implies the other.

II. Modern

Culture and Economy are separate

Economy is accorded a superior status because of its relevance to the creation of "productive" value

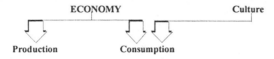

ECONOMY	Culture
Production	Consumption

III. Postmodern-postindustrial

New perspectives on the relationship between Culture and Economy

Culture subsumes Economy

CULTURE

Economy	Government	Ideology
Education	Family	
Institutions	Production	Consumption
Symbolic Systems		

Figure 2.1. Relationship Between Culture and Economy

ing in many parts of the world with the diffusion of information, communication, and transportation technologies.

The implications of global cultural diffusion are several. We need to understand the nature of the impact, the local resistances and adaptive strategies to external influences, and the modifications to externally imposed cultural phenomena by giving them a local coloring.

Ethnicity, Nature, and Scope

This book is about ethnicity and consumer behavior. Ethnicity is a catch-all collective term that has replaced several other identifiers—race, religion, language group, nationality, religion, and so forth—as a way to determine the social identity of groups, under the claim that although these different identifiers may be more precise and objective in their meaning, they may be inadequate in today's complex world. As a theoretical construct, ethnicity has acquired a central position in cultural studies in its ability to accord a separate status to people belonging to differentiated groups. It combines such elements as race, language group, and religion into schemes of identity formation. Accordingly, to cite Nash (1989), the "building blocks of ethnicity" (p. 5) are the body (a biological component expressed as blood and genes, commonly shared among group members), a language, a shared history and origins, religion, and nationality. Quite often, however, the term *ethnicity* is used euphemistically as a substitute for these identifiers. For example, it is not uncommon for a survey questionnaire to contain the question "What is your ethnic background?" and then to provide response categories that are simply a jumble of racial (White, Black) and religious (Jewish, Moslem) categories.

Barth (1969), in a systematic investigation of ethnicity, first suggested that ethnicity is not merely an agglomeration of other identifiers. To quote him, "the critical focus of investigation becomes the ethnic boundary and not the cultural stuff that it encloses" (p. 5). For Barth, the constitution of the ethnic boundary, the mechanics of boundary maintenance, and the mythohistorical rationale for the group formation are extremely important in ethnic identity and differentiation. Thus, some of the ethnic groups in the United States, for example, such as African Americans, Whites, Jews, and Hispanics, may each use different criteria for identity. The first two groups are racial in character, but Arabs and Iranians are not included among Whites, although racially they are closer to many Southern Europeans. The term *White* usually is applied to people of European ancestry and may connote that they follow the Christian religion. African Americans are identified by skin color as well as genes, no matter what their religion or nationality. As Eriksen (1993) pointed out:

> In the United States, . . . any individual who has the slightest phenotypical trace of African origin is classified as "black." So when a famous American professor in black history came to Trinidad in 1989 to give a lecture . . . the Trinidadian audience was startled to discover that the man was nearly white. (p. 83)

Thus, when discussion occurs within the context of a country such as Trinidad, it is the lightness or darkness of the skin and not the imputed African gene that makes up the ethnic category. Hispanics usually are identified on the basis of language (Spanish) and nationality (Mexicans and other Central and South Americans), unless they have European ancestry, in which case they are called Hispanic Whites. Jewish people sometimes are included among Whites, but they may be separated by their religion.

Such permutations make it more difficult to pin down the concept of ethnicity than in the case of the other terms, such as religion, nationality, and race. (I must hasten to add, however, that in this postmodern world, even such terms as race and nationality have become problematic. See Anderson, 1983/1991.) The question is, who defines ethnicity? According to Barth (1969) and many others (De Vos, 1975; Eriksen, 1993), the basis of ethnicity is self-identification of the members mediated by the perceptions of the others. There are two sets of principles that operate within ethnicity: the inclusionary-exclusionary principle and the difference-identity principle. By excluding, one establishes difference. By including, one establishes identity. Both are, therefore, closely related. The inclusionary-exclusionary principle states that a group tries to include only people who display preapproved characteristics and excludes the others. For example, to be called a White, the relevant characteristics are religion (Christian), skin color, and European extraction. The presumption here is that this group has a distinct value system and cultural patterns.

In recent years, the term *ethnicity* has evolved in prominence and significance over the other identifiers, which have yielded to ethnicity as a more powerful indicator of identity formation because it is both subjectively claimed and socially accorded. Globally, the ethnic phenomenon poses the most serious challenge to traditional views regarding nationalism, pluralism, and modernism. Ethnic boundaries have become contentious issues leading to political and power struggles. Ethnic groups that feel marginalized have become forces of resistance. For example, as Friedman (1990) pointed out, "Ethnic and cultural fragmentation and modernist homogenization are not two arguments, two opposing views of what is happening in the world today, but two constitutive trends of global reality" (p. 311). Tambiah (1989) took the question of ethnic boundaries one more step beyond Barth (1969) and suggested that ethnic boundaries have led to ethnic conflicts in many countries. Ethnicity seems to have the potential to generate a more comprehensive theoretical framework for the study of social distinction and social differentiation, although at the same time it unfortunately facilitates the division of the world, with insidious ease, into "us" versus "them."

Originally, ethnicity referred to as-yet unassimilated or unassimilable, relatively well-differentiated minority groups within a larger population. These groups were called *ethnics*, a noun form to describe the groups. The presumption was (and still is) that the term *ethnic* should not be applied to a group in its host cultural setting if such a setting does, indeed, exist. For example, Mexicans are considered an ethnic minority in the United States but by definition cannot be considered so in Mexico. Nevertheless, scrutinizing the language we use, we hear a different story. Many North Americans seem to view Mexicans ethnically (that is, as a subordinate cultural group), regardless of whether they are referring to Mexican immigrants in the United States or to citizens of Mexico. There is also the obverse and curious side to this logic: In no part of the non-White world are the Whites considered an ethnic group, even though they may be in a minority. *Ethnic* thus has come to mean people of secondary status in the eyes of a dominant global group. The term *ethnic* clearly originated with North Americans, Anglo-Saxons, and West Europeans, mainly to describe people of other cultures, frequently in inferior terms. For the most part, *ethnic* has come to mean an ideologically fashioned term to describe groups who are culturally and/or physically outside the dominant cultures of the day. Out of curiosity, I looked for the meaning of *ethnic* in *Webster's Third New International Dictionary* (1986). The first entry is, "of or relating to Gentiles or to nations not converted to Christianity," and one must read the third entry to find "having or originating from racial or linguistic groups" (p. 781). For my study, I prefer the prefix *ethno-* to the word *ethnic* because it seems less confusing if not less hegemonic. The only entry in the dictionary for the term *ethnos* is "of nation, people, caste, tribe" (p. 781). The choice is clear.

ETHNICITY AND CONSUMER BEHAVIOR

The burgeoning interest in the topic of ethnicity among consumer researchers in the United States demonstrates just how important this area of research has become. The increase in consumer research interest is partly a result of the changing ethnic landscape of the United States, especially in the states of California, Texas, Florida, and New York,[3] which have been affected by recent immigrants from Mexico, Latin America, and Asia. There is a heightened awareness that the recent immigrants are less likely to assimilate into the mainstream of American life to the extent most of their predecessors did; thus, these newcomers are more likely to retain their cultural identities. Consequently, the metaphor describing the American ethnic landscape as a melting pot is being supplanted by the "tossed salad" or "cultural mosaic" metaphors (Glazer & Moynihan, 1975; Hegeman, 1991). Ironically, just at the time when the ethnic tensions in the social sphere have become a cause for concern among mainstream political leaders, marketers—driven more by economic opportunities than by social realities—are eyeing ethnic populations as market segments. Thus, for the marketing practitioner, the consumption patterns of new immigrants are sufficiently different and their numbers are sufficiently large that they cannot be treated as marginal populations. Clearly, marketers are driven by profits and bottom lines, and their desire to understand the behaviors of ethnic groups certainly is not motivated by transcendental considerations. Consumer researchers, who play a critical role in the study of marketing dynamics, now are charged to show a genuine interest in understanding ethnic groups and their practices.

In the field of consumer behavior, ethnic research is not recent. The first wave of ethnic-oriented studies was reported in the literature in the mid-1960s to the late 1970s and focused primarily on Blacks. See Engel, Blackwell, and Kollat (1978) for a summary of these studies. The second wave of studies started appearing during the mid- to late 1980s, with the onset of increased growth in the Latin American and Asian immigrant populations in the United States and also as part of the general awareness of ethnic developments among consumer scholars. Coincidentally, fewer studies have been reported on Black consumers.

One of the first specific consumer-oriented studies involving ethnic populations was Hirschman's (1981) analysis of Jewish consumption patterns. Other examples include key studies on Hispanics by Penaloza (1994), Stayman and Deshpande (1989), and Zmud and Arce (1992). The latter two of these studies follow positivist approaches to consumer science by treating ethnicity as a social psychological-demographic construct. The aim of such studies is to establish a relationship between ethnicity as an independent variable and consumption as a dependent variable. Most discussion within these studies centers on the method of analysis, measurement of ethnicity as a construct, and its explanatory power as a concept. The problem of ethnicity as an existential condition and the problems of the ethnic groups and their coping strategies seldom are invoked because that is not the focus of these studies. The subject's point of view is not a major consideration in these and similar studies. The interpretive questions in these studies are necessarily limited because ethnicity is treated as a scientific construct leading to a reductionism of sorts, and ethnicity is regarded as just any other demographic variable, such as disposable income or household size.

Of course, there is merit to this type of research. For one thing, by making ethnicity an important variable, researchers emphasize that it has come of age. By making it a scientific, analytical unit, they say that it can be treated as a value-free construct. The problem with such treatment is that ethnicity becomes a faceless variable in research, and researchers make no attempt to provide an understanding of what it means to be a member of an ethnic group.

One of the few exceptions to a purely positivistic approach to the study of ethnicity in consumer research and one that broadens the mainstream ethnic research is the recent work of Penaloza (1994) on Hispanic immigrants. Penaloza's work, which began in the mid-1980s and is still continuing, is the result of more than 6 years of close observation and participation in Hispanic communities. She trained herself in the Spanish language and immersed herself in the culture of Hispanics—essentially a requirement if one wants to pursue studies of this type. Her understanding of the Hispanic culture allowed her to examine socialization and acculturation processes of this group, the trials and tribulations of this ethnic community, and the strategies of coping. Penaloza has demonstrated that ethnic reactions to mainstream culture are determined by strategies of both acceptance and resistance. Ethnic assimilation into the mainstream is both traumatic and cathartic, and the dynamics of this cannot be captured in a typical positivistic research mode.

It is my feeling that ethnic research will benefit when one goes beyond using standard positivistic research methods because the epistemological position of the researcher might become too rigid to capture the existential condition of the researched subjects in a meaningful way. The typical researcher tends to objectify consumption research data with the objective of scientific pursuit. This conflicts with the state of mind of the researched, who subjectivize consumption experiences. Clearly, these two positions can sometimes stand in opposition to each other to the detriment of appropriate research outcomes. If the researcher is truly interested in developing an understanding of consumers, he or she should develop an epistemology that is grounded in the subjects' point of view.

Three other examples, which concern Asian Indian immigrants, are Jain and Costa (1991), Joy and Dholakia (1991), and Mehta and Belk (1991). The complexity of doing ethnic research is clearly illustrated in these studies, which reveal that it is not possible to deal with ethnicity merely as another variable. Ethnicity becomes a cultural condition with profound consequences to the nature of consumption experiences among different groups.

Although not explicit, ethnic consumer studies can be considered cross-cultural or comparative because the researcher, in describing the relationship between ethnicity and consumption, establishes the cultural significance of ethnic consumption. A major difference between ethnic and cross-cultural or comparative studies lies in the fact that one is mainly intracultural and the other is intercultural. Ethnic studies always have as their implicit or explicit focus the relationship between the ethnic group and the dominant group.

Comparative and Cross-Cultural Research

The issue of comparative versus cross-cultural research in the social sciences is quite old and dates to the period of Durkheim. The nature of the debate has changed over the decades and has, indeed, become more complex. The issue has several aspects. Some center on the positivist approach to research versus the subjectivist-interpretivist approach. Then there are the goals of research: description, comparison, and generalization[4] (see Table 2.1). Description involves a detailed account of facts as observed and gathered by the researcher, along with his or her impressions of the people, settings, practices, and institutional arrangements. Under description, one may also include interpretation. Thus, Geertz's famous ethnographic work on the Balinese cockfight falls under description or, more specifically, under "thick description," as he labeled it (Geertz, 1973, p. 6). Comparison may be viewed as a logical extension of description in that two or more cultures are examined along one or more pertinent dimensions. Comparison in this sense means cross-cultural comparison. Researchers speak of generalizations when comparisons lead to valid generalizations across cultures on the basis of cross-cultural similarities. Table 2.1 lists the relative merits of the three levels of research. Of critical importance here is that in moving from description to generalization, researchers lose a lot of richness of data and begin to make unrealistic assumptions about the nature of reality. The positivist tradition aims to generate universal principles of behavior across different cultural settings. The following quotes highlight the principle of generalization in cross-cultural research:

Cross-cultural research provides an essential component of valid generalizations about human society. (Burton & White, 1987, p. 143)

The typical cross-cultural study is directed toward the analysis of a relatively small number of traits over a relatively large number of societies. (Udy, 1973, p. 253)

TABLE 2.1 A Comparative Analysis of Description, Comparison, and
Generalization

Factors	Description	Comparison	Generalization
Status of data	Focused data	Comparative data	Limited data
Richness of data	Very rich	Very rich	Low quality
Data gathering	Inductive	Inductive/Deductive	Deductive
Strategic use of research	Understanding	Differentiation	Universalization
Testable hypotheses	Minor importance	Major importance	Major importance
Positivism, interpretivism	Interpretivism, subjectivism	Interpretivism, subjectivism	Positivism, subjectivism
Nature of theory	Primary	Secondary	Tertiary
Realism	High	High	Low
Speculation	Low	Low	High
Data accuracy	High	High	Low
Credibility of analysis	High	High	Low

> Cross-cultural analysis makes sense only in an intellectual context that
> stresses the fundamental general similarities among separate societies that
> are different in detail. (Udy, 1973, p. 254)

Positivism in the social sciences has taken two different positions,
one pertaining to scientific generalization and the other arising out of
structuralism-functionalism. Scientific generalization refers to the discovery of lawlike regularities across cultures relative to the observed
phenomena. Structuralism-functionalism is a particular view of the
world as an organized system consisting of various parts with different
functional capabilities but with common systemic goals. Both positions
are for the most part ahistorical and treat culture in synchronistic terms.
On the other hand, in the subjectivist tradition (as opposed to the positivist tradition), emphasis is on differences between cultures and not on
similarities, but there is a recognition that cultural differences can be

explained by common theoretical categories appropriately modified for cross-cultural research. Here, the purpose of the theoretical categories is to make comparisons possible but not to make an assumption that generalizations are necessary or desirable.

An aspect of cultural studies that needs to be mentioned here is a lack of clear distinction between the terms *comparative* and *cross-cultural*. These two terms have different origins. I have seen researchers also use the term *cross-cultural comparative methods*. Comparative study is a disciplinary approach used in sociology and anthropology and goes back to the time of Durkheim (1912/1964) at the turn of the century. According to him, comparative sociology is not a particular branch of sociology, but rather it is sociology itself, insofar as it ceases to be purely descriptive and aspires to be a positivist science. The basic difference appears to be that a cross-cultural study must include at least two different cultures as part of the same field study, although it is possible to conduct a comparative study using a single cultural setting but making comparisons with other cultures using textual information rather than field data.

The term *cross-cultural* is more recent and is much looser in its orientation.[5] Cross-cultural comparison originated as a method of generating and testing hypotheses derived from the positivistic paradigms in the social sciences that tend to regard comparisons within a unified framework.

Cross-cultural research spans several basic social science disciplines. Most relevant here are the fields of anthropology, sociology, and psychology, which study, respectively, cultural, societal and social structural, and individual behaviors. Of course, there is a tremendous overlap among the three fields, so much so that Berry, Poortinga, Segall, and Dasen (1992) have argued for the necessity of doing multidisciplinary work. Each of these fields has its own orientation in terms of the subject matter and methods used. Traditionally, cross-cultural psychologists have tended to be very positivistic. Sociologists have tended to be slightly less so, whereas anthropologists have used interpretive methods. It must be recognized that in the Western (North American, to be more exact) academic world, both psychology and sociology, in contrast to anthropology, historically have operated inside a given culture and are, therefore, late entrants into the cross-cultural scene. On the other hand, anthropology's focus has always been on other cultures, and, only recently, in fact, have anthropologists turned their attention to the study of their own cultures. See the noted anthropologist Ortner's (1991) *Reading America* for a development of this theme. Because both cross-cultural psychology and comparative sociology appeared on the scene much after these two disciplines had established themselves intraculturally, they have tended to carry with them the epistemological and methodological baggage of their original disciplinary orientations. Typically, therefore, psychologists and sociologists rely on theories and frameworks that are basically unicultural (or monocultural), and their main research efforts are directed toward the application of their unicultural theories to cross-cultural settings. This has led many researchers to assume that the fundamental properties of behavior must be the same in all cultures, with only situational differences. There have been, however, some recent exceptions to this type of thinking (Berry et al., 1992).

A discipline in its own right, cross-cultural psychology has developed into a major area of inquiry in the past 20 years or so. The founding ideas of the field may be traced to B. B. Whiting and J. W. Whiting (1975) and Triandis and Lambert (1980). For a comprehensive survey of the field, a very good reference seems to be Berry et al. (1992). Applications to the field of management can be found in the influential work of Hofstede (1980) and in the fairly exhaustive theoretical discussion of Erez and Earley (1993). At the risk of simplification, the basic tenets of cross-cultural psychology may be summarized as follows. As the term *psychology* suggests, the focus of attention is individual behavior or, more specifically, individual psychological behavior, which is shaped by cultural factors. A major goal of cross-cultural psychology is to "test the generality of psychological laws" (Triandis & Lambert, 1980, p. 3). A similar statement can also be found in Berry et al. (1992), "In essence psychologists seek to transport their present hypotheses and findings to other cultural settings in order to test their applicability in other (and eventually in all) groups of human beings" (p. 3). A derivative goal is to explain whether psychological differences may possibly be due to cultural variations. In sum, cross-cultural psychology studies *individual* human behavior across cultures using psychological theories with the goal of exploring or establishing their universal applicability.

In the field of consumer behavior, cross-cultural researchers typically have followed the approaches of psychologists and, to a much lesser extent, of sociologists. They tend to test monocultural concepts in multicultural settings. Their bias in favor of psychology stems from the dominance of consumer psychology in American academe.

Another type of studies that cross-cultural consumer researchers undertake can more accurately be described as cross-national comparisons. Such studies are more common in economics and the policy sciences. Examples include standard economic studies involving different national economies, World Bank reports, and multinational investment reports in which the focus may be on such variables as gross national product (GNP), sales and turnover, disposable income, and so on—these variables presumably being objective measures that need no cross-cultural translation. Here, although the researchers deal with various macroissues that are local in nature (e.g., lack of education, poverty, health standards, etc.), the approach is structural and not cultural. Obviously, there are situations in which uniform methods and measures are appropriate. Unfortunately, many economically oriented consumer studies are conducted without regard to the intrinsic values of the questions studied. In such studies, categories are reduced to noncultural or quantitative idioms. Poverty is studied abstractly as a condition related to or in terms of lack of education, educational programs, infrastructure, adequate housing, subsistent wages, and so forth. In these studies, seldom does one find researchers studying poverty phenomenologically: The object of their study may be poverty, but it is never poor people. In particular, economists trained in the neoclassical tradition cannot deal with the whys and wherefores of their questions, either in historical or cultural terms, and they avoid, therefore, culture-theoretical explanations.

CROSS-CULTURAL RESEARCH AND CONSUMER BEHAVIOR

Until recently, very few serious research articles on cross-cultural research have appeared in consumer research journals and publications.[6] Nevertheless, the recent surge in activity suggests an important beginning in this area.[7] The work of Russell Belk must be acknowledged as among the most significant so far in cross-cultural consumer behavior. Other recent work on comparative consumerism has provided an exposure to various consumer trends in major parts of the world. Recent published research has focused on a variety of settings—affluent Asian cultures, such as Japan (Anderson & Wadkins, 1991; Sherry & Camargo, 1987), Korea (Ko & Gentry, 1991), and Hong Kong (Tse, Belk, & Zhou, 1991); developing Asian cultures, such as India (Joy & Dholakia, 1991; Mehta & Belk, 1991; Venkatesh, 1994; Venkatesh & Swamy, 1994) and China (Tse et al., 1991); developing African cultures (Belk, 1988); and emerging Eastern European markets, such as Romania and Turkey (Ger, Belk, & Lascu, 1993) and Poland (Witkowski, 1993). There also has been frequent mention in the press during the past 2 years of marketing and consumerist-oriented developments in these societies. The general theme pursued in these articles and popular studies is one of how these different cultures are adopting Western-style consumeristic tendencies while trying to retain their traditional and indigenous value systems.

In analyzing the developments across these different regions, two approaches can be seen. The first approach points to the commonalities in these developments that warrant generalizations regarding global consumer trends. The other approach emphasizes the peculiarities of each region with a reminder that there are deep-seated differences in the way consumer trends are unfolding and, therefore, that superficial similarities may hide real cultural differences. I believe that there is some truth in both positions. It is in this context of both similarities and differences that the present analysis is carried out.

Typical cross-cultural research studies involve a comparison of two countries or regions (sometimes more), usually the United States (or Canada) and another country. The following are some examples of recent studies: Europe and Turkey and the United States (Ger & Belk, 1990); Romania and Turkey (Ger et al., 1993); Canada and Germany (Rudmin, 1990); and the United States and the Netherlands (Dawson & Bamossy, 1990). Rudmin (1990) used cross-cultural psychological methods to study German and Canadian data on motivations for ownership. The scales and constructs he used were developed in the North American context and then applied to the German data. Interpretations of the results were based on theories developed mostly by American social theorists, Dewey and Mead. One could argue that Canada and Germany are comparable because they share Eurocentric perspectives and, therefore, that it is not necessary to take into account differential cultural norms and behaviors. This is a matter for further investigation in cross-cultural work.

In Dawson and Bamossy's (1990) study, the issue of materialism is examined with reference to the Netherlands and the United States. This study is similar to Rudmin's in terms of the positivistic methods used. Nevertheless, there is a clear differentiation in the interpretation of results on the basis of the different historical and sociocultural forces prevailing in these countries.

Ger and Belk's study (1990) involves a comparison of samples from the United States, Europe, and Turkey on the construct of materialism. The scales were developed in the American context and then adjusted, as deemed appropriate, for use with other samples. In the first half of the study, Ger and Belk discussed the methodology and scale construction in a manner similar to the two studies cited above. Their work, however, does contain a very detailed discussion of the results from the cultural standpoint. They examined the results and accounted for the differences and similarities using cultural arguments.

If I were to rank these studies in terms of cultural absorption (the term as it is used here connotes neither positive nor negative value), Rudmin is the least culturally absorptive, and Ger and Belk, the most. The cultural arguments in Ger and Belk's study, however, are presented only to interpret the results, not to illuminate their study's design. Had Ger and Belk examined the notion of materialism in different cultural settings, perhaps the very character of their research would have been different. By that, I mean that materialism as has been handed down in the North American context has a certain history to it and is embedded in its own cultural processes. Unless one examines this sociocultural context, the term *materialism* may not represent the same meaning in another context. Although Ger and Belk's study is certainly very significant in terms of the cultural discussion provided, I wonder if their results would be the same if they had discussed the cultural origins of the categories they used for their comparisons.

Why Ethnoconsumerism?

Why ethnoconsumerism? And why now? As mentioned earlier, the study of ethnoconsumerism follows the intellectual tradition of the comparative research methods and cross-cultural studies. The debates and issues of comparative studies are numerous and will not be repeated here. Nevertheless, some important issues need to be elaborated. One of the early approaches to cross-cultural studies is due to Ralph Linton (1945), who dealt with the notion of *modal personality*. A modal personality is one that occurs in a society with a certain empirical regularity and mirrors, in general, patterns of social interactions and work. It is Linton's argument that the individual's identity is constituted by his or her culture. This is a much stronger argument than the one that holds that culture merely influences the individual's behavior. In terms of consumption practices, the stronger argument is reinforced in a sociocultural-historical analysis carried out by Norbert Elias (1982) through his work *The History of Manners*. His is a clear demonstration of how the European culture, although undergoing changes of its own over a period of 400 or 500 years, created its own cultural product, the modern European individual as we know him or her today. Essentially, Elias's work deals with the I-We balance of individual behavior, in which *I* refers to behavior that is individualistically derived, and *We* refers to behavior that is collectively and culturally derived. The sliding between I-We is at the heart of the issue in any cultural analysis. Durkheim (1915/1965) also raised the idea of collective consciousness to signify the notion that individuals survive in shared environments of experiences, events, and meanings.

Echoing the issues raised by some of these early cultural theorists, ethnoconsumerism forces researchers to look at the individual not just as an individual but as a cultural being, as a part of the culture, subculture, and other group affiliations. It is the study of the consumer (his or her personality, cognition, and mental constructs) and the values systems, symbolic belief systems, rituals, and everyday practices all interwoven into a holistic view of the consumer. More precisely, the ethnoconsumerist approach is multilayered:

1. The study of the cultural (symbolic and belief systems, norms, and ritualistic practices)
2. The study of the social (social organization, social institutions, etc.)
3. The study of the individual (personality, cognition, behavior, mental constructs, etc.)

THEORETICAL RATIONALE

It is generally recognized that those social sciences whose focus is the study of various cultures across the globe have developed from Western epistemology—or, more specifically, from American epistemology—and that the cultural realities of the subject culture do not contribute to the theoretical categories but only to the content of research. (Incidentally, this is generally true of the field of marketing and consumer behavior.) This has led to certain disenchantment within some circles. In recent years, it has developed into a major debate in the social sciences. One of the first major thinkers to join the critical side of the debate was Clifford Geertz (1983), who addressed this question in his seminal work "From the Native's Point of View." He has influenced not only his own field of anthropology but also the social sciences in general. The debate has gone on in anthropology for several years, with Marcus and Fischer (1986) evincing one of the more provocative dimensions to the debate. The field of anthropology has been most concerned with these issues, primarily because its whole focus is the study of other cultures.

It is in this context that McKim Marriott's (1990) notion of ethnosociology as a framework for the study of different cultures is very appropriate. In line with Marriott's proposal, I propose a framework that I call *ethnoconsumerism* to study consumer behavior in different cultures. The arguments presented by Marriott for developing the field he called *ethnosociology* are very instructive and are stated here. Because his work is on India, his reference point is India. But the arguments he raises are applicable to other contexts well.

1. The social sciences as practiced in India today have developed from thought about Western, rather than Indian, cultural realities, and therefore cannot be used effectively to frame questions for which the answers lie in Indian realities and institutions. Therefore, we need social sciences that deal with Indian realities.

2. All social sciences, Western or otherwise, are ethnosocial sciences. All are parochial in scope.

3. Because thought originating outside of Europe and America has not yet been recognized as social science, the world has had to manage thus far with ethnosocial sciences of only one limited type—Western.

4. The term *ethno-* must not be viewed as a backwater of the social sciences but as an existential or definitional condition.

5. As a result of the above, the application of Western categories, such as "individuals," "social structures," "kinship," "classes," "rules," "oppositions," "solidarities," "hierarchy," "authority," "values," "ideology," "sacred," and so forth, risk imposing an alien ontology and epistemology on those who attempt an analysis of a particular culture.

6. Similarly, many Western conceptual distinctions simply cannot be transported into the framework Indian thought. Example of these distinctions include Marx's "material base and superstructure," as well as Durkheim's "sacred and profane," Lévi-Strauss's "nature and culture," Weber's "class and status," and so forth. This is because Indians have their own conceptions of the connections between matter, actions, thoughts, and words, and these are imbued with certain relational properties that are not commonplace in Western thought.

EXAMPLES OF ETHNOCONSUMERISM

Here, I will briefly discuss different studies that illustrate various points I have raised about ethnoconsumerism. This is meant to be not an exhaustive critique of the studies but a look at them exclusively from the point of view of ethnoconsumerism. The first study, by Yau (1988), is based on his doctoral dissertation. Yau provided a detailed historical analysis of Chinese values dating from the Confucian and Buddhist periods. Given the fundamental belief systems prevailing among the Chinese, he argued that the notion of consumer satisfaction, its expression, and the consequent action would be totally different from a typical situation in the West. Because of a particular value concept known as *yuarn* (karma), the Chinese are less likely to blame the product when it fails and are apt to attribute such product failures to their own fate. Although Yau engaged in a discussion of Chinese value systems, the theoretical or classificatory framework is the value-orientation model developed by Kluckhohn and Strodtbeck (1961). This model is introduced not at the level of categories but at the level of the overall framework itself. Thus, the framework includes such fundamental orientations as man-nature, man-himself, relational, time, and personal activity. This framework is at a higher order and, hence, is more fundamental than Hofstede's (1980) categories (individualism and collectivism, etc.) that are already culturally derived and so do not permit easy translation into a cross-cultural setting.

In a series of studies, Belk and Pollay (1985; Pollay, 1986, 1988) jointly and singly have discussed the cultural value systems as derived from advertising in the North American setting. Clearly, the cultural values extracted from an examination of hundreds of ads from a 60-plus-year period reveal that these values are fundamental to American cultural life and have found their way into the consumer culture. Belk and Pollay's work can be considered a good example of ethnoconsumerist research. Essentially, one can interpret their work to mean that American consumer culture has its own ethnological dimensions and that the mainstream American culture provides an example of an ethnically constituted culture that holds Protestant, Eurocentric values. Once we consider these cultural values as ethnoconsumeristic, by implication, we would be treading on shaky ground were we to apply the same set of values in cross-cultural contexts without regard to the substance of the cultures in question.

Consider, for example, a value that is very basic to American culture: materialism (the American version). Its historical roots are in a combination of evangelical idealism, individualism, exceptionalism, Protestantism, and the capitalist subversion of asceticism. In discussing materialism, one cannot ignore its origins and treat the concept purely synchronically. When Ger and Belk (1990) chose to study materialism in Turkey, one asks, out of necessity, what the roots of materialism are in the Turkish context. Is there anything analogous to American materialism? If not, would it make sense to use a cultural category so fundamental to American culture, in which materialism is regarded as its basic defining character? I do not think one can transport a cultural category without regard to its historical context. This is not to say, however, that Turkey is not materialistic or that it could not become materialistic. I am also fully cognizant of the fact that human history is full of examples of cultural categories that have been transported cross-culturally and taken root in their new settings. Buddhism in China and Christianity in Scandinavia are cases in point. Similarly, food habits have been transported across cultures: Tea drinking among the English did not become prevalent until much after British colonial contact. Nevertheless, a discussion of the historical, sociocultural roots is very essential in this type of research. The point I raise regarding Ger and Belk's work is to question not its overall insights and fruitful cultural analysis but an aspect of it that has relevance to my discussion of ethnoconsumerism.

Geertz's work on caste in Bali (as analyzed in Howe, 1987) has shown that there are some crucial differences between Bali and India in the study of caste systems, although both are Hindu societies. Although Balinese culture borrowed heavily from the Sanskritic culture of India, its social structure has no Indian influence and is similar to the Indonesian social system. Thus, an intercultural comparison of caste would not produce meaningful results, whereas a study of Hindu religious rites would. Another example is the sacred-profane dichotomy, which originally was developed by Durkheim and was adopted more recently by Belk, Wallendorf, and Sherry (1989) in their work. A comparison of India and the United States on the sacred and the profane dimension would present quite a few problems. In the American culture, the terms *sacred* and *profane* are used as semantically similar to *good* and *bad*. As Veena Das (1987) has noted, in the Indian context an argument has been made that "the dichotomy of sacred and profane which dominated the Durkheimian sociology of religion has very little relevance in the Hindu context, since these are not antithetical in Hindu belief and ritual" (p. 114). Alternatively, to the extent that sacred and profane represent a dichotomy, Das argued that *sacred* refers to life (or purity) and *profane* refers to death (or impurity).

Clearly, what I consider to be the best example of an ethnoconsumerist approach to consumer behavior is the recent work by Arnould (1989) on innovation diffusion and preference formation in the Nigerian culture. Arnould directly confronts the applicability of Gatignon and Robertson's (1985) framework, which has received a lot of attention in the consumer behavior literature. He began with a sociocultural and historical analysis of consumption in Zinder, dating from the precolonial era. From a historical analysis, he proceeded to give a contemporary structural perspective of Zinder society. Here, the focus is on the impact of market-mediated exchange on the consumption schemes of a traditional society. Using both macro (world systems) and micro (everyday transactions) theories of behavior, plus a descriptive analysis of the current economic order, Arnould is able to demonstrate the challenges inherent in applying Western (North American) theories of consumer behavior in a non-Western setting. Two of his conclusions are most instructive:

> Analyses of Nigerian data demonstrate the need to reconstrue the constructs employed in diffusion of innovations research for non-Western cultural contexts. . . . Innateness and emulationist theories underlying the standard diffusion of innovation models are shown to be ethnocentric, thereby lacking explanatory power in alternate contexts. (p. 262)
> By systematic study of particular macro-economic, social-structural, political, and cultural variables, the process of preference formation, innovation, and the diffusion of innovation can be elucidated. (p. 263)

A final study that is central to my own work here is de Pyssler's (1992) cultural analysis of the adoption of two-wheelers (motor scooters) in India. This is one of the most fascinating pieces of writing to appear in a consumer research publication. The study is at the intersection of what de Pyssler called *political economy* and *cultural economy*. Perhaps because it appeared in conference proceedings, it does not go into the depth of analysis that Arnould's (1989) article displayed, but it provides substantial evidence of what an ethnoconsumerist study could be. De Pyssler has provided a clear-sighted, historical analysis of the technology itself, its design, and its cross-cultural semiotics. After a discussion of the transformation of the meaning of the motor scooter in different cultural settings (Italy, Britain, and India), the article provided a narrative analysis of what *scooter* means to various Indians. The first part of the study accomplishes exactly what a cultural analysis is supposed to do, that is, de Pyssler took the subject's point of view in regard to a technology that was basically alien to the Indian scene at the time of its introduction more than three decades ago. Then the focus shifts to how Indians have adapted themselves to this technology, giving it a meaning wholly different from that given it by the Italians or the British. What is an elegant feminine icon in Italy becomes a technology of the rebel (punk rock groups) in England but in India is viewed as a utilitarian family vehicle. Here one does not impose the cultural categories of meanings from outside but generates them from the cultural ambiance of the setting. From the point of view of ethnoconsumerist discussion, one problematic aspect of the study comes in the latter half when de Pyssler began to discuss his findings by imposing two frameworks whose origins are Western in nature, McCracken's (1988) and Hebdige's (1988). There is no question about the standing of these two cultural theorists, but one must question why their framework was used to discuss Indian experiences.

SOME GENERAL GUIDELINES TO FOLLOW
IN DOING ETHNOCONSUMER RESEARCH

Increasingly, cultural studies are becoming more confusing and confused. On the one hand, fear is growing that the spread of new communication technologies and rampant consumerism introduced by the multinationals may make the world monocultural. According to Appadurai (1990), the global cultural scene is now witnessing two opposing, yet simultaneously occurring movements: the homogenization and heterogenization of cultures. Homogenization represents a submission to global culturalism; heterogenization offers resistance to it. In this melange of cultural juxtaposition, the cultural theorist does not risk elaborating theories of generalization but is quite content to provide comparative descriptions of intracultural themes. Operationally, it does not make sense to put different cultures on linearly measured scales under the assumption that in every culture the scale measures the same phenomenon. Even if it does, do the high and low points of the scale have the same significance in different cultures? The problem stems from the fact that when different cultures are compared, the variable does not have the same ontological property at all points in the scale. Suppose one wants to measure high modernization versus low modernization. One cannot use, say, a measure of the number of coke cans consumed or television sets sold as the best way to measure modernization. Cross-culturally speaking, one cannot make an assumption that higher numbers and lower numbers of culturally variant measures are symmetrically related. Thus, there is an acute problem in intercultural studies using similar measures or variables.

I have already discussed Geertz's analysis of the caste system in Bali and India and also the difficulty in applying Durkheim's sacred and profane distinction to the Indian situation. Neither warrants repetition except the point that one must be careful when pursuing cross-cultural or ethnoconsumerist analysis on the basis of measures developed in monocultural contexts.

Without meaning to suggest a full-fledged technique for conducting ethnoconsumerist research, in the following I suggest some guidelines for performing a cultural analysis. A cultural analysis is essential for developing an ethnoconsumeristic understanding of a given culture.

1. First, identify the cultural framework.
2. From the cultural framework, derive cultural categories.
3. Interpret and provide meanings for cultural categories.
4. Establish relationships between cultural categories.
5. Identify and investigate relevant cultural practices and pertinent socio-economic trends.
6. Identify relevant cultural objects and establish meanings.
7. Describe the consumer environments of interest and describe specific consumer behaviors. Interpret both the consumer environments and behaviors using the categories and their meanings.
8. Interpret findings in a way that the reader understands that, ultimately, the interpretation is based on the researcher's own perspective.

Here are some explanations to the terms used in the previous guidelines. A cultural framework represents a theoretical structure on the basis of cultural categories derived from two key elements: the *field view* and the *text view*. The field view is a descriptive account of current practices, subjective impressions and statements of people living within a cultural group, a record of relevant cultural symbols, and descriptions of relevant domains of experiences. The text view refers to historical-sociocultural themes of the culture embedded in texts, local histories, value systems, and archival sources. Cultural categories are theoretical concepts that are specific to the culture under study. Cultural categories must be carefully articulated and focused. They should also have relevance to the consumer environments that are included in the study. All cultural categories have meanings associated with them, and these meanings are generated internally within the culture and cannot be imposed externally from outside.

A key point to remember is that researchers who want to pursue ethnoconsumerist research need to combine two basic requirements of research: (a) knowledge of cultural texts and material and (b) in situ fieldwork or some equivalent. Doing only fieldwork, as ethnographers do, is not sufficient because cultural practices have origins and histories that cannot be evaluated purely on the basis of current practices. Nor can a researcher hope that fieldwork can be meaningfully substituted by data-gathering efforts, administering questionnaires to cross-cultural convenience samples. This practice has become so rampant as to raise important questions regarding the validity of such studies. Furthermore, although the "native's" point of view is clearly important in this type of work, sometimes the natives may not have a good understanding of the historical origins of their practices. In these cases, the researcher has to rely on other material, such as cultural texts, archival information, commentaries, and other written documents. Studying cultures cannot be reduced to "naive empiricism." Cultural patterns may display universal attributes and/or idiosyncratic patterns relative to other cultures, but the researcher should not be looking for either of these situations but instead be accommodating both possibilities.

Ethnoconsumerism in the Indian Context

FOUR QUESTIONS ON CONSUMPTION IN INDIA

With apologies to Ramanujan (1990), I ask the following four questions:

Is there an Indian approach to consumption?
Is there *an* Indian approach to consumption?
Is there an *Indian* approach to consumption?
Is there an Indian approach to *consumption?*

To the first question the answer is, there *was* an Indian approach to consumption, which has changed over the years because of a variety of influences. This question is a historical one. The question addresses the issue of how consumption patterns have varied or changed over time and of what the nature of consumption culture is now compared to in the past.

The second question requires an answer that there is more than one approach to consumption in India, depending on the region and cultural group one is studying. It is, however, possible to imagine an Indian approach to consumption.

The third question attempts to elicit the answer that there may be something uniquely Indian about consumption that will not be found in non-Indian settings. The answer to this question comes from a cultural analysis of everyday practices, symbolic systems, value orientations, and behaviors arising from them. This question is central to the spirit of ethnoconsumerist approach.

The last question raises the issue of whether something called *consumption* is itself a historical construct, a product of industrial revolution in much the same way production is. In other words, is it appropriate, in the context of consumption, to include cultures that have not been an essential part of modern industrial history? Can the

production-consumption nexus as conceived in the capitalist ethos, critiqued by Marx, appropriated by 20th-century socialism, and theorized
by Weber be applied legitimately to India? The answer to this question
is not a simple yes or no, for although countries such as India did not
directly participate in the early industrial history of the world, they
were forced, as victims of colonial expansion, to play a role in the world
industrial development.

With this background to the problematic of consumption, I shall now
discuss a specific application of ethnoconsumerist approach to India.
Interested readers may refer to some additional work of mine relating
to India (Venkatesh, 1994; Venkatesh & Swamy, 1994).

AN ETHNOCONSUMERISTIC APPROACH
TO HOUSEHOLD TECHNOLOGY

Adoption and Use

I shall give an illustrative account of the ethnoconsumerist approach
to a study that I conducted recently in India. My research project was
concerned with issues relating to the adoption of household technologies by Indian families. My earlier work dealt with similar issues in the
American context (Venkatesh, 1985; Venkatesh & Vitalari, 1992). The
site selected for my recent study was the city of Madras in southern
India.

The aim of the study was to document and critically analyze the uses
of modern household technologies by Indian families and their experiences with them. I addressed two main research questions in this study:
How do people relate to everyday technologies of the household as
cultural objects, and what are the social implications of the relationships that people develop with respect to those technologies? Thus, the
approach taken here may be called a sociocultural analysis of technological adoption and use.

The focus of analysis was at the microlevel, or the level of the household. I was more interested in the role of technology in the daily lives
of the people, or the relationship between people and technologies
from a cultural perspective. Such a cultural understanding of technologies has not been the subject of systematic research, although in the past
some contributions to this field had come from the works of Spicer
(1952), Foster (1962, 1969), and a few others. More recently, Singhal and
Rogers (1989) conducted important research on the diffusion of tele-

vision and VCRs in India with implications for the popular cultural practices in Indian communities. A similar study was undertaken by Manuel (1993) to study the impact of cassette technology on popular music in North India.

To explore the research issues concerning household technology adoption in India, I have developed an ethnoconsumerist framework consisting of four major components: (a) the cultural context, (b) modernization in the Indian context, (c) the rising consumerism in India, and (d) the technological context. These I describe briefly in the following sections.

The Cultural Context

Anyone studying India cannot take it merely on its face value. No amount of fieldwork will yield important insights into India unless this is also accompanied by a cultural understanding that can be obtained only by a knowledge of the secondary sources. A society that has an uninterrupted history dating back to more than 3,000 years has strong cultural and historical roots that cannot be easily unraveled but must be understood nevertheless. In this seamless web of complexity, one has to pick a few important threads as a way to gaining meaning into the cultural presence of India.

Indian Cultural Ethos. The basic cultural code of Indian life can be conceptualized in the following terms: (a) its social structure (caste hierarchy and extended family system), (b) the role of religion (both as a spiritual doctrine and as a way of life) and the cosmic role of the individual, and (c) pluralism in life patterns and experiences. From the Western point of view that emphasizes material order, Indian society might appear to be full of contradictions, juxtapositions, and irreconcilable internal differences. As Veena Das (1987) and Marriott (1990) have pointed out, much of what goes by the name *Indian culture* has strong religious roots. Any researcher who wishes to gain a true understanding of the cultural categories will benefit by becoming familiar with the essence of the sacred texts that, in the Indian context, are philosophical discourses that codify much individual and social behavior.

In the West, religion stands in opposition to science, to rationalist thought, and, in fact, to modernity, which is the defining philosophical and cultural position of the West in the last 400 years. Science and religion are understood in oppositional terms, science representing the materiality of life and religion representing its spiritual dimension. Such a distinction is totally absent in Hinduism and in Indian culture, in which spiritualism and materialism are not considered opposites. In fact, Indians believe that the material world and the spiritual world belong to the same realm of experience. Indians do believe in the notion that life can be both spiritual and materialistic at the same time without any implied antagonism. Similarly, the concept of secularism, another Western idea, is totally absent within the Indian cultural scheme except as a borrowed idea from the West. Indians either ignore secularism in their daily lives or wear it like a necessary garb in dealing with the West.

Indians believe that objects have symbolic meanings at three levels: aesthetic, functional, and spiritual. In contrast, the Western notion of the objective world extends to its aesthetic and functional dimensions only. Significant about the Indian experience is the spiritual coloring that is readily accorded to material objects. This is an important part of the Hindu cosmology and must be given serious consideration in the study of Indian consumer culture.

One of the first things to be learned from India's sociocultural history is the role of religion in the daily life of Indians. Hinduism, which is the primary religion of the country, is not an organized theological movement but represents a way of life that has evolved over many centuries. Hinduism represents a complex system of daily practices, rituals, beliefs, and symbolic patterns that overlap various aspects of social life. From cosmological doctrines that define how the physical and spiritual world is constituted to more mundane aspects of life, Hinduism provides the framework to understand all these matters.

Another aspect of Indian cultural life has to deal with time. Time is neither historical nor chronological. Time is essentially cyclical. Similarly, birth and death are not considered two finite events but two stages in one's continuous existence. Thus, the time before birth and after death have concrete meanings for many Indians. Because of this, the individual experiences take on different meanings because the Indian is prone to establish associations with people dead and gone.

The implications of Indian cultural ethos to the adoption of new technologies needs to be investigated if one believes that technology should be viewed as part of the cultural system. Although I establish in a separate research monograph what bearing the socioreligious character of Indian culture has on the adoption of technologies, my intention in this chapter is to demonstrate that a cultural analysis of technology adoption necessarily implies that to derive appropriate cultural categories, one has to have a sound understanding of the cultural ethos of India.

Modernization in the Indian Context

Technology adoption is clearly linked with the issues of modernization. Modernization is generally viewed both as a process and as an end-state (Schnaiberg, 1970). Schnaiberg investigated the change process occurring through modernization, especially in the context of the family or the household. On the basis of some previous studies, he noted that there is a hypothesized shift from an extended family system to a nuclear family system, consonant with individual mobility (social and geographic). He further postulated changes in the structure of production and consumption functions at home, declining importance of primary groups, greater dependence on impersonal resources (e.g., media) for information, and decline in religious involvement. Schnaiberg conducted a study of 803 Turkish households in the city of Ankara and evaluated them on six dimensions: media usage, extended family ties, declining religiosity, nuclear family role structure, environmental orientation, and production/consumption orientation. Because the study was conducted in a "developing" country, the findings are broadly applicable to the Indian situation. Schnaiberg found that all these dimensions were correlated with modernism. At the theoretical level, it means that even in non-Western societies, the process of urbanization and modernization and the impact of new technologies will grossly parallel the developments in Western industrialized societies. One should not forget that there could be exceptions to this. For example, Iran's recent history indicates that modernization over the years had the opposite reaction of pulling the country toward religious formalism.

In the Indian context, the early work of Srinivas (1966) is very relevant to the present study. Srinivas discussed social change in terms of Westernization, industrialization, urbanization, and secularization. Westernization results in the introduction of new institutions (elections, newspapers, etc.) and modifications to old institutions. It introduces such things as Western technology, clothing, eating practices, and scientific and rationalistic viewpoints. Modernization is related to Westernization. It is a general term that includes Westernization, industrialization, and secularization. Countries may prefer the term *modernization* to Westernization because it does not have the negative connotation of having to give up what is good within the indigenous culture. Vajpeyi's (1982) research explored the attitudes, opinions, perceptions, and beliefs of the Indian elites toward modernization. His findings showed that the Indian elites supported the idea of social change through modernized developments as long as the traditional value system was not negatively affected. In many non-Western societies, modernization has become a value-laden term because its main challenge lies in the discovery of relevant ideology. The urge for modernity is commingled with the urge for identity. In India, the dominant cultural values are hierarchy, holism, continuity, and transcendentalism. There is a fundamental socioreligious outlook in which religion and personal life are neither separate nor antagonistic. Singer (1972) has discussed vividly what happens when a traditional culture such as India modernizes.

Rising Consumerism in India

Consumerism is used here in the sense of the development of consumer-oriented tendencies, marked by the availability of a variety of manufactured consumer goods and active advertising of the products in various media. Part of the rising consumerism in India may be cast in the general context of global tendencies in consumerism. Recent work suggests that global diffusion of consumerism has been aided by the expansion of multinationalism, the diffusion of telecommunication and satellite technologies, the general dissatisfaction with socialist political regimes, and emerging economic successes in East Asian countries. Certainly, recent moves in India echo these developments.

What is happening in India may also be described in postmodern terms. Indian development does not follow standard chronological sequences observed in some Western societies. Models of social change do not follow any known patterns of change. Modernist methods found in the conventional social sciences have limited value when the objective is to capture change in non-Western cultures. This is because modernist thinking is regimented, very rationalistic, and (pseudo)scientifically oriented. Postmodernist thinking accommodates nonlinear thinking and is open-minded when it comes to alternate or nonorthodox patterns. For example, some new technologies in India are diffusing faster than some old technologies. So, one cannot use the historical progression of the West as a model to study India. The Indian consumer scene is replete with what might be misinterpreted by the modernist to be contradictions and the juxtaposition of opposites (and therefore, non-natural), but in reality they represent highly symbolic modes of behavior, much of which must be understood within the Indian cultural framework.

In sum, I have identified 13 different factors to describe India as an emerging consumer society. Although these factors are not to be considered exhaustive, they are representative of the movement of India toward a consumer-oriented society. The factors are:

- A burgeoning middle class, its changing values, and pent-up consumer demand
- Changing women's roles, women's labor participation, and the changing structure of the family (Liddle & Joshi, 1986; Sharma, 1986; Wadley, 1977)
- Rising consumer aspirations and expectations across many segments of the population
- Increased consumer spending on luxury items aided by past savings and the introduction of the credit system
- New types of shopping environments and outlets
- Media proliferation, satellite and cable television, and the thriving film industry
- Media sophistication and familiarity with English language among media people and a wide segment of the population
- High degree of consumer awareness and sophistication across different segments
- The emergence of traveling Indian consumers—immigrants in the United States and England, overseas workers, tourists, and professionals—and their exposure to worldwide consumer products
- Strong domestic consumer goods manufacturing sector
- Resurfacing of hedonistic cultural elements after centuries of dormancy
- Entry of multinational corporations into India
- The emergence of the rural consumer sector

The rising consumerism as reflected in the above factors are hypothesized to have considerable impact on technology diffusion and adoption.

The Technological Context

Underlying Issues. Some of the very early work by anthropologists and archaeologists is concerned with the relationship between technology and material culture (Kroeber, 1923; Tylor, 1878; Wissler, 1929). Using an evolutionist interpretation, they tended to view technologies (such as fire making, cooking, and pottery) in the context of societies advancing from one stage of development to the next. A related perspective on technology has dealt with the issues of diffusion (Rogers, 1962). Diffusion is the process by which new ideas are transferred from one social unit to another within the same culture. Analytically, these approaches regard technologies as an external force acting on the system. Such cause and effect approaches are still used for studying technology and social change.

Televisual Culture. The televisual culture in India is marked by strong consumerism and commercialism. Singhal and Rogers (1989) have already established how influential the television has become as a cultural and entertainment medium. Television reaches the four corners of India as no other technology has done in the country's history. The next development within the context of television is consumer advertising. Consumer advertising is burgeoning with the arrival of satellite TV, or more specifically, Star TV. A mix of domestic and multinational brands are advertised on Star TV, for example, Bajaj scooters, Stayfree sanitary napkins, Pepsi's Hostess Chips, and McDowell Whiskey, to name just a few. The diffusion of consumerism is further accelerated by the sponsoring of sports, concerts, and other entertainment for the public. The participation of industries in the cultural production system is on the increase.

New Technologies. Indian economy is also changing with the advent of new technologies. Ironically, the traditional technologies have not had much impact on Indian consumer. For example, very few of the recent changes in India can be attributed to the telephone or the automobile, both of which have existed in India for a long time. These same technologies have had profound impact on Western industrial economies in the last five decades. The telephone system in India is highly underdeveloped and is run by the government. It is indeed the object of many jokes and ridicule in India. In the case of automobiles, the impact has been minimal because very few Indians could afford the automobile.

On the other hand, there are some other technologies that have made a difference in Indian life, for example, the motor scooter, the television and the VCR, and other household appliances such as the refrigerator and the cooking stove. The motor scooter and the motorcycle have become ubiquitous because of their affordability and maneuverability. Many young families and individual professionals, both male and female, use motor scooters as personal transportation.

Consumer Technologies/Electronics. Many of the revolutionary changes in India can be attributed to the emergence of consumer technologies. The first effect of this is the access to electronic information and entertainment (Manuel, 1993). More specifically, the electronic media influences tastes in music and increases exposure to various entertainment forms from different cultures. This is also a prelude to what one might call the development of a mass culture society. Another consequence of this electronic technology is the development of the material culture.

India in the Global Technological Context. Four developments have begun to change the general nature of inquiry relative to technology. First, the rise of postindustrialism and information technologies has sensitized researchers to a radically different technological environment that is not amenable to standard modes of inquiry that were originally developed to investigate material technology. Second, the modern technologies have begun to interconnect the world in unprecedented ways, giving a new meaning to the world order. This interconnectedness seems to imply the emergence of a universal language of technology that could potentially bridge cultural differences. Third, the ascendance of Eastern countries such as Japan, Korea, and Taiwan as the producers of modern technologies and the accompanying rapid diffusion of modern technologies within those countries has prompted researchers to view technologies in a nondevelopmental, culture-specific framework. Thus, for the first time in several centuries, the sources of some new technologies are no longer located in the Western hemisphere. Finally, as Appadurai (1988) has pointed out in a different context, countries such as India that are experiencing new levels of material success have begun to view their cultural practices in a self-conscious, self-reflective fashion without using Western yardsticks of what is acceptable and not acceptable.

These developments stand in contrast to the notions of modernization and Westernization, which dominated earlier thinking on the subject (Srinivas, 1966). Previous research on India has dealt with issues of social change occurring because of modernization and Westernization. Although modernization was used as a broad concept dealing with urbanization, social mobility, and new media experiences, Westernization was identified with social and cultural patterns dealing with clothing, eating, language, and the like.

Recent work by Singhal and Rogers (1989) has focused on the cultural shifts occurring within the Indian entertainment scene as a result of the arrival of television and VCRs. The technological diffusion of both television and VCRs has been rather astonishing and cannot be completely explained by economic variables such as disposable income and standard of living. In fact, their diffusion pattern is unlike that of some other technologies such as the telephone, refrigerator, and the automobile. It seems more to do with the patterns of culture than mere economic processes.

One can, of course, venture an explanation to the Indians' adoption of modern household technologies in terms of class ideology and consumption styles, as Appadurai (1988) attempted to show with respect to certain aspects of food consumption. But this is not plausible because the historical role that food has played in Indian culture has no parallel in the adoption of technologies. Nevertheless, it is evident from Appadurai's work and the work of more recent authors that one has to look for a contemporary theme to better explain the various cultural shifts. For example, Singer (1989) has characterized the current Indian cultural scene in terms of "the coexistence of the past and the present" (p. 8). This is in direct contrast to some earlier views that tended to represent past and present in antagonistic and hierarchical terms. Thus, modernization and Westernization were regarded as both superior and antagonistic to traditionalism. This view is beginning to fade because the current research on India seems to suggest that the Indians are shaping their culture in ways different from those of an earlier generation.

With these various factors in the background, the following research questions were raised in the study:

- What role does technology play in the life of the household?
- How is technology viewed symbolically or materially? How does it fit into the rest of the symbolic and material system of the household, and how do technological objects relate to family values and other family possessions?
- How do families accumulate household technologies? In what order?
- What sociocultural significance can be attached to the process of acquiring technologies?
- What concepts of technology do members of the household have?
- How are the concepts formed, and how are they articulated?
- What cultural meanings are attached to technological products?
- How are the technologies used? By whom? With what frequency?
- How are members socialized into the use of technologies?
- How are decisions made regarding the acquisition of technologies?
- To what extent are social and gender roles reflected in the use of technologies?
- What impacts have these technologies had on the life of the household?

These research questions provided the basic structure for the empirical investigation (the field view of Indian consumer culture). The broader theoretical issues (the text view) emerged from the four major components of the ethnoconsumerist framework discussed previously. Together, these two elements (the field view and the text view)[8] provided a valuable framework for the research undertaken here.

In conclusion, I have illustrated an application of the ethnoconsumerist approach to the study of technology adoption and diffusion in the Indian context. Four major components of the ethnoconsumerist framework were identified. Although no attempt was made to establish possible theoretical and empirical connections among the components, some broad relationships were discussed as illustrative of the ethnoconsumerist approach. In due course, more rigorous arguments will be developed and presented. More to the point, however, is the idea that ethnoconsumerism is a new approach to studying consumer behavior both intraculturally and cross-culturally. It has several merits and has the potential for filling an intellectual void in cross-cultural research.

Appendix:
A Personal Intellectual Note

This chapter reflects to some extent my own existential condition, being a product of two cultures (or, perhaps, of neither). Recently, I had a chance to do fieldwork in India, and, as must be obvious to some seasoned researchers, I found it difficult to apply to the Indian situation the principles of consumer behavior that I had learned so assiduously in the American academic scene. My general training in the United States has given me the perspective that consumer behavior must be regarded in universal terms—that is, the point of departure for research is the discovery of similarities between different consumer settings, although the differences can be explained in terms of some idiosyncratic variables. The general idea is to impose a universal theoretical framework on different cultural settings, with a proviso that researchers are entitled to expect behavioral differences at the level of practices. The framework is sacrosanct, and the rest is a matter of detail.

For some of the reasons detailed above, I am also guilty of not being familiar with consumer research studies published outside the United States. After being away for a year in India and Denmark, I have become painfully aware of my own intellectual limitations caused by the academic condition in American universities, which is influenced by institutional and structural factors—institutional and structural because the attitude of the American academic environment to external scholarship extends from benign neglect to indifference. Although consumer behavior is a global phenomenon and the impact of American consumer culture is truly global, it is hard to understand how insular (and patronizing) American consumer research scholarship is to scholarship from outside the United States (unless it is modeled after it). By "American scholarship," I do not mean, so much, scholarship produced by native-born Americans scholars but by scholars working within the American institutional environments regardless of their origins. Here I must add that there are many intellectual differences among native-born American scholars who themselves represent many different perspectives. In fact, my main argument in this chapter is inspired by the work of McKim Marriott, an American South Asianist from the University of Chicago. It is also true that many North American-trained scholars, after returning to their home turf, simply apply American approaches to their own research problems.

Finally, although it is not uncommon for scholars outside the United States to read major journals and texts published in the United States, there is very little that goes on in the other direction. In the study of cross-cultural or comparative research, this shortcoming of U.S.-based researchers becomes an acute deficiency. One can understand, of course, that language could be a major hurdle, but this does not have much face validity because many non-U.S. publications are available in the English language. Parenthetically, one might add, marketing practitioners more than the academics seem to be better grounded and are waking up to the danger inherent in being insular from the social processes in the rest of the world. This does not mean that they do not have their own agendas that may run counter to local needs.

Notes

1. Because the term *native* seems to have acquired a negative connotation (although this is not how Geertz used it), perhaps we should consider something more neutral, such as, "the culture's point of view."

2. For a detailed analysis of the notion of culture in marketing, see Costa (1993).

3. In this section, I address the issue of burgeoning interest in ethnic consumption patterns among consumer researchers. Although the topic of ethnicity and the sociopolitical issues are globally widespread and are discussed widely by social theorists in various countries, the specific issue of consumption patterns of ethnic communities as a subject of market economy is not discussed in such detail outside the United States. Perhaps it is only natural—the United States being a consumer society par excellence with a high degree of marketing activism and specialization and a long history of inventing new markets for goods and services—that the consumer angle has first appeared here. It is only a question of time, however, before this spreads to marketing constituencies in other parts of the world and legitimizes the intellectual inquiries of consumer scholars about the consumption patterns of their own ethnic groups. The question of ethnicity has

become an important issue with the recent influx of Asian and Latin American immigrants in the United States. The immigrant issue is a recurrent theme in American history, but in the last hundred years, different groups have attracted similar attention.

4. The discussion on description, comparison, and generalization is based on Holy (1987).

5. The most problematic research in this area is by Hofstede (1980), who is one of the most influential researchers today. His work, despite its impact, is not as culturally sensitive as it is claimed to be by him and his supporters.

6. For important contributions to cross-cultural research in consumer behavior, see Tan and Sheth's (1985) edited volume based on the conference in Singapore. See also van Raaij and Bamossy (1993).

7. Emphasis on cross-cultural and comparative studies is also reflected in recent international conferences. Examples include the first Marketing and Development Conference held in Istanbul, Turkey (1987), followed by conferences in Zagreb, Yugoslavia (1989), New Delhi, India (1991), and San José, Costa Rica (1993). In 1985, the Association for Consumer Research held its first International Conference in Singapore. The year 1992 seems a key year in this sequence: the first European Conference of the Association for Consumer Research in Amsterdam (June 1992), the Conference on Culture and Marketing at University of Odense, Denmark (May 1992), and the First International Conference of the Macromarketing Group in Nijenrode, the Netherlands (May 1992).

8. The terms *field view* and *text view* are discussed in Veena Das (1987) and are directly adopted here.

References

Anderson, B. (1991). *Imagined communities: Reflections on the origins and spread of nationalism* (2nd ed.). London: Verso. (Original work published 1983)

Anderson, L., & Wadkins, M. (1991). Japan: A culture of consumption? In R. H. Holman & M. R. Solomon (Eds.), *Advances in consumer research* (Vol. 18, pp. 129-134). Provo, UT: Association for Consumer Research.

Appadurai, A. (1988). How to make a national cuisine: Cookbook in contemporary India. *Comparative Studies in Society and History, 30*(1), 3-24.

Appadurai, A. (1990). Disjuncture and difference in global cultural economy. In M. Featherstone (Ed.), *Global culture: Nationalism, globalization and modernity* (pp. 295-310). London: Sage.

Arnould, E. (1989). Toward a broadened theory of preference formation and the diffusion of innovations: Cases from Zinder Province, Niger Republic. *Journal of Consumer Research, 16,* 239-267.

Barth, F. (1969). Introduction. In F. Barth (Ed.), *Ethnic groups and boundaries: The social organization of culture difference* (pp. 9-38). London: Allen & Unwin.

Belk, R. W. (1988). Third world consumer culture. In E. Kumcu & A. F. Fırat (Eds.), *Marketing and development: Toward broader dimensions* (pp. 103-127). Greenwich, CT: JAI.

Belk, R. W., & Pollay, R. W. (1985). Images of ourselves: The good life in twentieth century advertising. *Journal of Consumer Research, 11,* 887-898.

Belk, R., Wallendorf, M. R., & Sherry, J. F. (1989). The sacred and profane in consumer behavior: Theodicy in the odyssey. *Journal of Consumer Research, 16,* 1-38.

Berry, J. W., Poortinga, Y. H., Segall, M. H., & Dasen, P. R. (1992). *Cross-cultural psychology: Research and applications.* Cambridge, UK: Cambridge University Press.

Burton, M. R., & White, D. R. (1987). Cross-cultural survey today. *Annual Review of Anthropology, 16,* 143-160.

Campbell, C. (1987). *The romantic ethic and the spirit of modern consumerism.* Oxford, UK: Basil Blackwell.

Costa, J. A. (1993, August). *Culture and marketing.* Paper presented at the Macromarketing Conference, University of Rhode Island, Kingston.

Das, V. (1987). The sacred and the profane in Hinduism. In V. Das (Ed.), *Structure and cognition: Aspects of Hindu caste and ritual* (pp. 114-131). Delhi: Oxford University Press.

Dawson, S., & Bamossy, G. J. (1990). Isolating the effect of non-economic factors on the development of a consumer culture: A comparison of materialism in the Netherlands and United States. In M. E. Goldberg, G. Gorn, & R. W. Pollay (Eds.), *Advances in consumer research* (Vol. 17, pp. 182-185). Provo, UT: Association for Consumer Research.

de Pyssler, B. (1992). The cultural and political economy of the Indian two-wheeler. In J. F. Sherry & B. Sternthal (Eds.), *Advances in consumer research* (Vol. 19, pp. 437-442). Provo, UT: Association for Consumer Research.

De Vos, G. (1975). Ethnic pluralism: Conflict and accommodation. In G. De Vos & L. Romanucci-Ross (Eds.), *Ethnic identity: Cultural continuities and change* (pp. 1-22). Chicago: University of Chicago Press.

Douglas, M., & Isherwood, B. (1979). *The world of goods: Towards an anthropology of consumption.* New York: Norton.

Durkheim, E. (1965). *The elementary forms of the religious life.* Glencoe, IL: Free Press. (Original work published 1915)

Durkheim, E. (1964). *The sociological method.* Glencoe, IL: Free Press. (Original work published 1912)

Elias, N. (1982). *The history of manners.* New York: Pantheon.

Engel, J. F., Blackwell, R. D., & Kollat, D. T. (1978). *Consumer behavior* (3rd ed.). Hindsdale, IL: Dryden.

Erez, M., & Earley, P. C. (1993). *Culture, self-identity, and work.* New York: Oxford University Press.

Eriksen, T. H. (1993). *Ethnicity and nationalism.* London: Pluto.

Firat, A. F., & Venkatesh, A. (1994). *The making of postmodern consumption* (Working paper). Irvine: University of California.

Foster, G. (1962). *Traditional cultures and the impact of technological change.* New York: Harper & Row.

Foster, G. (1969). *Applied anthropology.* Boston: Little, Brown.

Friedman, J. (1990). Being in the world: Globalization and localization. In M. Featherstone (Ed.), *Global culture* (pp. 311-328). London: Sage.

Gatignon, H., & Robertson, T. S. (1985). A propositional inventory for new diffusion research. *Journal of Consumer Research, 11,* 849-867.

Geertz, C. (1973). *The interpretation of cultures.* New York: Basic Books.

Geertz, C. (1983). From the native's point of view. In C. Geertz, *Local knowledge: Further essays in anthropology* (pp. 55-70). New York: Basic Books.

Ger, G., & Belk, R. W. (1990). Measuring and comparing materialism cross-culturally. In M. E. Goldberg, G. Gorn, & R. W. Pollay (Eds.), *Advances in consumer research* (Vol. 17, (pp. 186-192). Provo, UT: Association for Consumer Research.

Ger, G., Belk, R. W., & Lascu, D.-N. (1993). The development of consumer desire in marketizing and developing economies: The cases of Romania and Turkey. In L. McAlister & M. L. Rothschild (Eds.), *Advances in consumer research* (Vol. 20, pp. 102-107). Provo, UT: Association for Consumer Research.

Glazer, N., & Moynihan, D. P. (1975). *Ethnicity: Theory and experience.* Cambridge, MA: Harvard University Press.

Goody, J. (1993). Culture and its boundaries. *Social Anthropology, 1*, 9-32.

Hebdige, D. (1988). *Hiding in the light: On images and things.* London: Routledge.

Hegeman, S. (1991). Shopping for identities: "A nation of nations" and the weak ethnicity of objects. *Public Culture, 3*(2), 71-92.

Hirschman, E. (1981). American Jewish ethnicity: Its relationship to some selected aspects of consumer behavior. *Journal of Marketing, 45*, 102-110.

Hofstede, G. (1980). *Culture's consequences: International differences in work-related values.* London: Sage.

Holy, L. (1987). Description, generalization, comparison: Two paradigms. In L. Holy (Ed.), *Comparative anthropology* (pp. 1-21). Oxford, UK: Basil Blackwell.

Howe, L. (1987). Caste in Bali and India: Levels of comparison. In L. Holy (Ed.), *Comparative anthropology* (pp. 135-152). Oxford, UK: Basil Blackwell.

Jain, R., & Costa, J. A. (1991). Research progress report: Fragrance use in India. In J. A. Costa (Ed.), *Gender and consumer behavior* (Vol. 1, pp. 77-84). Salt Lake City: University of Utah.

Joy, A., & Dholakia, R. R. (1991). Remembrances of things past: The meaning of home and possessions of Indian professionals in Canada. *Journal of Social Behavior and Personality, 6*(6), 385-402.

Kluckhohn, F., & Strodtbeck, F. (1961). *Variations in value orientation.* Westport, CT: Greenwood.

Ko, G., & Gentry, J. W. (1991). The development of time orientation for use in cross-cultural research. In R. H. Holman & M. R. Solomon (Eds.), *Advances in consumer research* (Vol. 18, pp. 135-142). Provo, UT: Association for Consumer Research.

Kroeber, A. L. (1923). *Anthropology.* New York: Harcourt, Brace.

Liddle, J., & Joshi, R. (1986). *Daughters of independence: Gender, caste and class in India.* London: Zed.

Linton, R. (1945). *The cultural background of personality.* New York: Appleton-Century.

Manuel, P. (1993). *Cassette culture: Popular music and technology in North India.* Chicago: University of Chicago Press.

Marcus, G. E., & Fischer, M. M. J. (1986). *Anthropology as cultural critique: An experimental moment in the human sciences.* Chicago: University of Chicago Press.

Marriott, M. (1990). Constructing an Indian ethnosociology. In M. Marriott (Ed.), *India through Hindu categories* (pp. 1-40). New Delhi: Sage.

McCracken, G. (1988). *Culture and consumption.* Bloomington: Indiana University Press.

Mehta, R., & Belk, R. W. (1991). Artifacts, identity, and transition: Favorite possessions of Indians and Indian immigrants to the United States. *Journal of Consumer Research, 17*, 398-411.

Nash, M. (1989). Ethnicity: Meaning and vicissitudes. In M. Nash (Ed.), *The cauldron of ethnicity in the modern world* (pp. 1-28). Chicago: University of Chicago Press.

Ortner, S. B. (1991). Reading America: Preliminary notes on class and culture. In R. G. Fox (Ed.), *Recapturing anthropology* (pp. 163-190). Santa Fe, NM: School of American Research Press.

Penaloza, L. (1994). Atravesando fronteras/Border crossing: A critical ethnographic study of immigrant Mexicans. *Journal of Consumer Research, 21*, 32-54.

Pollay, R. W. (1986). The distorted mirror: Reflections of the unintended consequences of advertising. *Journal of Marketing, 50*(2), 18-36.

Pollay, R. W. (1988). Keeping advertising from going down in history—unfairly. *European Journal of Marketing, 22*(6), 7-16.

Rabinow, P., & Sullivan, W. M. (1987). The interpretive turn. In P. Rabinow & W. M. Sullivan (Eds.), *Interpretive social science: A second look* (pp. 1-32). Berkeley: University of California Press.

Ramanujan, A. K. (1990). Is there an Indian way of thinking? An informal essay. In M. Marriott (Ed.), *India through Hindu categories* (pp. 41-58). New Delhi: Sage.

Rogers, E. M. (1962). *Diffusion of innovations.* New York: Free Press.

Rudmin, F. W. (1990). German and Canadian data on motivations for ownership: Was Pythagoras right? In M. E. Goldberg, G. Gorn, & R. W. Pollay (Eds.), *Advances in consumer research* (Vol. 17, pp. 176-181). Provo, UT: Association for Consumer Research.

Sahlins, M. (1976). *Culture and practical reason.* Chicago: University of Chicago Press.

Schnaiberg, A. (1970). Measuring modernism: Theoretical empirical explorations. *American Journal of Sociology, 76,* 399-425.

Sharma, U. (1986). *Women's work, class, and the urban household.* London: Tavistock.

Sherry, J. F., & Camargo, E. G. (1987). May your life be marvelous. *Journal of Consumer Research, 14,* 174-188.

Singer, M. (1972). *When a great tradition modernizes: An anthropological approach to Indian civilization.* Chicago: University of Chicago Press.

Singer, M. (1989). A changing American image of India: The prospect of a civilization. In C. M. Borden (Ed.), *Contemporary Indian tradition* (pp. 1-18). Washington, DC: Smithsonian Institution Press.

Singhal, A., & Rogers, E. (1989). *India's information revolution.* New Delhi: Sage.

Spicer, E. H. (Ed.). (1952). *Human problems in technological change.* New York: John Wiley.

Srinivas, M. N. (1966). *Social change in modern India.* Berkeley: University of California Press.

Stayman, D., & Deshpande, R. (1989). Situational ethnicity and consumer behavior. *Journal of Consumer Research, 16,* 361-371.

Tambiah, S. (1989). Ethnic conflict in the world today. *American Ethnologist, 16*(2), 335-349.

Tan, C. T., & Sheth, J. (1985). *Historical perspective in consumer research: National and international perspectives.* Singapore: Association for Consumer Research and the National University of Singapore.

Triandis, H. C., & Lambert, W. W. (Eds.). (1980). *Handbook of cross-cultural psychology: Vol 1. Perspectives.* Boston: Allyn & Bacon.

Tse, D. K., Belk, R. W., & Zhou, N. (1991). Becoming a consumer society: A longitudinal analysis of print ads from Hong Kong, The People's Republic of China, and Taiwan. *Journal of Consumer Research, 15,* 179-201.

Tylor, E. B. (1878). *Researches into the early history of mankind and the development of civilization* (3rd ed.). London: John Murray.

Udy, S. H., Jr. (1973). Cross-cultural analysis: Methods and scope. *Annual Review of Anthropology, 2,* 253-270.

Vajpeyi, D. (1982). Modernity and industrial culture of Indian cities. *Journal of Asian and African Studies, 18*(1-2), 74-97.

van Raaij, W. F., & Bamossy, G. J. (1993). *European advances in consumer research.* Provo, UT: Association for Consumer Research.

Venkatesh, A. (1985). A conceptualization of the household technology interaction. In E. C. Hirschman & M. B. Holbrook (Eds.), *Advances in consumer research* (Vol. 12, pp. 189-194). Provo, UT: Association for Consumer Research.

Venkatesh, A. (1994). Gender identity in the Indian context: A sociocultural construction of the female consumer. In J. A. Costa (Ed.), *Gender issues and consumer behavior* (pp. 42-62). Thousand Oaks, CA: Sage.

Venkatesh, A., & Swamy, S. (1994). India as an emerging consumer society: A critical perspective. In C. J. Schultz II, R. W. Belk, & G. Ger (Eds.), *Research in consumer behavior: Consumption in marketizing economies* (pp. 193-224). Greenwich, CT: JAI.

Venkatesh, A., & Vitalari, N. (1992). An emerging distributed work arrangement: An investigation of computer-based supplemental work at home. *Management Science, 38*(12), 1687-1706.

Wadley, S. S. (1977). Women and the Hindu tradition. In D. Jacobson & S. Wadley (Eds.), *Women in India: Two perspectives* (pp. 113-140). New Delhi: Manohar.

Webster's Third New International Dictionary. (1986). Springfield, MA: Merriam.

Whiting, B. B., & Whiting, J. W. (1975). *Children of six cultures: A psychocultural analysis.* Cambridge, MA: Harvard University Press.

Williams, R. (1981). *Culture.* London: Fontana.

Wissler, C. (1929). An introduction to social anthropology. New York: Oxford University Press.

Witkowski, T. (1993). The Polish consumer in transition. In L. McAlister & M. L. Rothschild (Eds.), *Advances in consumer research* (Vol. 20, pp. 13-17). Provo, UT: Association for Consumer Research.

Yau, O. H. M. (1988). Chinese cultural values: Their dimensions and marketing implications. *European Journal of Marketing, 22*(5), 44-57.

Zmud, J., & Arce, C. (1992). The ethnicity and consumption relationship. In J. F. Sherry & B. Sternthal (Eds.), *Advances in consumer research* (Vol. 19, pp. 443-449). Provo, UT: Association for Consumer Research.

3

Marketing and the Redefinition of Ethnicity

DOMINIQUE BOUCHET

Human civilization depends on the diversity of cultures and ethnic identities.

Georges Devereux[1]

If the market were a lake, some marketers would just skim its surface. Many would be satisfied to take its surface temperature; a few would really care to investigate its deeper currents. But all would splash around to avoid drowning in it, greatly altering its fascinating surface on which each person tries to see his or her own reflection. In my view, marketing is today, more than ever, confronted with the problem of this splashing around. In fact, marketers can no longer avoid this tumultuous activity. An example of the splashing around is the way marketers currently react to the problems related to cultural diversity in Europe.

Many of the important issues with which marketers are confronted are related to the ways consumers identify themselves and the ways marketers identify the market. The intensification of internationalization and the loosening of cultural bonds challenge marketers. Marketers are increasingly asking questions such as: Should one advertise differently in Germany than in France? How can we cope with ever-changing lifestyles? What is the importance of cultural identity and cultural diversity in the market? In short, marketers wish to know how to cope better with cultural diversity. Europe after Maastricht and the collapse of the Soviet empire make it even more relevant to deal with the market, ethnicity, and cultural identity. But many marketers tend to adopt an attitude toward ethnicity and cultural identity in which they consider the market from the outside, without really realizing that their understanding of it and the actions they take toward it in fact contribute to further manifestations of cultural identity and ethnicity.

The first relevant point is that the theories and concepts used to analyze cultural entities, national specificity, and ethnicity do not just build on neutral objective definitions; they are the result of political struggles. Thus, the cultural differences and ethnic relations that are experienced in today's Europe can be explained by historical choices. These cultural differences and these relations should not, therefore, be considered as given once, for all. The importance of being aware of the historical nature and relativity of the conceptual framework prompts a more reflective and reflexive approach to the problems of ethnicity. This is, of course, even more necessary in marketing because marketing can be said to be one of the more central institutions of late modern society (Bouchet, 1991; see also Laufer & Paradeise, 1982/1990). Marketing, in its way of dealing with cultural diversity and ethnicity, has a tremendous impact on the further development of cultural identity and influences the future of what today are called ethnic groups and nations.

The second important point is that cultural identity in today's Europe is not organized in the same way as it was a few decades ago. The concept of ethnicity, which was once central to the understanding of cultural identity, no longer plays the same role. Identity and culture are still, of course, intertwined, universal phenomena. But the anchoring points of cultural identities are not what they used to be; when one refers to ethnicity in present-day Western Europe, one refers to something totally different. Ethnicity is no longer the point of departure or the necessary cultural reference, nor is it based entirely on historical background. Rather, ethnicity is the result of the nonintegration and of the destructuralization of the cultural community. Currently, ethnicity emerges because people experience a difference in the way they refer to the nation-state, to the past, and to the future. Ethnicity today has more to do with cultural loss than with cultural ties, more with the loss of a future than with the loss of a past. What remains, though, is the political character of the definition of ethnicity and cultural identity and the central opposition between those in favor of emphasizing cultural origins and those in favor of assimilation and an open future.

The third point is threefold and deals with the consequences of the emergence of a new understanding of both marketing and ethnicity. The understanding of actors within the field of marketing has a tremendous impact on the development of cultural identity; this should not be surprising because marketing is a constitutive part of today's culture. This redefinition of ethnicity should have a tremendous influence on marketing once this fundamental change is really understood by actors in marketing. I will try to show that today's ethnicity deals with the uncertainty of identity.

I will therefore first ask whether similar tendencies to those witnessed in Europe can be found in many other parts of the world, especially in the United States, even though ethnicity traditionally has a different basis in the United States than it does in Europe. Second, I will allude to what is at stake when marketers use ethnicity inappropriately. Third, I will stress the consequences that a further development of these tendencies might have for marketing and society.

Problematic Concepts

As a French historian stated in 1929:

> We are almost never confronted with impartially classified facts to combine as we please. We come up against traditional, more or less arbitrary selections of events and interpretations against collections of ideas and documents that have become classic: In brief, against "important problems" set, at times centuries ago, under the influence of customs, ideas and needs that are no longer ours. (Febvre, 1984, p. 13; translated from the French; all original quotes available from the author)

No wonder, then, that the concepts that are often used to describe the situation of some of the newcomers to European society can be misleading; they were produced in times when social science cared less for objectivity and reflexivity.

Western Europe has become host to many different groups of people during recent decades, and with the help of modern television, these groups seem to be omnipresent. Many older residents get the feeling that they are witnessing an invasion. One of the main issues of recent European politics has been the assertion that Islamic fundamentalism is spreading into the very heart of Europe.

Recent dramatic changes that have taken place in Eastern Europe and the former Soviet republics have opened new markets and created far-reaching economic and political challenges. As the historian Eric Hobsbawm (1992) stated:

> That ethnic-linguistic separation provides no sort of basis for a stable, in the short run even for a roughly predictable, ordering of the globe is evident in 1992 from the merest glance at the large region situated between Vienna and Trieste in the west, and Vladivostock in the east. (p. 184)

Nevertheless, the reference to ethnicity is ascendant, and marketers and politicians do have to refer to what is often called "the ethnic situation."

Defining Ethnic Groups and Ethnicity

Words that are used to describe and analyze the ethnic situation are taken from the old vocabulary of social science and politics. One talks about "ethnic groups" living in "ghettos," for instance. But these terms do not lead to a greater understanding of the situation. The term *ghetto* was originally applied to the Jewish quarter of prewar European cities, but most people now use the term to refer to "any urban area, often deprived, which is occupied by a group segregated on the basis of religion, colour or ethnicity" (Abercrombie, Hill, & Turner, 1984, p. 95). A ghetto is "a highly-congested ethnic slum" (Reading, 1977, p. 94), "a segregated community, usually racially or culturally homogeneous, within a larger community" (Theodorson, 1969, p. 174).

The term *ethnicity* is one that is not as easily understood as that of ghetto, although it is often used in connection with it. As stated above, a very commonly used paperback dictionary of social sciences provides a very short definition of a ghetto as "a highly-congested ethnic slum" (Reading, 1977, p. 94). But what does the term *ethnicity* cover? Comparing this short definition to the other definitions quoted here gives the feeling that ethnicity is a broader concept than religion, than color, and maybe even than culture.

Of course, it has long been evident that one should make a distinction between a group that claims ethnic distinctiveness and one that has distinctiveness imposed on it by some more powerful group. But this distinction is just the start of a greater understanding of cultural identity that draws attention to the play of mirrors that occurs in identity building.

According to the 1989 Merriam-Webster definition, *ethnicity* refers to "ethnic quality or affiliation;" an *ethnic* is "a member of an ethnic group; a member of a minority group who retains the customs, language, or social views of his group." The adjective *ethnic* is defined as: "of or relating to large groups of people classed according to common racial, national, tribal, religious, linguistic, or cultural origin or background" (Merriam-Webster, 1989, CD-ROM edition). Yet social scientists commonly make a distinction between a *tribe* and an *ethnic group*. The ethnic group designates a group of a certain size, sharing the same language and culture but not necessarily the same territory, although there is implicit reference to a common territory (Smith, 1991; see also Horowitz, 1985, especially Chap. 1 & 2; Smith, 1986, especially Chap. 2).[2] The term *tribe* usually refers to a smaller group. But all words are culturally biased and have a history and an origin; development of the concepts of tribes and ethnic groups are related to the outbreak of modernity.

The cultural and historical dimension of the concept, however, does not seem to have caught the interest of the many researchers within the field of ethnicity. A. C. Taylor (1991) remarked that ethnicity, even if often used and politically central, is one of the notions less theorized about in anthropology. Many researchers use the concept in an uncritical way; Isajiw (1974) pointed out that

> there are too many, indeed too many, studies that pretend to give us explanations of various phenomena connected with ethnicity yet in effect give us at best descriptions of various correlates of ethnicity, simply because they fail to make the link between the empirically observed phenomena and any theory that may provide the explanatory import. The link, of course, would be a logically sufficient definition of ethnicity. (p. 112)

What is necessary, he claimed, is an explicit definition of ethnicity that itself would provide a connection to a more general theory.

Noting that very few researchers of ethnic relations ever define the meaning of ethnicity, Isajiw (1974) examined 65 sociological and anthropological studies dealing with one or another aspect of ethnicity and came up with a composite definition of ethnicity as "a group or category of persons who have common ancestral origin and the same cultural traits, who have a sense of peoplehood and *Gemeinschaft* type of relations, who are of immigrant background and have either minority or majority status within a larger society" (p. 118). Discussing this composite definition, he then pointed out that it is not the common ancestral origin as such that is important, for all human beings ultimately have common ancestry; it is the ancestors or their descendants who can be said to have possessed the same cultural traits, as distinguished from persons and their ancestors with different cultural traits. He concluded that common origin in this sense indicates that a person is born into a group that shares certain cultural traits and therefore becomes socialized into them.

One should remember, however, that researchers also are socialized into cultures. Their definitions and their beliefs often reflect this embeddedness. According to Weber (1968), ethnicity is a matter of belief; he called ethnic groups "those human groups that entertain a subjective belief in their common descent because of similarities of physical type or of custom or both, or because of memories of colonization and emigration" (p. 389). Of course, such an emphasis on belief reflects the European political experience. In North America, mainly because of the so-called melting pot, one would be inclined to attach less importance to belief and focus more on the involuntary aspects of ethnicity. Indeed, Isajiw (1974) concluded with a general definition of ethnicity as referring to "an involuntary group of people who share the same culture" (p. 120). Isajiw thus emphasized that the person has no choice as to the specific cultural group that provides for him or her the basic process of socialization. One could even end with a conception that gave no room for choice, whereby ethnicity would be seen as the result of a socialization process to which individuals who belong involuntarily to specific groups are submitted.

There seems to be a rising dimension of choice in the so-called ethnic groups of Europe, however. I do not agree, therefore, with Breton and Pinard (1960) when they claimed that "a person does not belong to an ethnic category by choice. He is born into it and becomes related to it through emotional and symbolic ties" (p. 474). On the contrary, I argue that the deterministic and objective conception of ethnicity is becoming somewhat obsolete. The dimension of choice is increasing, as people

provide themselves with an ethnic identity by a creative cocktail making, the ingredients of which are suggested by the diversity of images
they confront in a postmodern society. A redefinition of ethnicity is
therefore necessary.

The concept of ethnicity should not be maintained in its original form
once and for all and cannot be rooted in so-called objective data. Ethnicity is, of course, a loaded concept, which either reflects the *Zeitgeist*
or functions as a guideline for an investigation or another type of action. This is true for most of the social concepts, all of which indicate
how those who use them not only see but create differences. One of the
most fundamental differences that people make regards their identity,
their sense of belonging (Bouchet, 1994a).

Of course, one could still dream of finding an objective way to cate-
gorize. But it appears that all such ways lead to—and most often also
originate in—prejudice and discrimination. It is easier to see that the
uses and definitions of the concept of ethnicity reflect different cultural
perspectives. Isajiw (1974), for instance, pointed out that "the European
usage of the concept reflects, of course, the European experiences of
ethnicity" (p. 113). It is strange, though, that Isajiw had to use the concept as if it had an objective content: He wrote "experiences of ethnicity." In fact, ethnicity is not experienced but created, denied, or
maintained. The point is that it is not something that was there before
being experienced. The concept is one of the many expressions of ways
of creating the social bond.

And the social bond changes. That is why it is no longer true—if it
has ever been[3]—that "definitions referring to ethnic groups in Europe
never conceive them as subgroups of a larger society" (Isajiw, 1974,
p. 113). Isajiw wrote that the term *ethnic group* is not used very often in
European sociological literature. Instead, the preferred terms are *nation*
or *nationality*. He contrasted this conception to the North American one,
in which reference to political and territorial boundaries is not central
and the notion of subsociety is critical. Nevertheless, it is now true, as
we shall see, that the concept of ethnicity in the 1990s can be used in
Europe to refer to subsocieties.

In fact, ethnicity and the phenomena to which it relates should be
considered in a historical perspective, taking into account the radical
changes that have occurred regarding personal and national identity.
Related concepts are those of lifestyles, subcultures, and globalization.
Related phenomena are immigration, massification, and secularization. Even such concepts as those of marketing and segmentation have
an impact on ethnicity. The endeavors of marketers to find ways of

segmenting the market provide mirrors for identification and pictures for prejudice.

Ethnos, Culture, and Cultural Identity

As Suzanne Citron (1989) once wrote in concluding her study of the French national myth, "What we regard as 'our' history follows from a manipulation of the past by the elites on duty or in support of the different powers" (p. 279). Indeed, the concepts used to deal with the perception of one's own cultural identity in confrontation with other human beings express the cultural choices made by those who have the power to create and develop the new differences. The story of the whole set of words—*culture, identity, ethnic group, tribe, race, people, nation,* and the like—is the story of the building of a frontier between those who provided the definitions of the differences and those who had to accept the discrimination.

Derived from the Greek *ethnos,* which stands for *people,* the word *ethnic* long remained an ecclesiastical term. Latinized and then made French and English, the term served as an indication of a difference between those who did and those who did not acknowledge the God of the Bible. Indeed in Merriam-Webster (1989), the first definition of the adjective *ethnic* is *heathen.* Secular language will designate those groups of people in other cultures with the words *people* or *nation* before the words *race* and *tribe.* This became more common, particularly in the 19th century, as the word *nation* was seen more and more to connote *civilization* or *culture* in the original meaning of those words (see Beneton, 1975; Boudon, 1992; Boudon & Bourricaud, 1982; Elias, 1939/1979; Williams, 1976).[4] *Nation* was then used to distinguish "civilized" states and people and, at least in French, to designate the subject of a historical destiny (Amselle & M'Bokolo, 1985). The use of these terms is strongly dependent on a specific understanding of a particular way of being together in the world, of a particular way of identifying oneself as part of a group—in other words—of a culture.

The concept of *race*—now referring to physical criteria—was considered too global, and in French was replaced by the word *ethnie* to designate what was felt to be less than a nation but somehow akin to it. In fact, *ethnie* designated the lack of something that was thought to be superior; the French substantive *ethnie* was defined in negative terms. The outbreak in usage of these terms was strongly related to the demands of the colonialist system. The naming, categorizing, and dividing of the subjugated populations, assigning them physical and cultural borders, contributed to the self-understanding of the colonialist culture and to the enclosure of those who were defined as outsiders (Amselle & M'Bokolo, 1985). The elements of the social science that worked on this newly delimited field were to be called *ethnology* or *ethnography*. But here again the cultural differences of Europe had an impact on the ways in which the various traditions developed.

Different Nations of Europe

The same words can be used throughout the ages, but their meaning does not remain the same. The signification of the words *people* and *nation* has indeed evolved since the Middle Ages, when they were used interchangeably. This evolution is not purely linguistic but can be said to be a social one. Gérard Noiriel (1992) stated that these terms have been progressively elaborated by individuals involved in political and social struggles, in which one of the essential stakes was precisely the definition of those words. Norbert Elias (1939/1979) captured the marked differences between Germany on the one hand, and Britain and France on the other; the tensions that were manifest in the concepts gave expression to the self-understanding of these societies. Eric Hobsbawm (1992) showed how those concepts evolved differently in different nations to result in different types of nationalism. Louis Dumont (1991) analyzed the specificity of two different ways of building up a cultural identity in European history: that of France and that of Germany (see also Blackbourn & Evans, 1991). The core problems of the issues of ethnicity and cultural identity originated in the ideological developments in Germany and France two centuries ago.

In France, as has been shown by François Furet and Mona Ozouf (1979), the modern speculation about the nation emerged in the 18th century and was at once caught up in the political struggles between those in favor of aristocracy and those in favor of the elite of the third estate. Internal politics were already at stake in the discussion of the question of nation. The aristocrats endorsed "an 'ethnic' conception" (Noiriel, 1992, p. 8) on the basis of victorious origin and blood rights; the philosophers of the Enlightenment defended an assimilationist conception of the nation.

As Hobsbawm, Noiriel, and other historians have pointed out, the French conception of what a nation is, as well as the French penchant for assimilation, owes much to the political situation and interest of the intellectual bourgeoisie of the time. To bring into disrepute the preten-

sions of aristocracy was a rebuff that meant denying origins any important role in the foundation of the national community. To decide on
assimilation and to adopt the thesis of the "contract social" was a way
to challenge and battle the privileges of the nobility. Nevertheless, as
these principles evolved into the French standpoint about the nation
and were freed from their original context, those very principles would
later, under other conditions, be used to solve other types of problems,
such as immigration.

In Germany, things turned out differently, which helps to explain
some of the important contemporary cultural differences between
France and Germany. The German conception of the nation emerged
from a different political background; the German intellectual bourgeoisie had not reached the same position as they had in France or in
Great Britain. In Germany, a much greater gap separated the aristocracy from an enlightened bourgeoisie, which could not participate
much in internal affairs. In France and Great Britain, the intellectuals
did not have this political background and did not feel the same frustration concerning the status of culture and the constitution of a nation.
French and British intellectuals had a large audience within a prosper-
ous and broad-minded bourgeoisie and an enlightened aristocracy;
their education had definitively been granted a central importance, and
their nations had been long established. As a result, the most radical
difference between the French and the German political fundament of
national identity is that in Germany, foreign affairs and not internal
affairs, as in France, were at stake.

Napoleon's troops invaded the states of the former German empire.
Reflections on events in Europe at the time did not take a similar direction. The modern discussion about nation, culture, civilization, and the
like was biased in the opposite way. As such, the debate was not so
much influenced by the fight against the aristocracy as by the reaction
against the universal pretensions of the French philosophers and the
Napoleonic invasion. For these reasons, there was little focus in Germany
on internal differences and little reflection on the problems of assimilation. This variation in approach can still be traced in today's different
codes of and debate about nationality on both sides of the Rhine.

Because the discussion of *nation* in Germany was affected by a different type of relationship between the intellectual bourgeoisie and the
aristocracy, the majority of intellectuals became more inclined in such
an ideological matter to adopt an ethnic definition of the nation: a definition that would have been much more difficult to develop in France
for the simple reason of the ethnic diversity of that country. As Noiriel
(1992) put it:

Whereas what haunts theoretical thought in France is the transition from ethnic diversity to national unity, in Germany, since the unity of the people is taken for granted, intellectuals strive to detect the constitutive elements of this unity in order to maintain them and enhance their significance in reaction to the French domination that justifies invasion by a universal conception of the nation. It is therefore by no means accidental if the main fundament of the German conception of the nation is precisely the rejection of universalism. (p. 10)

The Changing Reality of the Concept of Ethnicity

Of course, something has happened since these concepts were taken from antiquity and given a new content. The concept of tribe survived the disfavor of evolutionism and was often used by functionalists to designate societies organized without a state. The relationship to territory became more important, as may be seen from reading Evans-Pritchard (1940), for example. Shapera (1958) and Gluckman (1965) demonstrated the capacity of so-called tribes to adapt their political institutions to new situations; this contributed to the outbreak of the term *tribalism* to designate conservative behavior within those societies, a term that is still used in a disparaging manner to designate behavior in societies without a state.

Some of the important works that have dealt with the notion of ethnicity are those of Bennett (1975), Cohen (1978), and Despres (1975), who made clear that "ethnic identities which are self-ascribed need not correspond to the identities which others impose" (p. 193).[5] Many have contributed to the discussion: Nicolas (1973) insisted on the fact that the members of an ethnic group assert their differences with their neighbors; Nadel (1942/1971) emphasized that the most important criterion is that the members claim that they belong to the ethnic group; Fortes (1945) considered the borderlines at the horizon of the ethnic group to be paramount. Beyond those lines, the relationships of cooperation and opposition are only occasionally significant, Fortes remarked. Mercier (1968) and Nadel (1942/1971) emphasized that one should not consider an ethnic group outside of the larger sociogeographic and historical context. It is important not to have too rigid a perspective on ethnic groups; one should have a historical perception of them.

Marshall Sahlins (1968) and E. R. Service (1962) have reintroduced the use of the term *tribe* as connected to a universal state of development, that of the "neolithic revolution." The main idea is that in the tribal grouping mode, what today are called politics, economics, and religion are not organized in separate institutions but function within the relations of kinship and that hierarchy is organized in homogeneous segments in general opposition to one another. Maurice Godelier (1977) has shown how the crisis of the concept of tribe illustrates important empirical and theoretical anthropological problems. Other anthropologists have discussed the use of the term *tribe* to describe Mediterranean social alliances relying on marriage as having an important impact on status and politics in those countries since antiquity ("Tribus," 1987).

The old conception of tribes and ethnic groups as discrete entities with their own culture, their own language, and their own psychological identity is no longer central in anthropology. In the 1960s the works of Erving Goffmann (1959), Fredrik Barth (1969),[6] and others showed that an ethnic group is an ascriptive category whose continuity rests on the maintenance of a frontier and, therefore, depends on the ever renewed codification of cultural differences between neighboring groups.

As indicated, it has been shown that in colonial times what were called ethnic groups were in fact politically constituted from the outside. Also stressed has been the fact that it was the stereotypes of neighboring groups that produced the so-called cultural identity of the tribe or ethnic group.[7] It is now clearly understood that ethnic groups always crystallize—today as in the past—on the basis of political interactions with other groups, just as it is also now evident that what is said to be ethnic is only one aspect of identity and culture; ethnicity merited neither being reified nor being raised to such a central epistemological status.

This should particularly be kept in mind when dealing with the resurgence of "ethnic problems" in contemporary Europe. In colonized territories, the ethnicist discourse was used by colonialist groups to legitimize a certain way of acting toward other groups. The same type of phenomenon is occurring today in Europe, where those concepts are used to organize an understanding of social interaction and social change.

Because any identity has to derive inspiration from the available symbolic system, it is not only the members of the dominant group who believe in the reality of the concept. Those who are identified by the dominant group as belonging to an ethnic group can also choose to identify themselves with some of the characteristics with which they have been attributed. I am not saying that there is no characteristic that preexists the confrontation with the dominant group; however, the importance given to those characteristics and the perceived group borders are not predetermined or unchangeable. The characteristics are just partial elements that could enter into many other types of symbolic and political systems.

The importance given to ethnicity by the "ethnic group" itself will always depend on a series of factors. Examples of the type of factors that historically have had an effect on cultural and personal identities are an accelerating urbanization, the failure of political claims, the setback of class struggle, the breaking of existing social bonds (such as family ties or work connections), radical changes in some persons' status, and the calling into question of existing institutions or parts of the symbolic system such as the importance of the national image or the meaning of work. In the following section I will use Daniel Bell's (1975) 20-year-old analysis of the rising salience of ethnicity to stress what has changed lately and what is radically different in today's Western Europe as compared with American society 20 years ago.

Cultural Syncretism

In the early 1970s, Daniel Bell (1975; reproduced in Bell, 1980) remarked that in the preceding decade and in widely divergent societies, there had been a resurgence of ethnic identification as the basis for effective political action. Analyzing the major social trends that were reworking the structures of society, Bell tried to find an explanation for the salience of ethnic groups.

Most of the major social trends Bell listed then are still important today. The tendency toward more inclusive identities has led large numbers of people to abandon inherited ways and beliefs as outdated and to find new modes and creeds of uncertain validity, spreading throughout entire societies and creating a sense of uprootedness. Like many sociologists, Bell saw that a major influence in the breakup of older parochial beliefs was the greater mingling and jostling of peoples, resulting in stylistic borrowing and exchange in cultural syncretism.

It was not cultural syncretism that was the most important factor in 1975, however; Bell suggested that the most important form of inclusiveness was political: "Today there are strong tendencies toward wider economic and social unities, yet no real 'civil theology' to bind them. . . . In fact, it is where the 'civil theology' has broken down, or where it cannot be created, that one finds the centrifugal forces of separatism gaining strength" (p. 144). That is why, Bell claimed, ethnicity becomes a reference: "In these instances one would expect the rise of parochial forces to provide psychological anchorages for individuals; and ethnicity is one of these" (p. 144). As the desire for some particular or primordial anchorage becomes intensified, "ethnicity becomes more salient because it can combine an interest with an affective tie. Ethnicity provides a tangible set of common identifications—in language, food, music, names—when other social roles become more abstract and impersonal" (p. 169). In other words, people want to belong to smaller units and find in ethnicity an easy attachment.

Bell (1975) saw a major source of the salience of ethnic groups in American life in the rise of a "communal society," in the "politicization of society" affecting the communal lives of persons. He was referring to the fact that a shift from market to political organization had occurred: More and more decisions that had previously been left either to the market or to private negotiations were then under the purview of political entities. Because a market is dispersed and the actors are largely invisible, it is difficult to identify responsible parties; whereas in politics, "the spread of decision-making forces the organization of persons into communal and interest groups, and this multiplication of groups increases community conflict" (p. 144; 1980, p. 187). Individuals are compelled to join groups in order not to be excluded from the decisions; each group exercises veto powers and checks each other's purposes. Thus, any individuals who thought that their own participation would lead to the type of action they wanted end up being frustrated. As the need for group organization becomes more necessary, ethnic grouping, Bell argued, becomes a ready means for demanding group rights or providing defense against other groups.

At the same time, the redefinition of equality led to greater expectations from society. Tied to the value of achievement, equality has always been central in North America. Nevertheless, there has been an evolution from "equality of conditions" to "equality of opportunity" and further toward "equality of result." This pervasive revolution of rising expectations has changed every political citizen into a social claimant. The expression of political rights has often been reduced to the claim of entitlement to social rights.

In addition, according to Bell, industrial society places greater emphasis on skill as the basis of position and privilege, achievement becoming linked with technical competence, thereby leaving the political route as virtually the only major means available for unskilled individuals and groups to upgrade themselves in society. The development of skilled labor results also, as described by many sociologists (Gorz, 1980; Lecher, 1986) in the erosion of class identification.

In this context, concluded Bell (1975), claims are made on the basis of ascriptive or group identity, rather than on individual achievement. "What takes place, then, is the wedding of status issues to political demands through the ethnic groups" (pp. 170-171). And just as Bell (1960) prognosticated in the concluding chapter of his *The End of Ideology* that the new ideology of the last third of the 20th century would be drawn from the Third World, he also saw in this new ideology the rising importance of the ethnic reference in politics.

Ethnicity and Fragmented Management

According to Daniel Bell, the salience of ethnicity had much to do with the transition from market to politics. Nevertheless, in the 1990s, in Western Europe at least, politics are not preeminent. As I have asserted elsewhere, (Bouchet, 1994b), in postmodern society there is a tendency toward fragmented management, in which one claims that one does not need to legitimate anything, relying instead on one's own created symbolism. Georges Balandier (1985) expressed it well:

> It is the end of politics to the advantage of fragmented management of people and administration of things or, alternatively, in favor of the social, becoming a milieu (difficult to identify) capable of absorbing everything. It is the end of representative systems or, at the least, the crisis of representation; politics represents only itself and speaks only for itself; those represented no longer regard themselves as such, they are no longer implicated by their adhesion, but by the emotion (and its variations) and the changing beliefs submitted to the special effects produced by means of techniques. It is the arrival of power as spectacle and simulation, an indirect manner of announcing its end as reality. The age of the media imposes the permanent power of pictures, and thus the necessity of basing power on them; but the continued sensationality trivialises, it effaces the distance and the separation without which politics no longer has its own place, it replaces the secrecy (one of the weapons of the powers-that-be) by noise. The game of unconfessed complicities would mean that those subjected would adapt to absolute theatrocracy, and would accord more interest to the changes of program than to the programs for carrying out changes in society. The representation would be that of the spectacle; the power would no longer be maintainable except in becoming simulation and being satisfied with what is a simulation of civil rights. (p. 11)

The inscription of ethnicity in a societal context is, therefore, different today than in the times of political commitment. What is interesting is precisely this lack of possibility to express oneself politically, the lack of connection between identity and politics. The ethnic reference is no longer, as Bell thought, a way to express the demands of a group. Ethnicity does not express commitment to a group but rather the withdrawal from a group. It has more to do with style than with politics.

This political evolution is made easier by the further technical developments that have taken place in the economy and that have led to a redistribution of work qualifications (Robin, 1989). Today, even skilled labor is confronted with the insecurity of unemployment, and education is no longer a guarantee for economic integration. In addition, the educational system no longer dispenses social integration. Some high schools function more as a day care center[8] than as a place in which one is supposed to learn common knowledge and values. Even there, the future is not promising and the present often rather boring. Young people are challenging the authority of their teachers by creating embarrassing situations. Because school is supposed to be under secular control and the same for everybody, some students ask for special treatment and want to express—among other things, in their clothing (for example, the *tchador*)—their ethnic background (Bouchet, 1993).

Yet in my view, the most interesting remark by Bell (1975) on the rising importance of ethnicity 20 years ago is that

> ethnicity, in this context, is best understood *not* as a primordial phenomenon in which deeply held identities have to reemerge, but as a strategic choice by individuals who, in other circumstances, would choose other group memberships as a mean of gaining some power and privilege. In short, it is the *salience* not the *persona* that has to be the axial line for explanation. And because salience may be the decisive variable, the attachment to ethnicity may flush or fade very quickly depending on political and economic circumstances. (p. 171)

It is precisely this dimension of choice that appears to be the dynamic element in ethnicity today. In the following, I will argue that it is not the choice between two alternatives, that of the culture of the ancestors and that of the society in which one lives. What those people who refer to ethnicity in Western Europe today are confronted with is not like two different pairs of glasses but much more like a kaleidoscope. They have to build a self-identity on the basis of heterogeneous elements. They are combining those elements as a "do-it-yourself" person constructs something by using whatever comes their way. This is called, from the French, *bricolage*.

Ethnicity as Bricolage

Bricolage, at least since the writings of Lévi-Strauss (1962),[9] has referred to a creative activity that is improvised, is adapted to the materials at hand, and is not really part of an overall project. Ethnicity in postmodern Europe (Bouchet, 1994b)[10] is more bricolage than ever. It is not the continuation or the importation of an already existing cultural system, but rather the creation of a lifestyle. Ethnicity in today's Europe is, like new religiosity, à la carte.

The media talk a lot about a new wave of religiosity. In fact, however, this new religiosity has not much in common with the old one. People did not choose their religion in the old days. They were born into it, and they could not imagine changing it to adopt another one. Today's new religions have much more in common with today's malls than with yesterday's churches. The possibility of choice cannot be ignored. Everybody knows that there are alternatives. Within the same society, one has the choice among a variety of religions; such a choice was totally unimaginable in former times.

Something similar can be said about ethnicity today. In Western Europe, the idea that ethnicity is a key element of identity making among young immigrants of the second generation has become prominent in the media. Nevertheless, the way ethnicity enters into identity making is quite different from before.

Contrary to what appears in mass media, what is experienced is not the invasion of a foreign culture developing an enclave. It is not the transposition of a community coming from outside that keeps its identity, its ritual, its religion, its cuisine, its clothing, its language. It is not the reminiscence of tradition that is carried through modern times. It is the building of new and often individual identities on the basis of elements from a diversity of cultural representations and practices. One of the observers of the so-called ethnic groups of present-day Western Europe, Olivier Roy (1991), remarked:

> Ethnicity is an invention by the actors themselves of a new identity perceived and claimed in terms of exclusion through the creation of a code made up of borrowings from the modernity of the country of reception as well as from the fantasized past of a defunct community, a code formed more from the silence of the elders than from their speeches. (p. 40)

Roy (1991) pointed out, for example, that in the so-called Arabic communities, Arabic is not the primary language, and the Islamic religion is not really practiced and is used only on a symbolic level. Roy observed that it is the fast of Ramadan that is the most respected religious practice. He risked an interpretation of this phenomenon by saying that the importance of Ramadan may be because of its demonstrative and festive aspect, but it may also be because of all the religious observances, Ramadan demands the least knowledge and learning.

This phenomenon is mentioned by many a researcher observing Western European ethnic behavior. Isabelle Taboada-Leonetti (1990) called it *"identité volontariste"* (p. 76; see also Camilleri, 1980; Malewska-Peyre, 1983). Carmel Camilleri (1990) called it *"identité de principe"* and described the young people descended from immigrants who "continued to assert their affiliation to the group of Maghrébins whose traditional values they almost totally rejected, whilst they adopted the culture of the French to whose society they refused to affiliate" (pp. 91-92). Maurizio Catani (1989) stated that regardless of family education, the dominating social reality for this segment of French youth is that of the society in which they were born, even though they spend a few weeks once in a while at their grandparents' place in their parents' country of origin. Catani insisted that the generational conflicts that occur when young people choose their clothes and their sexual partners do not differ in nature—although they very often are more intense— from those experienced by contemporary French families of old stock.

Influenced by Dumont (1983), Catani (1989) stressed that what is central is that "young people complete what the preceding generations undertook: the individualization process" (p. 125). Catani also emphasized that the immigrant populations are somehow breaking up the national reality of European populations:

> The young people of foreign background empty the social organization, hitherto purely national and very recently cautiously European, of its meaning, because they belong to networks of cultural references and interests considerably broader generally than those that a number of representatives of the "public authority" and the majority of the natives of French origin have experienced physically and mastered intellectually. (p. 133)

The real question today regarding identity is: How will the generations influenced by the kaleidoscopic media construct their personal identities and social groups? Maurizio Catani (1983) stressed the confrontation within our value system:

Thus since our system of values virtually forces the subject, in the majority of cases, to identify himself by differentiating himself from his family origins, in what way will the observed subject combine two contradictory demands: the *continuity* of family sentiments and the education received, which is centered on *individual development*, characterized by the traits of our civilization, *liberty* and *equality?* The case of the children of immigrated parents is only one version of the general case. (p. 118)

This may be an important point. What we are observing among so-called ethnic groups might give us an idea of the type of identity difficulty and social problems that confrontation with a fast-changing socialization base may generate. As the inherited landmarks of identity making turn into ever-changing mirages, cultural identity loses its obviousness and spontaneity. Whether one likes it or not, whether one is a member of an ethnic minority or not, bricolage remains the only way to navigate. The way young people of the second generation of immigrants from a quite different culture react today to the challenge of identity may provide an indication of more general trends in the marketplace.

Olivier Roy (1991) stated that young people of the second generation of immigrants originating from a quite different culture are not transplants from an ethnic group that would have brought with it traditions and ways of life. They reinvent, fabricating new identities on the basis of bits and pieces of memories borrowed from the former generation, of fantasies induced by the modern media. They have at their disposal the models not only of the old family or clan structures but also of modern individualism and postmodern tribalism (Bouchet, 1994b; see also Maffesoli, 1988, 1992). The way they group and the way they isolate themselves owe much more to the postmodern culture of the country in which they now live than to the original culture of their parents. The youth are at odds with the cultural models of their parents, who usually still dream of integration or have a nostalgic relationship with the community structures of their country of origin.

In Olivier Roy's (1991) opinion:

If an "ethnicity" emerges it is precisely because people experience a difference on top of a cultural loss. The reconstruction of an identity is thus necessarily effected on a code of behavior consisting of borrowings from the host society: clothes, music, fast food and language, all of it broken, dismantled and reassembled—from backslang to break dance. Ethnicity is also a bricolage. (p. 41)

This "cultural loss" is also experienced by the parents. It has been noticed that it is in fact some of the parents frightened by the behavior—or the integration—of their children who choose Islam, somewhat as Catholics choose to practice their religion to provide a model of morality for their young children. But by so doing, parents also produce a bricolage similar to that of their children because they generate a symbolic community that is not ethnic but religious, on the basis of a social situation characterized by social change and not by continuity.

The role played by religion is indeed representative of the radical changes in so-called ethnic groups. The *Beurs*[11] know almost nothing about Islam. What seems to interest them is the provocative force of the word. The characteristics of the traditional understanding of ethnicity (as expressed in the previously quoted Isajiw's [1974] composite and general definitions, for instance), do not very well suit groups who "are of immigrant background" but are not "involuntary," do not "share the same culture," and do not "have a sense of peoplehood and *Gemeinschaft* type of relations" (pp. 118, 120).

Within the sociological tradition, the term *Gemeinschaft* refers to "relationships encompassing human beings as full personalities rather than single aspects or roles of human beings. These are relationships characterized by a high degree of cohesion, communality, and duration in time" (Nisbet & Perrin, 1977, p. 98):

> The most obvious and historically persistent types of *Gemeinschaft* are kinship groups, village communities, castes, religious organizations, ethnic groups, and guilds. In each of these the whole personality of the individual tends to be involved, and in each of them the claims of the social unity upon the individual tend to be nearly total. (p. 98)

In fact, the father of the concept, Ferdinand Tönnies, "derived all of the substance of his typology of *Gemeinschaft* from medieval village, family, and clan" (Nisbet, 1966/1970, p. 16). Here is one of Tönnies's (1887/ 1963) central quotes:

> The theory of *Gesellschaft* deals with the artificial construction of an aggregate of human beings that superficially resembles the *Gemeinschaft* insofar as the individuals live and dwell together peacefully. However in *Gemeinschaft* they remain essentially united in spite of all separating factors, whereas in *Gesellschaft* they are essentially separated in spite of all uniting factors. (p. 64)

The Totem of Ethnicity

How can we use such a term to characterize young people who have more in common with hooligans, Hell's Angels, and hip-hops than with Amish, guilds, or dwellers of an American Chinatown? It is neither the reference to a common past nor the perpetuation of a cultural bond that characterizes the socialization processes encountered in those ethnic groups of present-day Western Europe. Their relationship is not an involuntary one, and there is no guarantee that it will endure. With respect to the works of Tönnies and Nisbet (see previous quotes), the generations of the so-called ethnic community of today are "essentially separated in spite of all uniting factors." It can even be said that single aspects or roles play a greater importance in every individual than "the claims of the social unity." In other words, their "we" is more an "I" than the reverse.

Occurring are the building of an identity and the establishment of solidarity groups within a society whose social bond is very loose. The "ethnic groups" in Western Europe have more in common with skinheads, punks, hippies, and Rastafarians than with the Guyanese or the Jews. When elaborating their personalities and grouping themselves, individuals are influenced mainly by the boredom of their living conditions, the annoyance of their image as perceived by the dominant Other (which includes the mass media), the breakdown of their family structure, the loss of their parents' authority, the maladjustment of the education system, the loosening of the social bond, the fascination of consumption, the legitimacy of superfluity and mediocrity, the slackening of political commitment, and the resurgence of violence and force.

The virtual impossibility of connecting to an existing social bond at the macrolevel makes it necessary to unite at the local level. The negative image, which is almost impossible to reverse, makes it easy to choose the provocative attitude of an accepted negativity. The maladjustment of a school system, which no longer functions as an integrating institution but reinforces the feeling of frustration and the legitimacy of demand, encourages claims of singularity. The lack of future perspective leads to rejection. The lack of opportunities of integration and the dark future for employment make it easier to display rejection as an identity trait.

Like hooligans (Buford, 1991) or Heavy Metal fans, ethnics establish a mythical identification with what is pictured negatively and make incantatory references to their own norms. Ethnic groups can praise Saddam Hussein or despise Jews, just as some were fond of Castro,

Stalin, or Mao in the late 1960s (the main difference being that there is now no real reference to politics and no serious interest for political theories). Hooligans are proud of being among the few who dare practice extensive violence; they derive an identity from it. They need neither to know a lot nor to think much to do so. Many young people, referring proudly and provocatively to an ethnic background, adopt the same attitude. Some of them proclaimed sympathy for Saddam Hussein, others with the Koran, without even knowing anything about Hussein or the Koran other than the negative image they had among the dominant Other group. Just as youngsters choose their music style and pin-up posters of idols with enthusiasm, present-day ethnic groups use the images at their disposal to erect totems.

Nonetheless, this intended crystallizing of identities around the totem of ethnicity is unfeasible. In a world in which the points of reference are constantly changing place and form and in which the cultural foundations reveal their arbitrary semantic substance (Bouchet, 1985; see also Bouchet, 1987a, 1987b), it is difficult to erect anything except style.

Ethnicity as Style

Traditional ethnic groups kept their traditions. Postmodern ethnic groups keep up with their styles. They are not so much interested in their roots as in the way they see themselves. They do not so much refer to their ancestors as to the eyes of their contemporaries. They do not seek the approval of their parents but the disapproval of a society that does not provide them with possibilities for integration. It is not so much their differences they express as it is their refusal. It is not so much the content of a culture that interests them as the appearance of a form. Ethnicity is, more than ever, image and style.

Although "individual members of the same subculture can be more or less conscious of what they are saying in style and in what ways they are saying it" (Hebdige, 1979, p. 123), the subversive implications of style appear more and more clearly. Not being integrated is becoming a value among those people born of immigrant parents who do not find possibilities of integration. Nonintegration becomes the goal of frightened citizens and demagogic politicians.

In her recent study of violence in cities, Sophie Body-Gendrot (1993) stressed that ethnicity is the synthesis of several characteristics, whereby each element becomes more or less intense, depending on the circumstances. She emphasized that one of the most important of these circumstances is whether integration within society is functioning or not.

This point is also accentuated by Olivier Roy (1991), who wrote that "ethnicity is not therefore the point of departure but the result of the non-integration and the destructuralization of the community of origin, which has not known how to impose its values: the family is no longer the transmitting station" (p. 42). It is not only that the original community fails to communicate ancient values, however; it is also that the host community does not provide integrating values and does not allow a more integrating channel for the expression of the identity problems with which ethnic groups are confronted. Maurizio Catani (1989) put it this way: "As they cannot be formulated on an immediate social level, the ideological and economical choices of this part of the population will invariably be expressed on a more individual and underground level" (p. 133).

Of course, this is a vicious circle, as the societies taking in the ethnic groups—in the words of Carmel Camilleri (1990)—"identify their immigrants by means of an ethnic categorization as they belong to the less accepted groups" (pp. 91-92). This type of phenomenon is not alien to the individuals of ethnic groups themselves; ethnicity logically has to be self-referent. In the words of Georges Devereux (1978): "The treating of ethnic identity as an ideal self-model, composed of predicative statements of a psychological type, is, in terms of strict logic, an adulterated ethnic identity, i.e., one already contaminated by the ethnic personality self-model" (p. 142).

In other words, the whole ground of identity and of cultural difference is favorable to paradox (Bouchet, 1991). This should not be surprising—identity is always paradoxical. One must remember the words of Pierre Tap (1986): "There is, in my view, only paradoxical identity, place, real or imaginary, and source of conflicts and illusions, spaces varying with changing frontiers, times reconstructed by memory or marked by projects and utopias" (p. 12).

Ethnicity is part of this imaginary and paradoxical construction. "Ethnicity becomes assertion and demand of an identity," wrote Françoise Morin (1986), aware that ethnicity is "a dynamic concept that must be understood as an answer to a change of a social situation" (pp. 57-58). Ethnicity has become a way of reacting to social change, whereas it was formerly more a way of avoiding it. It is no longer the articulate expression of conformity to inherited unambiguous principles but the creative claim to nonintegration in a multicultural and rapidly changing society.

The Change of the Nature of Ethnicity

In conclusion, postmodern ethnicity is not the transfer or even the rebuilding on Western European territory of imported ethnic groups. It is the original and contemporary shaping of provocatively claimed ethnic groups by putting together heterogeneous elements borrowed from different cultures. It is a bricolage making use of a diversity of cultural motives from different origins and strongly influenced by the mirror image provided by the dominant Other and the overwhelming media.

The fact that the dominant Other still has a strong tendency to obscure (scotomize) any other characteristic than the ethnic origin should not prevent the researcher from seeing not an ethnic group in the traditional meaning of the word but a postmodern subculture. Table 3.1 summarizes some of the fundamental differences that I see in the way ethnicity has functioned as a reference in traditional, industrial, and postmodern societies.

What Is at Stake
When Marketing Plays With Ethnicity

A WORLDWIDE TREND

In view of the previous discussion, one may consider whether ethnicity in other parts of the world is not also evolving toward a new situation. Ethnicity is a historical category whose content owes much to the way the dominant groups look at the ethnic minorities. The reference to ethnicity is different when the socialization process relies more on mass media, the authority of the older generation is weak, and the range of identity is large.

There was a great difference between what were, years ago, referred to as ethnic groups in the United States and what is experienced in present-day Western Europe. Although ethnic groups in America were very much influenced by the emerging American culture, they contributed more to it than they were influenced by it. The society into which the different ethnic groups were "melting" was not at all as homogeneous as, for example, Scandinavian societies now receiving refugees from former Yugoslavia.

Nonetheless, the radical changes that occur in the imaginary of the postmodern (Bouchet, 1994b) societies might result in a diminution of

TABLE 3.1 Functions of Ethnicity in Societies

Ethnicity/Society	Traditional	Industrial	Postmodern
Main characteristic	Persona	Salience	Provocation
Identity principle	Evidence	Expression	Demand/Claim
Kind of "choice"	Ascribed	Strategic	Spectacular
Organizational principle	Affirmation	Attachment	Bricolage
Main function	Mirror	Megaphone	Totem
Main institutional reference	Religion	Politics	Style
Main political form	Conformism	Commitment	Withdrawal
Main conflict	War	Exploitation	Exclusion
Main subject	Us	We	Me
Time orientation	Focus on past	Loss of past	Loss of future
Social change	Not registered	Avoided	Reacted to
Mode of expression	Syntactic	Pragmatic	Semantic
Main cultural focus	Sectarianism	Syncretism	Eclecticism
Main cultural source	Homogeneous	Ambivalent	Heterogeneous
Main cultural filter	Dogma	Ideology	Kaleidoscope
Main social role	Orthodox	Diehard	Harbinger

the importance of this structural difference. For instance, the logic of ethnicity among Native Americans and Mexican immigrants in North America might be greatly affected by the social changes of recent decades. As the postmodern condition becomes salient, as the way the dominant Other looks at those people evolves,[12] it might become true that the so-called ethnic groups in North America have much in common with Western European "ethnic groups."

The same holds true in Eastern Europe. Although it appears that the ethnic references in the different groups are in opposition in the civil war in former Yugoslavia, it can be said that, even there, it is not only the past that haunts but also the radical changes of the imaginary of the future. Nevertheless, the role played by nationalism all over Europe is clear, and the impact of modern consumption culture cannot be denied. In the near future, the role played by marketing will be even more prominent in providing elements for identity making all over the world. The marketing of cigarettes, for instance, is already striking in most East European countries. And what is usually called "the American lifestyle" is familiar to more and more people on this planet. Even though they cannot always adopt the lifestyle in practice, there are many who adopt it in their dreams.

An important consequence of this is that the mirror built by marketers will have an increasing impact on the way people will refer to ethnicity in the future. As I have discussed in this chapter, ethnicity today expresses an identity problem and is a bricolage of the images provided by consumer society. Today, more than ever, ethnicity deals with the uncertainty of identity.

THE DYSFUNCTIONALITY OF ETHNIC IDENTITY

Somehow, what the reference to ethnicity expresses has much more to do with the evolution of identity in general than with the origin of one's local and historical identity. What is happening in the subcultures of descendants of immigrants might well be harbingering the situation of many people of this planet who, confronted with the postmodern sources of identity making such as international marketing and satellite television and with the difficulties of political expression on a world market dominated by transnational companies, will have to define new ways of being persons and groups.

To do so, if they want to remain *animal symbolikum* (Cassirer, 1944) and *politikon zon* (*Aristotelis: The Politics of Aristotle*, 1976; Chatelet, 1986; Mairet, 1993), human beings will always have to symbolize their experience, to search for meaning.[13] This process seems to be more difficult today than in the past, however, because there is less opportunity for reflection.

In his seminal work "Ethnic Identity: Its Logical Foundations and Its Dysfunctions," Georges Devereux (1978) argued that "a hypercathecting[14] of the ethnic identity leads, in effect, to a reduction of the subject's relevant class identities to one only—and thus to the annihilation of the individual's real identity" (pp. 171-172). The word *class* is used in Devereux's chapter in a logical-mathematical sense only. He meant that any human being's identity is made up of a variety of relationships to the cultural environment (in Devereux's vocabulary: a person's class identities). Most persons have—fortunately—multiple social attachments that cross-cut one another. What is alarming is when this conglomeration is negated, this variety denied, and one chooses to stress only one reference, to hypertrophy one dimension. It is not only when one chooses to emphasize the ethnic identity that this type of problem takes place. The same occurs every time only one of a person's class identities is deemed relevant. And this does not have to be a choice. It is in the interaction between "I" and the Other that people define themselves through connections with others. It can be those Others that impel the simplification of complex identity. Under the Nazis, the Jews were gradually stripped of all their relevant class identities, save only their Jewish identity, and, in the process, were denied personal identities (Antelme, 1957).

According to Devereux (1978), it is dysfunctional at the level of the individual as well as at the level of society when one reduces someone else or oneself to such unidimensionality. He warned of some catastrophic tendencies in our societies:

> The contemporary scene abounds with examples of persons stripping *themselves* of all their potentially meaningful class identities, ceasing to be *anything* but Xs, where X denotes a real or spurious *ethnos*. This process is more impoverishing than ever today, when one's ethnic identity can structure only increasingly limited segments of one's total potential repertoire. Hence, the moment A insists on being *only* and *ostentatiously*—an X, twenty-four hours a day, large segments of his behavior, which cannot, by hook or by crook, be correlated with his ethnic identity, are deprived of any organizing and stabilizing "skeleton." His behavior therefore tends to become increasingly chaotic, particularly when he operates as a member of an actual group. (p. 172)

In Devereux's (1978) opinion, an insistent or obsessive stressing of and clinging to one's ethnic (or any other "class") identity reveals a flaw or a lacuna in one's self conception as an "*induplicably multidimensional* entity" (p. 173). Devereux gave the example of the Nazi SS who pleaded that in performing atrocities, they only obeyed commands. Such persons implicitly affirmed that SS status took precedence over all other group identities including membership in the human estate. Having shown that any person's identity is fundamentally multidimensional, Devereux made the following statements:

Sane and mature persons do not hypercathect their ethnic identity or any other class identity. An excessive stressing of one of one's several class identities, such as ethnic identity, simply seeks to shore up a flawed self and an uncertain and shaky awareness of one's identity as a person. . . . The current tendency to stress one's ethnic or class identity—its use as a crutch—is prima facie evidence of the impending collapse of the only valid sense of identity: one's differentness, which is replaced by the most archaic pseudo-identity imaginable. (pp. 173-174)

Devereux (1978) made reference to the so-called identity crisis of our times, suggesting that it cannot be resolved by recourse to the artificial props of collective identities: of ethnic, class, religious, occupational, or any other "assistant identity." According to him, it can lead only to a renunciation of identity to fend off what is apprehended as a danger of total annihilation. He considered the evolving and assuming of any massive and dominant class identity whatever as a first step toward such a "protective" renunciation of true identity. "If one is *nothing but* a Spartan, a capitalist, a proletarian, or a Buddhist, one is next door to being nothing and therefore even to not being at all" (p. 174).

Other researchers have focused on the polarization of postmodern cultural identity. Olivier Clain (1990) stated:

It is this polarization of cultural identity between national culture and rationalist and universalist ideology that is progressively disappearing in societies in transition toward postmodernity. In the same way the manifest expression and the demand for a cultural identity tend to get confused with the defence and promotion of a collective identity made autonomous on the basis of its particularity (age, sex, profession, sexual orientation, standing, etc.) and, more generally, on the demand for particular rights; and it is around the mobilization implied by the demand for particular rights that identity groups are gradually going to form. (p. 1212)

In other words, the segmentation of society is more and more structured by an ever-changing and hazardous demand on the market than by a well-defined cultural heritage.

In his recent book about the problems that democracy is facing today, Michel Wieviorka (1993) saw in the reemergence of ethnicity the symptom of a social crisis:

The signs in countries such as France, Belgium or Germany that bear evidence of the beginning of ethnicity may very well be interpreted as the transitory marks of a societal crisis, the expression of a deregulation of national societies, which ought, in one way or another, to dissolve once and for all these totally destructurized societies, or, on the contrary, re-establish them in a renewed or maintained form of integration. (p. 154; see also Gosselin & van Haecht, 1994)

Democratic societies seem unable to integrate the newcomers, to propose some project that can be shared without destroying the core democratic principle. According to Wieviorka (1993), the emerging new notion of ethnicity is now challenging our democratic societies. Are they capable or not of managing the cultural differences that they, for a very large part, produce themselves? How will they manage those cultural differences? Will the social actors who are making use of those cultural differences be able to control what they are doing? Wieviorka wondered whether this ascending reference to ethnicity is not pathological. He argued that one can see in it

a provisory pathology, suited to groups that waver between the counter-culture and mass-consumption, between community affiliation and integration; it is subject to social difficulties and to racism, and in various modes of cultural expression, finds the means of translating the subjectivity of these groups in a transitory way. (p. 154)

Wieviorka also insisted on the fragility of postmodern identity making. Referring to developments in Great Britain, in the United States, and in the Netherlands, he ventured a postmodern interpretation

making ethnicity one of the most symptomatic expressions of bypassing modernity and insisting on the image of a still provisory construction in a society defined by cultural fluctuations in perpetual change, without other actors than those created by transitory states of the market who disappear as rapidly as they appear. (p. 155)

Charles Taylor (1992) connected the problem of identity with the lack of project, an idea that I also expressed in a former article (Bouchet, 1991), but let me quote Taylor here:

The problem of identity as it appears at present results from the fact that every democratic country needs a common identity in the sense of a "form" in which its citizens see themselves as bound to their co-citizens in the same project, a project that does not necessarily tie up with other human beings outside, but that unites them in one unit, as one common actor. (p. 59)

The sadly missed Yves Barel (1984) has contributed greatly to a better understanding of what he called "the society of emptiness." He defined the social void as "an incapacity of human beings and human actions *to provide meaning in common*" (1982, p. 167). And he emphasized that "the first manifestation of this social void was the breaking off of the necessary dialogue between the population and the institution that represents it, between the periphery and the center" (p. 24). Maybe we should consider the growing number of people excluded from the center of society as a symptom of a cultural crisis and bear in mind what Alain Touraine (1994) explained in his last book: "Democracy's raison d'être is the acceptance of the Other" (p. 268).

Conclusion

It might be worth taking all this into consideration when considering which strategy to adopt on the European market nowadays. As the next generation is becoming inspired by the overwhelming and ubiquitous modern media, making use in one way or the other of the reference to ethnic identity in marketing might contribute to a simplification of the personality structure of a whole generation seeking meaning. The responsibility of marketers increases as the importance of other socializing institutions fades. In my opinion, marketers should not satisfy themselves by only looking at the surface of the lake to find out whether ethnicity is a factor they could play with. They should reach a deeper understanding of the forces at stake. All social representations are always interrelated in some way. Ethnicity no longer expresses a reference to the traditions of the past but a manifestation of the bewilderment of the present, confronted with the loss of the outdated certain future. Ethnicity is a dynamic concept related to changing social relations. Today ethnicity is not so much the expression of existing roots but the provocative avowal and claim of a disturbed identity.

As I have shown, there are still some constitutive differences to be traced in today's Europe. The way theoreticians, politicians, and marketers deal with these constitutive differences will continue to shape the world. But the emergence of multinational marketing strategies and activities, together with the correlated ubiquity of modern media, has brought new conditions that have an impact on the way present-day consumers identify themselves. The mixing of populations with different backgrounds and the complications of integration of the new generations in a society facing the difficulties of its confrontation with new types of limits (those of not accepting limits) result in radical changes in the way people identify themselves and assemble.

Postmodern ethnicity is not the perpetuation of an ancestral bond. Neither is it the transfer or even the rebuilding on Western European territory of imported ethnic groups. It is, as I stressed in the previous discussion, the original and contemporary shaping of provocatively claimed postmodern identities by putting together heterogeneous elements borrowed from different cultures. It is a bricolage making use of a diversity of cultural motives from different origins and strongly influenced by the mirror image provided by the dominant Other and the overwhelming media, including the marketing signs and symbols.

This situation is a real challenge for contemporary marketing. It is a combined knowledge of the roots of the cultural differences of European societies, understanding of the social situation of present-day social groups, comprehension of the risks at stake, and intelligence of the responsibilities involved that will lead us toward a more complex practice of marketing, theoretically and practically.

In a special issue of the influential journal *Esprit* dedicated to the identification of Europe, Paul Thibaud (1991) wondered "if the national non-belonging which is manifesting itself throughout Europe is merely that of *homo economicus*, if it does not also express a whiff of indifference or even of resentment towards the State" (p. 51). It could be argued that the two phenomena are intrinsically related—the market-integrating political and economical aspects of the same reality: that of changing the patrimony of references as to how we elaborate our multidimensional and changing identities. The way marketers will act on the market will have an impact not only on what will be bought and sold but also on the future of European nations and of the functioning of markets. Traditional segmentation and market analysis techniques are not necessarily adapted to the emerging new market structure. Today's marketing has to give a higher priority to the investigation of its embeddedness in society, including its impact on society at the macrolevel.

Today's marketers should not ignore that they are actors having much greater responsibility than just selling products, services, or ideas. Playing with ethnicity is possible. Playing with fire is also fun. One has to be aware of the risks at stake, however. Marketing strategists should seriously consider the consequences of their use of ethnicity and their contribution to identity making—because the market is never a given but is continuously constructed.

Notes

1. Georges Devereux (1928-1930) asserted this when he was not quite 20 years old in the famous regional periodical *Böttcherstrasse* (see Devereux, 1978, p. 173).

2. Smith (1991) listed "six main attributes of ethnic community (or *ethnie*, to use the French term):

    1. A collective proper name
    2. A myth of common ancestry
    3. Shared historical memories
    4. One or more differentiating elements of common culture
    5. An association with a specific 'homeland'
    6. A sense of solidarity for significant sectors of the population" (p. 21).

3. Isajiw's sample does not seem to include much European literature. The studies were taken from American or American-like journals. To reach a better understanding of the concept, one has to take into account the history of Europe.

4. This information was derived from *Dictionnaire de l'Ethnologie et de l'Anthropologie* (Bonte & Izard, 1991), *Encyclopédie Philosophique Universelle, Volume 2: Les Notions Philosophiques* (1990), *Encyclopædia Universalis* (1990), and *Encyclopædia Britannica* (1974).

5. Leo Despres (1975) concluded the volume with the following:

> To summarize, the papers which comprise this volume suggest that prevailing conceptions of ethnicity are perhaps too ambiguous in their overall construction to significantly advance the comparative study of ethnic phenomena beyond the work of Barth. Clearly such phenomena are multidimensional. They simultaneously engage elements that tend to be conceptualized differently in reference to the analysis of cultural systems, organized groups, and individual transactions. Unless these elements are ordered within some more systematic and inclusive theoretical framework, it will be difficult to derive and comparatively establish generalizations in respect to poly-ethnic societies. (p. 194)

6. As Barth (1969) wrote in his introduction:

> These essays try to show that ethnic boundaries are maintained in each case by a limited set of cultural features. The persistence of the unit then depends on the persistence of these cultural differentiae, while continuity can also be specified through the changes of the unit brought about by changes in the boundary-defining cultural differentiae. (p. 38)

According to Barth (1969), the critical feature is the characteristic of ascription: self-ascription and ascription by others. "A categorical ascription is an ethnic ascription he says when it classifies a person in terms of his basic, most general identity, presumptively determined by his origin and background" (p. 13).

7. Jean-Loup Amselle expressed similar ideas in other books:

> One sees how much his definition (of the idea of an ethnic group) is colored by ethnocentrism and how much it depends on the conception of a nation-state in the territorial sense, a conception of a discount state. (Amselle, 1990a, p. 972)

Each existing ethnic group is itself the result of the disintegration of the pre-colonial "economy world," so that the problematics of local societies which the transposing of these changes bring about in the theoretical sphere are also an integral part of the colonial ideology and of the race theory on which it is based. (Amselle, 1990b, pp. 227-228)

This last book of Amselle (1990b) criticizes the widespread tendency to extract, purify, and classify different types in all domains (political, economic, religious, ethnic, and cultural). Such a *discontinuiste* (intermittent) approach is, according to Amselle, one of the foundations of the European domination of the rest of the world. However, one can oppose to it a *logique métisse* (hybrid logic), an approach emphasizing continuity, indistinctness, and syncretism. Such an approach can be useful when studying the way we look at ethnicity in present-day Western Europe by helping us avoid insisting too much on the distinction and helping us find a syncretism in the different ways groups function within society.

8. The headmaster of a *lycée technique* in the northern suburbs of Paris once said that his foremost function was not to teach his pupils anything but to make sure that they were kept inside for the peace of the neighborhood. And in fact when some of his pupils visited a Danish Gymnasium, they spent a good deal of their time shoplifting in the local malls.

9. In his book *La Pensée Sauvage*, Claude Lévi-Strauss (1962) claimed an analogy between mythical thinking and bricolage. François Jacob (1981, second chapter, especially pp. 69-77), made the same analogy of bricolage for the evolution process. Bricolage is the French word for "do-it-yourself" but with the idea—as opposed to in engineering—that one uses materials at hand for producing something with no clear purpose in mind and which—and this is also important—is not a part of a general project.

10. The main point of concern here is that the possibilities of choice offered to identity making are much less determined than a few years ago.

11. A *Beur* is a young Arab of the second generation, born in France of immigrant parents.

12. May I risk the comment that there seems to be less racism and less self-confidence in present-day North America.

13. As Albert Camus once wrote: "*L'homme est un animal qui veut du sens.*" I will paraphrase this by writing: The difference between human beings and the other animals is that humans demand meaning.

14. To cathect is to invest with mental or emotional energy.

References

Abercrombie, N., Hill, S., & Turner, B. S. (1984). *Dictionary of sociology*. Harmondsworth, UK: Penguin.

Amselle, J.-L. (1990a). Ethnie [Ethnos]. *Encyclopædia universalis* (Vol. 8, p. 972). Paris: Corpus.

Amselle, J.-L. (1990b). *Logiques métisses: Anthropologie de l'identité en Afrique et ailleurs* [Hybrid logics: Anthropology of identity in Africa and elsewhere]. Paris: Payot.

Amselle, J.-L., & M'Bokolo, E. (Eds.). (1985). *Au cœur de l'ethnie: Ethnies, tribalisme et etat en Afrique* [In the heart of ethnos: Ethnos, tribalism, and state in Africa]. Paris: La Découverte.

Antelme, R. (1957). L'espèce humaine [The human race]. Paris: Gallimard.

Aristotelis: The politics of Aristotle (rev. text with introduction, analysis and commentary by F. Susemihl & R. D. Hicks). (1976). New York: Arno.

Balandier, G. (1985). Le détour [The detour]. Paris: Fayard.

Barel, Y. (1982). La marginalité sociale [Social marginality]. Paris: Presses Universitaires de France.

Barel, Y. (1984). La société du vide [The society of emptiness]. Paris: Seuil.

Barth, F. (Ed.) (1969). Ethnic groups and boundaries: The social organization of culture difference. Bergen-Oslo, Norway: Universitets Forlaget.

Bell, D. (1960). The end of ideology. Glencoe, IL: Free Press.

Bell, D. (1975). Ethnicity and social change. In N. Glazer & D. P. Moynihan (Eds.), Ethnicity: Theory and experience (pp. 141-176). Cambridge, MA: Harvard University Press.

Bell, D. (1980). The winding passage. New York: Basic Books.

Beneton, P. (1975). Histoire de mots: Culture et civilisation [History of words: Culture and civilization]. Paris: Presses de la Fondation Nationale des Sciences Politique.

Bennett, J. (1975). The new ethnicity: Perspectives from ethnology (Proceedings of the American Ethnological Society). St. Paul, MN: West.

Blackbourn, D., & Evans, R. J. (Eds.). (1991). The German bourgeoisie. London: Routledge.

Body-Gendrot, S. (1993). Ville et violence [City and violence]. Paris: Presses Universitaires de France.

Bonte, P., & Izard, M. (Eds.) (1991). Dictionnaire de l'ethnologie et de l'anthropologie [Dictionary of ethnology and anthropology]. Paris: Presses Universitaires de France.

Bouchet, A. T. (1993). L'ecole française et la laicité [French school and secularity]. Merino, 17, 1-16.

Bouchet, D. (1985). Når sandheden løper ut i sanden, og stranden ikke lenger finnes under asfalten, er kun poesien tilbake [When the truth runs out of sand and the beach is no longer found under the asphalt, then only poetry remains]. Profil, 4, 76-79.

Bouchet, D. (1987a). Erkjennelse uten grunnlag [Knowledge without foundation]. Profil, 1-2, 100-103.

Bouchet, D. (1987b). Videnskab som kunstform [Science as an art form]. Paradigma, 1(2), 15-21.

Bouchet, D. (1991). Kulturens paradoks: Om det samfundsmæssiges levevis [Culture's paradox: About the nature of the social]. Paradoks, 1, 6-13.

Bouchet, D. (1994a). The concept of identity (Working paper). Odense, Denmark: Odense University, Department of Marketing.

Bouchet, D. (1994b). Rails without ties: The social imaginary and postmodern culture: Can postmodern consumption replace modern questioning? International Journal of Research in Marketing, 11(4), 405-422.

Boudon, R. (Ed.). (1992). Traité de sociologie [Treatise of sociology]. Paris: Presses Universitaires de France.

Boudon, R., & Bourricaud, F. (Eds) (1982). Dictionnaire critique de la sociologie [Critical dictionary of sociology]. Paris: Presses Universitaires de France.

Breton, R., & Pinard, M. (1960). Group formation among immigrants: Criteria and processes. Canadian Journal of Economics and Political Science, 26, 465-477.

Buford, B. (1991). Among the thugs. London: Norton.

Camilleri, C. (1980). Les immigrés Maghrébins de la seconde génération: Contribution à une étude de leurs évolutions et de leurs choix culturels [Second-generation immigrants from the Maghreb: Contributions to a study of their evolution and cultural choices]. Bulletin de Psychologie, 33(347), 985-995.

Camilleri, C. (1990). Identité et gestion de la disparité culturelle: Essai d'une typologie [Identity and management of cultural disparity: A tentative typology]. In C. Camilleri, J. Kastersztein, E. M. Lipiansky, H. Malewska-Peyre, I. Taboada-Leonetti, & A. Vasquez (Eds.), *Stratégies identitaires* [Identity strategies] (pp. 91-92). Paris: Presses Universitaires de France.

Cassirer, E. (1944). *An essay on man.* London: New Haven.

Catani, M. (1983). l'identité et les choix relatifs aux systèmes de valeurs [Identity and the choices regarding value systems]. *Peuple Méditerranéens, 24,* 117-126.

Catani, M. (1989). De la marseillaise à la jeunesse Beur [From Marseillaise to Beur youth]. In H. Boll-Johansen (Ed.), *L'identité française: Colloque à l'Université de Copenhague le 20 et 21 novembre 1987* [French identity: Conference at Copenhagen University, November 20-21, 1987] (pp. 117-145). Copenhagen: Akademisk Forlag.

Chatelet, F. (1986). Aristote. In F. Chatelet, O. Duhamel, & E. Pisier (Eds.), *Dictionnaire des œvres politiques* [Dictionary of political works] (pp. 16-28). Paris: Presses Universitaires de France.

Citron, S. (1989). *Le mythe national: L'histoire de France en question* [The national myth: The history of France in question]. Paris: Les Editions Ouvrières/Etudes et Documentation Internationales.

Clain, O. (1990). Identité culturelle [Cultural identity]. *Encyclopédie philosophique universelle: Vol. 2. Les notions philosophiques* [Encyclopedia of universal philosophy: Vol. 2. Philosophical notions] (p. 1212). Paris: Presses Universitaires de France.

Cohen, R. (1978). Ethnicity: Problem and focus in anthropology. *Annual Review of Anthropology, 7,* 379-404.

Despres, L. A. (1975). Toward a theory of ethnic phenomena. In L. A. Despres (Ed.), *Ethnicity and resource competition in plural societies* (pp. 187-207). La Haye-Paris: Mouton.

Devereux, G. (1928-1930). *Böttcherstrasse, 1-2,(2).*

Devereux, G. (1978). Ethnic identity: Its logical foundations and its dysfunctions. In G. Devereux (Ed.), *Ethnopsychoanalysis: Psychoanalysis and anthropology as complementary frames of reference* (pp. 136-176). Berkeley: University of California Press.

Dumont, L. (1983). *Essais sur l'individualisme* [Essay on individualism]. Paris: Seuil.

Dumont, L. (1991). *Homo aequalis II: L'idéologie allemande: France-Allemagne er retour* [German ideology]. Paris: Gallimard.

Elias, N. (1979). *The civilizing process* (2 vols.). Oxford, UK: Basil Blackwell. (Original work published 1939 as *Über den Prozess des Zivilisations*)

Encyclopædia britannica. (1974). London: Encyclopædia Britannica.

Encyclopædia universalis. (1990). Paris: Encyclopædia Universalis.

Encyclopédie philosophique universelle: Vol. 2. Les notions philosophiques [Encyclopedia of universal philosophy: Vol. 2. Philosophical notions]. (1990). Paris: Presses Universitaires de France.

Evans-Pritchard, E. E. (1940). *The Nuer.* London: Clarendon.

Febvre, L. (1984). *Au cœur du religieux du XVIe siècle* [In the heart of the religious of the 16th century]. Paris: Le Livre de Poche.

Fortes, M. (1945). *The dynamics of clanship among the Tallensi.* London: Oxford University Press.

Furet, F., & Ozouf, M. (1979). Deux légitimations historiques de la société française au XVII, Mably et Bouillanvilliers [Two historical justifications of French society during the 18th century, Mably and Bouillanvilliers]. *Annales, 34*(3), 438-450.

Gluckman, M. (1965). *Politics, law and ritual in tribal society.* Chicago: Aldine.

Godelier, M. (1977). Le concept de tribu: Crise d'un concept ou crise des fondements empiriques de l'anthropologie? [The concept of tribe: Crisis of a concept or crisis of the empirical foundations of anthropology?]. In M. Godelier (Ed.), *Horizon et trajets Marxzistes en anthropologie* [Marxist horizons and paths in anthropology] (Vol. 1, pp. 188-235). Paris: Maspéro.

Goffmann, E. (1959). *The presentation of self in everyday life.* New York: Anchor.

Gorz, A. (1980). *Adieux au prolétariat* [Farewell to the proletariat]. Paris: Galilée.

Gosselin, G., & van Haecht, A. (Eds.). (1994). *La réinvention de la démocratie: Ethnicité et nationalisme en Europe et dans les pays du sud* [The reinvention (or remaking) of democracy: Ethnicity and nationalism in Europe and in the countries of the south]. Paris: L'Harmattan.

Hebdige, D. (1979). *Subculture: The meaning of style.* London: Methuen.

Hobsbawm, E. J. (1992). *Nations and nationalism since 1780* (2nd ed.). Cambridge, UK: Cambridge University Press.

Horowitz, D. (1985). *Ethnic groups in conflict.* Berkeley: University of California Press.

Isajiw, W. W. (1974). Definitions of ethnicity. *Ethnicity, 1,* 111-124.

Jacob, F. (1981). *Le jeu des possibles: Essai sur la diversité du vivant* [The game of the possible: Essay on the diversity of living]. Paris: Fayard.

Laufer, R., & Paradeise, C. (1990). *Marketing and democracy: Public opinion and media formation in democratic societies.* New Brunswick, NJ: Transaction. (Original work published 1982 as *Prince bureaucrate: Machiavel au pays du marketing.* Paris: Flammarion.)

Lecher, W. (1986). Zum zukünftigen Verhältnis von Erwerbsarbeit und Eigenarbeit aus Gewerkschaftlicher Sicht [About the future perspectives of the relationship between wage labor and self-employment in a trade union perspective]. *WSI Mitteilungen, 3,* 356.

Lévi-Strauss, C. (1962). *La pensée sauvage* [The savage mind]. Paris: Plon.

Maffesoli, M. (1988). *Le temps des tribus: Le déclin de l'individualisme dans les sociétés de masse* [Tribe time: The decline of individualism in mass societies]. Paris: Méridiens Klincksieck.

Maffesoli, M. (1992). *La transfiguration du politique: La tribalisation du monde* [Transfiguration of politics: The tribalization of the world]. Paris: Grasset.

Mairet, G. (1993). *Les grandes œuvres politiques* [The great political works]. Paris: Le Livre de Poche.

Malewska-Peyre, H. (1983). L'image de soi des jeunes délinquants immigrés [The image of young immigrant delinquents]. *Bulletin de Psychologie, 36*(359), 363-376.

Mercier, P. (1968). *Tradition, changement, histoire: Les Somba du Dahomey septentrional* [Tradition, change, history: The Somba of northern Dahomey]. Paris: Anthropos.

Merriam-Webster. (1989). *Dictionary* (CD-ROM ed.).

Morin, F. (1986). Identité ethnique et ethnicité: Analyse critique des travaux Anglo-Saxons [Ethnic identity and ethnicity: A critical analysis of the Anglo-Saxon works]. In P. Tap (Ed.), *Identités collectives et changements sociaux* [Collective identity and social change] (pp. 57-58). Toulouse, France: Privat.

Nadel, S. P. (1971). *Bysance noire: Le royaume des Nupe du Nigeria* [Black Byzantium: The kingdom of the Nupe in Nigeria]. Paris: Maspéro. (Original work published 1942)

Nicolas, G. (1973). Faits ethniques et usages du concept d'ethnie. *Cahiers Internationaux de Sociologie, 54,* 95-126.

Nisbet, R. (1970). *The sociological tradition.* London: Basic Books. (Original work published 1966)

Nisbet, R., & Perrin, R. (1977). *The social bond* (2nd ed.). New York: Knopf.

Noiriel, G. (1992). *Population, immigration et identité nationale en France XIXe-XXe siècle* [Population, immigration, and national identity in 19th to 20th century France]. Paris: Hachette.

Reading, H. F. (1977). *A dictionary of the social sciences*. London: Routledge & Kegan Paul.

Robin, J. (1989). *Changer d'ère* [Changing era]. Paris: Seuil.

Roy, O. (1991). Ethnicité, bandes et communautarisme [Ethnicity, gangs, and community]. *Esprit, 169,* 37-47.

Sahlins, M. (1968). *Tribesmen*. Englewood Cliffs, NJ: Prentice Hall.

Service, E. R. (1962). *Primitive social organization*. London: Random House.

Shapera, I. (1958). *Government and politics in tribal society*. London: Watts.

Smith, A. D. (1986). *The ethnic origin of nations*. Oxford, UK: Basil Blackwell.

Smith, A. D. (1991). *National identity*. London: Penguin.

Taboada-Leonetti, I. (1990). Stratégies identitaires et minorités: Le point de vue du sociologue [Identity and minority strategies: A sociological point of view]. In C. Camilleri, J. Kastersztein, E. M. Lipiansky, H. Malewska-Peyre, I. Taboada-Leonetti, & A. Vasquez (Eds.), *Stratégies identitaires* [Identity strategies] (pp. 43-83). Paris: Presses Universitaires de France.

Tap, P. (1986). Introduction. In P. Tap (Ed.), *Identités collectives et changements sociaux* [Collective identity and social change] (p. 12). Toulouse, France: Privat.

Taylor, A. C. (1991). Ethnie. In P. Bonte & M. Izard (Eds.), *Dictionnaire de l'ethnologie et de l'anthropologie* [Dictionary of ethnology and anthropology] (p. 242). Paris: Presses Universitaires de France.

Taylor, C. (1992). Quel principe d'identité collective? [Which principles for a collective identity?]. In J. Lenoble & N. Dewandre (Eds.), *L'Europe au soir du siècle* [Europe in the evening of the century] (pp. 59-66). Paris: Editions Esprit.

Theodorson, G. A. (1969). *A modern dictionary of sociology*. New York: Harper & Row.

Thibaud, P. (1991). L'Europe: Essai d'identification [Europe: Essay of identification]. *Esprit, 176,* 47-62.

Tönnies, F. (1963). *Community and society* (C. Loomis, Trans. & Ed.). New York: Harper Torchbook. (Original work published 1887 as *Gemeinschaft und Gesellschaft*)

Touraine, A. (1994). *Qu'est-ce que la démocratie?* [What is democracy?]. Paris: Fayard.

Tribus en Afrique du Nord et au Moyen-Orient [Tribes in North Africa and the Middle East] [Special issue]. (1987). *L'Homme, 102.*

Weber, M. (1968). *Economy and society* (Vol. 1). New York: Bedminster.

Wieviorka, M. (1993). *La démocratie à l'épreuve: Nationalisme, populisme, ethnicité* [Democracy put to the test: Nationalism, populism, and ethnicity]. Paris: La Découverte.

Williams, R. (1976). *Keywords: A vocabulary of culture and society*. London: Fontana.

4

Consumer Culture
or Culture Consumed?

A. FUAT FIRAT

The purpose of this chapter is to provide some insights into the character and the position of culture in contemporary society. The basic argument will be that culture is increasingly becoming a consumable, marketable item. Consequently, individuals of our day are more and more consuming cultures rather than belonging to any one culture. The body of the chapter tries to follow the history of this evolution of culture into becoming an item for consumption. Specifically, I discuss the story of culture in modern society with some emphasis on its paradoxical transformation into a marketable item as modernity matures and enters into a postmodern age. It seems necessary to review this (hi)story to make sense of contemporary changes.

It can be said that as the 20th century ends, culture has (re)gained an importance that it had, paradoxically, lost in modern society. This is paradoxical because, as shall be discussed later, modern society privileged culture over nature yet, at the same time, declared culture to be bound by or dependent on only one of its dimensions: the economy. The initial emphasis on the economy as the determining moment within culture later culminated in a separation of culture from economy, causing the two to be signified not as inclusive but as largely

exclusive of each other, taking on separate and at times even oppositional meanings and roles.

Modern Culture

Modern culture was predicated on the idea that human society,
armed with scientific knowledge and technologies based on this
knowledge, could control most of nature's negative effects on human
life and thereby improve human existence. Nature presented a reality
to the human being, a reality that "was (out) there" and independent of
the human being who had been and was a part of this nature and this
reality. But, using correct methods and tools, the human being could
find out about this reality, this nature, accurately represent it in theories
and models, and modify its effects to increase control over his or her
life and to progress toward fulfilling his or her potential as the knowing
and acting subject. It was this belief and this purpose that structured
the modern culture and largely shaped modern society. There was, indeed, a goal to being human, a project to be realized, objectives to reach,
and targets to fulfill. Thus, modern culture was a driven one with its
eyes on the future and its feet securely planted on the material ground,
in reality. Reaching the goals—realizing the project—required commitment, order, and universal, valid principles.

Modern thought emphasized and largely operated through separations of phenomena into distinct and proper categories, especially
into dualistic, binary, and oppositional categories. Active-passive,
valid-invalid, true-false, rational-emotional, feminine-masculine, and
production-consumption were some of the binary categories that determined modernist ways of thinking. It was mostly through such separations that modernity tried to establish norms and order. Indeed,
normativity or the establishment of norms was a major quest for modernism (Habermas, 1983; Steuerman, 1992). After all, modernism had
completely discarded the norms of an earlier order: an order that depended on and that was established by the faith in a supreme power.
The normative order that modernism discarded was largely constructed on the basis of monotheist religions. As a matter of fact, in
modern society, which was defined by project(s) of emancipation, one
of the emancipations sought was from powers outside of the human
being and his or her material conditions (Lyotard, 1992). Modernity
called for a *knowing subject*, as opposed to a *being subject* (Dreyfus, 1991).
The life of the premodern being subject was determined by her or his

fate, an experience of merely *being*, carrying out the inexorable direction(s) of his or her preordained fate.

Yet modernity did not discard the *idea* of *order*. It merely transferred it from one of spiritual order to one of material order (Rorty, 1979). An order had to have its norm(al)s, and, consequently, modernism embarked on the search for those of the material order. Of course, science played the most important role in this search. Science and the scientific method advocated correct (proper) as opposed to incorrect (improper) ways of searching. Specifically, the norms were constructed through categories that opposed one another, thereby identifying the proper and the improper—those that enlightened the way to the norm(al) and the abnormal. Those categories that corresponded to the proper were, then, imbued with meanings of superiority. Those that corresponded to the improper were imbued with inferior meaning.

Modern culture argued that the purpose of knowing was the emancipation of the human subject, now no longer a subject *to* a supreme being but a subject *of* one's own, who could act on her or his own accord. Knowing about his or her circumstances and conditions enabled this subject to break free from the impositions of these conditions or at least to control some of their implications and limitations to create better, improved living conditions. This, as a matter of fact, was the modern project: to improve human lives by controlling nature through scientific technologies (Angus, 1989). Science was the domain and the means of the knowing subject. Through scientific principles, by following the rules of scientific inquiry, the modern subject could develop valid and accurate representations of the reality around her or him. Furthermore, such accurate and unbiased representations of reality were allowed through yet another separation: the separation of the mind and the body.

The biological constitution of the subject, the body, was fairly constrained within its nature: its genetic, chemical, physical determinations and limitations. Being so dependent, the body could not have an objective, disinterested perspective into its own existence. Therefore, unbiased representations of the elements of the reality into which the body was immersed required an ability to distance oneself from the everyday and profane existence. Immersed experience was too involved and interested to provide objective observations and knowledge. The Cartesian subject, on the other hand, one that was conceptualized as having a mind separate and independent of the body, could achieve the task of objective knowing (Rorty, 1979; Russell, 1945). The mind could stand detached and aloof when the body was immersed in and constrained by its nature. From its privileged, detached, and distanced position, the mind could afford a disinterested yet acute and accurate gaze, observing, measuring, and producing knowledge that truly represented the real.

Many of the notions of superiority and inferiority that modern culture developed were based on such privileging of the detached observer as opposed to the immersed participant. There was too much feeling and emotion, touching and involvement in immersion, qualities that, according to modern scientific thought, distracted from accurate measurement and knowledge rather than providing further and more in-depth information and understanding. When and if the scientist, the observer, the knower felt, she or he could no longer be objective. The scientist should not feel (what things felt like) oneself but needed to be *informed* by multitudes of research subjects who experienced the emotions (as to how things felt) and to *observe* their (re)actions. It is no wonder, then, that the *word* and the *visual* were privileged in modernity. They became the basic tools and the guides of the mind, and the visual—the sense that was most accommodating of the distanced, detached "observation" as opposed to touching, smelling, hearing, and tasting—took on a special status. The modern culture became largely a visual culture trusting sight above all, enjoying and seeking the visual above all (Berger, 1972; Foster, 1988; Levin, 1993). After all, it was Galileo's telescope and Brahe's observations that expanded the modern subject's horizons and liberated one from servitude to gods, and it was the visual arts and crafts of da Vinci and Michelangelo and the like that enabled the appreciation of the beauty of that which was real.

In the clean separation of the mind and the body, the body represented nature and the mind represented culture. Body was indeed the nature of the human being, in all respects. It was reproduction, sensation, digestion, and defecation. The mind constituted and constructed human culture, one's ways of knowing—traditions of reflection, of understanding self and its conditions. The mind was reason! Consequently, the mind and anything related to it was privileged in modernism. The mind and its ability to reason were sacred, the only salvation for the knowing subject—because they were the only way to objective, accurate, valid knowledge. All that was important for the human subject, all that mattered, had to be done through reason, or it would be doomed to failure because only the mind could provide true knowledge and point to the correct directions and decisions. The body was for profane experience—to eat, sleep, and fulfill the sensations. According to the modern way of thinking, to enjoy, recreate, and replenish one would refer to bodily functions, but when any important activity was to be performed, one needed to refer to reason. Nature (body) was, of course, present and necessary, and one ought to know it. Nevertheless, when substantive, consequential decisions about the future of society were to be made and public, political action was to be taken, then one had to have the necessary culture (mind). Thus, as previously mentioned, culture and the mind were privileged and considered superior in modernity. In the oppositional, polar categorizations of mind-body, and culture-nature, body and nature came to be signified as inferior.

Yet culture itself fell victim to further separations and oppositional categorizations. Originally, in the modern separation between nature and culture, nature represented that part of the human condition that was given or determined independent of human action. Culture, on the other hand, was the totality of the human experience that was not given by nature but was humanly created, woven, and produced. As modern society further developed, however, the cultural experience became compartmentalized into its components, such as the economic, the social, the political, and the *cultural*. Culture, therefore, came to signify only a certain component of what it used to be. Within this compartmentalization, the economy gained the upper hand because it was the component that related most to the material welfare and wealth of nations. The emphasis on the material in modernism repressed the symbolic along with the spiritual and relegated such phenomena to a state of being determined and shaped. It was the material conditions that determined, the economy that shaped the culture (Marx, 1939/1973; Weber, 1927). Culture became considered as part of a *superstructure* that was molded by the conditions and relationships in the *infrastructure* (Parsons, 1937/1968). The infrastructure was specifically constituted by the economic relationships and the material assets of the society, such the railroads and the highways, the industrial base, and the natural resources. Therefore, in modern society, the economy took center stage, and it became considered the engine of society.

The Modern Challenged

The above story (narrative) of modernity is increasingly challenged in contemporary philosophy as well as in the arts, architecture, literature, and the social sciences. Culture has started to (re)gain a primary role in conceptualizations of social change and determination. Many perceive and call for a recognition of the symbolic and the cultural over the material and the economic as the engine(s) of society. Even the privileging of the economy in modern society was a symbolic act: When culturally the economy was signified to be the most important core of society, it became so. After all, the wise ones (Adam Smith and others) preached it, the capitalists practiced it, and the masses believed in it. The important thing in modernity was to expand the pie (read *pie* as the gross national product/wealth of nations/capital accumulation) so that all subjects (the human beings) could get a larger piece of the pie and thus take greater control over their material conditions and improve their lives. According to the critics of the modernist narrative, however, it was all just that—a narrative, a story that was culturally, symbolically woven, bought into, further woven, and (re)produced as the "reality" of modern society. In this society, the most important determinant, the all-important provider of the promised "better life," was material wealth and accumulation. This accumulation was made possible and mediated by the market. It was realized through commodities (products, services, etc.)—objects that were desired and, therefore, valued in the market.

The (re)production of modern reality in the image of the modern imaginary—the modernist narrative that captured the imaginations—has been called hyperreality by some postmodernist thinkers (Baudrillard, 1983; Eco, 1986). *Hyperreality* is the becoming real of what is (was) hype or simulation. It is the cultural process that renders simulation or hype "realer than real" (Massumi, 1987). Postmodernist insights into modern culture reveal that although the "official" rhetoric of modern society insisted that a reality outside and independent of the human will existed, the social realities of modern society were largely constructed. Consider, for example, the urban environments, the cities, as the most imposing reality of modern life. Clearly, these were completely constructed realities that, in turn, greatly determined social relationships. In many respects, our (sub)urban realities continue to be (re)constructed presently as simulations of imagined (maybe more so than lived) urban experiences of the past or, in some cases, of the future. The thematized wharf areas, downtown centers, and renovated sections of cities are witnesses to this phenomenon, and they dominate our realities as the simulations are increasingly replicated (Andersen, 1994).

World fairs and other global events allowed the cities to represent their cultures in terms of spectacular structures and landscapes that became the symbols that promoted the culture (for example, the Eiffel Tower in Paris). These were most exciting and meaningful to a visual, voyeuristic culture: a culture of tourism. Many of the spectacles were, indeed, monumental proofs for the achievements of the industrial modern society. Seeing (observing) them left little doubt about what the modern society could accomplish (Buck-Morss, 1991). These spectacles, extracted and abstracted from local culture, became the representations of that culture. They translated and were translations of culture; they fulfilled the visual needs of the culture. Each modern culture asserted its existence and established its "originality" through these spectacles (spectacular products, structures, etc.) that translated its qualities into cultural meanings. For a visually oriented modern world, this was the best, if not the only, claim to existence, and each culture that found ways of translating its qualities into marketable experiences (be they croissants or hamburgers) extended its existence even beyond its original borders.

It could be argued that, with time, modern society has reinforced the marketization of *all* experience, and the market has become the only locus of legitimization in society. Human society, which resolved its affairs through different means such as politics, kinship relations, and social contracts, has increasingly come to resolve politics, kinship, and social interaction through the market, as evidenced in the marketing of presidential candidates, for example. The advent of postmodernism has further reinforced this trend because the postmodern sensibility calls for an end to the repression of cultural tendencies that are already strong in modern society by the modernist rhetoric to liberate and practice those tendencies unabashedly (Hassan, 1987; Huyssen, 1984). The postmodern stance is not to try to dominate conditions by imposing one single (meta)narrative (a single, totalizing ideological story system) on the increasingly fragmenting and spectacularized (symbolic) conditions of human existence but to playfully, even if critically, employ these conditions in allowing the sampling of varied and experimentable lifestyles and states of being by the consumers of society.

The Postmodern Existence

Indeed, at the end of the 20th century, at the culmination of the modern society in, specifically, the West (the "First World"), the term *consumer* has come to define the human experience (Ewen, 1988). In an overwhelmingly marketized existence, individuals experience practically all aspects of their lives as consumers. Not only has consumption come to signify all sorts of activity—that is, all activity is considered as an act of consumption, from consumption of church services to consumption of interpersonal relations—but the consumers have become more and more consumed with the act(s) of consumption (Kling, Olin, & Poster, 1991; Postman, 1985). Outside their homes (in which consumption of food, television, etc., is continuously experienced) and their workplaces (where work experiences are consumed), consumers of the (post)modern society are spending most of their time in shopping environments (such as malls and restaurants), in theme parks, and in tourism (Sorkin, 1992; Venkatesh, 1991).

Perceiving or conceiving life as a consumption experience was not highly regarded in the modern narratives (Brewer & Porter, 1993). Rather, production and being productive were privileged in modernist rhetoric. With the end of modernity, this has largely changed in experience, if not completely in rhetoric. Studies show that the purpose for most of the postmodern generation is to consume—and to consume brand names that represent sensational images (Dunn, 1992; Moyers, 1989a; Ritchie, 1992; Zinn, Power, Yang, Cuneo, & Ross, 1992). Production and what one does as a producer serve largely to provide the means to consume. Both for the one consuming and for those who judge, who one is tends to be represented and communicated through what one (can) consume(s). As the saying may go, "You are what you eat, wear and drive, . . . in short, you are what you consume." For the postmodern generation, image, including the self-image, is the most important statement, and one is not limited to making a single statement (Ewen, 1990; Kaplan, 1987; Moyers, 1989a). One can, indeed, sample (self-)images as one samples fragmented, momentary life experiences, as one moves through the different situations in life, playing varied roles, such as the mother, the manager, the homemaker, the wife, the lover, the friend. Each moment may require, indeed does require, a different self-image to be marketable, likeable, and attractive (Fırat, 1992a).

For the critic who adheres to modern ways of thinking, the image switching, the representation of different selves in different situations, is a loss of self, a violation of *character*. To the postmodern consumer, it is liberation from imposed (modernist) narratives of necessity of a character, of *an* authentic self (Dreyfus, 1991). It is a freedom to creatively construct and reconstruct self, to experience different ways of being. Rather than being constrained with a single existence that may be both imposed and repressive, the ability to sample and switch images is a way of finding one's own expression(s) (Hutcheon, 1988; Wilson, 1989).

Postmodernists, such as Baudrillard (1975, 1981), dismiss the primacy given to production in modernist narratives and demonstrate that value, which modernists consider to be a property of the product and to be created in production, is determined in consumption, through sign-value. Value is constructed through the meanings imbued in the images represented by things (products, objects) (Fırat, 1992b; Fırat & Venkatesh, 1993). In the postmodern sensibility, therefore, consumption is not just a destruction or devouring of value. It is not a profane activity that is to be hidden, not to be made public or flaunted. On the contrary, it is where meanings are decided and where the individual can lay claim to his or her images and statements (Breen, 1993). This postmodern orientation is well observed in the behaviors of consumers of the First World (Ewen, 1988). They indicate a preference for image products and brand names, such as Nike shoes, BMW automobiles, and Levi's jeans. Consumers who can afford it do, indeed, make their personal statements through what they consume, and others judge them on the basis of what they consume (Featherstone, 1991). This form of statement has become so important and real to consumers that several people have been killed by others who wanted their tennis shoes, and school children fight with their parents to get them to purchase brand-name clothing for them to wear. If they do not wear brand names, they are often subject to ridicule and scorn by classmates.

The consumption orientation reaching its epitome in the final hours of modern society and into the postmodern culture has reinforced the voyeuristic tendencies in modernism. The consumer has increasingly become a consumer of experiences, seeking not only things (objects, material items) but also meaning and excitement in the moments experienced (Kroker, 1992). Image brands and products are preferred because they allow experiences that are sought after. Clearly, the visual arts and media, especially film and television, have played a role in this trend by reinforcing the primacy of the visual that was already privileged in modernism. The metaphors of objective knowing in modern thought were almost exclusively visual: "observation," "seeing is believing," "a picture is worth a thousand words." The centrality of the written word in modernity required sight (and reading, which was itself a visual experience). Both reading and writing, primarily visual experiences, were the essence of literacy, the most revered sign and medium of knowing, and further established the primacy of the visual, although paradoxically. It was paradoxical because what was seen, the visual image, ironically overrode the written word—"a picture is worth a thousand words"—especially with the advent of the photograph and, then, film and video. In the televisual culture, the two (visual image and the written word) have come to be considered oppositional, the visual image dominating the word (Moyers, 1989b) and, in many a critic's mind, destroying literacy and knowledge (Gitlin, 1986; Kellner, 1990; Newcomb, 1979). Yet the contemporary consumer is, indeed, a consumer of the visual image(s) on a screen, in shop windows, or on the "tour." It is not only a coincidence that tourism, that voyeuristic experience in modern society, is now the largest industry in the world. The tourist is the metaphor for the consummate consumer of our time

(Canan & Hennessy, 1989)—one who samples, tours, and experiences the images and the sights, watching and observing other people, places, and objects, as well as her or his own self-image(s) from the perspective of the other, in the mirror image (Fırat, 1992a; Gallop, 1985).

Globalization of Fragmentation

Brand names and images are increasingly becoming the spectacles for the global tourist. They can now be found all around the world, conjuring the same and similar meanings and experiences. This is largely because of global communications, specifically in terms of visual images from television and films, music videos, and advertising spots (Belk, 1988; Costa & Bamossy, 1993; Dholakia & Fırat, 1988). As many international marketing organizations are well aware, market segments transcend national boundaries, forming global alliances of consumers. Those who cannot decipher each other's languages decipher the images of each other's consumption and can place (position) each other on social maps that cross cultural boundaries. The images of consumption are already well globalized, and this phenomenon is already widely observed. Markets are globalizing (Huszagh, Fox, & Day, 1986; Levitt, 1983) and so are the symbols (in terms of brand names and advertising images) that signify the meanings for each moment in life. There are growing pressures to unify economies, currencies, and markets (as apparent in the European Community movement) to keep up with trade and financial institutions, which have already largely globalized. The fast diffusion of information technologies and the exponential growth in mobility and ability to communicate across all boundaries indeed seem to make all borders nominal and almost superficial.

Wherever in the world one is, it seems that one can have a bottle of Coca-Cola and eat a McDonald's hamburger, rent a Toyota, listen to Madonna and Sting tunes, enjoy a croissant for breakfast, and follow one's favorite soap opera on television brands (Panasonic, RCA, Sony, etc.) that are in the remotest corners of the world. On the one hand, such diffusion of brands, programs, and products continuously feed the fears, especially among observers of these trends from the Third World countries, that many cultures are being overtaken by others, that many a culture is now endangered (Alavi & Shanin, 1982; Featherstone, 1990; Keane, 1990). On the other hand, globalization of information is (re)creating a touristic interest in different cultures and in experiencing them. It might be this interest that results in the rejuvenation of Little Tokyo,

Little Italy, and Chinatown sections in major cities around the world. One can find upscale Italy on Rodeo Drive (Via Rodeo) in Beverly Hills, California, or the "American experience" complete with its KFCs, McDonald's, skating rinks, and many other brand names and stores at the Galeria shopping mall in Istanbul, Turkey.

At the same time that such globalizing tendencies are greatly felt, there is fragmentation in different respects around the world. Independence sought by different ethnic groups are often creating conditions of civil war and political struggle. There are mounting calls to recognize different lifestyles, family formations, and social organizations (Weston, 1991). There is a weakening of uniformity and universality in approaches to living and being in general. In the United States, for example, the idea of a melting pot seems to give way to the idea of a (cultural) mosaic. The tendency to recognize and respect different ethnic, religious, social, and ideological cultures and allow them to exist in their own ways seems to be gaining strength. This is, indeed, a leaning that seems to reverse the modernist quest for a universal, singly rational order of (or for) progress.

The two trends of globalization and fragmentation may at first glance seem contradictory and paradoxical. Yet what seems to be occurring is a globalization of fragmentation. All images, products, brand names, and lifestyles that create excitement, sensation, attraction, and interest can and do find their markets. The consumers, regardless of their nationalities and countries, are willing to experience and sample the different styles and cultural artifacts, if at different times and for different purposes. Globalization, therefore, does not seem to be an event in which one form or style dominates and eliminates all others. Rather, it is the diffusion of all different forms and styles all around the world. Because the postmodern consumer experience is not one of committing to a single way of being, a single form of existence, the same consumers are willing to sample the different, fragmented artifacts. The consumer is ready to have Italian for lunch and Chinese for dinner, to wear Levi's 501 blue jeans for the outdoor party in the afternoon and to try the Gucci suit at night—changing not only diets and clothes but also the personas and selves that are to be (re)presented at each function.

Indeed, the experience of the consumer in today's market is fragmented, yet the same fragments are possible to experience across the globe. There is what may be termed an "enclavization" of experience. For example, the differentiation between the "developed" and "underdeveloped" countries no longer seems to hold. In underdeveloped countries one encounters the same rich lifestyles that one can in developed countries, and dire poverty, such as homelessness, can be found in developed countries just as in underdeveloped countries. Whether in developed or underdeveloped countries, however, these experiences are generally isolated from each other. The rich rarely interact with the poor, encountering them only in the streets and in the media. Each live in enclaves, "protected" and divided from each other. It seems paradoxical, especially to the modernist observer, that such contradictory tendencies exist together and simultaneously. Poverty grows within riches and wealth flourishes among poverty. Regional wars, local armed conflicts, and ethnic strife expand at the same time that a rhetoric of peace and democracy increasingly dominates around the world. Yet even those countries and groups in armed conflict or in conflict over ideologies are found to trade with each other in the global market through common intermediaries. These experiences are also greatly fragmented, within (physical and/or mental) enclaves, concurrent and common across national boundaries. Thus, there is a globalization of fragmentation in all respects. Poverty is everywhere, wealth and riches everywhere—America in every country and every country in America. The epitome of this phenomenon is the World Showcase at the Epcot Center in Disney World, Florida, where tourists can visit France, England, China, Morocco, Norway, and so on and experience their sights, sounds, and tastes. Yet this is only the intensified, theme park version of what takes place in everyday places, in cities and shopping malls. Themes, the simulated experiences of different cultures, lifestyles, and existences are, indeed, to a greater degree becoming the everyday experiences (Sorkin, 1992). This can be seen in the (re)created renovated sections of cities, the wharf areas, city centers, shopping centers, and the like. The simulated theme areas attract so much interest and traffic that they are, then, replicated and become the *norm* for our (sub)urban existence, constituting our (sub)urban reality (Andersen, 1994). Furthermore, the contemporary consumer seems to want to sample and experience different themes rather than a single urban theme. Thus, to a growing extent, we find the (sub)urban experience as fragmented sets of themes, each rarely unique, because once they find a consuming audience they reappear across cities, regions, and continents.

Postmodern Culture

As expressed earlier, the postmodern call has reinforced the tendencies discussed previously with its insistence on liberation from universal forms, systems, and "reality." Fragmentation and the freedom to touristically visit and experience different forms of existence that come with it are celebrated by the postmodernists. The modernist narratives that call for commitment to a single system that will emancipate all are evidenced to have brought, instead, conformity, oppression, and righteous totalitarianisms of all sorts. Therefore, the postmodernists call for an acceptance of different styles and realities as simply different, neither superior nor inferior to each other. Postmodern culture has institutionalized, in the everyday experiences of its consumers, the playful switching of (self)-images, the tolerance for acting and being different—not to commit to any form of being forever but to try and retry each. Furthermore, no single commitment is to be taken too seriously because it is understood that each has paradoxical outcomes, that times may require change. Rather than stick to one thing no matter what, the postmodern sensibility finds it more prudent and more fun to come and go, to adopt, change, and readopt forms and styles when and as required to achieve that which is selected as the (momentary) goal. Because every single goal has contradictory outcomes for the individual and for the community, the idea is not to select a single one forever but to creatively, playfully, and critically construct and reconstruct balances.

The postmodern culture is a culture of the *now and here* (Gitlin, 1989). The consumer of this culture is unlike the modern subject who committed oneself to a future project and sacrificed the present for the future. The postmodern consumer is unwilling to commit oneself to any single project, as already discussed, and wants to experience the past and the future now and here. Thus, the popularity of the thematized simulations can be understood. Those simulations that attract and capture the imagination are multiplied and recreated and become the frequent experiences, the realities of existence in the (sub)urban environments. The themes are generally cultural, representing the Roman (as at Via Rodeo or at the Forum at Caesar's Palace in Las Vegas, Nevada), the Scandinavian (as in the case of many re-creations of Scandinavian villages in the United States), or the past or the future (e.g., simulations of past San Francisco earthquakes at the San Francisco pier attraction and the visits to planets at film studio theme parks). In this sense, the touristic consumer visits and experiences these cultures, all here and now, moving from one to the other as time and interest and other resources allow.

Thus, postmodern culture is the reculturation of social existence. The idea that the economy is all powerful and determining has created only one form of existence: the modern. Yet things are changing, although, currently, rather paradoxically. To the postmodernist, trying to resolve the paradoxes is a futile quest because they exist in every development;

rather, one has to play with the paradoxes and create balances. At the same time that the economic is reintegrated as part of the cultural and the markets that were the foci of economic activity in modernity are becoming recultured, culture itself is becoming a commodity for the market. Cultures of all types—ethnic, national, regional, and the like—that are able to translate their qualities into marketable commodities and spectacles find themselves maintained, experienced, and globalized. Cultures that cannot or do not (re)present themselves in terms of marketable qualities, simulated instances, experiences, and products are finding themselves divested of members. In particular, traditional cultures, which are dying because of the encroachment of the market, find that the way to keep their members interested in maintaining their culture is to involve the young people in the marketization of the culture, especially as touristic spectacle, through their music, dances, food, clothing, and ornamental items. This allows the youths to have incomes and, thereby, the ability to participate in the larger global market. Whether a Native American culture in southwestern United States, one in Kashmir, India, or an aboriginal culture in Taiwan, cultures are either fading away or finding ways to make themselves marketable. Cultures that cannot succeed in translating some of their qualities into spectacles or commodities seem to vanish only to become museum items.

Culture Consumed

The consumer culture that has marketized everything has, paradoxically, transformed culture itself into a consumable item (Sherry, 1987). Consequently, today, culture is no longer so much what people belong to but increasingly something that they consume. In postmodern times, culture is likely to become the most popular commodity sought because it satisfies so many of the tendencies in the modern that are becoming liberated by the postmodern. Perhaps most important, culture allows not only being a spectator, a voyeur, satisfying the visual gaze, but also being totally immersed into the experience.

The postmodern, in liberating the tendencies that were already in the modern despite the modernist rhetoric, has liberated the sensual and the sensational, specifically, the senses other than the visual that were relegated to an inferior status in their contribution to reason and knowledge. The postmodern consumer, in rejecting the privileged categorizations of all types and in being willing to accept difference rather than a stratifying (superior-inferior, sacred-profane, rational-emotional) normative system, exhibits a great desire to immerse her- or himself into experiences, rather than remain solely an observer. Thus the advent of and the great excitement about interactive, integrative technologies that will allow greater immersion, participation, and interaction for the consumer, such as virtual reality (Bylinsky, 1991), are understandable. The postmodern sensibility that celebrates such technologies invites a form of literacy that is multifaceted, multimedia, and multisensory. The postmodern consumer, therefore, will be literate and *know* through immersion, virtually or actually, into cultures, at once experiencing and learning by allowing information to reach him or her through different forms: sight, sound, touch, smell, and taste. This is the postmodern merging of genres (Hassan, 1987), the equalizing of the visual with other senses and of reason with other means of interpretation and perception. The postmodern consumer is seeking to learn and understand culture not through detached and distanced observation and reading but through immersed experiencing. In this sense, as well, culture is not just something to study and be informed about but something to exist in, experience, and consume. Again, not a single culture but all cultures that are marketed and represented here and now will be experienced.

Clearly, there are many philosophical and even moral implications of culture as a consumable that will worry and distress many, especially the modernist minds. The commodification/marketization of culture may also dispute the postmodernist assertion that the end of modernity is also the end of metanarratives; that totalizing, universalizing ideologies and systems are gone; that with postmodernism comes fragmentation, multiplicity of narratives, realities, and truth regimes (Foucault, 1980; Lyotard, 1984). The postmodern idea has been that when the singular dominance of the economic ends and the multiplicity of culturally signified regimes of truth begin, the era of metanarratives will be over. Yet when all cultural signification is mediated through the market and through commodification, despite the fragmented existence of different and competing cultures, (life)styles, images, and brands, the market itself and marketing—as the market's conscious practice to make anything marketable, (re)presentable as attractive—become the new universal. There is, maybe, a difference in the sense that what is now universal is not the end product (the idea system or culture) but the process. This process of survival through marketization is highly conducive to fragmentation (Fırat, 1992b) because anything that can be attractively represented can find a market and be momentarily experienced. Thus, no single culture can any longer claim universality or exhibit dominance except the *culture of fragmentation.* Fragmentation, through the process of marketization, becomes the new metanarrative. This may be the ultimate paradox of postmodernity.

The Question of Cultural Identity

Progression of modern society has created substantive transformations in the character of culture, as suggested by the previous discussions. From encompassing all that was constructed through human agency (all that is not given by nature), it fragmented into its components, such as the economic, the social, and the political. Later, it came to signify a domain separate and different from its earlier components, finally relegated to constituting a part of the superstructure that was largely determined by the infrastructure, specifically, the economic and the material (Marx, 1939/1973; Parsons, 1937/1968). With the culmination of the many tendencies in modernity, culture has become even further fragmented into qualities that are representable as marketable commodities.

The fragmentation generally experienced in contemporary culture is conducive to the fragmentation of cultures into their singular qualities, such as their food, attire, music, art, dance, shopping environments, and popular media items. Then, any and all such qualities that can be translated into marketable commodities represent the vitality and the continuity of a culture. At the same time, such isolation of singular qualities from the culture in which they were originally embedded provides these qualities a relative autonomy from the culture from which they emerged. It becomes possible to resignify each quality, to invest it with some new meanings that indeed make it more alluring, seductive, and marketable to the different (touristic) consumer markets. In effect, each quality so commodified begins to create its own hyperreality (Baudrillard, 1983; Eco, 1986). This process, although allowing the culture to preserve its livelihood, also provides the seeds for its transformation into something different, specifically, into a more commercial entity (Canan & Hennessy, 1989; Costa & Bamossy, 1993; Rossel, 1988).

Thus, sustaining cultural identity through commodifying and marketizing it becomes a paradoxical success. Is a culture so marketized true to its original identity? Is a culture that ensures its livelihood through commodifying its qualities preserving what it originally was, or is it preserving something different from the original although resembling it in some respects? Is it at all possible to think of a stable or stagnant cultural identity?

Clearly, even without the existence of markets, cultural identities must have gone and did go through transformations. In any era, a stagnant culture must have lost its hold over most of its subjects. In our contemporary culture, however, despite the dominance of the economic market in all respects, there is a general tendency among most scholars and intellectuals to consider changes in cultural identity due to the forces of a commercial market as abhorrent. The idea that *identity* is lost when changes occur because of the commercialization in the market seems to dominate. It is curious that at the same time the commercial market is expanding its influence, it is considered to represent that which is vulgar. This paradox is indeed telling about the contemporary culture's images of itself and, maybe, contributes to our understanding of the cynicism and the loss of commitment that are apparently on the increase in postmodern times (Gitlin, 1989; Huyssen, 1984).

If cultures transformed even before they had to survive in and through the market, were they able to preserve their identities then? What is it that makes us think that identity is lost when the commercial market is involved? Similar debates seem to be happening in the communications field, specifically as researchers study the impacts of commercial media from economically advanced countries on the cultural identities of the peoples of economically less developed countries (Ferguson, 1993, Şahin & Aksoy, 1993; Schlesinger, 1993). The "violation" of the "host" culture is more evident in these cases because there is the occasion of one culture "imposing" itself on another. Yet even in this case, there is a disagreement among scholars as to whether the incursion of the commercial elements of one culture on another does indeed cause a loss of identity for the invaded culture. Some researchers find that commercial invasion is less harmful than other forms of invasion because, they argue, a commercial invasion allows elements from all cultures to survive as long as they are marketized (Ferguson, 1993; Schlesinger, 1993). Compare this to military cultural invasions, for example, in which elements from the host culture may not be allowed to sustain themselves under any circumstance.

Yet is any invasion of any type really able to completely dominate and determine culture? And given time, changing generations, technology, and so forth, is any culture really able to completely preserve its identity? The answer to both questions, it seems clear, is no. The issue has never really been one of either stagnation or perfect preservation of any cultural identity. All cultures had to (re)present some allure to their members to have some historical continuity. This chapter has demonstrated that today the dominant form of (re)presenting allure is commodification and marketization. In the past, the dominant forms have changed. At times it has been more force and less allure. Members of a culture have been subjected to strategies of fear and repression through physical force to make them conform. At times, social, communal, convivial support, and companionship have been the means of making members of a culture feel happy, content, and appreciated, thereby loyal to and appreciative of the culture, wanting to preserve it. Yet in every case, whether slow or fast, changes have occurred in all cultures; myths have been modified, and different values and behavior patterns have gained popularity. The issue is, therefore, where the changes come from and who likes the changes and who does not, who finds the changes advantageous and who does not. Consequently, different preferences have developed, giving different means for change a good or a bad name.

In the end, therefore, the issue is one of *power:* where the power to change or preserve culture lies. Also at issue is whether or not the form of power allows all members of culture to participate in the process of change. Furthermore, in the case in which popular participation is not allowed, the issue becomes one of who participates and who cannot. In this sense, the problem should not be with the market; after all, it is just another form of legitimation (Habermas, 1973) and mediation in society. The problem is that many scholars conclude that the market has fast become the only locus of legitimation and that it does not allow a fair and equal participation by all. Because of its current emphasis on the economic, the market has favored and continues to favor the needs, wishes, tastes, and preferences of some (generally a minority) over others. In the end, the struggle is not with the fact that cultural identity changes or even with the fact that currently the market plays an overwhelming role in it but with the fact that the power to signify, represent, and communicate forcefully what is acceptable, seductive, attractive, and meaningful is not evenly distributed. Our dissatisfaction regarding the offerings in the commercial market would be much less if such offerings did not limit our abilities to have a greater say in which cultural qualities ought to be preserved and what changes ought to occur in others.

Perhaps the greatest contribution from integrating the postmodernist insights with our varied perspectives is the recognition that we may have been asking futile questions under the influence of universalizing modern narratives. Too much effort has been spent on determining what is right and, consequently, what is wrong on the basis of foundations (theological, ideological, or scientific) that were, in their heyday, considered to be universal, indubitable, and superior. Postmodernist insights, on the other hand, enable us to (re)appreciate change and the paradoxical nature of all that is good and *right*, as well as all that is bad and *wrong*. Recognition of the hyperreal makes us become aware (once again, because the modern metanarratives may have suppressed our earlier awareness of certain things) that cultural identities have been historically constructed, then transformed and reconstructed, on the basis of different forms of legitimation and mediation in society, each of which promoted different bases and forms of power (Fırat, 1993; Toffler, 1991). It may be time to turn our attention, therefore, from describing cultural identity to describing changes in identity and to understanding the forms (processes of legitimation and mediation) and means (power) whereby change occurs.

References

Alavi, H., & Shanin, T. (Eds.). (1982). *Introduction to the sociology of "developing countries."* New York: Monthly Review Press.

Andersen, K. (1994, January 10). Las Vegas, U.S.A. *Time*, pp. 41-42.

Angus, I. (1989). Circumscribing postmodern culture. In I. Angus & S. Jhally (Eds.), *Cultural politics in contemporary America* (pp. 96-107). New York: Routledge.

Baudrillard, J. (1975). *The mirror of production*. St. Louis, MO: Telos.

Baudrillard, J. (1981). *For a critique of the political economy of the sign*. St. Louis, MO: Telos.

Baudrillard, J. (1983). *Simulations*. New York: Semiotext(e).

Belk, R. W. (1988). Third world consumer culture. In E. Kumcu & A. F. Fırat (Eds.), *Marketing and development: Toward broader dimensions* (pp. 103-127). Greenwich, CT: JAI.

Berger, J. (1972). *Ways of seeing*. London: British Broadcasting Corporation.

Breen, T. H. (1993). The meanings of things: Interpreting the consumer economy in the eighteenth century. In J. Brewer & R. Porter (Eds.), *Consumption and the world of goods* (pp. 249-260). New York: Routledge.

Brewer, J., & Porter, R. (Eds.). (1993). *Consumption and the world of goods*. New York: Routledge.

Buck-Morss, S. (1991). *The dialectics of seeing: Walter Benjamin and the Arcades Project*. Cambridge: MIT Press.

Bylinsky, G. (1991, June 3). The marvels of "virtual reality." *Fortune*, pp. 138-150.

Canan, P., & Hennessy, M. (1989). The growth machine, tourism, and the selling of culture. *Sociological Perspectives*, 32(2), 227-243.

Costa, J. A., & Bamossy, G. J. (1993). Ethnicity in developing countries: Implications for marketing and research. In L. V. Dominguez (Ed.), *Marketing and economic restructuring in the developing world* (pp. 408-415). Madison, WI: Omnipress.

Dholakia, N., & Fırat, A. F. (1988). Development in the era of globalizing markets and consumption patterns. In E. Kumcu & A. F. Fırat (Eds.), *Marketing and development: Toward broader dimensions* (pp. 79-101). Greenwich, CT: JAI.

Dreyfus, H. L. (1991). *Being-in-the-world: A commentary on Heidegger's "Being and time,"* Division I. Cambridge: MIT Press.

Dunn, W. (1992). Hanging out with American youth. *American Demographics*, 14(2), 24-35.

Eco, U. (1986). *Travels in hyperreality* (W. Weaver, Trans.). San Diego, CA: Harcourt Brace Jovanovich.

Ewen, S. (1988). *All consuming images: The politics of style in contemporary culture.* New York: Basic Books.

Ewen, S. (1990). Marketing dreams: The political elements of style. In A. Tomlinson (Ed.), *Consumption, identity & style* (pp. 41-56). London: Routledge.

Featherstone, M. (1990). *Global culture: Nationalism, globalization and modernity.* London: Sage.

Featherstone, M. (1991). *Consumer culture and postmodernism.* London: Sage.

Ferguson, M. (1993). Invisible divides: Communication and identity in Canada and the U.S. *Journal of Communication, 43*(2), 42-57.

Fırat, A. F. (1992a). Fragmentations in the postmodern. In J. F. Sherry, Jr., & B. Sternthal (Eds.), *Advances in consumer research* (Vol. 19, pp. 203-206). Provo, UT: Association for Consumer Research.

Fırat, A. F. (1992b). Postmodernism and the marketing organization. *Journal of Organizational Change Management, 5*(1), 79-83.

Fırat, A. F. (1993). Powershift [Book review]. *Journal of Marketing, 57*(3), 139-141.

Fırat, A. F., & Venkatesh, A. (1993). Postmodernity: The age of marketing. *International Journal of Research in Marketing, 10*(3), 227-249.

Foster, H. (Ed.). (1988). *Vision and visuality.* Seattle, WA: Bay.

Foucault, M. (1980). *Power/knowledge: Selected interviews and other writings* (C. Gordon, Ed.). New York: Pantheon.

Gallop, J. (1985). *Reading Lacan.* Ithaca, NY: Cornell University Press.

Gitlin, T. (Ed.). (1986). *Watching television: A Pantheon guide to popular culture.* New York: Pantheon.

Gitlin, T. (1989). Postmodernism: Roots and politics. In I. Angus & S. Jhally (Eds.), *Cultural politics in contemporary America* (pp. 347-360). New York: Routledge.

Habermas, J. (1973). *Legitimation crisis.* Boston: Beacon.

Habermas, J. (1983). Modernity: An incomplete project. In H. Foster (Ed.) & S. Ben-Habib (Trans.), *The anti-aesthetic: Essays on postmodern culture* (pp. 3-15). Port Townsend, WA: Bay.

Hassan, I. (1987). *The postmodern turn: Essays in postmodern theory and culture.* Columbus: Ohio State University Press.

Huszagh, S., Fox, R. J., & Day, E. (1986). Global markets: An empirical investigation. *Columbia Journal of World Business, 20*(4), 31-44.

Hutcheon, L. (1988). *A poetics of postmodernism: History, theory, fiction.* New York: Routledge.

Huyssen, A. (1984). Mapping the postmodern. *New German Critique, 33,* 5-52.

Kaplan, E. A. (1987). *Rocking around the clock: Music television, postmodernism, and consumer culture.* New York: Routledge.

Keane, J. (1990). *Media and democracy.* London: Polity.

Kellner, D. (1990). *Television and the crisis of democracy.* Boulder, CO: Westview.

Kling, R., Olin, S., & Poster, M. (Eds.). (1991). *Postsuburban California: The transformation of Orange County since World War II.* Berkeley: University of California Press.

Kroker, A. (1992). *The possessed individual: Technology and the French postmodern.* New York: St. Martin's.

Levin, D. M. (Ed.). (1993). *Modernity and the hegemony of vision.* Berkeley: University of California Press.

Levitt, T. (1983). The globalization of markets. *Harvard Business Review, 83*(3), 92-102.

Lyotard, J.-F. (1984). *The postmodern condition: A report on knowledge.* Minneapolis: University of Minnesota Press.

Lyotard, J.-F. (1992). Missive on universal history. In J. Pefanis & M. Thomas (Eds.) & D. Barry (Trans.), *The postmodern explained* (pp. 23-37). Minneapolis: University of Minnesota Press.

Marx, K. (1973) *Grundrisse: Foundations of the critique of political economy*. New York: Vintage. (Original work published 1939)

Massumi, B. (1987). Realer than real: The simulacrum according to Deleuze and Guattari. *Copyright, 1*, 90-96.

Moyers, B. (1989a, November 8). Image and reality in America: Consuming images [Episode of *The Public Mind*]. Public Broadcasting System.

Moyers, B. (1989b, November 22). Image and reality in America: Illusions of news [Episode of the *The Public Mind*]. Public Broadcasting System.

Newcomb, H. (Ed.). (1979). *Television: The critical view* (2nd ed.). New York: Oxford University Press.

Parsons, T. (1968). *The structure of social action* (Vols. 1 & 2). New York: Free Press. (Original work published 1937)

Postman, N. (1985). *Amusing ourselves to death: Public discourse in the age of show business*. New York: Penguin.

Ritchie, K. (1992). Get ready for "Generation X": Soon the primary market, and very unlike aging boomers. *Advertising Age, 63*(46), 21.

Rorty, R. (1979). *Philosophy and the mirror of nature*. Princeton, NJ: Princeton University Press.

Rossel, P. (Ed.). (1988). *Tourism: Manufacturing the exotic* (Document No. 61). Copenhagen: International Work Group for Indigenous Affairs.

Russell, B. (1945). *A history of western philosophy*. New York: Simon & Schuster.

Şahin, H., & Aksoy, A. (1993). Global media and cultural identity in Turkey. *Journal of Communication, 43*(2), 31-41.

Schlesinger, P. (1993). Wishful thinking: Cultural politics, media, and collective identities in Europe. *Journal of Communication, 43*(2), 6-17.

Sherry, J. F., Jr. (1987). Cultural propriety in a global marketplace. In A. F. Fırat, N. Dholakia, & R. P. Bagozzi (Eds.), *Philosophical and radical thought in marketing* (pp. 179-191). Lexington, MA: Lexington Books.

Sorkin, M. (Ed.). (1992). *Variations on a theme park: The new American city and the end of public space*. New York: Noonday.

Steuerman, E. (1992). Habermas vs. Lyotard: Modernity vs. postmodernity. In A. Benjamin (Ed.), *Judging Lyotard* (pp. 99-118). London: Routledge.

Toffler, A. (1991). *Powershift*. New York: Bantam.

Venkatesh, A. (1991). Changing consumption patterns. In R. Kling, S. Olin, & M. Poster (Eds.), *Postsuburban California: The transformation of Orange County since World War II* (pp. 142-164). Berkeley: University of California Press.

Weber, M. (1927). *General economic history*. London: Allen & Unwin.

Weston, K. (1991). *Families we choose: Lesbians, gays, kinship*. New York: Columbia University Press.

Wilson, E. (1989). *Hallucinations: Life in the post-modern city*. London: Hutchinson Radius.

Zinn, L., Power, C., Yang, D. J., Cuneo, A. Z., & Ross, D. (1992, December 14). Move over, boomers: The busters are here—and they're angry. *Business Week*, pp. 74-82.

5

Interest Groups
With a Noble Face

EUGEEN ROOSENS

Ethnicity, ethnic group, ethnic identity, ethnic minority, multiethnic society, multicultural society, nation, nationalism, nation-state, and *ethnonational* are terms that frequently appear in today's media, in political discourse, and in daily life in general. At first glance, their meaning seems to be nonproblematic: Everybody is supposed to know what they point at. To make things worse, social scientists use the same expressions, mostly with different, technical connotations.

Because analytical tools are always constructs implying theoretical assumptions, I will first sketch a theoretical framework to elucidate the terms used in this chapter. In the second part of this chapter, I will look at the realities these analytical concepts are meant to signify.

Ethnic Groups

Fredrik Barth's *Ethnic Groups and Boundaries* (1969) is considered a landmark in the development of the anthropology of ethnicity. Before Barth's publication, most scholars tended to conceive of an ethnic group as a population of common descent, possessing a common culture. It was assumed that ethnic groups were distinct because they were the bearers of dissimilar cultures and that cultures were different because they had developed in relative isolation. With global communication increasing, contact between cultures would reduce cultural differences and, therefore, differences between the bearers of these cultures, the ethnic groups. Being an ethnic group and living in relative isolation seemed to go hand in hand. In those days, culture was generally considered as a rather homogeneous, holistic package of cultural traits. These academic representations fit very well the imagery involved in the popular notion of the American melting pot (Schlesinger, 1992): When human beings hailing from different ethnic backgrounds come together, cultures fuse, and a new human being, a new nation is born.

In some particular situations, things may indeed develop along these lines: Cultural traits merge and peoples amalgamate, or dominant majorities absorb allochthonous minorities. Usually, however, the fusion of the ethnic groups does not automatically flow from processes of cultural transformation, absorption, or amalgamation. In most cases the scenario is different.

As Barth made clear in his theory, ethnic articulation tends to increase when two or more ethnic groups enter into contact. This phenomenon is very visible in the context of immigration. Although it is true that many aspects of the migrant culture are transformed, the profile of the migrant group, with its own genealogical and cultural background, tends to stiffen in contact situations. To read the facts correctly, it seems more appropriate, then, to highlight the way the bearers of the culture behave: They are not passive human beings, marked and differentiated by their respective cultures. These groups of human beings emerge as active social formations, "social vessels," whose members ascribe themselves to that type of entities and are seen by both insiders and outsiders as belonging. Ethnic groups are not cultural but social entities *in the first place*.

In Barth's view, ethnic groups use only a limited number of elements of their respective cultures to constitute an ethnic boundary, through which they differentiate themselves from other similar groups. It is not culture that makes things happen but humans who use their respective cultural traits, selectively and conveniently, as ethnic boundaries. To understand how ethnic groups and ethnic relations function, ethnic boundaries are *the* relevant topic to study, not the cultures as contents or holistic fields. Needless to say, the "we" of the ethnic group always implies a "them"—the outsiders—who belong to another similar group. In this sense, ethnic groups are instruments of inclusion and exclusion.

It is beyond doubt that the ways ethnic boundaries are constructed and maintained are essential to understanding ethnic phenomena. The creation and maintenance of boundaries by means of cultural or phenotypical elements, however, do not make groups or categories of people into ethnic groups or ethnic categories per se (Roosens, in press). To be sure, origins do figure in Barth's landmark contribution, but in my view, this notion has not been elaborated on nor given an adequate place in the model, the distinction between culture and ethnic group absorbing full attention. Studies on migration in Europe especially reveal that a *complementary* perspective is needed. What makes migrant groups ethnic, in my view, is that they refer to a specific and distinct origin. Members of ethnic groups or ethnic categories always develop and keep alive—or even create from scratch—representations about their beginnings and their ancestors (Horowitz, 1985; Roosens, 1992). This applies to native ethnonational groups but is especially the case with immigrants. In the massive chain migration fluxes that started after World War II and stretched well into the 1970s, family and kinship networks have played a prominent role. Chain migrations operate mostly with the help of family and kinship connections or via friends or former neighbors one considers as kin. Very often, kinship members constitute the only link between the immigration site and the place of origin. Unlike boundaries, which make people different from each other and maintain ethnic division, origins inversely make people identical within the same group, creating and maintaining ethnicity from the inside. A minimal reference to outsiders in general—to those who do not belong—and thus to a boundary in general suffices to make the conception of an in-group possible. Concrete interaction with a *specific* out-group is not required, for the same reason that being and feeling a member of a kin group does not necessarily imply a strong opposition with neighboring families.

When the chips are down and the migrants feel secure enough to position themselves vis-à-vis the surrounding natives, the relations with the folks who stayed behind and with their own migrant community serve as the starting point to form an image of their "own people," their "own nation," their "own ethnic group." Folk genealogy, using phrases such as "the same blood" and "people of one kind," combined with folk history, keeps alive images of a mythical past one has in common with the home region (Smith, 1988). Family, kin (Harris, 1990), and ethnic or ethnonational group are mixed up so that family relations seem to stretch into the field of the ethnic network and the ethnic group. Affection and emotion that are generated and nourished by the kinship network and the family are projected on the imagined ethnic group or nation (Anderson, 1991; De Vos & Romanucci-Ross, 1975; Epstein, 1978).

In this perspective, ethnic identity then can best be defined as a feeling of belonging and continuity in being (staying the same person(s) through time), resulting from an act of self-ascription and/or ascription by others to a group of people who claim both common ancestry and a common cultural tradition (Hutnik, 1991). Ethnic identity can take its drive and pattern from an interplay of oppositions with outsiders, but it mostly combines this source of differentiation with an internal source of identification. One of these two sources can be more important than the other, depending on historical circumstances and situations.

The combination of the origin metaphor with the boundary metaphor allows for a more complete elucidation of the polyvalent character of ethnicity. Ethnicity can stress division and opposition in humanity but must not necessarily do so. It always involves a form of "standing on its own" and thus of independence and of being distinct from others, but this "being a people" must not unavoidably be defined in opposition to specific, concrete outsiders. References to a common origin and a vague "non-we" suffice. A group of people can think and feel about their past and celebrate their common origin without necessarily stressing ethnic exclusion. This is why ethnicity can be represented as a pacific, "natural" form of social organization that does not necessarily lead to hostility—just as having different parents does not unavoidably turn neighbors into rivals. A myth about common origin in a distant past can even unify ethnic or ethnonational groups without dissolving their distinct ethnic identities, as the movement for Flemish-Dutch unification illustrates.

Ethnic Group and Nation

In daily discourse, *ethnic group* and *nation, ethnicism* and *nationalism* are frequently interchanged. This further obscures a number of phenomena, making a careful analysis impossible. One likes to think with Anderson (1991), Gellner (1983), Hobsbawm (1992), and many other social scientists and historians that the nation, the nation-state, and nationalism are recent phenomena. The late 18th and the 19th centuries may have been the heyday of nation building. Building a modern nation in this phase of history implied the bridging of different ethnic origins, different languages, and divergent localisms. In this sense, nation building contained a broadening of the social perspective and group formation.

Anderson (1991) defined the nation as "an imagined political community—and imagined as both inherently limited and sovereign" (p. 6). It is imagined because it is impossible to meet the other members of the community, however small the community. A nation is represented as a community in that its members, at least in their imagination, relate as comrades in a type of imagined friendship and equality, whatever their real socioeconomic differences. Besides, a nation is imagined as limited: Beyond its boundaries lies another, similar nation.

In Anderson's (1991) view, this imagination of the nation was made possible because sacred languages, intertwined with their respective religions, ebbed away, and sacred rules lost their legitimation in the same phase of history. The discovery of the world by Westerners, technological development, and especially print capital, which made possible the spreading of printed text from the 16th century on, gradually introduced another global perspective. Deep down, the fear of death and the loss of meaning caused by the crumbling of established values may have been, according to Anderson, powerful additional factors in bringing about the modern nation as a new frame of reference. Gellner (1983) also stressed the modernization of culture, more specifically, the spreading of "high culture" as one of the conditions of modern nation building.

Whatever the historical processes involved in the nation building of the late 18th century and the following decades, one thing is certain: Nation building did contain a broadening perspective. One may even think with Hobsbawm (1992) that it was one step short from developing a universal platform for humanity. Or to put it another way, there was more conjunction than disjunction involved in the process. It must be clear then, that the ongoing process of bringing about and keeping alive what is called a nation in the last two centuries of European history should certainly not be confused with today's revival and creation of ethnic groups and categories that are occurring in Canada, the United States, and several countries of Europe. Usually, the ethnic groups or self-defined nations that emerge or reemerge in recent times are infranational and divide the encompassing nation-state.

Smith's work *The Ethnic Origins of Nations* (1986) shows that there is a historical continuity between the ethnic group and the modern nation, so that many elements of the modern nation are not so modern as some may believe. Modern nation building always uses an ethnic group or category as its kernel or core to start from. And although it is true that a modern nation cannot be reduced to be an ethnic group, both formations, as societal entities, have much in common. In both entities an imagined past or a myth of origin provides a common beginning.

Sometimes, as with the French Revolution, the quality of citizen and the republican character of the nation are stressed, but at least for a part of the nation, common ancestry and forms of folk genealogy are invoked and used as structuring elements. At least part of the nation is "of one blood," descending from the same ancestors. Also, after a few generations, other citizens who initially did not share the ancestors of the founding group may forget their own origins and join the founders of the nation-state, honoring a common, imagined ancestry. Even if many insiders are aware of the doubtful national origins of certain subgroups, a convenient silence protects the seamless solidarity of the newly knit nation. Often, a dialectical process of mutual reinforcement develops between the *mythomoteur* and the efforts to stick together against outside competitors or political enemies. Exactly the same processes of boundary formation and boundary maintenance operate in the case of both the nation-state and the ethnic group.

A series of nations that are termed *ethnonational* display exactly the same kinship and family imagery as most ethnic groups. Hitler, Mussolini, and others represented the nation as a huge family. It is striking that these family metaphors come to the fore especially in times of crises, racism, and xenophobia. This, of course, is not surprising. The family metaphor offers something reassuring and caring by touching a string of deep feelings of togetherness, unconditional belonging, and absolute origins. These feelings are a formidable tool not only to pull together but also to keep or push the stranger out (Harris, 1990).

Analytically speaking, a type of nation whose ideology is strongly based on common origins and on the kinship and family metaphor (such as Japan) differs from a type of nation such as the United States, in which republican citizenship and *jus soli* are predominant. The first type, the ethnonation, is, of course, structurally and functionally closer to the ethnic group than the second. But the second type also generally contains an ethnic core.

Both types of nations differ from the ethnic group by the degree of political self-determination they enjoy. One important expression of this autonomy is their own territory, the homeland. A political entity need not be fully independent to be a nation, however. It can be part of an encompassing state or even a part of another encompassing *nation*-state, so that its citizens belong twice to a nation. In federal Belgium, for example, it is expected that Flemish citizens are both loyal Flemings and loyal Belgians.

A remarkable interplay of notions, concepts, and imagined groups is taking place in today's public discourse and debate. The expression *national communities* instead of *ethnic minorities* or *ethnic groups* can be heard in the United States. Some ethnic groups are described as *nationalistic*. Other ethnic groups who try to achieve a far-reaching political independence call themselves nations, as some native Canadian peoples do (Roosens, 1989). In terms of international political ethics, there is nothing wrong with trying to become a nation. The United Nations symbolizes the legitimacy of this idea. For decades, the nation has been universally considered as the building block of humankind. Therefore, trying to become a nation should not be condemnable per se unless the building of a new nation implies the violent destruction of an enclosing nation-state from the inside.

Usually, ethnic or ethnoterritorial groups who try to get recognition as a nation break away from an encompassing state or nation-state. This unavoidably appears as a process of fraying, decomposing, and deconstructing. This *micro*nationalism, although going in the opposite direction of the nation building of the 19th century, uses the same types of symbols, identical feelings, and identical forms and even the same contents of ideology, with disjunction replacing conjunction. It appears from these phenomena that exactly the same mobilizing factors can be used in two opposite directions. It follows that the term nationalism, as indistinctly used in popular discourse, can signify two opposite processes.

Ethnicity in the United States and Ethnicity in Europe: A Comparison

In the United States, it has often been assumed for almost two centuries that immigrants coming from all possible parts of the world would forget their past as members of other nations or ethnic groups to become Americans. As recent history from the 1960s on has been showing, ethnic self-profiling, or ethnicity, has reemerged in all possible ethnic groups and categories, especially among the so-called ethnic minorities (Glazer & Moynihan, 1975). The United States provides an extremely clear case in which ethnic groups can be observed in their relationship with a state and a nation. From the beginning, nation building in the United States has been trying to make people transcend their ethnic origin and belonging. As a matter of principle, loyalty to the American people implied a relativizing of the original ethnic membership. Practically, however, the dominant English-speaking White minority has been forcing the others to adapt to their language and lifestyle. Being an American looked suspiciously close to being or imitating a White Anglo-Saxon Protestant (WASP). But at the official ideological level, an American was and had to be an American in the first place, not a Briton, or a French, or a Swede, or an Italian. The American state was and still is an institution that organizes the monopoly of enforcement, directed and supervised by a regime that in principle stands for equality and nondiscrimination among ethnic groups.

In recent years, ethnicity has come so much to the foreground that some scholars talk about the "disuniting of America" (Schlesinger, 1992), and leading weeklies publish well-documented articles on the fraying of the United States. Barth's (1969) theory, especially his concept of ethnic boundary, allows one to highlight ethnic relations in the United States as an interactive game in which being recognized as an ethnic group and being taken seriously as a player are, at least in part, questions of bargaining and negotiation. The processes on the American scene dramatically show how much ethnic categories and ethnic groups are intentional constructions that can be highly instrumental in achieving specific utilitarian goals, as well as expressive in providing human beings with a face of their own and a setting to belong (Roosens, 1993; Trueba, Rodríguez, Zou, & Cintron, 1993). The ethnic mosaic of Canada provides a similar vista (Roosens, 1989).

Since the late 1940s, northwestern Europe has actively attracted a growing number of immigrants. The first flow came in as guest workers, intending to return to their country of origin as soon as they reached their target—making plenty of money in a short time. Many of them, however, stayed on and were joined by their families. Considered in terms of population, many parts of northwestern Europe, especially cities, have become de facto multiethnic and multinational, in the sense that people from different ethnic and national backgrounds are living now within the same social spaces.

More recently, countries such as Spain, Portugal, Italy, and Greece, which used to be typical *emigration* countries, became *immigration* countries, attracting many people from the south and the east. It is a matter of political and governmental discussion in European countries today if, or under what conditions, they should assume their multicultural and multiethnic character explicitly and devise a consequent policy. The Netherlands may be the only country, until now, that officially adopted the epithet of being (since the beginning of the 1980s) a multiethnic society. Some European countries, such as Belgium, already were composed of "native communities," containing more than just one people or ethnic group well before the arrival of recent immigrants. But the question of multiethnicity, *new style,* came to the fore in the conflicts between autochthons and allochthons in almost all the countries of Europe. The violent reactions of significant numbers of xenophobic and racist groups, culminating in physical confrontations in which people were killed and thousands of migrants severely molested in some European countries, made the migration question into a main political issue. In this general atmosphere, local ethnonationalism has been flaring up, terrifying the immigrants with attempts to convince them to "go home."

In this perspective, ethnic relations and particularly the question of multicultural society has been associated with violence, crime, xenophobia, mutual distrust, and intolerance. For huge numbers of autochthons, it seems difficult to discuss these questions without releasing some anger or emotion. The setting up of a multiethnic and/or multicultural society does not sell as a positive task for the future as a means to contribute to a better, new world order. Migration is felt, rather, as a mishap that never should have occurred. It is especially unclear how a harmonious society should be constructed in which Muslims and natives of various Christian religions and other worldviews can live peacefully together.

Although similarities between the United States and Europe in the field of ethnic structures and ethnic relations are increasing, differences remain as well. To begin with, all Americans, except Native Americans (and African Americans, who came under force), are descendants from immigrants, and mostly they remember. If they forget, Native Americans will bring it up. Although the history of America shows distrust toward newcomers, in layer after layer of influx—California today is a case in point—there were no myths about distant origins, making believe that the "genuine Americans" had been present from time immemorial. Besides, although migrants stemming from the same region tend to concentrate, ethnic and national categories have been widely spread and mixed all over the United States (Glazer, 1983; Portes & Rumbaut, 1990). This U.S. perspective makes the immigrant less of a stranger than is the case in Europe, where vast majorities of Europeans strongly believe that their ancestors have been living on the native soil for centuries, even "from the very beginning." European masses and governments, even if they actively fight racism, are very resilient in their refusal to accept the multiethnic and multicultural character of the state in which they live. Again and again, it is requested that immigrants adapt, meaning that they should vanish and become absorbed into the local population as much as possible.

In this perspective, the widely used term *multicultural society* is striking very different chords and is defined and perceived in divergent ways by the various ideological and political groupings and currents. Moderate liberal politicians and mass media figures use the term to introduce the idea that the millions of migrants who came to the north are likely to stay and that migrants have become immigrants; more-over, the allochthons are not likely to give up their cultural identity and thus will stay different from the natives in many ways. The idea of a multicultural society is fashionable in quite a number of circles. In stressing the notion of culture, however, the term understates a fact that the native masses might not be prepared to swallow, namely, that the minorities intend to stay *ethnically* or *ethnonationally* different while claiming all sorts of rights, voting rights included. The term *cultural* is much softer than *ethnic* in that the notion of culture, even in social science discourse, is vague and more prone to overlap than *ethnic*. It is perfectly possible to compare my culture with the culture of other people and to discover that there are striking similarities without feeling threatened in my cultural identity. The term *ethnic*, on the contrary, is strongly divisive. My ethnic self-definition will always be exclusive with respect to people who belong to another ethnic group. Thus, attitudes associated with "one's own culture" can be very different from attitudes related to "one's ethnic identity." I can feel perfectly at home in my mother tongue and consciously enjoy cultural traits such as "our own" cuisine and celebrations while rejecting ethnic chauvinism and disliking the idea of cutting up humankind into ethnic pieces.

Some circles consider multicultural society as an abomination. Best-selling books such as Schlesinger's *The Disuniting of America* (1992) associate the idea of multicultural society with the historiographic revisionism of extreme Afrocentrism. Multicultural society is also rejected as utter nonsense by ultra-right-wing and xenophobic movements such as the *Vlaams Blok* in Flanders (Roosens, 1992). Neither the United States nor Europe has come to terms with the idea, let alone the implementation, of a genuine multicultural society. Up to now, even the definition of the term remains unclear, confusing, and sloganizing, covering a diversity of political agendas (Eldering, 1993).

Why Now?

NEW INTERNATIONAL ETHICS

After World War I, the idea that every nation deserves independence and its own state was launched by President Wilson, to the despair of some of his close collaborators who foresaw catastrophes if too many nations or aspirant nations moved in that direction (Moynihan, 1993). After World War II, a new strong impulse in the same direction was given. Being confronted with the unspeakable facts of the Holocaust, the whole world reacted in horror. The principle that every human group on earth should have the right to exist and to express and develop its own culture and beliefs was loudly proclaimed and widely publicized. This idea has grown into an internationally accepted norm. As a matter of principle, every human group that considers itself a nation can ask the moral backing of the international community of nations to pursue its destiny. Dozens of peoples, ethnic groups, nations, and nations-to-be have been claiming this right ever since.

Less than 2 decades after World War II, decolonization was spreading and Western dominance came to an end. All over the world, peoples have been fighting for the right to exist and the idea that all human groups are of equal value, that no people should be subjugated by any other. Although trespassing of this norm is frequent, the rule still holds at the level of principles. All these developments have encouraged a return to the ethnic or ethnonational group as a form of social organization, implying more political independence (Glazer & Moynihan, 1975).

TRANSFORMATIONS WITHIN THE STATES

Moreover, from the 1960s on, changes have occurred in many industrialized states, making membership in certain macroforms of organization less attractive and norms and frames of reference hazy and diffuse. These phenomena became very visible in the United States, Canada, and northwestern Europe in the late 1960s when all honorable institutions—religious and political authorities, universities, schools, churches, businesses, the family, and so forth—were discredited. These far-reaching gulfs of criticism contributed to anomie all over the industrialized world. Many people were no longer sure what to believe or to what groups to adhere (Glazer & Moynihan, 1975). Moreover, culture contacts and culture confrontations increased, and cultural relativism became rampant also among the masses. One realized, suddenly, how values could be different from place to place, from people to people. All this coincided in recent decades with the growth of immense international organizations that had not yet developed enough "soul" or "civil theology" to inspire thrust and orientation. The United Nations and the European Union are still, today, clear cases in point (Bell, 1975).

In addition, authority at the level of individual daily life has been shrinking. Few people openly assume moral authority anymore. The wealthy and influential have almost disappeared as identification figures. The leveling of the socioeconomic classes has received more impetus. Increasing incomes have allowed people of the lower class and lower middle class to dress as the well-to-do and to drive flashy cars. Hence, it has become impossible to tell the rich from the poor in very many contexts of daily life.

On top of all this, still other frames of reference crumbled. Communism and socialism had already been diversifying and splitting before the beginning of the 1970s. Chinese communism marked itself off from Soviet communism and differed from African socialism and Eurocommunism. Existing encompassing value systems, such as communism in Russia and in the former Eastern European countries, lost their face. Ethnicity and ethnoregionalism reemerged in almost all of these countries.

Wars among nation-states, which tend to reinforce internal cohesion among composing ethnic groups, were no longer fought. Heroic "discoveries" of new parts of the world had ceased. State-national ideologies and myths became outdated. The seemingly unlimited economic expansion showed its limitations, and huge environmental problems arose (Bell, 1975).

The aforementioned developments reduced the power of attraction of the nation-states, which kept and still keep ethnic groups together (Schlesinger, 1992). Issues that really matter seemed to become more and more supra- or infranational (Hobsbawm, 1992).

Membership in encompassing, universally oriented, conjunctive churches and religious congregations was plummeting, although the importance of divisive, "tribally oriented" religions was on the rise. Christian as well as Islamic currents divided huge numbers of people and became dangerously fanatical, especially when they coincided with ethnic or ethnonational divisions.

Still other social formations that tended to keep people together lost much of their attraction. As Bell convincingly showed in 1975, class struggle had become less attractive than before. Due to technological developments, the number of manual workers had sharply declined, whereas white-collar jobs had been on the increase. The polar opposition between the capitalists and the proletarians had been bridged by a gliding hierarchy of jobs and professions, and the worker unions had been *talking* the heat out of the battle. In this sense, most laborers have been alienated from their class struggle. Negotiations have taken the place of physical struggle and confrontation.

Nation-states, conjunctive churches, and class struggle all used to cut across ethnic and ethnonational groups and thus mitigate ethnic oppositions. With the receding of these institutions, ethnic division, opposition, and confrontation came to the fore. Ethnic groups and ethnonational formations, which appear as primordial, provide to an increasing number of people schemes of orientation and identification, at least for the time being.

ETHNIC STRATEGIES IN THE WORLD OF INTEREST

As discussed previously, the evolution of international power relations has in the last 40 years produced a context in which the principle of equality among humans and nations has come to the foreground, setting a favorable climate for the use of ethnicity as a weapon. Hundreds of populations who identify as ethnic groups or nations and who feel disadvantaged, repressed, or colonized have since emerged as claimants. They usually start their militant activity by asking cultural autonomy and the financial means to guarantee this autonomy. In the climate of principled equality among citizens and ethnic groups that prevails in industrialized democratic societies, freedom of cultural expression cannot be denied. Moreover, cultural expression is almost impossible to control outside the context of public parades or state-controlled institutions. A refusal by those in power is liable to be widely publicized as discrimination, oppression, or racism if confrontation occurs between groups with different phenotypical traits. Very frequently, mass media are informed about the incident. This way, local confrontation catches international attention and puts majority authorities under formidable pressure, especially when violence or violent coercion is involved.

Once cultural autonomy is deemed safe, the militant ethnic group tends to proclaim that cultural autonomy without economic infrastructure is not viable. Once a relatively solid economic basis is acquired, many ethnic groups openly militate for more political power and even for independence.

If minorities succeed in getting the idea accepted that equality should mean not only "equality in chances" but also "equality in results" and affirmative action or a quota system is set up, ethnic belonging becomes a weapon in quite a number of cases. Whether quota systems are justified or not, they do confirm ethnic categories and groups in their existence and do reinforce mutual opposition and competition. In a country such as the United States, in which citing and suing are widespread and political correctness is in vogue, the fraying and fragmentation of society are no wonder (Roosens, 1993).

People who compete for material interests, status, or power and who are successful on grounds of ethnic belonging tend to use all available ethnic or cultural justifications. Pride about one's ancestors and origins is often used as a motive to claim one's dues. Many militant ethnic groups promulgate the idea of belonging to a "big family" and promote feelings of togetherness to build up strength. They act as "interest groups with a noble face." It is striking how "being different" is invoked and used as a tool to acquire more and more of the same material goods, status, and power positions that make people look so similar (Roosens, 1989).

A Link With the Marketplace

Because cultural items and places of origin can figure as expressions or symbols of ethnic identity in a world in which many cultural items are produced as commodities (Hannerz, 1992), they readily relate ethnicity to the world of goods. Cultural items in the field of music, literature, and other forms of art and tourist travel appealing to ethnic feelings, such as looking for one's roots in the country of origin, are frequently processed as commodities in the marketplace. So are ethnic dresses and foods.

The recent celebration of *Cinco de Mayo* by the Mexican American communities in Los Angeles is a case in point. Although the May 5 battle of Puebla in 1862, in which Mexican freedom fighters were victorious over the French, is commemorated in Mexico, it is not considered as a particularly important day of celebration. In California, however, the commemoration has been wielded by ethnic leaders as a symbol and emblem of liberation since the 1960s. The *Los Angeles Times* (Hayes-Bautista & Rodríguez, 1994) reported that about 500,000 people, mostly Mexican Americans and other Latinos, participated in the celebrations. With several music festivals taking place in the city, this was clearly a highly visible happening.

Hayes-Bautista and Rodríguez (1994), two researchers with Latino backgrounds, were preparing a book about the Latinization of California and published the article in the *Los Angeles Times* commenting on the events. They reported about a celebrated Latino disc jockey who is the owner of a popular radio station and one of the organizers of the music festivals: "Hidalgo, who arrived in this country 10 years ago and picked strawberries up the coast in Oxnard before breaking into radio, admits that the celebration is a commercial matter, yet its real value is in encouraging Southern California's Latinos to revel in their numbers and their strengths" (p. B7).[1] So the festivities were profitable for business and a forceful expression of ethnic revival to the customers.

Moreover, Hayes-Bautista and Rodríguez (1994) stressed that with 500,000 of them celebrating in the city of Los Angeles, Mexican Americans did not see themselves as a minority but as a majority, proud of their own language and culture. The *banda* music was considered as a mighty expression of Mexican (American) identity. The article said that the Los Angeles version of *banda* was so successful that even journalists from Mexico City had been calling to learn the recent trends in L.A. Mexican (!) *banda*. This suggests that the leading trend in genuine Mexican music is set not in Mexico City but in Los Angeles, meaning that Mexican Americans in Los Angeles have an authentic culture of their own and that they have become part of the American mainstream while maintaining their own language and culture:

> Bilingualism is becoming the norm among Latinos, not because of education policy but because of the market forces. Television and radio, videos and compact disks, supermarket chains and jumbo jets keep the old language and customs alive. *Banda*, the traditional Mexican musical style that has been given new life by contemporary bands' up-tempo interpretations, took the Mexican world by storm. Former gang members have told us that donning sombreros and cowboy boots—the requisite *banda* gear—makes them feel like they're back to being Mexicans. . . . While it was assumed that the only way to become a true American was to strip away all other experience, today it is evident that strong ethnic and cultural identities actively reinforce what were considered quintessentially American values. Adherence to tradition translates into strong family and religious ties as well as healthy work ethic. (Hayes-Bautista & Rodríguez, 1994, p. B7)

Alert businesspeople will notice a golden opportunity here: Nothing is so manipulable, flexible, and reinterpretable as cultural and folk expressions of ethnic or ethnonational feelings. They even pass as eminently patriotic. At the same time, these expressions seem so eminently noble and selfless that they readily sell at quite profitable prices, especially on days of ebullient celebration.

Note

1. Quotes from D. E. Hayes-Bautista and G. Rodríguez, "Perspectives on Latinos: L.A.'s Culture Comes Full Circle," *Los Angeles Times*, May 5, 1994, p. B7. Reprinted with permission of the authors.

References

Anderson, B. (1991). *Imagined communities: Reflections on the origin and spread of nationalism* (rev. ed.). London: Verso.

Barth, F. (1969). *Ethnic groups and boundaries: The social organization of culture difference.* Boston: Little, Brown.

Bell, D. (1975). Ethnicity and social change. In N. Glazer & D. Moynihan (Eds.), *Ethnicity: Theory and experience* (pp. 141-174). Cambridge, MA: Harvard University Press.

De Vos, G., & Romanucci-Ross, L. (Eds.). (1975). *Ethnic identity: Cultural continuities and change.* Palo Alto, CA: Mayfield.

Eldering, L. (1993). Cultuurverschillen in een Multiculturele Samenleving [Culture differences in a multicultural society]. *Comenius, 49,* 9-26.

Epstein, A. (1978). *Ethos and identity: Three studies in ethnicity.* London: Tavistock.

Gellner, E. (1983). *Nations and nationalism.* Oxford, UK: Basil Blackwell.

Glazer, N. (1983). *Ethnic dilemmas 1964-1982.* Cambridge, MA: Harvard University Press.

Glazer, N., & Moynihan, D. (Eds.). (1975). *Ethnicity: Theory and experience.* Cambridge, MA: Harvard University Press.

Hannerz, U. (1992). *Cultural complexity: Studies in the social organization of meaning.* New York: Columbia University Press.

Harris, C. (1990). *Kinship.* Buckingham, UK: Open University Press.

Hayes-Bautista, D. E., & Rodríguez, G. (1994, May 5). Perspective on Latinos: L.A.'s culture comes full circle. *Los Angeles Times,* p. B7.

Hobsbawm, E. (1992). *Nations and nationalism since 1780: Programme, myth, reality.* Cambridge, UK: Cambridge University Press.

Horowitz, D. (1985). *Ethnic groups in conflict.* Berkeley: University of California Press.

Hutnik, M. (1991). *Ethnic minority identity: A social psychological perspective.* Oxford, UK: Clarendon.

Moynihan, D. (1993). *Pandaemonium: Ethnicity in international politics.* Oxford, UK: Oxford University Press.

Portes, A., & Rumbaut, G. (1990). *Immigrant America: A portrait.* Berkeley: University of California Press.

Roosens, E. (1989). *Creating ethnicity: The process of ethnogenesis.* Newbury Park, CA: Sage.

Roosens, E. (Guest Ed.). (1992). *The insertion of allochthonous youngsters in Belgian society* [Special issue]. *Migration, 15.*

Roosens, E. (1993). Culturele Gelijkheid in de VS: Een economisch Wapen [Cultural equality in the U.S.: An economic weapon]. In P. Wymeersch (Ed.), *Liber amicorum Marcel d'Hertefelt: Antropologische opstellen* (pp. 229-242). Brussels: Afrika Studies.

Roosens, E. (in press). The primordial nature of origins in migrant ethnicity [Lecture for "The Anthropology of Ethnicity: A Critical Review"]. Amsterdam: Het Spinhuis.

Schlesinger, A. (1992). *The disuniting of America: Reflections on a multicultural society.* New York: Norton.

Smith, A. (1986). *The ethnic origins of nations.* Oxford, UK: Basil Blackwell.

Smith, A. (1988). The myth of the "modern nation" and the myths of nations. *Ethnic and Racial Studies, 11*(1), 1-26.

Trueba, T., Rodríguez, C., Zou, Y., & Cintron, J. (1993). *Healing multicultural America: Mexican immigrants rise to power in rural California.* Washington, DC: Falmer.

PART II

Case Studies and Applications

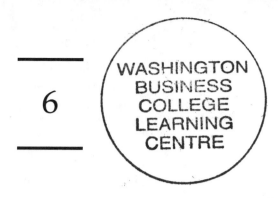

6

The Cultural Past in the Present: The Meaning of Home and Objects in the Homes of Working-Class Italian Immigrants in Montreal

ANNAMMA JOY

MICHAEL HUI

CHANKON KIM

MICHEL LAROCHE

This study used an ethnographic approach to advance the understanding of the meaning of home and possessions to working-class[1] Italian immigrants in the city of Montreal. Italian identity has an experiential base conveyed through language and values as well as a structural base conveyed through the home and objects in it. Although importance is given to both in the process of acculturation by immigrants, the sacralization and demarcation of space and objects within it continue to be

AUTHORS' NOTE: The authors gratefully acknowledge the funding received from the Social Sciences and Humanities Research Council of Canada. We thank Christine Coté, Marisa Bove, and Adrienne and Roy Toffoli for their help in the process of collecting data. In particular, we acknowledge the assistance and hospitality of Marisa Bove's entire family, who took an avid interest in this research project.

145

central to these immigrants' definitions of "self." Home and hearth are central to immigrant identity because family is everything. Through tangible and visible means, Italian immigrants invoke their cultural past into the cultural present—more so into the cultural present of their children. Through the organization of space and objects, they create an atmosphere that both reflects their past and shapes their future.

Objects and architecture are visible and tangible markers of a culture (Appadurai, 1986; Arnould, 1989; Belk, Wallendorf, & Sherry, 1989; Bourdieu, 1977; Clark, 1986; Cohn, 1979; Creighton & Ford, 1961; Csikszentmihalyi & Rochberg-Halton, 1981; Dholakia & Levy, 1987; Duncan, 1981; Handlin, 1979; Holdsworth, 1977; McCracken, 1988, 1989; Wallendorf & Arnould, 1988; Wright, 1981). They reflect cultural categories and principles centrally held by groups or individuals. When individuals move from one culture to another, some of these taken-for-granted objects, assumptions, and principles may be left behind, and other modes of spatial organization and building forms may be adopted. Swidler (1986) suggested that in contexts marked by such uncertainty, individuals invest meaning in familiar material objects and reorganize space to confront other cultural values and ways of being. Objects in that sense become extensions of the self (Belk, 1985, 1988) and are mechanisms by which individuals bridge cultures.

This study focuses on one immigrant community—working-class Italians in Montreal. We examine the link between values cherished by members of the group and the manifestations of such values in the homes they live in and the objects they possess. The working-class Italian immigrants who were interviewed are very selective in their approach to what is appropriate to their ideas of self. They are concerned with the reconstruction of what they judge to be their past—to invest meaning in particular objects and to display them. They keep these objects in special places that are publicly seen but rarely used. They are also collectors in that they acquire objects they hope to bequeath to their children. Their passion for collecting and displaying is heightened by the uncertainties in the new context. It is a personal statement and a reflection of the world(s) they live in (Belk et al., 1989). We begin with a general examination of how the cultural past is invoked into the cultural present.

THE CULTURAL PAST IN THE PRESENT

Remnants of the past exist both in a tangible form, as in objects, and in an emotional form, as in people's minds and hearts. There is a structural base as well as an experiential base from which individuals can draw their inspiration. The motivations for preserving the past are based on the assumption that this interpreted past will enrich the present. They are also rooted in the perception of a future that would be impoverished if the past as well as the present were not a part of it (Bloch, 1976; Gmelch, 1980). For Italians (as is also the case for other immigrants) with children growing up in Canada, the desire to bequeath to their children what is unique and special to their culture is counterbalanced by the seductive influences of the host culture (Lopreato, 1970).

Every individual has a special way of interpreting the past. A precise understanding of and importance given to the past will differ, depending on various experiences, and will give rise to new interpretations. Although the contexts may vary, the process is an ongoing one. Furthermore, this personalized sense of the past is communicated to others as well as to oneself. For some immigrants, it may take the form of engaging in activities in which their parents were involved. For instance, making wine from imported grapes is more important to certain individuals than to others. Consequently, it forms the cornerstone of a personal sense of identity.

Each individual also shares in the past of others, however—the culture to which he or she belongs. This cultural past is more than the sum of the individual pasts of its members and is socially constructed. It is the larger canvas against which individual pasts are created and to which people make reference (Clifford, 1989; Davis, 1979; Geertz, 1973). For immigrants, this sense of the past is heightened in the new culture and is celebrated within the context of newly formed Italian cultural associations. In contexts of migration, individual as well as cultural identity comes under constant scrutiny and is subject to change. Language and behavior as much as objects and building forms help to recover and reshape identity. Italian immigrants, like others, are caught up in the process of making sense of their past and giving direction to their future. They collect, conserve, singularize, display, and interpret (Appadurai, 1986; Migliore, 1988).

THE MEANING OF "HOME" AND OBJECT ORIENTATION

For many people in North America, the idea of owning a home is central to their definition of self and expressive of their deeper sentiments about family, kinship, and social status (Dholakia & Levy, 1987; Joy & Dholakia, 1991; Perin, 1977; Tuan, 1982). McCracken (1989) has argued that "homeyness" is an important outcome of the transactions between people and their homes and contributes to the creation of an environment "dense with symbolism" that serves to draw and keep the members of the family together (pp. 172-173). The home provides people with what Belk (1991) called "place identity" and nurtures and protects them as much as their own bodies do (p. 121).

Bourdieu's (1977) notion of *habitus* is useful in understanding the use of space and, in this context, the idea of home. *Domestic habitus* refers to the commonsense, taken-for-granted social ways that are unreflexively learned during the process of socialization. Culture in this sense refers to what people do more than what they say or think. People in general are not conscious of the practices that are closest to their cultural being. People have to dwell in a house to reproduce the habitus objectified by it. How they do so is clearly an outcome of their childhood socialization, the way in which space is structured in their present dwelling, and the nature of their interactions outside of the home. Thus, an understanding of the culture is possible through an examination of the habitus in the context of the home (Robben, 1989).

Although the dream of many families and individuals may be to own a home, it is not always simple or possible to do so, particularly in the larger cities in which crowding and poverty are rampant. An analysis of homelessness (Hill, 1991) is indeed indicative of the precariousness of the American dream of home ownership and also points to societal and structural problems that make it impossible for people to own homes. Furthermore, as Hill noted, without the basic context of a permanent home, individuals are less likely to acquire larger collections of certain objects.

The material manifestation of a culture, particularly through objects, has long been an issue in ethnographic studies (Sahlins, 1976). In recent consumer research, it has achieved much currency through the work of McCracken (1986) and the subsequent works of Arnould (1989); Arnould and Price (1993); Belk, Sherry, and Wallendorf (1988); Mehta and Belk (1991); and Sherry and Camargo (1987) to name just a few. McCracken's (1986) thesis is that cultural meaning is located in consumer goods and that this meaning is constantly in transit from the culturally constructed world to the consumer. The key idea is the mobility of the good and, consequently, the meaning associated with the good as it is appropriated by the individual.

In the case of immigrants, both the goods and the individual consumers have been in transit. In a sense, the first generation always considers itself in transit and as upholding the myth of eventual return. Goods that they have brought with them are stable reminders of this cherished past. Meanings vested in these goods are not expected to change because such change would result in uncertainty in the minds of these newcomers.

Furthermore, even if people are restricted in terms of the number of goods that they can bring from their past, they carry in their heads memories of material objects and artifacts that acquire special status when they migrate. For instance, the idea of a home in which one grew up or of special places becomes a concrete image that sometimes get translated in material ways in the new context.

Among second-generation immigrants, the wish for stability through objects becomes less of a concern, and further accommodation to cultural contexts occurs. This particular process is hastened by the negative and positive constraints that exist in the new context. The wish to be part of the mainstream culture as well as negative outcomes if one does not comply may operate to ensure that what was once unmistakably an aspect of the culture may no longer remain so.

The previous discussion, however, may give the false impression that cultural change is minimal among first-generation immigrants and inevitable in subsequent generations. Cultures are not static but rather continuously evolving over time and space, and every generation negotiates the outcomes of such cross-cultural encounters. Furthermore, in the case of working-class Italians, poverty in the country of origin and the wish to overcome the same were overriding concerns—particularly for first-generation immigrants. This took many forms, some of which deepened the networks among families and heightened their sense of being Italian. It is important to keep in mind that a linear model of adaptation with assimilation as the outcome is not very useful in understanding the creation and maintenance of ethnic consciousness.

A final dimension critical to the understanding of the meaning of home as part of the acculturation process is gender (Pivato, 1986). Although both husbands and wives were interviewed to explore the meaning they attach to home and garden, the focus of our probing and analyses was on women. Consequently, much of the narrative revolves around the information provided by the women and the stories of their lives in both the first and second generation. It is also particularly important to note that most of the women interviewed worked both inside and outside of the home. Although our interviews did not focus on what they did outside the home, it was clear that they placed a great deal of emphasis on their role in producing and maintaining a beautiful home and garden. Although both men and women contributed to the purchase of a home, the emotional investment in the home seemed to be greater for women. In the same vein, it must be noted that men, more than women, invested themselves in their gardens. The products from the garden were processed by both groups, however: The men made the wine; the women canned the tomato sauce and the fruit preserves.

ACCULTURATION

The literature on cultural contact tends to view immigrants as moving along a continuum that has assimilation as its ultimate goal. This model views immigrants as merging with the host culture over time (Glazer & Moynihan, 1975; Gordon, 1964). Acculturation, on the other hand, views individuals as architects of their own identities and considers the degree to which newcomers learn the values and ideas that are native to another culture (Joy, 1989; Kiefer, 1977; Yinger, 1985). Yet individual action is constrained by structural and psychological forces and is dependent on the relative bargaining power of the groups in question (Padilla, 1980). The existence of the cultural past of the host culture is as monumental as the cultural past of the immigrants themselves. Positioning oneself between the two cultures is and has been difficult for a number of immigrant groups (Valeria, 1987; Williams, 1989). Thus, for Italians, the question of what it means to be Italian becomes very significant in the new cultural context.

The complexity associated with acculturation and its impact on consumption are captured in some of the more recent works in consumer behavior (Deshpande, Hoyer, & Donthu, 1986; O'Guinn & Faber, 1985; Valencia, 1985; Wallendorf & Reilly, 1983). The reconstruction of the cultural past in the light of the present is a subjective process and has an important impact on how much of the present will be appropriated and incorporated (Hirschman, 1981). The issues dealt with in this study have less to do with universal patterns of adjustment to a given norm than with particular forms of ethnic consciousness and identity. In the following section we outline the approach we used in gathering and interpreting data.

Method

This study was done during the course of a year and is part of a larger and longitudinal project on ethnicity and consumption. The approach was basically ethnographic in nature and involved both participant observations and in-depth interviews. Three research assistants helped in the interview process, two of whom were Italians. Thus, triangulation of researchers was possible. Because two of the assistants were of Italian origin, any queries, assumptions, or issues were dealt with immediately as they emerged in situations. The study may have taken longer, had they not been Italian. Both these assistants had participated in the earlier collection of questionnaire data on various other ethnic groups in Montreal. Although Italian names are used to identify informants, these names do not refer to the actual people who were interviewed. Italian names are used only to allow us to create a particular context for the reader.

Naturalistic inquiry has been challenged on a number of dimensions, and important criticisms have been leveled at it concerning its ability to produce scientific knowledge (Calder & Tybout, 1989). In particular, concerns relating to reliability and validity of data have been raised. The counterclaims provided by a small body of ethnographers focus on credibility (which takes into account believability and adequacy of the interpretations made of the phenomenon), transferability (its applicability to other contexts), dependability (the effort made to construct as stable an interpretation as possible, realizing the inherent stability of the phenomenon), confirmability (on the basis of the research notes and journal maintained by the researchers), and the integrity of the researcher in providing an interpretation that is not based on lies, evasions, or misinformation (Altheide & Johnson, 1994; Denzin, 1994).

For the most part, the acceptability of this approach lies in the prolonged participation and observation of the phenomenon, triangulation of methods and researchers, regular interaction of researchers, negative case analysis, debriefing by peers, and reflexive journals maintained by the researchers.

SENSE MAKING AND INTERPRETATION

As mentioned earlier, the data for this study were collected during a fairly long period. Because two of the research assistants were of Italian origin, establishing rapport and gaining access to the community was not difficult. Because they both spoke the same dialects as those of the Italians interviewed, interpretation was also not a major problem. The investigators attended Italian functions, monitored media discussions on or about the Italian community, frequented stores in which Italians shopped, and photographed homes and neighborhoods in which the members of the community lived.

All participants were told of the purpose of the interviews and were free to discontinue at any point in the study. During the interviews, we were conscious of the fact that we did not want to use participants as "objects." Over time and with the help of the Italian assistants, we were able to get closer to those we interviewed and also to respond frankly and openly to the questions that were asked of us. The fact that we were all immigrants opened up the dialogue. As much as we learned about the lives of these individuals, we also learned about ourselves.

Our research assistants recalled instances when women who were interviewed noted that they were really surprised that an immigrant woman (meaning myself, the first author) could be a university professor. They also felt that I was pressured into publication and possibly overworked because of my gender and my immigrant status. After my initial surprise that they could have doubted my status because of my ethnic background (because I see myself primarily as an academic and I sought to use this specific distancing mechanism), I was relieved, because I felt that they saw me not only as a researcher but also as a woman and as an immigrant. It was no longer tedious for me to write about them as the Other. I was the Other in their eyes, and now, through my writing, I had become the Other as well. As Oakley (1981) pointed out, "there can be no intimacy without reciprocity" (p. 49).

Interviews were done within 60 families in a variety of locations in Montreal. The city is broadly divided into francophone and anglophone areas. The immigrant groups have tended to concentrate around the peripheries of both spaces and, with time, have moved into central districts as well. The majority of these interviews, however, centered on three predominantly Italian neighborhoods, although some involved interviews with Italians who had moved into anglophone areas. Thus, we were able to obtain information on the original settlements, the secondary residential developments, and the more recent movement to the suburbs.

Data were collected in the form of field notes, audiotapes, and photographs. Each member of the team kept a diary, and weekly meetings of the investigative team were held. This allowed for the formulation of a number of possible interpretations of behaviors and ideas as they emerged in the field.

DEBRIEFING BY PEERS AND MEMBER CHECKS

Research findings were discussed with a number of researchers who were unfamiliar with this project or this type of analysis. We also had a chance to discuss the findings with a few sociologists and anthropologists who worked in the field of ethnicity. We used their input to sharpen our own understanding of the phenomena and to redirect some of our own concerns in the field.

In addition, we provided information to members of the community to verify whether we were on the right track in our explanations. They not only offered suggestions but also embellished the discussion of some of the topics to which they were drawn. We feel this project has created an awareness among some members of the Italian community regarding their identity and their future in Canada. In this context, it is important to raise issues relating to the ethical dimensions of doing research. It is clear that we honored the concept of informed consent. In addition, the questions of privacy, identification, and confidentiality were also taken into consideration. But more important, we were aware of our intrusion into their lives. Our role in creating a heightened sense of self through intensive probing is only one side of the coin. The alternative explanation is that, confronted with Otherness, they were engaged in self-reflection as well. In this context of interpreting what *home* means to working-class Italians in Montreal, Martin and Mohanty's (1986) discussion of the meaning of home to the creation of the self is appropriate and important. They note that insofar as identity is conflated with home and community and is based on comfort and familiarity, being bereft of home is like being bereft of the self.

WRITING ABOUT OTHERS

Both husbands and wives were included in an interview. The primary respondents were the women, although questions pertaining to gardens and the maintenance and financing of the home were often answered by the men. In some instances, the grandparents and children were included, although the exchange with the latter group was mostly informal. Both first-generation immigrants and Canadian-born Italians were interviewed, although the focus of this paper is on the first generation. The age range of the first-generation immigrants was between 40 and 80 years. The age of the Canadian-born Italians ranged from 18 to 30 years. All members of the first generation had been in Canada for at least 15 years and had been responsible for the sponsorship of many members of their kin networks from the villages and towns from which they came. In terms of geographic origins, they can be broadly divided into two groups—Italians from the middle and those from the south of Italy. We had roughly equal numbers of both in the sample interviewed. In some instances, the husband was from the north and the wife from the south or vice versa, given that many of them married in

Canada. Questions pertaining to family income and social status were not asked in the interview, but information was gathered about the educational background, occupation, and work history for all members of the household including grandparents. It was clear from the interviews that the predominant number of immigrants were from rural and poor backgrounds. They were barely literate in their dialect and were untrained or unskilled workers. On arrival, most men worked in unskilled jobs around the port and the railway tracks, and the women found jobs in the factories. When they could find alternate employment that was generally better, they moved to larger houses. Today the men continue to work as janitors, factory workers, small entrepreneurs, and construction workers.

A NOTE ON THE INTERPRETIVE PROCESS

In studies of a qualitative nature, what we observe and study in situ gets translated into field notes, photographs, audiotapes, and field journals. This sifting of information gathered and the creation of field texts is done entirely by the field researchers. None of these artifacts speak for themselves or can be considered outside of the context and of the person who shaped them. During the course of the year, we were acutely aware of the various types of respondent texts that we gathered. They included oral histories, family stories, memories, letters, conversations, photographs, and other material artifacts. As informants told the stories of their lives, they relived their experiences and provided us with the ingredients for retelling them. These stories in turn reflected their feelings, hopes, remembrances, histories, and future directions. In the final analysis, each story is the outcome of a negotiation between the researchers and the respondents. The presence of the researcher can overpower any other voice, particularly the voices of those interviewed, or the researcher can selectively present her or his own voice and balance it with the selective presentation of the voices of others.

Clearly, such a choice of whose voice and what message to insert is central to the truth and verisimilitude of the text. Sometimes, several quotes from various respondents are used to make a point. Yet in other instances, a single quote that typically represents the views of various respondents is used. Supportive documentation from published works is mingled with the voices and always identified by the source in the text. Ultimately, we, the authors, are the final arbiters in the narrative process. Authority rests with us, although we try to invoke multiple voices in the text.

A BRIEF HISTORY OF THE
ITALIAN COMMUNITY IN MONTREAL

The history of the Italians in Montreal is a microcosm of the history of the Italians in Canada. We rely largely on the works of Boissevain (1976) and Zucchi (1988) for this information.

There were three waves of immigrants from Italy. The first came around the turn of the century, the second in the early 1920s, and the third after World War II. Each wave was constrained and shaped by the immigration laws of the time (Hawkins, 1972). Between 1951 and 1961, of the 216,000 Italians who came to Canada, 56,000 settled in Quebec. Furthermore, according to Boissevain (1976), of the 108,500 persons of Italian origin in Quebec, 101,000 were residents of Montreal. In this study, we focus on the group who came after World War II from the middle and southern parts of Italy because they represent more than half of the total Italian population in Montreal.

Because chain migration is characteristic of Italian entry into Canada, it is not surprising that new arrivals lived with members of the family or with close friends. It was only when they had accumulated enough money to rent or purchase homes that they moved out of the core areas. Thus, intimacy was maintained through close ties among members of the same village or town (the *paesani*). Although geographic origins were a principal concern in neighborhood formations, the overriding factor seems to have been proximity to relatives.

Because these immigrants came to Canada to improve their economic status, one of their aspirations was to buy a house. This is not unique to the group that we studied but can be substantiated historically. As Boissevain (1976) noted:

The drive to buy a house, to own property is one of the fundamental reasons why the immigrant left his own country. It is only when he has acquired a house that he begins to put down roots in his new homeland. The importance of owning property and thus providing a focal point for future generations of his family is a value which the immigrant has brought with him from Italy. In order to meet this housing demand, whole sections of Montreal are being constructed by Italian builders for Italians. (p. 1)

Within the first 10 years of their arrival, Italians worked very hard to buy a house. They saved until they had enough to make a down payment. Once they owned a place, the next step was to pay off the mortgage. Once that was done, they saved again to buy expensive living room and dining room furniture. The desire to make money and the emphasis on savings, a house, a television set, and other valuable possessions have thus resulted in extreme importance being placed on material things. These findings again are not unique to the people we studied but also applicable to other Italians as well, as Boissevain (1976) noted.

For these Italians, however, material success was not based on a spirit of individualism and individual accumulation that is characteristic of North American culture (McCracken, 1988) but rather on a group ethic centered around the family. The family was and continues to be everything. This was their reason for coming to Canada, and this continues to preoccupy the minds of both the Canadian-born Italians and their parents. As one informant who echoed the sentiments of many others noted:

> The foremost factor in making me feel Italian is the strong family ties. This includes my husband and children as well as both our parents as well as brothers and sisters on both sides of the family. My parents are old, but we would never place them in an old folks' home in their declining years. We will always take care of them as long as they live. Likewise, we feel that our children can stay as long as they want. Even when they are married, we would like them to stay with us or at least close to us. (Rosa, 48, factory worker)

This particular individual, as others, was quite conscious of the priority Italians place on various aspects of their identity. The language, religious values, the cuisine, the consumption and use of Italian goods, the savings account in the Italian bank, the importance given to the ownership of home and filling it with objects from Italy, and the careful cultivation of the garden were all common themes. In the final analysis, the family, symbolized by the home, was the hub around which participants defined themselves. It is within this context that we can focus on the home and the attachments to objects in the home for the participants.

Ethnographic Narratives

MEMORIES OF GROWING UP IN ITALY AND EARLY SETTLEMENT IN MONTREAL

Memories of the past were particularly important to many of the informants because they seemed to provide a rationale for their activities in the new culture. They also used these memories as a vehicle for teaching their children to value what they currently have. Although work inside and outside the home seemed to be divided along gender lines, both men and women talked about the common hardships their respective families had faced in Italy. The memories of growing up in the towns and villages from which these immigrants came are revelatory of such impoverished backgrounds:

> We had only one coat for all occasions, one pair of shoes, and one set of clothes. If this wore out, we had none. Whatever we could grow and sell we did in order to buy salt, cheese, and occasionally some meat. (Angela, 53, factory worker)

Donato, likewise, talked about his home in Italy:

> We were poor. We did not have many things. My mother had to wait for the chicken to lay an egg which she sold in order to buy our pasta. The house was very small and had a first and second floor. On the first floor, there was the kitchen, the storage area, the *catina* as well as the stalls for the animals. There were two bedrooms upstairs. There were several of us in the family. (Donato, 58, construction worker)

Survival primarily meant being able to live off whatever piece of land the family owned or had access to. On that small piece, Italians grew what they could and consumed it all. As a long-time resident observed:

> Without the garden, we could not have survived. There we grew potatoes, tomatoes, onions, herbs, and a few figs and other fruits. This is all we had to eat. (Tony, 50, janitor)

For the children of these immigrants, stories of their impoverished past recounted to them by their parents may be somewhat difficult to relate to. One noted:

> My mother described living conditions in Italy during World War II. They were very poor—12 children. It was very difficult—they lived from day to day. They woke up every morning and hoped to be able to put some food on the table. Everybody went to work, including the kids. They did not go to school; they had to work in order to survive. (Sylvana, 28, bank teller)

The typical home these immigrants left behind had one or two rooms that housed both family and cattle. Because many came from agricultural backgrounds and because they lacked both education and skills, they were able to find only very low-level jobs in the city. Yet most of them opted to stay in the city rather than live on farms like other migrants such as the Portuguese in Canada, who made their way from working on the farms to finally owning them. Yet their links with land were not broken. They became engrossed in the idea of owning homes and having gardens:

> I had only one dress that I wore to work and did not have any other fancy clothes. I had two bus tickets every day and always took my own lunch. I did not even spend any money to buy a cola when I was tired. Every penny we saved in order to buy a home. (Candida, 50, factory worker)

Life in Italy and on their arrival in Canada was full of hardship. It is clear from their descriptions of gardens in Italy that the value placed on them was directly linked to their impoverished backgrounds. The meaning of gardens in Canada changed over time, however. Initially, subsistence was critical, and gardens symbolized hard work and making a living. Once those initial fears were overcome, gardens began to symbolize success, status differences, and productivity.

NEIGHBORHOODS AND SPATIAL ORGANIZATION

Although initial settlements centered around the factories in which these immigrants worked, the movement away from these centers occurred as soon as they could afford to buy homes. Italian neighborhoods in Montreal can be found in Notre Dame-de-Grace (NDG), Lachine, St. Laurent, Montreal North, St. Leonard, Rivière des Prairies, and, to a lesser extent, suburbs such as Kirkland and Dollard des Ormeaux. St. Leonard, where a number of our informants live, is a typical new settlement in which homes were constructed by Italian builders primarily for Italian immigrants. These newer areas have been populated by Italians since 1980, whereas the older communities have existed since the turn of the century. The major street that borders this neighborhood is lined with stores that sell products from Italy. Most of these are fresh pasta stores, cheese shops, grocery stores specializing in Italian foods, Italian pastry shops, butcher shops selling Italian sausages and meats, Italian furniture stores, Italian restaurants, and espresso coffee houses, as well as the occasional sporting bar. In addition, there is the branch of the national bank of Italy and several car dealers that service primarily the Italian market.

St. Leonard has an older as well as a newer part. In the newer area, the wealthier members of the community have built large marble single-family homes that resemble Italian villas in size and form. The rest live in triplexes owned by one family, although multiple families may live under the same roof. These triplexes are large and equivalent in size to the single detached homes of the wealthy. Other older areas of the city, such as Notre Dame-de-Grace in which some other members of the community live, are much more modest in design and consist of duplexes, semidetached homes, and single-family dwellings. Depending on its income and savings, a family was able to afford one of the above.

Both men and women worked hard to save enough money to buy a home. The maintenance and repairs associated with the home were generally taken care of by the men, whereas women furnished and beautified the home. Housework was predominantly "women's work," although certain types of activities such as wine making was done by the men. Typically, the multifamily dwellings in which most of our informants live have white or ochre brick facades decorated with geometric designs of a darker color brick, stairs and balustrades made of cement or marble, and in some cases, marble or cement columns that hold a portico made of one or the other material, as well as various assortments of statues and fountains on the front lawn (see Photos 6.1 and 6.2).

The design of villalike homes of the rich as well as of the triplexes is inspired by the architecture of the villas that dot the countryside and towns of Italy. According to Farber and Reed (1980), many of them have columned and pedimented porticos with archways that are small-scale replicas of the villas designed by Palladio. In many homes there are smaller proportioned ionic porches, high entrances, and wide marble stairways that are also inspired by Palladian architecture. The brickwork is also unique in character because of the preference for neutral tones such as white, beige, or yellow, marked only by distinctive geometric designs in the front of the house. These designs, once again, are a pale imitation of the complex, elaborate brickwork of the Baroque and more recent period as identified by Mars (1925). One participant, when asked to describe how she would identify an Italian home, remarked:

The houses would be neutral in color—not like the lovely red brick homes in the rest of Montreal. There would be arches, columns, lions, fountains, and statues of naked ladies in the front of these homes. Of course, the stairs leading to the house and the balustrades would be massive and made of marble or cement. (Vincenzina, 53, factory worker)

Photo 6.1. Entrance to Italian Home in Montreal

One man conveyed how home is central to his sense of self:

Italians love to own a home. It's like a nest and signifies where a person is born, lives, and where he or she grows up. If this nest does not belong to your parents, the family is considered less stable and, by extension, the persons are not considered stable. To be rooted in one place, to have security and stability are the reasons for owning a house. The children can say "it is my father's or mother's house or where I was born." Moving means changes, and the house serves as a refuge. (Remo, 50, construction worker)

As noted earlier, the most common dwellings owned by Italians are triplexes. The typical triplex has apartments for rent in addition to the

Photo 6.2. Exterior of Italian Home in Montreal

main living space of the family. Families prefer to rent these apartments out to married children or to aunts and uncles, although today the children prefer to establish themselves in other neighborhoods. This is not unlike the custom in Italy. As one informant observed:

> If the parents can afford it, they give their children a house or at least help them to buy a house. But if they cannot afford it, the next best solution is to offer them two rooms (once again, if they can afford it) in their own home. (Ada, 52, factory worker)

Thus, the spirit of the close-knit family continues to influence purchase behavior. Another informant, who was very aware of the importance of owning property in Canada, expanded on the importance of the home:

> Homes are very concrete, very secure—they are a roof over your head. Even if a house is very small, people own it. To come here, many families had to sell their homes in Italy and had to rent homes here on arrival. This is a step down the ladder—so as soon as possible, families saved enough to buy their own homes. They reestablished themselves in the community. In Italy, when a child married, the parents would build an extra room to

the house if they could not afford to buy them a house. This room is a separate "house," and the result is that rooms [read houses] are built on top of each other. They are not temporary solutions but permanent ones. (Giovanna, 54, seamstress)

When asked the reasons why he chose to buy a triplex, one informant replied:

My wife and I liked the apartment that we had decided to occupy. My in-laws would have their own apartment and privacy, yet they would be close by. Needless to add, the house is close to stores and the Metro, and the neighborhood is very quiet . . . mostly immigrants who have undergone hardships similar to us. (Rocco, 55, construction worker)

He was also very enthusiastic about the house itself. He noted:

When I saw this house (a triplex), the feeling was very good. My son and my wife felt it too. This truly is our dream house; I will never move away. The house is completely detached, and there is a lot of privacy. I am proud of this house which my wife and I worked very hard to own. It represents all our hard work. This house is the reward—for all the tears I cried when I first arrived and all the sacrifices I made when I left Italy. I worked 7 days a week, 120 hours a week, if you can believe that. I did that for years at 80 cents an hour in conditions where if a worker said a word he would be let go. So if you break open a brick of this house, my blood will probably come out.

Another participant talked about his home:

In 1963 when I arrived in Canada, I bought land. But in 1968 when I got married, I bought my first house, and my wife transformed the Canadian-style bungalow into a Mediterranean home. We put white stone in front of the house and used tiles for the roof. The area that leads to the door is made of white cement in the Romanesque style. Inside the house, we have marble floors and stairs, crystal chandeliers, ceramic floors in the kitchen, granite countertops, and two fireplaces. It is very Italian. (Traddiccio, 58, construction worker)

Second- and third-generation Italians, however, do not always speak with the same emotional attachment to homes or neighborhoods. As one observed:

Living in this neighborhood has its drawbacks. Everybody knows what you do, who you are going out with, and when you come back home. I do

not like that. I'd like to move away to the West Island or any other place
other than this neighborhood. (Sylvana, 25, student)

Another young Italian noted:

I would like to live in Westmount in one of those old houses. I think they
have a lot of character, and they are in many ways like the older homes in
Italy with high ceilings and large rooms. In these homes, it makes more
sense to have chandeliers, and columns, and marble floors, and so on. Otherwise, it seems too false and so exaggerated. (Angela, 28, bank teller)

SACRED CONSUMPTION

The predominant style of the homes that these immigrants owned
initially, as well as currently, is multifamily. A few Canadian-born Italians, however, have moved to the suburbs and own single-family cot-
tages and bungalows.

In all instances, the homes had to have gardens in which the families
grew tomatoes, parsley, corn, and other vegetables. Many informants
mentioned that they had brought with them from Italy cuttings of fig
trees to grow in their backyards. A special memory associated with
home in Italy was their fruit and vegetable gardens. As one of them
recalled with a great deal of pride:

The food we ate in Italy was grown in our own garden. You picked
enough of the things you needed for each day. It was simple but good.
We made our own cheese, bread, and the fruit and vegetables we grew in
our own garden. (Sophia, 58, garment worker)

Reminiscing about the home in which he grew up, one informant said:

My home was located on a mountain—it was beautiful. I remember my
mother . . . she was strong and hardworking. Another thing I remember is
the backyard which was covered with grass and had a fig tree in the center. We used to play there all day, and when we were hungry, we would
climb the tree, pluck the large black, juicy figs and eat them. I brought a
cutting from this tree to Canada and whenever I moved houses, I took this
tree with me. Every winter, I protect it with plastic and material . . . and
every summer it bears at least 30 figs. (GianFranco, 65, janitor)

The extension of the garden and fruit to the definition of self is also
revealing. One informant observed:

I am like a pear. A pear grows and ripens on a tree. I was born and raised
in Italy, but I ripened or matured in Canada. My blood and sweat were
poured in Canada and not Italy. I love this country, but I will never forget
my roots—they are Italian. (Enrico, 48, factory worker)

Another informant, talking about the importance of growing their own
tomatoes and preparing their own food, noted:

For Italians, the home is incomplete without a cold storage or *catina*. The
women make all their food there, and the men make their own wine and
store it in this place. We would never buy frozen or canned food unless we
had to and we knew what went into those packages. (Marianna, 58, garment worker)

Many spoke of bringing cuttings of plants from their homes in Italy and
lovingly tending them in Canada. Fig trees are special favorites, although plums and pears are also grown. Although initially the garden
was central to their subsistence activities, later it symbolized their success in the new country.

The demarcation of space and its sacralization through rituals and
other appropriate behavior is a dominant theme in the lives of the Italians who were interviewed. But their past is not up for sale, and outsiders who are invited to view it are a more intimate group. The home is
sacred—it is family, yet spaces within the home are for exhibit and display. In almost all instances, the basement constitutes the living space
for the family, with a kitchen, bathroom, family room, bar, and fireplace. The children work and play there while the adults cook, clean, or
watch television. The entrance to this area is through the garage, and
both family and friends enter the house this way. The furniture is simple, functional, and, as one of the informants described it, "homey." The
floors are made of ceramic tiles or marble, and there are no area rugs or
carpets covering the floor.

At the center of this lower level living space is the fireplace. Almost
all informants noted its importance as the hub of the house. The basement is also the area in which the wine is made from homegrown
grapes. A cold room or *catina* is thus indispensable to Italian families
because most of the food and wine is stored in this space. It is by way of
the ceramic or marble stairs that family and friends access the living and
dining rooms.

The typical home has a living room, a dining room, another kitchen,
washrooms, and bedrooms on the first floor. Access to this area through
the front door is possible but is rarely used except on special occasions
such as a wedding. The foyer is usually very large and is mostly unused.

Photo 6.3. Chandelier in Foyer of Italian Home in Montreal

It is characterized by the elaborate ceramic tiles or marble floor and the ceramic or crystal chandelier in the center. The chandelier hangs from a recessed, ornamental section of the ceiling outlined in gold or other bright colors and built up through the use of colored stucco (see Photo 6.3). The prevalent use of stucco occurs in most homes of the informants. It is commonly used in homes in Italy. According to Mars (1925), the technique of stucco supplanted terra cotta in the Baroque period and was very commonly used in many forms to suit the new style and taste. That this form of stucco should find its way into the homes of Italians in Montreal should come as no surprise, not only because the influence of Italian architecture is extensive in North America (Farber & Reed, 1980) but also because, as many informants noted, Italian builders use this concept of heritage to sell homes to members of the Italian community in Montreal.

The living room is usually on one side of the foyer, and next to it are the dining room and the kitchen. Across the hall are the bedrooms and washrooms. The floor covering in each of these rooms is usually ceramic or marble. On occasion, a family sets itself apart by having a decorative wooden floor in the living room. The chandeliers in the living and the dining rooms are also decorative, although smaller than the one in the foyer (see Photo 6.4).

Photo 6.4. Dining Room With Chandelier in Italian Home in Montreal

The usage pattern of rooms on this floor is of special significance. The bedrooms are used on a nightly basis. As one informant noted, "We come upstairs when we are ready to go to bed. When we wake up, we tidy our rooms and then go downstairs for the rest of the day." The living and dining rooms are occasionally used to celebrate anniversaries or weddings. The upstairs kitchen is used only in an emergency, although it is equipped with a self-cleaning stove and oven, a frost-free refrigerator, expensive cookware, china, and flatware. One informant talked about his home in the following manner:

> My son and I bought the house together, but we have two separate living areas. We have separate bedrooms and two kitchens. If we want to eat upstairs as on holidays, etc., then we eat upstairs. If we cannot get along, my wife and I can stay in the basement because we have our own kitchen and family room. (Agosto, 64, factory worker)

Jacinta likewise observed:

> I bought this house because of the Italian ambience. The basement contains a small kitchen, a full bathroom, a cold storage, and a large, furnished family room. It was not intended as a separate apartment, but it

does provide access to the garden. On the main floor, there is a large kitchen and a large living and dining space. Upstairs, there are four bedrooms and a bathroom. (Jacinta 48, garment worker)

The demarcation of space into day-to-day use and special occasion use fits very well with what Bourdieu (1977) referred to as *domestic habitus*. Given the rural background of most of those who were interviewed, the separation of space seems logical and normal and arises out of their taken-for-granted childhood experiences and dispositions. Many respondents stated that their understanding of how the rich live is based on descriptions in books on life in Italy. Their present situations are financially more secure, however, and are reflected in the architectural layouts of their current homes. It is also in these homes that they make a projection of what they understand as upper-class domestic habitus—hence the museumlike upstairs and the homey downstairs use of space. Thus, their current domestic habitus is a reflection of their present interactions outside the home and an outcome of the habitus learned in the context of their socialization in Italy. It is not surprising then that second-generation immigrants do not share in this domestic habitus with their parents. Indeed, second-generation Italians are not very positive about such arrangements. As one of them noted:

I hated this distinction between where we could play and where we could not. I did not like the idea that all the furniture was covered with a plastic until guests visited us or for special occasions. When I have my own house, I want to use every bit of space. (Bianca, 30, bank teller)

The few cases in which this sharp separation is not as apparent is in the homes of those who live in single detached homes in primarily anglophone suburbs. Even here, however, the family room with fireplace serves as the hub, and although Italians do not have two kitchens, the living and dining rooms are set apart for special occasions. The furniture in these rooms of informants who live in anglophone suburbs are invariably Mediterranean in inspiration, although they may not have been purchased in Italian furniture stores.

For the majority of the informants, however, the first floor of their homes is out-of-bounds for the children, and the furniture is usually under plastic wraps. On occasions when the furniture is used, such as for weddings, Christmas, or anniversaries, access is allowed but with certain constraints. Interaction in that space is formalized, for instance, through the use of the best china and crystal. Although regular cleaning and maintenance are part of the household chores, the preparations for

Photo 6.5. Living Room in Italian Home in Montreal

festive events are special. On such an occasion, silverware requires more polishing, teapots and cups need more careful attention when washing and drying, chandeliers are given an extra dusting, and the plants are given additional watering to mark the occasion and to set it apart from nonfestive days.

The furniture and objects in the living and dining rooms are special in yet another sense (see Photo 6.5). They are either made in Italy and purchased in Italian stores or made in Canada but bought in Italian furniture stores (see Table 6.1). Not all informants, however, opt for the Italian styles, and Louis IX and French Provincial furniture are found in some homes. Also, the Canadian-born Italians seem to be interested in Oriental- or English-style furniture. The furniture is not antique either, because although informants did note the value of antiques, they prefer the antique look to real antiques. Generally, they prefer new furniture, although when they first arrived, they could afford only second-hand furniture. As one of them remarked:

> When we bought our house, we bought everything new—living room and dining room sets, a 28-inch black and white television, a new refrigerator and stove. The rest of the objects you see here are gifts—housewarming

TABLE 6.1 Objects Identified by Informants as Either From Italy or Purchased in an Italian Store

Upstairs	
Living room furniture	Silver spoons
Dining room furniture	Tablecloths
Vases	Dolls
Trinkets	Small statues
Marble-top coffee tables	Pasta machines
Velour drapes	Bicycles (Torpedo)
Ceramic and/or marble floors	Skis and boots (Munari)
Crystal lamps and chandeliers, recessed in stucco ceiling	Hand-painted wooden napkin holders
Chinaware and crystal	Hand-painted porcelain dishes depicting the four seasons
Bedroom furniture	
Porcelain sculptures	Doilies
Espresso coffee pots	Homemade wine

gifts, gifts received at weddings, baptisms, first communion, and other important occasions. (Stephania, 55, garment worker)

Another also talked about the furniture her family owned:

The living room furniture is all made of solid mahogany. It is expensive but of very good quality. I bought this at an Italian store where I know I will get the best for a very good price. The dining room furniture is likewise bought at the same store, and it is solid oak and intricately carved. The details in the carving are beautiful, and I felt it was worth every dollar that I paid. (Caterina, 50, garment worker)

There is great pride and joy in showing and discussing the objects in the home, especially in the living and dining rooms. Italians consider them a tribute to Italy rather than a remembrance of their family's past. They are proud to be Italian, but it seems that Italy would be more proud of them. It is not merely an individual or family achievement but also a tribute to their heritage. One of the informants noted:

This part of the house is my way of remembering [Italy] . . . where I was born and raised for 18 years. I love thinking about it—a feeling of nostalgia fills me. (Lina, 55, homemaker)

She was quick to indicate that Canada is home now, however. She aptly described her situation as well as that of others in the community: "I came from Italy, but Canada is home." This sense of dual identity is displayed in her demarcation of space upstairs and downstairs. Her present is embodied in the family room with the hearth in the basement, where all the family's daily activities are accomplished. The upstairs, which is cared for like a museum (her children remarked), is symbolic of her past. This space is rarely used, yet the objects are lovingly cared for, singularized, and displayed as sacra. Although the house is not open for visitation or veneration as are the homes of the rich and famous, it acts as both a window to the outside world and as a looking glass for the informants. As one of the informants very proudly stated:

> We did not have the money in Italy. We were poor peasants that lived off the land. The home in which I grew up was small—basically one room with a large fireplace where we cooked, ate, played, and slept. If only people would see us today—Italy would be proud of us. (Louisa, 58, garment worker)

Each piece has a story, and this story is tied not only to memories and family but also to the concern for aesthetics and beauty that sets this space apart. The sculptures, the marble tables, ceramic or porcelain vases, lamps, and statues are all one-of-a-kind in informants' minds, although they were bought from Italian stores. Although to an outsider the furniture appears mass produced, to the informants it was fashioned out of special woods such as oak, mahogany, and rosewood with intricate carvings and rich upholstery (see Photo 6.6 of bedroom furniture). With each story, they singularize their furnishings and move them from the realm of commodities to that of art (Appadurai, 1986). It is as if they search for surrogate lineage through cultural display.

For most interviewed, the sanctum sanctorum is the dining room with its elaborate furniture. The wood is often solid oak and intricately worked. As an Italian furniture salesman observed:

> Italians prefer massive furniture even though they do not have the space to put it. It has to be elaborate and rich in appearance. They want quality and will not skimp on price. They are willing to wait till they have saved up enough to buy the furniture of their dreams. The tragedy is that once they own it, they never use it. (Johnny, 50, salesman)

Even in the modern split-level homes of the informants, they expressed a general unease about the use of space. One informant found it par-

Photo 6.6. Bedroom Furniture in Italian Home in Montreal

ticularly trying that her dining room was modern because, as she noted,

> I plan to buy a dining room set of dark wood and in a Mediterranean style. This house is not the right one for me. (Veronica, 48, seamstress)

The informants were also particular about filling the entire room with objects rather than leaving spaces empty. Every inch of the room had to be covered, although this principle did not apply to the walls.

The attitude toward fine china and crystal from Italy suggests that their perception is similar to that of private collectors. Although the status associated with ownership is very important, Italians also view these items dispassionately as *objets d'art*. They derive pure pleasure from looking at them and lovingly care for them. In a typical home, these include pieces that were received as wedding and housewarming gifts, as results of visits by family from Italy, and as gifts from their children. Many observed that although these are souvenirs, they are also more than that: They are beautiful objects that provide aesthetic pleasure.

Although furniture, crystal, and chandeliers are treated as art objects to be admired, informants made references to sculptures as well. One informant noted:

> It is in our blood—Italians love sculptures. They have many pieces in the living and dining rooms—angels, nude women, and saints. It is generally overdone. (Maria, 58, homemaker)

Visual art in the form of paintings, however, was not mentioned by any of the informants. Although the Italians interviewed do have paintings on the wall, these are usually of less importance to them. When asked about the two pictures that hung in her living and dining room, one informant said, "These were gifts given to us when we bought the furniture." This rather casual observation about a central wall piece came as a surprise, although she remarked, "Paintings can never reflect our achievements and our desires."

Books, likewise, are not regarded as cherished objects in the homes of these informants. Although occasional reference was made to study areas or the use of a wall unit to store books, the inspiration borne out of books was not identified by these informants.

Photographs were mentioned as special objects. They were usually framed like paintings and adorned the walls of the living rooms or foyers. The importance of photographs was noted by both parents and children. Photographs were identified as evocative of special relationships between husbands and wives, children and parents, and of family get-togethers. One informant had a 2-foot by 5-foot photograph of herself and her husband taken on their wedding day. It hung in the foyer. Although this is rather unusual because of its size and the public nature of the display, she was very particular about it. She liked questions relating to it, and the most valuable memory she associated with it is the way her husband looked at her on their wedding day.

Another informant, who had two photographs of his home and town in Italy given to him by a young nephew, remarked:

> The first is the picture of my house in Italy. The second is the view of the village on the mountain where I was raised. The scene is beautiful, so green. All those lovely olive trees . . . I hope my children will want these photographs someday . . . to show it to their children and their children's children. (Guiseppe, 65, retired)

The demarcation of space, the sacralization of it through special rituals and special occasions, and the singularization of each object with a story all help the process of acculturation of these informants. With the help of the sacra and the use of it on special occasions and with each new telling of the story of their lives, they are able to let go of some of their past. There is a sense of loss, but it is somewhat mitigated by their focus on the present. By re-creating a memory of their Italian heritage through furniture and objects, they have managed to let go of a tie that binds them to the country of origin. They move metaphorically between their country of origin and their country of residence as they move between the two floors of their homes. There is thus no great experience of loss—and no myth of return. Their cultural past not only is in their hearts and minds but also is embodied in the objects and furniture. It has been refabricated within the walls of their home. The re-creation of this "little Italy" allows them to merge their cultural present with that of the host country. They are by no means assimilated, yet their desire to return to their country of origin has long ceased to exist.

Gift giving among members of the immediate household as well as among more distant relatives and friends is, as discussed previously, central to the maintenance of identity. Initially, when asked about it, informants were not graphic about its importance. In the identification of objects in the home (mostly made in Italy or purchased in Italian stores), however, informants went through the collection and identified the occasion on which they received each item, as well as the names of the gift givers. Parents are expected and wish to provide their children with as much material wealth as they can afford.

Trousseaus are therefore started very early and include such items as bed linen, tablecloths, kitchen linen, nightgowns, and a wide assortment of cookware, china, and flatware. The status of the family is measured primarily by what they give their daughters, although today some of the younger generation do not want to receive these gifts. Yet the bond of friendship and affection built through careful choice and purchase of these objects is conveyed through the remarks of both parents and children. As one informant noted:

> Linen is a tradition. If you leave the house, you leave with linen. Linen is the basic gift. It is usually collected when a girl is barely in her teens. You may buy many other things, but it is important to have bedsheets and towels. All other gifts are based on what the groom and bride want. (Agnessa, 55, homemaker)

A local Italian bank manager also observed:

> Italian parents will not think twice about giving expensive gifts to their children. They will forgo their own vacations in order to save and give their children dining room and living room sets. It is very expensive, but they give with no reservations quality goods. (Franco, 60, bank manager)

But not all kids raised in Canada approve of their parents' choice in such matters, as one observed:

> My mother wanted to give my sister a trousseau for her wedding. She wanted to collect things for her—but my sister did not like the idea. She told my mother "you have your taste and I have mine. I will buy what I want when the time comes." There were no family heirlooms because my parents were very poor when they came. They had one trunk, not even a leather suitcase. (Marisa, 28, student)

One particular occasion in the middle of an interview was memorable—when the daughter remarked that her parents would have liked her to have their dining room furniture. She had been married several months but had not yet furnished her dining room. When the mother looked very reproachfully at her, the daughter lovingly yet clearly told her parents that she would prefer money instead to buy the furniture of her dreams. Although the amount was quite a large sum, her mother responded quickly that she would finance the purchase. The mother noted:

> Ideally, I would love to give you my own dining room set. It has not been used except for family occasions, and I would love for you to keep it as a memory of good times. However, since you want to buy your own, I cannot stop you. At least I will pay for it so that you will always think of the home you grew up in when you have your own family gathered around you at the table.

The sadness in the mother's voice was very clear, and the daughter was very conscious that she had touched a wound. The objects that the mother owned and wished to bequeath were a part of her, and giving them to her daughter meant that she was giving part of herself.

This pattern of gift giving had been altered by living in Canada because the children wanted to make their own choices. For earlier generations, such choices were made by elders, and the younger generation accepted them. Canadian-born Italians, however, are creating changes in this established structure.

Although materialism and abundance of objects and ownership of property seem to be uppermost in the minds of most of the informants, a few did note that objects have begun to displace people and relationships. Although this was not a dominant theme, it still balances our understanding of how meaning is constructed in the homes and objects of working-class Italian immigrants to Montreal.

Conclusions and Future Directions

This study is an exploration of the meaning of home and consumption styles of Italian immigrants in Montreal. Italian immigration to Canada began around the end of the last century and continues to the present. The focus in this study has been on immigrants and their offspring who came after World War II, mostly from the middle and southern parts of Italy. Our choice was deliberate in that they represent the majority of Italian immigrants in Montreal. Furthermore, the focus on a few families in one city has important limitations—yet this study outlines in some detail the concerns and values of the group in a microcosm. Clearly, more studies that examine particular sociocultural and regional factors that affect the acculturation process are necessary to understand the creation and maintenance of ethnic consciousness.

Although class is not explicitly explored, it plays a critical role in providing the parameters of consumption for the families interviewed. The focus is on first-generation informants who had virtually no education and no skills to offer in the job market. They also came from rural and poor backgrounds. Yet many of them emphasized the importance of owning homes and gardens that not only guaranteed subsistence but were also symbols of productivity and success. Thus, the importance of class in understanding consumption cannot be overlooked (Costa & Belk, 1990).

In addition to class, gender seems to play a role in the consumption process. Although male and female roles are fairly well demarcated, both men and women worked outside the home to save money to buy homes. Household activities were primarily women's work, although repairs and construction-related activities were done by men. Clearly, more research on changes in gender roles and perceptions is needed to better understand the intricacies of acculturation.

Home is everything. It is not merely a structure or a roof over their heads—it is family. The walls enclose the intimacy and the warmth among members of the household. Objects concretize these feelings and emotions, although the occasional informant lamented the loss of such warmth through the growing centrality of objects and possessions in the home. Each object reveals a part of the identity of those who own it and is thus a window to the world(s) they live in.

Home also serves as a looking glass, reminding Italians of who they are in a Canadian context. Italians demarcate and sacralize space in the home as a tribute to their heritage. Insofar as they move between sacred (a little Italy) and secular spaces in the context of their own homes, they have strengthened a link to their past. Their cultural past is thus in their present, and, as long as they can see it in a tangible form, their longing for the past is channeled into attempts to become more conscious about their present—more important, the present in which their children live. The children have viewed their cultural past in the demarcated spaces and objects and will continue to treasure some of it in their own homes. The ionic columns, the pedimented porches, the colored geometric shapes in the brick facades, the marble balustrades, and the gardens with grapevines will continue to be tangible markers of a culture, but the children will see these objects and markers more as a model of, rather than a model for, reality.

Note

1. The definition of *working class* follows from the work of Bourdieu (1990, 1991) in which he discussed the dialectical relationship between structure and agency in defining class. An individual's class position is a function of the amount and types of economic and cultural capital she or he possesses. Cultural knowledge, modes of speech, and thought are acquired through the socialization process and without much reflection. One's class is, of course, reinforced by institutional structures such as the church, schools, and so forth. Those who have large amounts of economic and/or cultural capital are "dominant" and will seek to dominate those with less capital. The formation of taste cultures is therefore based on material and cultural conditions of individuals, and, consequently, members of these classes will share similar interests and dispositions.

References

Appadurai, A. (Ed.) (1986). *The social life of things: Commodities in cultural perspective.* Cambridge, UK: Cambridge University Press.

Arnould, E. J. (1989). Toward a broadened theory of preference formation and the diffusion of innovations: Cases from Zinder Province, Niger Republic. *Journal of Consumer Research, 16,* 239-267.

Arnould, E. J., & Price, L. (1993). River magic: Extraordinary experience and the extended service encounter. *Journal of Consumer Research, 20,* 24-45.

Altheide, D. L., & Johnson, J. M. (1994). Criteria for assessing interpretive validity in qualitative research. In N. K. Denzin & Y. S. Lincoln (Eds.), *Handbook of qualitative research* (pp. 485-499). Thousand Oaks, CA: Sage.

Belk, R. W. (1985). Materialism: Trait aspects of living in the material world. *Journal of Consumer Research, 12,* 265-280.

Belk, R. W. (1988). Possessions and the extended self. *Journal of Consumer Research, 15,* 139-168.

Belk, R. W. (1991). Possessions and the sense of past. In R. W. Belk (Ed.), *Highways and buyways: Naturalistic research from the consumer behavior odyssey* (pp. 114-130). Provo, UT: Association for Consumer Research.

Belk, R. W., Sherry, J. F., Jr., & Wallendorf, M. (1988). A naturalistic inquiry into buyer and seller behavior at a swap meet. *Journal of Consumer Research, 14,* 449-470.

Belk, R. W., Wallendorf, M., & Sherry, J. F., Jr. (1989). The sacred and the profane in consumer behavior: Theodicy on the odyssey. *Journal of Consumer Research, 16,* 138.

Bloch, M. (1976). The past and the present in the present. *Man, 12,* 278-292.

Boissevain, J. (1976). *The Italians of Montreal.* Ottawa, Canada: Ministry of Supply and Services.

Bourdieu, P. (1977). *Outline of a theory of practice.* Cambridge, UK: Cambridge University Press.

Bourdieu, P. (1990). *In other words.* Stanford, CA: Stanford University Press.

Bourdieu, P. (1991). *Language and symbolic power.* Cambridge, MA: Harvard University Press.

Calder, B., & Tybout, A. M. (1989). Interpretive, qualitative, and traditional scientific empirical consumer behavior research. In E. C. Hirschman (Ed.), *Interpretive consumer research* (pp. 199-208). Provo, UT: Association for Consumer Research.

Clark, C. E. (1986). *The American family home, 1800-1960.* Chapel Hill: University of North Carolina Press.

Clifford, J. (1989). *The predicament of culture.* Cambridge, MA: Harvard University Press.

Cohn, J. (1979). *The palace or the poorhouse: The American house as cultural symbol.* East Lansing: Michigan State University Press.

Costa, J. A., & Belk, R. W. (1990). Nouveaux riches as quintessential Americans: Case studies of consumption in an extended family. In R. W. Belk (Ed.), *Advances in non-profit marketing* (Vol. 3, pp. 83-140). Greenwich, CT: JAI.

Creighton, T. H., & Ford, K. M. (1961). *Contemporary houses evaluated by their owners.* New York: Reinhold.

Csikszentmihalyi, M., & Rochberg-Halton, E. (1981). *The meaning of things: Domestic symbols and the self.* London: Cambridge University Press.

Davis, F. (1979). *Yearning for yesterday: Toward a sociology of nostalgia.* New York: Free Press.

Denzin, N. K. (1994). The art and politics of interpretation. In N. Denzin & Y. S. Lincoln (Eds.), *Handbook of qualitative research* (pp. 500-515). Thousand Oaks, CA: Sage.

Deshpande, R., Hoyer, W., & Donthu, N. (1986). The intensity of ethnic affiliation: A study of the sociology of Hispanic consumption. *Journal of Consumer Research, 13,* 214-220.

Dholakia, R., & Levy, S. (1987). The consumer dream in the United States: Aspirations and achievements in a changing environment. *Journal of Macromarketing, 7*(2), 4151.

Duncan, J. S. (Ed.). (1981). *Housing and identity: Cross-cultural perspectives.* London: Croom Helm.

Farber, J., & Reed, H. H. (1980). *Palladio's architecture and its influence.* New York: Dover.

Geertz, C. (1973). *The interpretation of cultures.* New York: Basic Books.

Glazer, N., & Moynihan, D. P. (Eds.). (1975). *Ethnicity: Theory and experience.* Cambridge, MA: Harvard University Press.

Gmelch, G. (1980). Return migration. *Annual Review of Anthropology, 9,* 135-159.

Gordon, M. (1964). *Assimilation in American life: The role of race, religion and national origins.* New York: Oxford University Press.

Handlin, D. P. (1979). *The American home: Architecture society, 1815-1915.* Boston: Little, Brown.

Hawkins, F. (1972). *Canada and immigration: Public policy and public concern.* Montreal: McGill Queen's University Press.

Hill, R. (1991). Homeless women, special possessions and the meaning of home: An ethnographic case study. *Journal of Consumer Research, 18,* 298-310.

Hirschman, E. C. (1981). American Jewish ethnicity: Its relationship to some selected aspects of consumer behavior. *Journal of Marketing, 45*(3), 102-110.

Holdsworth, D. W. (1977). House and home in Vancouver: Images of West Coast urbanism, 1886-1929. In G. A. Stelter & A. F. J. Artibise (Eds.), *The Canadian city: Essays in urban history* (pp. 118-140). Toronto: McClelland & Stewart.

Joy, A. (1989). *Ethnicity in Canada.* New York: AMS.

Joy A., & Dholakia, R. R. (1991). Remembrances of things past: The meaning of home and possessions of Indian professionals in Canada. *Journal of Social Behavior and Personality, 6*(6), 385-402.

Kiefer, C. (1977). *Changing cultures, changing lives.* San Francisco: Jossey-Bass.

Lopreato, J. (1970). *Italian Americans.* New York: Random House.

Mars, G. C. (1925). *Brick work in Italy.* Chicago: American Face Brick Association.

Martin, B., & Mohanty, C. T. (1986). Feminist politics: What's home got to do with it? In T. de Lauretis (Ed.), *Feminist studies/critical studies* (pp. 208-209). Bloomington: Indiana University Press.

McCracken, G. (1986). Culture and consumption: A theoretical account of the structure and movement of the cultural meaning of consumer goods. *Journal of Consumer Research, 13,* 71-84.

McCracken, G. (1988). *Culture and consumption: New approaches to the symbolism of consumer goods and activities.* Bloomington: Indiana University Press.

McCracken, G. (1989). Homeyness: A cultural account of one constellation of consumer goods and meanings. In E. C. Hirschman (Ed.), *Interpretive consumer research* (pp. 168-184). Provo, UT: Association for Consumer Research.

Mehta, R., & Belk, R. W. (1991). Artifacts, identity and transition: Favorite possessions of Indians and Indian immigrants to the United States. *Journal of Consumer Research, 17,* 398-411.

Migliore, S. (1988). Religious symbols and cultural identity: A Sicilian-Canadian example. *Canadian Ethnic Studies, 20*(1), 78-95.

Oakley, A. (1981). Interviewing women: A contradiction in terms. In H. Roberts (Ed.), *Doing feminist research* (pp. 30-61). London: Routledge & Kegan Paul.

O'Guinn, T. C., & Faber, R. (1985). New perspectives on acculturation: The relationship of general and role specific acculturation with Hispanics' consumer attitudes. In E. C. Hirschman & M. Holbrook (Eds.), *Advances in consumer research* (Vol. 12, pp. 113-117). Provo, UT: Association for Consumer Research.

Padilla, A. M. (Ed.). (1980). *Acculturation: Theory, models and some new findings.* Boulder, CO: Westview.

Perin, C. (1977). *Everything in its place.* Princeton, NJ: Princeton University Press.

Pivato, J. (1986). Italian women writers recall history. *Canadian Ethnic Studies, 18*(1), 79-89.

Robben, A. C. G. M. (1989). Habits of the home: Spatial hegemony and the structuration of house and society in Brazil. *American Anthropologist, 91*(3), 570-588.

Sahlins, M. (1976). *Culture and practical reason.* Chicago: University of Chicago Press.

Sherry, J., Jr., & Camargo, E. (1987). May your life be marvelous: English language labelling and the semiotics of Japanese promotion. *Journal of Consumer Research, 14,* 174-188.

Swidler, A. (1986). Culture in action. *American Sociological Review, 51,* 273-286.

Tuan, Y. (1982). *Segmented worlds and self.* Minneapolis: University of Minnesota Press.

Valencia, H. (1985). Developing an index to measure Hispanicness. In E. C. Hirschman & M. Holbrook (Eds.), *Advances in consumer research* (Vol. 12, pp. 118-121). Provo, UT: Association for Consumer Research.

Valeria, L. S. (1987). From Tuscany to the Northwest Territories: The Italian community of Yellowknife. *Canadian Ethnic Studies, 19*(1), 77-87.

Wallendorf, M., & Arnould, E. J. (1988). My favorite things: A cross-cultural inquiry into object attachment, possessiveness, and social image. *Journal of Consumer Research, 15*, 531-547.

Wallendorf, M., & Reilly, M. (1983). Ethnic migration, assimilation and consumption. *Journal of Consumer Research, 10*, 293-302.

Williams, B. (1989). A class act: Anthropology and the race to nation across ethnic terrain. *Annual Review of Anthropology, 18*, 401-444.

Wright, G. (1981). *Building the dream: A social history of housing in America*. New York: Pantheon.

Yinger, M. (1985). Ethnicity. *Annual Review of Sociology, 11*, 151-180.

Zucchi, J. E. (1988). *Italians in Toronto*. Montreal: McGill Queen's University Press.

7

Ethnicity and Consumption in Romania

RUSSELL W. BELK

MAGDA PAUN

Ethnicity is often encoded, preserved, and celebrated in consumption. At the level of individual consumption, prominent modes of ethnic expression include clothing, grooming, jewelry, foods, music, homes, and home decor. Even objects such as gravestones (Clark, 1987; Meyer, 1993) may announce individual ethnic identity. Not coincidentally, the majority of such objects are also used in the formal and informal rituals through which identity is enacted (Belk, 1992; Rook, 1985). At the broader level of group ethnicity, additional spheres of culture production and consumption are employed to help define ethnic identity, including religion, art, literature, museums, flags, education, spectator sports, entertainments, and various holidays and celebrations of culture—especially folk culture (e.g., Cawelti, 1990; Horne, 1984). This is not to say that consumption is the only way through which ethnicity is enacted. Certainly language, history, traditions, myths, roles, territories, values, norms, laws, and behaviors are all critical as well (Askegaard, 1991). But there is good evidence that consumption is a key marker (Douglas & Isherwood, 1978) of ethnic identity, both by those claiming ethnic identity and by those discriminating against ethnic minorities. For instance, in North America, consumption patterns involving homes, foods, cars, clothes, and various other possessions have proved to be key markers of both distinctive ethnic identity and assimilation into the dominant culture (e.g., Bih, 1992; Heinze, 1990; Joy & Dholakia, 1991; Levenstein & Conlin, 1990; Matz, 1961; Mehta & Belk, 1991; Plascencia, 1985; Wallendorf & Reilly, 1983). There are thus good reasons to attend both to consumption patterns in seeking to understand ethnicity and to ethnicity in seeking to understand consumption patterns.

The present chapter explores the role of consumption in defining Romanian ethnicity. Because the ethnic profile of Romania is historically volatile and because this history is a highly contested field on which the struggle for Romanian ethnic identities continues to be played out, we begin with a history of Romania and its ethnic groups. We then examine the role of consumption in defining contemporary ethnic identity for Romanians as a whole and for its two largest minority groups: Hungarians and Gypsies. Smaller minority ethnic groups such as Germans, Ukrainians, and Jews will not be considered in any detail. Besides historical analysis, this chapter relies on data gathered during the first author's year in Romania from September 1991 through August 1992. Participant observation, depth interviews, focus groups, and questionnaires were all employed in a broader study of the effects of economic and political changes on Romanian consumption patterns. The second author is a Romanian graduate student who is both a key informant and collaborator on this project. Additional methodological details can be found in Belk (1993).

We found differing strategic uses of consumption in defining ethnic identity among majority and minority Romanians. We attempt to understand these differences in light of historical, class, religious, and political factors in past and present-day Romania. In view of the ethnic violence and divisions that have arisen in surrounding Eastern European nations since the collapse of communism, the present struggles involving ethnicity in Romania are of more than passing interest. Since the fall of Nicolae Ceauşescu in December 1989, there have been a number of violent actions involving both Gypsies and Transylvanian Hungarians in Romania. Although these occurrences have been limited in comparison to neighboring clashes between Serbians, Croatians, and Bosnians in the former Yugoslavia or between Ukrainians and Romanians in the former Soviet Union, they are a part of the same general increase in Balkan ethnic tensions during this critical period of transition. At the same time, these frictions help to cast the role of consumption in the age-old ethnic tensions in Romania into a sharper and clearer light.

A Brief History
of Romanian Ethnic Groups

By one estimate, 90% of the nations of the world are multiethnic (Smith, 1991, p. 15). Furthermore, ethnicity itself may be a social construct more than it is a biological construct (Hobsbawm, 1992; Verdery, 1988). The potential fluidity of ethnic boundaries and the frequent use of ethnicity to stimulate nationalistic passions often make ethnicity and nation interdependent contested grounds. In such contests, consumption plays a significant role not only in marking but often in defining boundaries between nations and ethnic groups.

The present boundaries of Romania have been in place only since the close of World War II. Two of the three historic regions of Romania—Moldavia and Wallachia—were joined after Ottoman rule in 1877. The third, Transylvania, was added temporarily after World War I. Throughout its history, Romania has had numerous alterations in both its borders and the nationality of its rulers. Some of the earliest of these alterations are a source of a heated dispute because of missing links in Romanian history, and this controversy pertains to current issues of national and ethnic identity (Castellan, 1989). Appreciating the nature of this dispute is critical for understanding Romanians' desperate need to claim a history, homeland, and ethnic identity and for understanding how individual and aggregate consumption patterns bear on serving this need.

The area that essentially coincides with present-day Romania was once Dacia until it was conquered by Rome through battles in A.D. 101-102 and 105-106. The Romans ruled for approximately 165 years, after which the area was controlled by a series of other invaders from elsewhere in Europe and Asia. During the span of Roman control, the conquerors' Latin language was imposed and largely replaced the Dacian language. The Romans intermarried with the Dacians, and little of previous Dacian history remains. This much is relatively uncontested. Of dispute is the Daco-Roman thesis that the Romanized Dacians remained in this territory and provide a continuous ethnic link to present Romanians. The Daco-Roman thesis is the predominant view in Romania and glorifies the tenacity of Romanians (Hale, 1971).

There are two Romanian theories of the history of the Romanians after the Romans (see Gilberg, 1990). One is that the Romanians contributed to the culture of the less sophisticated invaders but eventually isolated themselves in the forests and Carpathian Mountains of Transylvania, where their isolation allowed them to maintain their language, culture, and traditions. The prominent Romanian historian Nicolae Iorga described the Transylvanian village political organizations supposed to exist at this time as "popular Romanias" to suggest their Daco-Roman roots (see Pascu, 1979/1982). The second theory is that the Romanians remained but were enslaved by the new conquerors. In the Romanian version of this theory, it is only their cohesion and commitment that allowed them to preserve their language, customs, and culture. On the other hand, Hungarians claim that during the invasions following Roman rule, the Daco-Romans fled across the Danube into what is now Bulgaria, leaving the northern territory, including Transylvania, to Slavs and others (e.g., Illyés, 1982; Ludanyi, 1983). In addition, the Hungarians claim that the Romanians who presently occupy Transylvania migrated there from their homeland in Wallachia in the 13th century, whereas Magyars had conquered the "barbaric" tribes of the region shortly before A.D. 900 and remained thereafter. Some versions also claim Hungarian roots in the area preceding the Magyar conquest. Romanians, on the other hand, see the Magyar conquest "as no more than a 'barbarian' and 'ruthless invasion' against the Daco-Roman indigenous tribes inhabiting Transylvania at that time" (Kurti, 1989, p. 23).

At stake in this controversy is the rightful ownership of Transylvania—an area that Romanians see as the birthplace of their nation and Hungarians see as a sacred site where they successfully fought against both the Ottomans and the Austrians. For Romanians, the Daco-Roman thesis provides a manifest destiny for keeping their native soil in Transylvania, whereas the Hungarians who live there see it as historically and rightfully belonging to Hungary (Verdery, 1991). Very little history of Romania was written or survives from these contested dark ages. Archaeologists from both sides claim that the archaeological evidence supports their theses, but in the absence of definitive evidence, this battle over history is perhaps best seen within the context of the uses of history to attempt to legitimize a particular present or future. As Kurti (1989) noted of these positions in the era before the fall of communism: "All too often, notions of Daco-Roman continuity and Hungarian ethnogenesis have been 'supported' by a new set of 'scientific' data and Marxist-Leninist interpretations of historical, linguistic, and archaeological 'facts' that amount to Romanian and Hungarian claims of 'rights' and 'cultural heritage' " (p. 22).

Gilberg (1990) summarized the view of Western scholars seeking to sort through these conflicting claims, with several points of consensus that emphasize the role of consumption in anchoring Romanian identity:

Romanian group identity, including language, customs, folklore, and perhaps even dress was preserved despite the repression meted out by countless conquerors and rulers, thereby demonstrating considerable staying
power, even in the face of great adversity. . . . Ethnic identity became
solidified over time because the group's symbols, myths, nostalgia, and
boundary markers (such as dress and rituals) became part and parcel of its
existence, whether the group lived together on common territory or was
spread out among others. Thus it should not be surprising that ethnicity
survived centuries of repression, as long as that repression did not destroy
the group's boundary markers and symbols of togetherness. (p. 23)

Thus, regardless of the validity of the Daco-Roman thesis, it seems clear
that individual and aggregate consumption patterns acted as key boundary markers that historically allowed Romanians to keep their Lati-
nate language and cultural identity intact in the face of numerous
challenges.

At present, the disputed area is part of Romania. In the past, Transylvania has changed ownership between the two countries on several
occasions. It was independent after Hungary was partitioned in 1526,
was again Hungarian in 1691, was Romanian from 1918 to 1940, was
Hungarian during part of World War II, and became a part of Romania
again following the war (Behr, 1991). Similar shifts in nationality have
occurred in other parts of Romania. Romania has been absorbed or
dominated by the Ottoman empire (administered by Phanariot Greeks
in Romania), the Hapsburg empire, and the Soviet bloc under communism. It has been invaded by Visigoths, Huns, Avars, Gepidae, Slavs,
Bulgars, Tartars, and others. Given the sequence of foreign domina-
tions that began with the Romans, the missing pieces of Romanian
history, the resulting uncertainty about Romanian ethnicity, the continuing conflicting claims concerning Transylvania and neighboring
Bessarabia and Ukrainian Bukovina (which were once parts of Romania and have largely Romanian citizenry), and the breakups of the
former Soviet Union, Czechoslovakia, and Yugoslavia in recent years,
it is certainly understandable that concern with ethnicity is strong in
Romania.

But although ethnogenesis in Romania and disputes over the rights
and nationality of Hungarians in Romania and Romanians in Bessarabia and Bukovina are key parts of the history of ethnicity in Romania, there is more to this history. As Beck (1986) noted, next to the
former Soviet Union, Romania has the largest number of ethnic groups
of any country in Europe. Besides Hungarians, the most significant
groups are Gypsies, Germans, Ukrainians, and Jews. The two world

wars significantly reduced the population of three of these ethnic groups in Romania. Illyés (1982) estimated that 700,000 to 800,000 minority Romanians were killed, disappeared, or were deported during World War II alone, of whom 350,000 to 400,000 were Jewish, 200,000 were German, and 150,000 to 200,000 were Hungarian. These estimates do not include the largely ignored loss of Romanian Gypsies during this war. Approximately 500,000 of Europe's (then) 1 to 2 million Gypsies perished along with Jews in Hitler's extermination camps; of these, 150,000 to 200,000 were Romanian (Fraser, 1992; Illyés, 1982; Oliner & Hallum, 1978). The German population in Romania was cut in half by the war and was further reduced when 40,000 were forced to resettle outside the country in 1951 (Illyés, 1982). In addition, several hundred thousand Romanian Jews and Germans were allowed to immigrate to Israel and Germany (in exchange for payments from these countries) after World War II (Campeanu, 1991). As a result, by 1970 there were only about 100,000 Jews left in Romania (Hale, 1971), and there are even fewer today. German Romanians were estimated at 350,000 in 1981 (Shafir, 1985); many more have left since the Romanian revolution in 1989. By contrast, out of the 23 million Romanian population, 2 to 2½ million are Hungarian (Gallagher, 1992) and as many as 3 million are Gypsies (Kinzer, 1992).

If the history of Hungarians in Romania is obscure, the history of Gypsies (*Ţigani* to Romanians, *Romani* or *Romi* to themselves) in Romania is nonexistent. It is most likely that Gypsies moved from northwestern India to Eastern Europe by the late 11th century (Crowe, 1991). In India they were Dravidians whom the local Rajputs had elevated from low to high caste by making them the warrior society of the region (Hancock, 1991). Following battles in what is now Afghanistan, they moved into Europe and initially became metalsmiths and craftspersons. But they were eventually enslaved for economic, military, social, and possibly racial reasons (Crowe, 1991). Although Romania has the largest concentration of Gypsies, they are now widely scattered throughout Europe and elsewhere, with pan-Gypsy unity being more myth than fact (Salo, 1982). In Romania, Gypsies were slaves from the 13th century through the mid-19th century. Although the languages spoken by Gypsies (chiefly the Vlach dialect in Romania) are variants of Hindi, there is no written language to record their history.

As Beck (1986) noted, the stereotypes associated with the ethnic and cultural division of labor in Romania have remained: A Gypsy is seen as a slave, a Romanian as a serf, and a Hungarian as a noble. Gypsies remain clearly at the bottom of this hierarchy and are the subjects of considerable hatred, prejudice, and scapegoating among virtually all

Romanians. This prejudice is strong even within the context of the universal low regard for Gypsies around the world. Oliner and Hallum (1978) summarized the epithets used to characterize them: "They were 'anti-Christs,' 'thieves,' 'bandits,' and purveyors of 'immorality, promiscuity, and pornography.' They were also accused of witchcraft and stealing children. At best, they were corruptors of the religious and social order" (p. 45). Gypsies, together with executioners, dealers in horseflesh and leather, and collectors of night soil, constitute what Barth (1969) termed a pariah minority group whose members cross the borders of taboo that exist in the dominant culture.

Despite continuing prejudice against Gypsies, they were considered part of the state under communism and offered jobs and schooling as well as the forced relocation and other consumption deprivations suffered jointly with other Romanians. Such equal treatment only served to heighten resentment by other Romanians. Before the revolution, Kideckel (1988) reported that "villagers often claimed that the cadre who implemented collectivization were gypsies while older informants suggested that their factory superiors were Ţigani who received high salaries, did no work, stole factory materials, and then blamed local Romanians" (p. 405).

Such scapegoating (here of Gypsies by Romanians) is certainly not without precedent elsewhere. For instance, in the mid-14th century when bubonic plague swept through Europe, the Spanish blamed it on the minority Jews and Muslims, the French blamed the minority English, and Eastern Europeans blamed the Christian minority for causing it (Breuer, 1982). Similarly, after the fall of Nicolae Ceauşescu, when Romanians were better able to appreciate and speak about the atrocities he committed, rumors quickly surfaced that he was part Gypsy (Beck, 1989a; Behr, 1991). It now appears that Gypsies were an important part of the Romanian revolution in Bucureşti (Beck, 1993), yet their heroism remains invisible to and unacknowledged by the majority Romanian population.

According to a 1993 study conducted by Bucureşti University, in Romania, where such things are generally taken for granted, only 4% of Romanian Gypsies have completed high school, only 20% have a refrigerator, and half of the adults are unemployed (Petreanu, 1993). Despite problems of poor health care, high illiteracy, and poverty among Romanian Gypsies, they have not been given the official recognition of other minorities. They remain largely outside the Romanian social welfare system and beneath the contempt of Romanian people. Indeed, despite a 900-year presence in Romania, Gypsies are not considered by the populace to be Romanians (nor do they consider themselves to be). In fairness, Romanians also keep a distance from Hungarian-Romanians and regard them as *nationalitatie conlocuitoare*, a cohabiting nationality.

Not surprisingly, woven among the issues of ethnic identity played out in Romania are various consumption markers at both individual and aggregate levels. Goods may play an even stronger role in marking Romanian ethnicity because Romanians lack distinct and homogeneous physical characteristics that might otherwise identify them (Gilberg, 1990). In the following sections, we analyze these consumption aspects of ethnicity in contemporary Romania and use them to help understand ethnic relations among Romanians. We approach this analysis in three sections: Romanian national identity, Hungarian-Romanian ethnicity, and Gypsy ethnicity. We conclude with a brief appraisal of the extensiveness of the role of consumption in Romanian ethnicity.

Consumption and
Romanian National Identity

HISTORIC MYTHIFICATION

The preceding discussion outlines some of the reasons that Romanians might well desire a common sense of ethnic identity: a history of foreign rule, a key missing link in Romanian history, resulting uncertainty about Romanian ethnicity, conflicting national claims in Transylvania, Bessarabia, and Bukovina, turmoil and uncertainty due to the dramatic changes in the Romanian economic system, and the ethnic breakups and battles in surrounding Eastern and Central European nations. In attempting to establish their identity, Romanians cite the fact that theirs is the only country in the region with a Latin-based language and is surrounded by a sea of Slavic language countries (Bulgaria, Serbia, and the former Soviet Union) as well as the Finno-Ugric language of Hungary. It is also significant that to ennoble his presidency, Nicolae Ceauşescu sought to connect himself to rulers going back more than 2,000 years to the Dacian kings. As Hale (1971) observed, almost immediately after he became Party secretary, Ceauşescu began to tour the country and visit or set up shrines to every possible national hero as well as museums, historic houses, monasteries, and fields of liberty. Fischer-Galaţi (1981) described the 1979 May Day celebrations in which Ceauşescu sought to have his name interspersed in speeches listing Romanian heroes going back to the Dacian king Burebista 2,050 years ago and claiming unbroken connections to Ceauşescu and to present-day

Romania. Similarly, one patriotic Romanian song describes the Dacian king Decebalus as diligent and a man of justice, and his skill and bravery are heralded in the ultimately losing battles against the Romans. In parallel fashion exhibiting "Dacian" traits, Ceauşescu was portrayed as brave in standing up to the Soviets during the communist era. A strong and consistent attempt was made to conflate Ceauşescu, Daco-Roman history, and the Romanian people into a single constellation of meaning during this period. Apart from adding Ceauşescu to this pantheon, however, the nationalist mythification of the Romanian past is not new:

> With the exception of the references to Ceauşescu and to communism there is little that is new in this historic fairy tale. For over one hundred years poets, patriots, and politicians, men like Bălcescu and Brătianu, Alexandri and Antonescu, Eminescu and Ceauşescu have spun similar versions of the Romanian epic. In essence, the Cinderellas of history, the Romanian people, were prevented from attaining national liberation, political unification, and social justice by wicked stepmothers such as the Hapsburgs, the Turks, and the Russians. To their rescue came the Prince Charmings of the 19th century, the rightful descendants of Decebalus, Trajan, Stephen the Great, Michael the Brave, the Romanian nationalists. These national heros outwitted the wicked stepmothers and fought off all other dragons too—Greeks, Hungarians, Jews. (Fischer-Galaţi, 1981, p. 328)

Notably, Trajan was the Roman conqueror of the Romanians in A.D. 106. Yet he is revered as the founder of Romania, as Benedict (1953) explained:

> Trajan, too, is a living folk hero, not as a Roman emperor subduing a distant outpost populated by their own ancestors, but as the founder, the "papa," of Rumania. . . . Rumanians see their history as a long struggle during which they have preserved their Roman tongue and their identity against conqueror after conqueror, and hence the myth that makes Trajan the father of Rumania is nationally indispensable. (p. 406)

A replica of the Trajan column (in Rome) memorializing his triumph resides in the Romanian National Historical Museum. Nevertheless, as Hungarian-born historian John Lukacs observed, "Official Rumanian propaganda and official Rumanian historiography claim that the Rumanians are direct descendants of Trajan's legions, which is as if Ronald Reagan were to declare his descent from Pocahontas" (quoted in Kaplan, 1993, p. 90).

The mythification of national histories and heroes is also far from new in the world of both communist and capitalist countries (Burke, 1992; Hobsbawm & Ranger, 1983; Lane, 1981; Schmidt, 1991). Whether the myths involve George Washington's chopping down a cherry tree, Scottish Clan Tartans, or Lenin's benevolence, nations and leaders have long sought to embellish history. But in Romania, there are additional external reasons (boundary conflicts) and internal reasons (Romanians' fierce pride in the face of foreign invasions and historic ambiguity) why much of this mythification can be seen as a celebration of ethnic purity. These myths are taught in the schools; celebrated in countless heroic names on streets, buildings, hotels, and plazas; reified in public statues, shrines, and currency depictions; codified in history books; and celebrated in songs, films, television programs, and public commemorations and celebrations. The most celebrated and popular Romanian poet, Mihail Eminescu, wrote many well-known poems celebrating Romania's Dacian, Roman, and medieval past and heroes. Like several other Romanian cities, Cluj (the Hungarian Kolozsvar) is often written and spoken of as Cluj-Napoca, adding its Latin name as a suffix. And the most popular car made in Romania is a copy of an old Renault named the "Dacia." It is accordingly impossible to walk the streets, watch television, or buy bread without constant reminders that to be a Romanian is to be from a proud race of Dacians.

RELIGION

In terms of aggregate consumption and national sense of self (Belk, 1988), there are a number of spheres in which the ideology of ethnic purity and national tradition is produced and consumed. One such sphere is religion. Although religion is often allied with ethnicity, in Romania, where 75% of believers are Orthodox, there is also strong nationalism associated with this religion (Kerr, 1992). As Romanian philosopher Nae Ionescu put it in the mid-1930s, "We are Orthodox because we are Romanian, and we are Romanian because we are Orthodox" (quoted in Hitchins, 1992, p. 1075). Christianity was brought to Romania by the Emperor Constantine in the 4th century (Gilberg, 1989), and Romanians have been Orthodox since a 9th-century occupation by the Bulgars (Kaplan, 1993). Following the Bulgar occupation, Orthodox priests not only presided in key rituals but also provided education to peasants, preserved the Romanian language, and contributed strongly to maintaining a sense of Romanian identity. Because the Romanian Orthodox church is not shared by the German, Hungarian,

Jewish, and Gypsy populations of Romania, it has long served as an ethnic marker with strong national symbolism (paralleling in some respects the situations in Bosnia [Bringa, 1993] and Albania [Reineck, 1993]). Communist leadership of Romania, although not actively acknowledging Orthodox religion, was careful to preserve many old monasteries, churches, and the priesthood of the church throughout the years of communism. Although Ceauşescu stopped short of official recognition of the church, he visited monasteries, supported priests with state funds, and allowed the printing of a small number (100,000) of bibles on state printing presses (Hale, 1971). Christmas and Easter celebrations were not as openly opposed or transformed as they were in the Soviet Union (Binns, 1980; Lane, 1981), and Romanians could still find for sale during the appropriate season such items as Christmas trees, Christmas tree ornaments, and chocolate *Moş Crăicun* ("old man Christmas") characters (all nonreligious objects), as well as red dye for hard-boiled eggs to crack in salute to the resurrection of Christ in Easter celebrations. Churches and monasteries were still able to supply beeswax candles for burning in tribute to the dead, and some tombstones still carried Orthodox religious motifs.

Nevertheless, in these as in other state uses of ethnic consumption signs and symbols, the public face did not always match the private. A Communist Party member who was observed attending church services placed his or her job and position in the party in jeopardy, workplaces were monitored for the traditional egg crackings at Easter time, and some churches were bulldozed. Since 1989, however, Romanians have been free to practice their religion, although an influx of foreign missionaries has begun to offer small challenges to the dominance of Orthodoxy.

FOLK CULTURE

Another broad sphere of public consumption attached to nationalism and the myth of Dacian-descended ethnic purity, and one that was more wholeheartedly and openly embraced by communist leaders than religion, is Romanian folk culture. Folk revivals have been common to European nationalistic movements for well over a hundred years and were seized on as highly consistent with communist glorification of the worker and peasant. Folk culture includes folk music, folk dance, folktales, folk art, folk architecture, traditional clothing, and traditional crafts (Coussens, 1984). The heroes of this folk culture are the

Romanian peasants. Here too there is an irony in the revival of Romanian folk culture that occurred in the Ceauşescu years. During the 1960s through the 1980s, Romania was vigorously pursuing a program of urbanization, industrialization, and homogenization of the country. Under this program of *sistematizare* (systematization), land was appropriated, traditional agriculture was collectivized, new cities were built to house peasants converted into factory workers, and local ethnic concentrations were dispersed as university graduates and others were intentionally sent to parts of the country distant from their homelands. Although some attempt was made to celebrate the new industrial state with holidays such as *Ziua Minerilor* (Miners' Day), *Ziua Tipographia* (Printers' Day), and *Ziua Petroliştilor* (Oil Workers' Day) and through the celebration of May Day as a workers' holiday (Kideckel, 1988), these holidays generated little public enthusiasm. Celebrations of folk culture, on the other hand, have been much more extensive and well received.

As with the open-air folk museums that sprang up in Norway, Sweden, and northern Europe in the 19th century, there are reconstructed villages exhibiting only the finest of once far-flung rural folk architecture in many large Romanian cities. Popular television fare continues to feature traditional songs (*doine*) performed by costumed singers and musicians playing traditional Romanian instruments such as *nai* (panpipes). Children attend various folklore summer camps around Romania. A number of festivals around the country continue to feature traditional folk costume, music, and stories. What such celebrations have in common is that they are nostalgic revivals of a folk culture that has largely disappeared. They are reminiscent of the Romanian "peasant" costumes placed in the Paris Exposition of 1890 and currently in the French Musée de l'Homme (Karnoouh, 1982). These garments were designed in the latest style of Parisian gowns with the single exception of their gold and silver embroidered patterns that are vaguely reminiscent of Romanian folk designs. On one hand, the selection of "peasant" garments by the newly founded Romanian state was intended to glorify the peasant, but on the other hand, the embellished artifacts created bore little resemblance to the sturdy clothes of the real Romanian peasant. Such restylized patterns persist in current presentations of Romanian folk culture.

These presentations are similar to the sorts of folk celebrations variously called "invented tradition" (Hobsbawm & Ranger, 1983), "staged authenticity" (MacCannell, 1976, p. 91), and "fakelore" (Dorson, 1976). In Beck's (1989a) view, Romanian folk culture under Ceauşescu became a commodity for consumption. In Kligman's (1988) view this was a nationalistic attempt to mystify and exploit the peasant as Other. Accordingly, peasant and worker review boards were set up under Ceauşescu to ensure that Romanian art, theater, and culture were folksy rather than dominated by the artistic intelligentsia (Gilberg, 1989). Codrescu (1991) elaborated:

> Ceauşescu's propaganda had made so much of the "peasant" that his reality was hard to fathom. One of the subtler crimes of nationalist propaganda is to make even the genuine unreal, to turn the world to postcard and caricature. One of the artistic tasks of the future will be to extract the peasant from the pseudopeasant, folk music from "folkloric ensembles," folk art from "popular socialist art." (p. 151)

More generally, what is confused here is the real and the hyperreal.

Coussens (1984) detailed the process of Romanian folklorization in the small Transylvania town of Buciumi-Salaj. She found that this city's singers and musicians not only participated actively in numerous *judeţ* (county) folklore festivals and competitions but also were frequently selected for national radio and television folklore programs. Nevertheless, not only were the selections of songs censored to exclude religious themes and include patriotic songs and praises to Ceauşescu, but only certain elements of folklore (those rewarded by television appearances and state-supported travel) were chosen by villagers for preservation and presentation. Gone are the traditional weavings, furniture, art, and other handicrafts, and in their place are the trappings of an incipient consumer culture:

> Buciumani no longer wear their most elaborate and beautiful costume for the Sunday promenade, but instead display the latest fashions from the local clothing store. There are no more Sunday afternoon dances in the village square. Spontaneous *şezători*—work bees—and evening social gatherings for singing, dancing, storytelling, and discussing the issues of the day give way to television viewing and other less social pursuits. Today's woven goods, still far from urban tastes, are even farther from traditional models, exhibiting bright, cacophonous colors and bold new designs. Icons on glass have been replaced by Italian religious prints or pictures from magazines. Household furnishings and decorations are purchased with an eye to urban styles. Weddings, too show the influx of urban and other regional influences. Modern young couples [marrying] dispense with many local traditions, sport long polyester gowns and suits, and hire a town-bred guitar and drum band. (Coussens, 1984, p. 133)

These trends have accelerated since the revolution as Romanian consumers spurn local clothing and other products in favor of longed-for Western and Japanese goods that represent the ideologies of modernity, consumer culture, and the good life (Drazin, 1994; Ger, Belk, & Lascu, 1993). But the paradox continues as staged celebrations of disappearing folk culture continue to grow in popularity as well. Thus, in these times of uncertainty, Romanians displace meaning into both the mythical past and hypothetical future (McCracken, 1988), with one foot in each, while straddling the more problematic present.

In the face of majority Romanians' use of official historic myths, religion, and folk culture to create and reinforce a sense of national identity, we next consider how Romania's two largest minorities use individual and aggregate consumption patterns to anchor their own ethnic identities. Anthony Smith (1991, p. 21) suggested that an ethnic community ideally shares six main attributes:

1. A collective proper name
2. A myth of common ancestry
3. Shared historical memories
4. One or more differentiating elements of common culture
5. An association with a specific "homeland"
6. A sense of solidarity for significant sectors of the population

We find, however, that the strategies used by Hungarians and Gypsies in Romania are quite different from each other and that both differ from the strategies employed by majority Romanians.

Hungarian-Romanian Ethnicity

LANGUAGE, EDUCATION, AND ETHNIC RELATIONS

In the years following World War II, Romania was one of the most responsive of Eastern European countries in its treatment of ethnic minorities. Hungarians, concentrated in the new Romanian area of Transylvania, were provided an education in Hungarian, an overly representative number of leadership positions, and full rights of Romanian citizenship (King, 1973). Educational opportunities included an excellent Hungarian university in the regional center of Cluj. The Romanian constitution of 1952 created an Autonomous Hungarian Region in Transylvania. Hungarian newspapers were published and

Hungarian inscriptions were put on tombstones. In part, these concessions may have been designed to placate Hungary over the loss of Transylvania. Shortly after the Hungarian revolt was suppressed by the Soviet Union in 1956, conditions also began to deteriorate for Hungarian-Romanians. Education in Hungarian began to be more and more restricted, and the Hungarian language university of Bolyai was merged with the Romanian language university of Babeş to become Babeş-Bolyai University. Hungarians began to be purged from party leadership positions. In 1960 the name of the autonomous region was Romanianized to become the Mureş-Autonomous Hungarian Region (similar changes were made in community, street, and school names). In 1968 the region was eliminated. During the Ceauşescu era (1965-1989), Hungarian cultural institutions were also shut down, and communications with and travel to Hungary were made more difficult (Gallagher, 1992). Not surprisingly, a strong political emphasis on ethnic nationalism does not bode well for ethnic minorities. Ceauşescu forbade public use of Hungarian, publication of newspapers in Hungarian, and Hungarian names for children (Kaplan, 1993). In the 1970s the tension grew so great that opposing camps of foreign anthropologists characterized the Hungarian situation in Romania as one of ethnocide by Romanians (Sozan, 1977, 1979) or chauvinism and irredentism by Hungarians (Romanian Research Group, 1979). On the basis of abuses of civil rights, especially among Hungarian-Romanians, American religious groups and Hungarian-Americans ultimately pressured the U.S. government (in 1988) to force Ceauşescu to renounce the Most Favored Nation status granted to Romania alone in Eastern Europe (in 1975) when he defied the Soviets (see Harrington & Courtney, 1991; Rady, 1992).

Surprisingly, in light of this official suppression of Hungarian ethnicity in Romania, Hungarians and Romanians united in the city of Timoşoara to spark the Romanian revolution. When the Romanian government sought to oust Lazlo Tokes, the Hungarian minister of the Reformed Lutheran church in Timoşoara, he became a symbol of human rights not only for Hungarians but also for Romanians, Germans, Serbs, and Gypsies of the region as well (see Codrescu, 1991). After these groups joined together in the bloodiest revolution in Eastern Europe, there was at least the brief hope that postrevolutionary Romania would be a place of multiculturalism and mutual respect. Initially, there was some evidence that this was occurring in Transylvania when the Hungarian newspaper reappeared, Hungarian language education was reestablished, and the new Romanian government allowed some radio and television broadcasts in Hungarian (Rady, 1992).

But this hope was quickly extinguished when ethnic violence broke out between Hungarians and other Romanians in the Transylvanian city of Tirgu Mureş (formerly known to Hungarians as Marosvasarhely) in March 1990, resulting in hundreds wounded and, according to some reports, eight deaths (Gallagher, 1992). The violence against Hungarians was orchestrated by members of *Uniunea Vatra Românească* (Romanian Hearth Union), which had been organized in opposition to the demands of Romania's ethnic minorities and swiftly rose to power following the revolution. Although a rival group, the Democratic Alliance of Hungarians in Romania (HUDR) has moved for Hungarian rights, including the reestablishment of an independent Hungarian language university in Cluj and mandatory bilingualism in Transylvania, these demands have only fueled the nationalist fervor of Romanians who see Transylvania as the cradle of Romania. Instead, names of schools and streets that still remained Hungarian have been Romanianized in Cluj since the revolution. With Hungarians constituting only 30% of the population in Cluj and only 20% in all of Transylvania, Hungarian candidates lost the autumn 1992 elections, and ethnic tensions appear certain to continue.

SENSE OF PLACE AND RELIGION

Hungarians are traditionally most heavily concentrated in urban areas of Transylvania, although this is the first generation in which other Romanians are slightly more urban than rural (Illyés, 1982). Hungarians, accordingly, stereotype other Romanians as peasants. An important part of ethnic identity, especially critical to Hungarian-Romanians, is having a sense of place. As such, the systematization program of Ceauşescu was seen as an attempt to deprive Hungarians of their roots in Transylvania and to disperse them so that they would be less than 10% of the population (their percentage of the total Romanian population is approximately 10%). But the systematization program threatened the rural roots of the Romanians as well. The plan, only partially carried out, was to reduce the number of villages in Romania from over 13,000 in 1985 to fewer than 6,000 in the year 2000 (Beck, 1991). Villages would be destroyed and reclaimed for communal farmland, and villagers would be moved to cities in which factory workers were needed. The threat from this plan thus struck at non-Hungarians as well and was an important factor precipitating the Romanian revolution. With the end of the systematization program following the revolution, Romanians have gained security in their sense of place, whereas Hungarians have gained assurance only that they can remain as Romanians in Transylvania. Because Hungary is currently refusing would-be emigrants from Romania, the Transylvanian Hungarians remain in limbo between two groups who do not want them.

A key consumption area that has provided a sense of Hungarian ethnic identity and continuity in Romania has been religion. Although the Romanian Orthodox religion is overwhelmingly non-Hungarian, the Roman Catholic Church, Reformed (Calvinist) church, Unitarians, and several other Protestant churches are overwhelmingly Hungarian and German (Hale, 1971; Illyés, 1982; Shafir, 1985). Although these churches were not actively encouraged (e.g., prayer books were allowed to be printed but only in limited numbers and with censorship) before the revolution, they were and remain officially recognized, and priests and ministers are paid by the state Department of Religious Affairs. Because key ritual events that help structure Hungarian life are performed in these churches, including baptisms, confirmations, and weddings (after state weddings have been performed first), they have been a critical element in sustaining Hungarian identity. Although all of these churches share a common Christianity with the Romanian Orthodox church, most of their important holidays (including Christmas and Easter) occur at slightly different times (see Verdery, 1983). Certain differences also exist in Orthodox Saint Days and weekly *zile de post* (days of fasting), which also serve as ethnic markers. In some parts of Transylvania, when Orthodox people encounter one another on the street, religious greetings such as "Praise Jesus" (*Laude-se Isus*) are used (see Kligman, 1988), but this is a greeting that does not necessarily exclude Hungarians. These greetings *were* used to exclude Jews in the highly anti-Semitic period preceding World War II in Romania (Jews are now almost totally absent in Transylvania). On the other hand, the seasonal greetings used during the Orthodox Easter do exclude Hungarians, except for the one year in seven when the ritual calendars of Orthodox and non-Orthodox churches coincide. Thus, in various ways, large and small, religion serves both as an anchor for ethnic identity among Romania's Hungarians and as a vehicle of exclusion for Orthodox Romanians. Without religious differences, ethnic differences almost certainly would be less distinct.

CLASS AND INDIVIDUAL CONSUMPTION

Hungarian ethnicity is associated with a number of other differences in Romania: values, behaviors, wealth, and even personality traits. Verdery (1983) explained:

"Being" a Romanian peasant meant many things, which tended to hang together over time. It meant large amounts of diminishing returns to one's labor, frequent sharecropping and some stealing, clever stratagems for getting by, celebrating saints' days, speaking Romanian mostly, worrying about hospitality to guests, preferring cattle, valuing sociability and good times, mourning one's dead properly—and it meant these and other things, year in and year out, in constant juxtaposition with clearly alternative ways of being that were not Romanian. There was "being" Magyar which meant (from the Romanian point of view) being quick-tempered and ready to take offense (and raise an insurrection), being belligerent, civilized but arrogant and cruel, dressing finely, drinking heavily and gambling, speaking Magyar, being Catholic or Calvinist. What Romanian could seriously admire most of that? . . . Being Romanian has also meant centuries of being survivors, principally by mechanisms other than overt conflict. . . . Germans and Magyars are disdainful of this approach, which they view as cowardly. Easy for them to say, having always had some degree of access to opportunity, to history, and to power. (pp. 389-390)

There are a variety of differences in clothing, music, food, and drink that both express and codify such differences. Traditional Hungarian foods are not the same as traditional Romanian foods. Hungarian language or Hungarian-dubbed videotapes are beginning to become common. Although Romanians eat *mamaliga, mititei,* and *sarmale,* Hungarians eat *tokány, gulyás,* and *paprikash.* Even though both cultures drink a clear brandy, there is a distinct ethnic difference between preferences for Romanian *țuica* and Hungarian *palinka.* Hungarians in Transylvania prefer filtered coffee to the thick Turkish coffee found elsewhere in Romania. And there is also often an insistence on the Hungarian name for things. For instance, a Hungarian clerk in a Cluj bakery was found to refuse to understand the word for bread until it was spoken in Hungarian.

There is also an inescapable sense that physically and economically the Hungarian (and German) areas of Romania are more similar to Western Europe than other parts of the country. There are more shops with a greater number of goods, more foreign goods, better preserved public buildings, more and larger free-standing houses, and cities and villages that are free enough of the drab communist apartment blocs that they might be mistaken for being in Western Europe. Service is more courteous and attentive in shops, restaurants, transportation, and other services compared with other parts of Romania. Innovations such as commercial film processing, supermarkets, new restaurant cuisines, new clothing styles, and foreign music, clothing, and automobiles tend to be visible in Cluj, Sibiu, and Timoşoara before they appear in Bucureşti, Galaţi, or Craiova. To some degree these differences are historical and geographical (given proximities to Western Europe), but more than this is involved. The traditional associations noted earlier (Beck, 1986) of Hungarian nobles, Romanian peasants, and Gypsy slaves continue to echo through daily life. Just as ethnicity is related to religion and geographic region, it is also related to the historical and reemerging class structure in Romania.

Gypsy-Romanian Ethnicity

HATRED OF GYPSIES

Not only in Romania, where they are found in greatest numbers, but also throughout Europe, Gypsies are the focus of consistent disdain and hatred. Non-Gypsy Romanians commonly revile Gypsies as lazy, dishonest, unscrupulous, immoral, loud, violent, uneducated, and above all, dirty. They are seen as nomadic beggars, thieves, black marketeers, entertainers, and producers and sellers of cheap and shoddy crafts. They are regarded as unwilling to conform, settle down, and work for a living. Stereotypes are a socially constructed consensus that often project personal fears of inadequacy onto another group with distinctive physical or material characteristics. The kernel of truth hypothesis (Campbell, 1967), however, suggests that the generalized stereotype of such a group is built around an exaggeration of traits that do in fact distinguish a minority group, at least as seen through the eyes of the dominant culture. We shall therefore consider the possibility that much or all of this stereotype may be based on a grain of "truth" (when seen from the cultural frame of Romanian values) and shall try to understand the actual characteristics that distinguish Gypsies, especially in the realm of consumption. By approaching these stereotypes from the point of view of both non-Gypsies and Gypsies, we hope to understand something of the bases for hatred between the two groups.

Gypsies in Romania, despite being in all likelihood the largest ethnic minority group, are not officially recognized as such. As Beck (1989a) summarized the situation:

> Romania has denied a distinctive Gypsy presence in the country and hence has disavowed a Gypsy role in Romanian state formation. Gypsies are perceived by officials and the population at large as outsiders of those people who are cultured or civilized. In other words, Gypsies are underestimated, devalued, peripheralized and ultimately invalidated. Such values can be understood in a context that has crystallized the socialist Romanian

state's efforts to generate a hegemonic Romanian culture and social relations, what ethnic minorities refer to as "Romanianization." (p. 4)

Since the revolution, the Romanian government has curried the favor
of Gypsy voters, but Gypsies clearly remain outside the mainstream.
They are notably absent from higher education and are poorly represented in lower grades. They have poor health, little land, and almost
no representation in government (Petreanu, 1993). Although there are
some prominent exceptions to these generalizations, it is clear that
whether by choice, exclusion, or both, Gypsies in Romania are a disen-
franchised group. If anything, hatred of Gypsies has increased since the
revolution. Verdery (1992) explained this trend as a result of the introduction of capitalism:

> Gypsies, long stereotyped as lazy and thieving, are now reviled either
> for not working (they are lazy, they steal), or for doing petty commerce.
> Under socialism, of course, *no-one* worked hard, and everyone stole; now,
> inflation increasingly drives people to hold two or even three jobs—and to
> be enraged at the thought that "lazy" Gypsies continue to live by "theft."
> As for the Gypsies' putative role in petty commerce—itself a form of theft—
> to it is attributed scarcities of goods and the terrible inflation of prices.
> Both these images of Gypsies obviously relate to market reform. (p. 9)

Since 1989, group violence against Gypsies has broken out in more
than a dozen different locations. In June 1990, thousands of hard-hatted
uniformed miners came to Bucharești and proceeded to use pipes and
sticks to pummel students, foreigners, and anyone who looked at all
radical (by sporting a beard, for instance). Following these battles, they
proceeded to the Gypsy parts of the city where they ransacked homes
and beat any dark-skinned "Gypsy-looking" people they encountered
(Gheorghe, 1991). Also in 1990, in the village of Mihail Kogalniceanu
near the city of Constanța on the Black Sea, a mob of 1,000 burned 30
Gypsy homes (Ingram, 1992). In 1992 in the small village of Valeni la
Posului, about 250 miles north of Bucharești, Gypsies were burned out
of their homes by 200 angry townspeople. In other areas Gypsies have
been killed by angry Romanians acting on rumors of Gypsy crimes
and taking out years of frustration and bitterness. Even when actions
are not this violent, acts of hatred against Gypsies have been increasing. Nor is Romania alone in this regard, as Ingram (1991) found in
Hungary: "The new freedom of speech in Eastern Europe has, unfortunately, brought with it the liberty to express hatreds openly. Anti-
Gypsy discrimination in jobs, education, and housing is a fact of life"

(p. 17).[1] Gypsies who have recently fled to Germany have met similar treatment (Kinzer, 1992), and about 40,000 a month are sent back to Romania (Ingram, 1992).

GYPSY CONSUMPTION PATTERNS
AS RESISTANCE AND SURVIVAL

Gypsies are regarded by other Romanians as foreign and unassimilable (Beck, 1989a). But for many Gypsies themselves, it is clear that they "don't want in" (Gmelch, 1986, p. 307). Nowhere is this clearer than in their consumption patterns. One evidence is the sizeable portion of Romania's Gypsies who prefer a nomadic existence to the ties of a permanent residence. As Gheorghe (1991) pointed out, throughout formerly communist Eastern and Central Europe, communities are attempting to eject Gypsies whom the state settled there in an effort to end their nomadicism. Thus, as has been true for hundreds of years, becoming nomadic is a means both of rejecting the majority system and of keeping alive by seeking new geographic and economic niches. Such a lifestyle further restricts educational and occupational possibilities, further marginalizes and impoverishes Gypsies, and makes deviant behaviors more necessary for survival as well as more likely as an outlet for frustrations.

It might be thought that under such circumstances, combined with hatred and opprobrium from other Romanians, Gypsies would suffer low self-esteem and even self-hatred. But as Oliner and Hallum (1978) found, Gypsies instead band together and offer communal support to other Gypsies. Furthermore, rather than keep a low profile and accept the feelings of inferiority that the dominant culture attempts to assign them, Gypsies instead flaunt their differences, cling tenaciously to their ethnic identity, and castigate the non-Gypsy oppressor as *gadjo*—a term that has connotations of rube, hick, yokel, peasant, and bumpkin. By dehumanizing the dominant culture in this way, not only is dignity preserved among Gypsies, but crimes against non-Gypsies take on different meanings, as Oliner and Hallum (1978) explained:

> Respect for *gadjo* property was not part of the *Romani* [Gypsies]. Indeed economic exploitation of the *gadjo* was commendable. Stealing from the *gadjo* was thus sanctioned, although such theft was restricted to subsistence needs and not for the accumulation of possession [according to the oral code of Gypsy justice of *Kris*]. . . . To take advantage of the *gadjo* successfully was simply a manifestation of Gypsy superiority and was a large part of Gypsy life. It included both the theft of products for their needs

(such as horses, firewood, a "stray" chicken, or vegetables), as well as "fortune telling" and the enactment of shrewd bargains. (pp. 51-52)

Other ways in which Gypsies resist the derision and claims of superiority of majority Romanians include a language that is unwritten and forbidden to teach to *gadjos*, elaborate jewelry, a fondness for gold-capped teeth, distinctive hats for men, and, for women, long braids, scarves, and brightly colored highly distinctive dresses. As Gmelch (1986) found in Spain, "In contrast to the neat and somber dress and rather reserved behavior of the people around them, [Gypsies] wear vividly colored clothing; their dress and hair styles are careless; and their body movements and deportment are characterized by boldness, loudness, spontaneity, and violations of street etiquette" (p. 323).

Gypsies are also prone to be conspicuous consumers in restaurants, bars, and automobile purchases, in comparison to majority Romanians. Their dress characteristics and manners are especially galling to the conservative and style-conscious Romanians (see Drazin, 1994). The two ethnic styles of dress are probably interdependent, as Romanians who are anxious to "elevate" their ethnic identity (especially the darker skinned Romanians of the Oltanea region who might be mistaken for Gypsies) no doubt seek to counterposition themselves from Gypsies through their clothing, music, and manners. Thus, Gypsy music, arts, crafts, and vendor merchandise are disparaged as kitsch.

Nevertheless, Gypsies specialize in being musicians and provide much of the music at Romanian wedding celebrations and funerals (see Beck, 1989b). In fact, the Lăutari are male Gypsy singers who have for centuries performed and preserved traditional Romanian poems, songs, and dance music, especially classic Romanian epic songs and ballads (Beissinger, 1991). Furthermore, the black market activities of Gypsies before the revolution have since been transformed into small shops and stalls selling clothing, small electronics, cosmetics, imported alcohol, cigarettes, musical tapes, used goods, and other hard-to-find products. As is traditionally true, Gypsies survive by cleverness in adaptation, by finding viable economic niches. Although Gypsies and Romanians dislike and distrust each other, they thus need and rely on each other.

GYPSIES AND POLLUTION

As noted earlier, the near-universal criticism of Gypsies in Romania is that they are "dirty." Other Romanians are apt to cite as evidence of their "dirtiness" and "uncivilized" character instances of Gypsies bringing their horses up several flights of stairs and into their apartments; lower strata Gypsy vendors and jewelers often sitting on the ground with their sunflower seeds, flowers, rings, cigarettes, and other wares they offer for sale spread on a towel on the sidewalk or directly on the dirt; and Gypsy beggars sitting or crawling on the streets, in train stations, and in front of retail shops. Such occurrences, together with their marginal status in Romanian society, lead to the label "dirty." As Frykman and Löfgren (1979/1987) argued, however, the label "dirty" is most often a *moral* judgment. Orwell (1937) called such labels

> the real secret of class distinctions in the west. . . . [No] feeling of like or dislike is quite so fundamental as a *physical* feeling. Race-hatred, religious hatred, differences of education, of temperament, of intellect, even differences of moral code, can be got over; but physical repulsion cannot. . . . It may not greatly matter if the average middle class person is brought up to believe that the working classes are ignorant, lazy, drunken, boorish and dishonest; it is when he is brought up to believe that they are dirty that the harm is done. (pp. 159-160)

In Douglas's (1966) terms, "dirt" is symbolic pollution of cultural values; it is "matter out of place" (p. 40). In this respect, the flamboyant Gypsy is clearly out of place in conformist Romanian society. Controlled as slaves until the mid-19th century, Gypsies had a place in Romanian society (Crowe, 1991). But as free men and women, Gypsies clearly do not fit. Flaunting their differences from other Romanians merely reinforces their societal pollution in the eyes of the dominant group.

Ironically, to Gypsies it is the *gadjo* who are dirty and polluting (Okely, 1983; Oliner & Hallum, 1978). According to the Gypsy concept of *marime*, pollution and defilement come from taking inside (the home, as well as the body) that which is dirty and belongs outside or to the lower stratum of the body in particular. This is sacrilege. Thus, Gypsies keep separate bowls and towels for washing the hands (because hands bring food into the body), clothes, and cooking utensils. To mix them is seen as highly polluting. Doing laundry, urinating, and defecating are all done outside the home if at all possible. Cats are not allowed in the house because they are unclean by virtue of burying their feces with their paws. To make matters worse, they potentially ingest their fur (dirtying the inner body) by licking their paws. Horses, on the other hand, do not lick themselves, symbolize freedom and mobility, and even filter water with their teeth in drinking it. Thus, they are considered perfectly clean. *Gadjos* are unclean in Gypsy beliefs but are all the more impure when they allow their pets to lick them, do their toilet and laundry inside, and wash their hands and their dishes in the same sink. Accordingly, contact with *gadjos* is kept to a minimum. For the Gypsy, it is the inner self that must be kept ritually pure, whereas the outer public self is a protection from impurity.

Summary and Conclusions

The preceding analysis suggests that consumption differences help to define and demonstrate minority and majority ethnicity in Romania. Ethnicity is an issue of special importance to majority Romanians and Hungarian-Romanians because of missing history that affects Hungarian claims to Transylvania and Romanian claims to a long and proud tradition inherited from Dacians and Romans. For majority Romanians, Gypsies are to blame for social ills and are the key group from which they wish to distinguish themselves. For this majority, Gypsies are "dirty" and "thieving," whereas for Gypsies it is the majority non-Gypsies who are contaminated and who are foolish oppressors who deserve any mischief that can be done to them in the interests of Gypsy survival.

Ethnic identity for majority Romanians is encoded chiefly through language, history, folklore, and appearance. This has been emphasized in commodified and packaged revivals of folk dance, music, songs, and costumes, mobilized by Romanian leaders to stir feelings of nationalism and patriotism for their political advantage. Religion, museums, and education are other key group ritual contexts of consumption in which these ethnic competitions are constructed and played out. It is not surprising that again the dominant culture has the upper hand in these aggregate spheres of consumption. In popular culture, the dominant group's control is less complete. For example, lower and middle-class Romanians are fond of both Gypsy and (recently) Turkish music. More affluent non-Hungarian Romanians in Transylvania look to Hungarians there as fashion opinion leaders. But in many foods, clothes, grooming styles, housing, and other visible expenditures, there remain significant differences between all three groups.

As Douglas and Isherwood (1978) have pointed out, consumer goods often become markers that form boundaries between groups. The present investigation has found that both public and private consumer goods can be a contested field on which symbolic battles of aggregate extended self are waged over conflicting ethnic values, national heritage claims, and status claims. Romania is certainly not unique in staging such battles or in using consumer goods as differentiating markers. It does, however, offer a vivid case of majority and minority ethnic groups using such goods to uphold feelings of ethnic identity, national continuity, and personal integrity. In all of these cases, for both minority and majority ethnic groups in Romania, consumption patterns ennoble individual sense of self, establish and preserve aggregate sense of past, and offer a means for achieving dignity. Although this is all well and good in a truly multicultural society, across groups within Romania these same patterns of consumption difference facilitate and perpetuate ethnic hatreds, violence, and discrimination.

Note

1. Reprinted by permission of *Ms.* Magazine, © 1991.

References

Askegaard, S. (1991). Toward a semiotic structure of cultural identity. In H. H. Larsen, D. G. Mick, & C. Alsted (Eds.), *Marketing and semiotics: Selected papers from the Copenhagen Symposium* (pp. 11-30). Copenhagen: Handelshøjskolens Forlag.

Barth, F. (1969). Introduction. In F. Barth (Ed.), *Ethnic groups and boundaries: The social organization of culture difference* (pp. 9-38). Boston: Little, Brown.

Beck, S. (1986). Indigenous anthropologists in socialist Romania. *Dialectical Anthropology, 10*(2), 265-274.

Beck, S. (1989a). Ethnic identity as contested terrain. *Dialectical Anthropology, 14*(1), 1-6.

Beck, S. (1989b). The origins of Gypsy slavery in Romania. *Dialectical Anthropology, 14*(1), 53-61.

Beck, S. (1991). What brought Romanians to revolt. *Critique of Anthropology, 11*(1), 7-31.

Beck, S. (1993). The struggle for space and the development of civil society in Romania, June 1990. In H. G. De Soto & D. G. Anderson (Eds.), *The curtain rises: Rethinking culture, ideology, and the state in Eastern Europe* (pp. 232-265). Atlantic Highlands, NJ: Humanities Press.

Behr, E. (1991). *Kiss the hand you cannot bite: The rise and fall of the Ceauşescus.* New York: Villard.

Beissinger, M. H. (1991). *The art of the Lăutar: The epic tradition of Romania.* New York: Garland.

Belk, R. W. (1988). Possessions and the extended self. *Journal of Consumer Research, 15*, 139-168.

Belk, R. W. (1992). Moving possessions: An analysis based on personal documents from the 1847-1869 Mormon migration. *Journal of Consumer Research, 19*, 339-361.

Belk, R. W. (1993). *Daily consumer life in Romania* (Working paper). Salt Lake City: University of Utah, David Eccles School of Business.

Benedict, R. (1953). History as it appears to the Rumanians. In M. Mead & R. Metraux (Eds.), *The study of culture at a distance* (pp. 405-415). Chicago: University of Chicago Press.

Bih, H.-D. (1992). The meaning of objects in environmental transactions: Experiences of Chinese students in the United States. *Journal of Environmental Psychology, 12,* 135-147.

Binns, C. A. P. (1980). The changing face of power: Revolution and accommodation in the development of the Soviet ceremonial system, Part II. *Man, 15,* 170-187.

Breuer, M. (1982). Orthodox Judaism in Eastern and Western Europe. In D. Kerr (Ed.), *Religion, state, and ethnic groups: Comparative studies on governments and non-dominant ethnic groups in Europe, 1850-1940* (Vol. 2, pp. 79-93). Hants, UK: Dartmouth.

Bringa, T. R. (1993). National categories, national identification and identity formation in "multinational" Bosnia. *Anthropology of East Europe Review, 11,* 69-76.

Burke, P. (1992). We, the people: Popular culture and popular identity in modern Europe. In S. Lash & J. Friedman (Eds.), *Modernity and identity* (pp. 293-308). Oxford, UK: Basil Blackwell.

Campeanu, P. (1991). National fervor in Eastern Europe: The case of Romania. *Social Research, 58,* 805-828.

Campbell, D. T. (1967). Stereotypes and the perception of group differences. *American Psychologist, 22,* 817-829.

Castellan, G. (1989). *A history of the Romanians* (N. Bradley, Trans.). Boulder, CO: East European Monographs.

Cawelti, J. G. (1990). Symbols of ethnicity and popular culture. In R. B. Browne, M. W. Fishwick, & K. O. Browne (Eds.), *Dominant symbols in popular culture* (pp. 83-95). Bowling Green, OH: Bowling Green State University Popular Press.

Clark, L. (1987). Gravestones: Reflectors of ethnicity or class? In S. M. Spencer-Wood (Ed.), *Consumer choice in historical archaeology* (pp. 383-395). New York: Plenum.

Codrescu, A. (1991). *The hole in the flag: A Romanian exile's story of return and revolution.* New York: William Morrow.

Coussens, R. (1984). Folk culture as symbol in contemporary Romania. In J. W. Cole (Ed.), *Economy, society and culture in contemporary Romania* (Research Report No. 24, pp. 129-138). Amherst: University of Massachusetts, Department of Anthropology.

Crowe, D. (1991). The Gypsy historical experience in Romania. In D. Crowe & J. Kolsti (Eds.), *The Gypsies of Eastern Europe* (pp. 61-79). Armonk, NY: Sharpe.

Dorson, R. M. (1976). *Folklore and fakelore: Essays toward a discipline of folk studies.* Cambridge, MA: Harvard University Press.

Douglas, M. (1966). *Purity and danger: An analysis of concepts of pollution and taboo.* London: Routledge & Kegan Paul.

Douglas, M., & Isherwood, B. (1978). *The world of goods: Towards an anthropology of consumption.* New York: Norton.

Drazin, A. (1994). Changing appearances in Romania. In C. Shultz, R. W. Belk, & G. Ger (Eds.), *Consumption in marketizing economies* (pp. 57-88). Greenwich, CT: JAI.

Fisher-Galați, S. (1981). Myths in Romanian history. *East European Quarterly, 15*(3), 327-334.

Fraser, A. (1992). *The Gypsies.* Oxford, UK: Blackwell.

Frykman, J., & Löfgren, O. (1979/1987). *Culture builders: A historical anthropology of middle-class life* (A. Crozier, Trans.). New Brunswick, NJ: Rutgers University Press.

Gallagher, T. (1992). *Vatra Românească* and resurgent nationalism in Romania. *Ethnic and Racial Studies, 15,* 570-598.

206 CASE STUDIES AND APPLICATIONS

Ger, G., Belk, R. W., Lascu, D.-N. (1993). The development of consumer desire in marketizing economies: The cases of Romania and Turkey. In L. McAlister & M. L. Rothschild (Eds.), *Advances in consumer research* (Vol. 20, pp. 102-107). Provo, UT: Association for Consumer Research.

Gheorghe, N. (1991). Roma-Gypsy ethnicity in Eastern Europe. *Social Research, 58,* 829-844.

Gilberg, T. (1989). Religion and nationalism in Romania. In P. Ramet (Ed.), *Religion and nationalism in Soviet and East European politics* (pp. 328-351). Durham, NC: Duke University Press.

Gilberg, T. (1990). *Nationalism and communism in Romania.* Boulder, CO: Westview.

Gmelch, S. B. (1986). Groups that don't want in: Gypsies and other artisan, trader, and entertainer minorities. *Annual Review of Anthropology, 15,* 307-330.

Hale, J. (1971). *Ceauşescu's Romania: A political documentary.* London: George G. Harrap.

Hancock, I. (1991). The East European roots of Romani nationalism. In D. Crowe & J. Kolsti (Eds.), *The Gypsies of Eastern Europe* (pp. 133-150). Armonk, NY: Sharpe.

Harrington, J. F., & Courtney, B. J. (1991). *Tweaking the nose of the Russians: Fifty years of American-Romanian relations: 1940-1990.* Boulder, CO: East European Monographs.

Heinze, A. R. (1990). *Adapting to abundance: Jewish immigrants, mass consumption, and the search for American identity.* New York: Columbia University Press.

Hitchins, K. (1992). Historiography of the countries of Eastern Europe: Romania. *American Historical Review, 97,* 1064-1083.

Hobsbawm, E. (1992). Ethnicity and nationalism in Europe today. *Anthropology Today, 8*(6), 3-8.

Hobsbawm, E., & Ranger, T. (Eds). (1983). *The invention of tradition.* Cambridge, UK: Cambridge University Press.

Horne, D. (1984). *The great museum: The re-presentation of history.* London: Pluto.

Illyés, E. (1982). *National minorities in Romania: Change in Transylvania.* Boulder, CO: East European Monographs.

Ingram, J. (1991, September/October). Hungary's Gypsy women: Scapegoats in a new democracy. *Ms.,* p. 17.

Ingram, J. (1992, October 18). At last a helping hand for Romanian Gypsies. *New York Times,* p. I5.

Joy, A., & Dholakia, R. R. (1991). Remembrances of things past: The meanings of home and possessions of Indian professionals in Canada. In F. W. Rudmin (Ed.), *To have possessions: A handbook of ownership and property* [Special issue]. *Journal of Social Behavior and Personality, 6*(6), 385-402.

Kaplan, R. D. (1993). *Balkan ghosts: A journey through history.* New York: St. Martin's.

Karnoouh, C. (1982). National unity in Central Europe: The state, peasant folklore, and mono-ethnism. *Telos, 53,* 95-105.

Kerr, D. (1992). Religion, state and ethnic identity. In D. Kerr (Ed.), *Religion, state, and ethnic groups: Comparative studies on governments and non-dominant ethnic groups in Europe, 1850-1940* (Vol. 2, pp. 1-26). Hants, UK: Dartmouth.

Kideckel, D. A. (1988). Economic images and social change in Romanian socialist transformation. *Dialectical Anthropology, 12*(3), 399-411.

King, R. R. (1973). *Minorities under communism: Nationalities as a source of tension among Balkan communist states.* Cambridge, MA: Harvard University Press.

Kinzer, S. (1992, September 27). Germany cracks down: Gypsies come first. *New York Times,* p. H5.

Kligman, G. (1988). *The wedding of the dead: Ritual, poetics, and popular culture in Transylvania.* Berkeley: University of California Press.

Kurti, L. (1989). Transylvania, land beyond reason: Toward an anthropological analysis of a contested terrain. *Dialectical Anthropology, 14*(1), 21-52.

Lane, C. (1981). *The rites of rulers: Ritual in industrial society—The Soviet case.* Cambridge, UK: Cambridge University Press.

Levenstein, H. A., & J. R. Conlin (1990). The food habits of Italian immigrants to America: An examination of the persistence of a food culture and the rise of "fast food" in America. In R. B. Browne, M. W. Fishwick, & K. O. Browne (Eds.), *Dominant symbols in popular culture* (pp. 231-246). Bowling Green, OH: Bowling Green State University Popular Press.

Ludanyi, A. (1983). Ideology and political culture in Rumania: The Daco-Roman theory and the "place" of minorities. In J. F. Cadzow, A. Ludanyi, & L. J. Elteto (Eds.), *Transylvania: The roots of ethnic conflict* (pp. 229-288). Kent, OH: Kent State University Press.

MacCannell, D. (1976). *The tourist: A new theory of the leisure class.* New York: Schocken.

Matz, M. (1961). The meaning of the Christmas tree to the American Jew. *Jewish Journal of Sociology, 3*(1), 129-137.

McCracken, G. (1988). *Culture and consumption: New approaches to the symbolic character of consumer goods and activities.* Bloomington: University of Indiana Press.

Mehta, R., & Belk, R. W. (1991). Artifacts, identity, and transition: Favorite possessions of Indians and Indian immigrants to the United States. *Journal of Consumer Research, 17,* 398-411.

Meyer, R. E. (Ed.). (1993). *Ethnicity and the American cemetery.* Bowling Green, OH: Bowling Green University Popular Press.

Okely, J. (1983). Why Gypsies hate cats but love horses. *New Society, 63*(1057), 261-263.

Oliner, S. P., & Hallum, K. (1978). Minority contempt for oppressors: A comparative analysis of Jews and Gypsies. *California Sociologist, 1*(1), 41-57.

Orwell, G. (1937). *The road to Wigan Pier.* London: Victor Gollanez.

Pascu, Ş. (1982). *A history of Transylvania* (D. R. Ladd, Trans.). New York: Dorset. (Original work published 1972 & 1979 as *Voievodatul Transilvaniei* [2 vols.], Cluj: Cluj Editura Dacia)

Petreanu, D. (1993, June 6). Gypsies live on fringes of society: Romania's community on brink of disaster. *Salt Lake Tribune,* pp. A10-A11.

Plascencia, L.F.B. (1985). Low riding in the Southwest: Cultural symbols of the Mexican community. In M. T. García, F. Lomelí, M. L. Barbera, E. Escoba, & J. García (Eds.), *History, culture, and society: Chicano studies in the 1980s* (pp. 141-175). Ypsilanti, MI: Bilingual Press.

Rady, M. (1992). *Romania in turmoil: A contemporary history.* London: I. B. Tauris.

Reineck, J. (1993). Seizing the past, forging the present: Changing visions of self and nation among the Kosova Albanians. *Anthropology of East Europe Review, 11,* 85-92.

Romanian Research Group (1979). On Transylvanian ethnicity. *Current Anthropology, 20,* 135-140.

Rook, D. W. (1985). The ritual dimension of consumer behavior. *Journal of Consumer Research, 12,* 251-264.

Salo, M. (1982). Introduction [Special issue on Gypsies]. *Urban Anthropology, 11,* 265-272.

Schmidt, L. E. (1991). The commercialization of the calendar: American holidays and the culture of consumption, 1870-1930. *Journal of American History, 78,* 887-916.

Shafir, M. (1985). *Romania: Politics, economics and society: Political stagnation and simulated change.* London: Frances Pinter.

Smith, A. D. (1991). *National identity.* Reno: University of Nevada Press.

Sozan, M. (1977). Ethnocide in Romania. *Current Anthropology, 18,* 781-782.

Sozan, M. (1979). Reply. *Current Anthropology, 20,* 140-148.
Verdery, K. (1983). *Transylvanian villagers: Three centuries of political, economic, and ethnic change.* Berkeley: University of California Press.
Verdery, K. (1988). Ethnicity as culture: Some Soviet-American contrasts. *Canadian Review of Studies in Nationalism, 15*(1-2), 107-110.
Verdery, K. (1991). *National ideology under socialism: Identity and cultural politics in Ceauşescu's Romania.* Berkeley: University of California Press.
Verdery, K. (1992). Comment: Hobsbawm in the East. *Anthropology Today, 8,* 8-10.
Wallendorf, M., & Reilly, M. D. (1983). Ethnic migration, assimilation and consumption. *Journal of Consumer Research, 10,* 292-302.

8

McDöner:
Döner Kebap and the Social
Positioning Struggle of German Turks

AYSE S. CAGLAR

Döner kebap is a fast food introduced and incorporated into the German market by Turkish migrants living in the Federal Republic of Germany (FRG). Although *döner* (in the form offered in Germany) is itself a new and hybrid product that developed through Turks' migration experience in Germany, it became *the* traditional ethnic food of Turks in the eyes of the Germans. Nothing else is as often quoted as *döner kebap* to refer to the positive effects of Turks' presence in Germany. Indeed it functions as a positive symbol in multiculturalist discourses, in contrast to the scarf worn by Turkish girls and women, which has become mainly a negative symbol in discourses concerning the lack of integration of German Turks.

Today around 1.8 million Turkish migrants live in the FRG. These migrants, recruited within the guest worker system designed to serve the labor needs of the host society, came to Germany after the first

AUTHOR'S NOTE: I would like to thank Gary Bamossy, Georg Elwert, and the two anonymous readers for their comments on an earlier version of this chapter. Of course, the final responsibility for the contents of the present work is mine alone.

209

bilateral agreement signed between Germany and Turkey in 1961. Since then they have been living in Germany and are economically well integrated into the society. During this 30-year period, these guest workers have become internally stratified, so that they are now present in almost all levels of German society. The 35,000 Turkish businesses run by German Turks have an investment figure of 7.2 billion German marks. Their turnover per annum is around 25 billion German marks (Zentrum für Türkeistudien, 1992, p. 2). As many as 87% of these Turkish businesses are active in food and catering (Şen, 1988), with the majority being owners of *döner Imbiss* stands (small fast-food stalls or snack bar restaurants offering *döner*).

Berlin, with its 140,000 Turkish residents, has the largest Turkish population of any German city. It is often called the largest Turkish city outside Turkey. Moreover, it has a very active and lively Turkish business life, with more than 6,000 Turkish business places. Today, due to *döner Imbiss* stands (over 800) abounding in its streets and to the 40 to 50 tons of *döner* produced daily, Berlin has come to be known as the *döner* center, *döner Metropole,* or *döner* paradise of Germany.[1]

Döner means "revolving" (*Redhouse Turkish-English Dictionary,* 1984, p. 311). *Kebap,* an Arabic word, is a generic term used for roasted or broiled meat. Thus, *döner kebap* means "meat roasted on a revolving vertical spit" (*Redhouse Turkish-English Dictionary,* 1984, p. 311). *Döner kebap* in Germany, referred to as *döner* or, interchangeably, *kebap,* is a "sandwich" of roasted spicy meat slices prepared in a quarter or one fifth of a Turkish flat bread (*pide*), garnished, depending on taste, with a combination of different sorts of salad (lettuce, tomatoes, cucumbers, red cabbage, onions) and topped with a choice of garlic yogurt or hot ketchup-like dressing.

Döner was introduced to Germany by Turkish migrants. Nevertheless, although produced and sold mostly by Turks and known as a Turkish food in Germany, *döner kebap* in the previously mentioned form is not available in Turkey. In Turkey, until the 1960s, *döner* was offered only as a main dish in restaurants (especially in specialized restaurants known as *kebapci*). With the rapid urbanization and the spread of fast food in the 1960s, *döner* appeared in the major cities of Turkey as a fast-food variety. The roasted meat slices, garnished with a pickle and sometimes with ketchup, would be sold in a sandwich bread or in a quarter of a loaf of bread. In this form, however, it never became, and still is not, as popular a fast food in Turkey as *döner kebap* is in Germany.

Since its appearance in the German fast-food market, *döner* consumption in Germany, particularly in Berlin, has showed a steady increase.

Today, *döner kebap* is firmly established in the German fast-food market. In 1992 the daily *döner* production was estimated by the producers to be a minimum of 40 tons for Berlin and 70 tons for Germany. Given that each *döner kebap* contains 80 to 90 grams of *döner* meat, this figure means production and consumption of 780,000 portions of *döner kebap* daily. This gradual incorporation of *döner kebap* into the fast-food diet of Germans was never accompanied by advertising campaigns targeting German customers, however.[2] Other than one or two advertisements (in German) in public places, *döner* trade is still thriving without advertisements.[3]

In the early 1990s, the market for *döner kebap* was expanding, and *döner* as an ethnic fast food was having its heyday. Nevertheless, signs of change in the marketing strategy of *döner kebap* were appearing. More and more Turkish *döner Imbiss* stands started to offer their "regular" ordinary *döner kebap* under names such as "McKebap," "Keb'up," "Mac's Döner," and so forth. An effort to underplay *döner's* ethnic connotations became apparent in these marketing efforts. It is difficult to explain this change solely in terms of economic forces because, at the time of this change, *döner* was selling better than ever as an ethnic fast food.

With its introduction into German society, this new food item took on novel meanings in its new context and underwent a process of change that continues today. Embedded in the social relations and set of meanings surrounding it, *döner* became an integral part of Turkish migrants' relations with the Germans and of Turkish identities in Germany.

The uses of goods are social, and goods carry social meanings. They have communicative value because of their symbolic and expressive functions (Douglas & Isherwood, 1979). Moreover, they act as markers. Thus, objects that have acquired intimate associations with a social group are integral to the development of the group identity and social relations of this group. In a similar way, food and food consumption have symbolic and constitutive functions in intergroup relations. "What people eat expresses who and what they are to themselves and to others" (Mintz, 1985, p. 13). Like other goods, food acts as a marker. Especially in cases in which particular food items are associated with ethnically and culturally differentiated groups, these items more often function as ethnic signifiers. *Döner* functions in German society as such. In exploring the way *döner's* meanings and images are manipulated and transformed in Germany, one also needs to examine the web of social relations of German Turks embedded in Germany and the transformations of these relations. This chapter focuses on the changes in *döner*'s marketing strategy and aims to explore the dynamics behind these in a broader context of the social positioning struggle of German Turks in German society.

A Brief History of *Döner Kebap*'s Incorporation Into the Berlin Market

As stated, *döner kebap* was introduced to Germany by Turkish migrants who were recruited as guest workers. Following the oil crisis and the consequent economic stagnation in 1973, the German government, like other European governments of countries experiencing immigration, officially banned the entry of non-European Economic Community workers to Germany. Although the number of foreign workers decreased in the postrecruitment period, the foreign population in Germany has continued to grow, however, because of the implementation in 1974 of the policy allowing migrants' families to enter Germany. The number of Turkish migrants increased from 910,500 in 1973 to 1,268,300 in 1979 in the FRG as a whole (Statistisches Bundesamt, 1991) and from 79,468 in 1973 to 100,217 in 1979 in Berlin (Statistisches Landesamt, 1991). The ratio of workers among foreign residents has continually decreased with this development.

Unemployment among foreigners rose from 0.7% in 1972 to 6.8% in 1976 (Castles, Heather, & Wallace, 1984, p. 185). Thus, the rise of unemployment, arrival of new family members of Turkish migrants seeking work, and some Turkish migrants' readiness to invest their savings in Germany paved the way to the self-employment of Turkish migrants (mostly as grocery store and *Imbiss* owners) and to *döner* production in Germany. According to one *döner* producer in Berlin, this link was very direct and obvious. He said: "The time unemployment appeared among Turks was the time Turks started *döner* business in Germany."[4] In fact, the very first *döner Imbiss* stands appeared around the central train station (Bahnhof Zoo) in Berlin in 1975, when unemployment was increasing among Turks. The number of *döner Imbiss* stands increased rapidly in the late 1970s, but they gained real momentum in the 1980s, reaching their peak when the Berlin Wall fell in 1989.

From the very beginning, *döner kebap* was marketed as a Turkish specialty and targeted Germans as its consumers. Today, according to *Imbiss* owners, 95% of *döner* consumers are German. This orientation toward German customers, however, should not be interpreted as *Imbiss* owners' desire to extricate themselves from their compatriots. It was based on economic considerations; German customers simply meant a greater market for *döner*. For this reason, in marketing *döner* in its new form, the "German taste" was the primary concern of Turkish *Imbiss* owners. This German taste had a substantial impact in orienting the changes in the composition and the taste of *döner kebap* until it reached its more or less standardized taste in Germany. This is not to say that Turkish migrants did not, and do not, consume *döner*. They did, and still do, but their percentage of its overall consumption was, and is, still very low. Since the second half of the 1980s, *döner* has been firmly incorporated, at least in Berlin, into the daily fast-food scene of *Hamburger, Curry Wurst, Bockwurst, Bulette,* and french fries.

Döner and *Pide:* A Symbiotic Success

The introduction and popularity of *döner kebap* was not without effect on the consumption and production of some other food items on the market. Moreover, it gave rise to new forms. The most important change of *döner* on its journey from Turkey to Germany was the substitution of the sandwich bun or the quarter of a regular loaf of Turkish bread by *pide* (Turkish flat bread). In Turkey, *pide* is not, as in Germany, a type of ordinary bread found on the market throughout the year. Although there are various forms of *pide* in Turkey, the *pide* sold in Germany throughout the year (mostly in Turkish stores and bakers) is available in Turkey only during Ramadan, the fasting month in Islam.

Imbiss owners give the following reasons for their preference of *pide* for *döner kebap:* its practicality in serving as a bread pocket thick and curved enough (one quarter or one fifth of the round flat bread) to hold the roasted meat, the salad, and the dressing; the smooth texture of its crust; and most important, its quality of being more filling than a sandwich bun but less so than a Turkish loaf of bread, which is believed to be too much for the German taste. *Döner*'s major effect on *pide* was to increase *pide* production drastically in Germany, especially in Berlin. *Döner* increased the demand for *pide,* thus consequently, its production. For this reason, the success of *pide* covaried with the success of *döner kebap:*

> When I started the business in 1975, there were five, six small Turkish bakeries. But I am the first to bake and sell *pide* [wholesale] in Berlin. *Döner Imbiss* stands of that time baked their own *pide* for their *döner kebap* in their own shops, in their small ovens. Today, there are over 70 Turkish bakeries producing *pide* in Berlin. How to say, it is *döner* which brought *pide* to this level. (Informant interview)

The figures of *pide* production also confirm the words of the owner of this Turkish bakery. Today, daily *pide* production is estimated to be around 200,000 pieces (loaves) in Berlin and over 500,000 pieces total throughout in Germany. Most important, it is estimated that at least 70% of this figure goes to *döner Imbiss* stands.

Although unintended, using *pide* for *döner kebap* changed the meaning and the connotations of *pide*. Among Turkish migrants in Germany, it lost its association with Ramadan. The fact that Turkish bakers in Berlin now produce a different type of *pide* as *ramazan pidesi* (*pide* for the Ramadan) whose form is slightly different (more of an ellipse), although its dough is the same, points to this decontextualization of the regular *pide* in Germany. The *ramazan pidesi* weighs a little more than a regular *pide*, has more sesame and black cumin on its surface, and is more expensive. Now, with the exception of one Turkish baker, all Turkish bakers in Berlin produce this new type of *pide* only during Ramadan. People queue for this *pide* in Turkish bakeries during Ramadan, although what would be a *ramazan pidesi* in Turkey but not considered as such in Germany remains unnoticed on the shelves. When asked for the reasons behind the introduction of this new *pide* as *ramazan pidesi* in Berlin, one baker answered that "*döner* business finished the *pide*. It had nothing left to do with the Ramadan." It is also noteworthy that all the *Imbiss* owners and the *pide* bakers interviewed use *pide* and *bread* interchangeably and most often refer to *pide* as "the bread." This is also an additional sign of *pide*'s recontextualization as a regular type of bread.[5] Now, in some *Imbiss* stands, *pide* has found its way into *Wurst* (sausages, mostly pork), and some *Imbiss* stands sell sausages within a slice of *pide*. Although most of these *Imbiss* stands are owned by Germans, some Turkish *Imbiss* stands also sell sausages in this fashion.

Döner kebap not only determined the scale of the production and consumption of *pide* to a large extent but also paved the way to *pide*'s incorporation into the fast-food market in Germany. Now, the latter is also established in this market, but *döner* dominates its symbolic field. It is noteworthy that *pide* finds its way as *Döner-Brot* (*döner* bread) to the other fast-food products such as falafel (see "Die Bohnen-Bulette," 1994).

Pide has contributed to the success of *döner* as has *döner* to *pide*'s popularity because *pide* played a very important role in *döner*'s competition with more familiar fast-food items in the market. Starting from the end of the 1970s, *döner* was portrayed in the German media as in strong competition with other fast-food types in the German market, namely, with *Hamburger*, *Bockwurst*, and the Berliner novelty, *Curry Wurst* ("Döner auf Berliner Art," 1992; "Döner Kebap: Ende unserer

Curry Wurst," 1982; "Döner Kebap macht der Curry Wurst," 1989). Surveys of the newspapers showed that among the consumers who were asked to compare these fast-food types and voice their preference, the proportion of those who preferred *döner* to other fast-food varieties was steadily increasing in Berlin.

Döner producers, *Imbiss* owners, and consumers more or less agree on the factors behind *döner*'s success. First of all, compared with *Curry Wurst* or *Bockwurst*, *döner*, with its substantial amount of "bread," spicy meat, and variety of salad and dressing, is a meal in itself. "It is not appropriate to compare *döner* to *Curry Wurst*, they are not comparable," said one *Imbiss* owner who owns 22 *Imbiss* stands in Berlin:

> One is a meal and the other is not. With a portion of *Curry Wurst* you could still your hunger only for a while, for that moment, but with one *döner kebap* you have your meal. It is settled. Instead of spending DM [deutsche mark] 2 or DM 2.50 on *Curry Wurst*, one buys a *döner* and it is all done. (Informant interview)

Pide plays an important part in this filling quality of *döner kebap*, which consumers always underscore. It is more filling than a sandwich bun but not as much as a quarter of an ordinary loaf of bread. When these qualities of *döner* are taken into account, it is apparent that *döner*, varying between DM 3 and DM 4, is a relatively cheap and practical fast-food meal.

There are also other factors accounting for *döner*'s success, including its attractiveness in terms of its ingredients and its aesthetics. The attractiveness of *döner* with regard to its ingredients vis-à-vis *Curry Wurst* or *Hamburger* needs to be contextualized within the healthy nourishment discourse that became popular especially in the second half of the 1980s. First of all, *döner* meat is mostly veal or beef, leaner in contrast to the pork in *Curry Wurst* or *Bockwurst* and thus more in line with the low-fat diet consciousness of the late 1980s.[6] The salad in *döner kebap*, a mixture of lettuce, red cabbage, onions, cucumbers, and tomatoes, topped with a yogurt dressing, is also attractive to those whose awareness of health and nutrition is shaped for the most part by an emphasis on a diet of fresh vegetables, salad, and yogurt. Moreover, all the ingredients of *döner* are fresh. *Döner* meat on the spit is supposed to be, and mostly is, consumed daily.[7] Being free from chemical ingredients, especially in comparison to *Curry Wurst* or *Bockwurst*, *döner* has a clear advantage over the latter.[8] The aesthetic attractiveness of the colorful salad in *döner kebap* topped with yogurt dressing should also be understood within the context of these discourses.

All these factors, combined with Germans' increasing desire since World War II for international and exotic food (Wildt, in press), established the ground for *döner kebap*'s success in Germany. *Döner* was gradually incorporated, at least in Berlin, into the fast-food diet of Germans. With the fall of the Berlin Wall, it became the number one fast food of the East Germans as well.

Marketing *Döner Kebap:* Up to 1989

In terms of German Turks' marketing strategies of *döner kebap* in the German fast-food market in Berlin, it is possible to differentiate two periods: the period from its introduction up through 1989 and the period after the fall of the Berlin Wall. The first stage, from the introduction of *döner* in the mid-1970s to the standardization of the composition and taste of *döner* meat in Berlin in 1989 by German authorities (*Berliner Verkehrsauffassung für das Fleischerzeugnis,* 1989), was characterized by small-scale individual production of *döner* in apartment basements or at Turkish restaurants or *Imbiss* stands. During this period, the taste, composition, and price of *döner* meat varied considerably. Although the meat of *döner kebap* in Turkey does not contain minced meat, this was, and still, is the basis of the *döner* produced in Germany, although the ratio to other ingredients varied. Consequently, the production costs of *döner* ranged considerably, depending on the ratio of the minced meat (sometimes reaching 80% to 90%) and on the other binding ingredients. It is noteworthy that this period was marked by fierce price wars among *döner Imbiss* stands. The price, even in the late 1980s, fluctuated between DM 1.80 and DM 3.50 for one *döner*.

To keep the quality of *döner* meat standard and to prevent *Imbiss* owners from using high ratios of minced meat and of binding or chemical ingredients in their fierce battle to cut down the cost, German authorities in Berlin officially defined the ingredients of *döner* meat (veal, beef, or lamb) and the ratios of ingredients (fat, spices, and percentage of minced meat). In 1991, the same regulation was adopted for all of Germany.[9] Under this regulation, only *döner* in line with the specified ingredients and ratios of ingredients are entitled to be sold as *döner kebap.* This regulation standardized the taste of *döner* meat to a great extent.

This setting of product norms for *döner* was initiated by some German Turks who were in the *döner* trade. They urged the authorities to take measures against the deteriorating quality of *döner* meat with the severe competition. Most of them looked on the new regulations very positively because the fierce price wars put them under pressure to cut the production costs by any means.

Moreover, this setting up of product norms was also seen as a type of official recognition and admission of *döner kebap* into the German market. When explaining these product norms, one *döner* producer said:

> Today *döner* is firm in Germany. Even the authorities have recognized this fact. They understood and appreciated its value and set regulations on its ingredients. *Döner* business is not like a jungle any more. There are standards. It is a serious business. You cannot put whatever you want and sell it as *döner!* (Informant interview)

Thus, this act was not considered as an unwanted interference of the German authorities in German Turks' affairs.

In the period until the regulations were implemented, the composition of *döner* meat varied, but the form of the *döner kebap* was fairly standard. Slices of spicy *döner* meat within a quarter of *pide*, garnished with a combination of salad and topped with the garlic yogurt dressing, was the *döner kebap* of this period. Little product differentiation existed; there was basically one type of *döner* with varying quality of *döner* meat.

The presentation and marketing of the *döner kebap* of this period were embedded in a folkloric discourse of Turkishness. *Döner Imbiss* stands offered this "Turkish" specialty in a highly accentuated oriental and folkloric atmosphere. Touristic Turkey posters, several types of souvenirs from Turkey, and colorful lights dominated the interior decoration of *döner Imbiss* stands of this period. The ethnic and exotic associations of *döner kebap* were at the forefront. In marketing *döner*, the *Imbiss* owners' strategy was to promote its Turkishness and exoticness; they exploited its ethnic associations.

Döner Kebap After the Fall of the Berlin Wall

Setting up product norms for *döner kebap* by the German authorities coincided with the fall of the Berlin Wall on November 9, 1989. A focus on the period starting from this date reveals that both the production of *döner* and its marketing went through—and are still going through—some important changes. The most striking characteristics of this stage are a substantial increase in *döner* production and the introduction of new *döner* varieties involving product differentiation and image renewal.

After the fall of the Berlin Wall and the reunification of the former German Democratic Republic (GDR) and the FRG, the number of firms producing wholesale *döner* increased rapidly in Germany, particularly in Berlin. Although the exact number of these *döner* meat factories is not available, they are believed to number between 25 and 30 in Berlin now. Other than four or five of them, however, these are still small family firms. As stated before, the daily *döner* production is estimated to be a minimum of 40 tons for Berlin and 70 tons for Germany. This amount is evaluated to be the saturation point for West Germany, but the former GDR is seen as an expanding and promising market for increased production. Consequently, Turkish migrants in *döner* businesses are investing rapidly in this part of Germany. In 1992, of the 115 Turkish firms active in the Eastern section of Berlin, 80 of them were restaurants and *Imbiss* stands offering *döner* (Blaschke & Ersöz, 1992). With complete incorporation of the former GDR market, daily *döner* production is anticipated to reach 100 tons in Germany. During this period, *döner kebap* was integrated into the German language. In 1991, *döner kebap* made its way into the authoritative German dictionary *Duden: Rechtschreibung der deutschen Sprache* (1991) as *döner kebap* (p. 214).

By 1991 new varieties of *döner kebap* appeared in the market. There was an apparent attempt at product differentiation by changing the composition of *döner* meat within the allowed limits and by changing the garnishings of *döner kebap*. Different varieties of *döner* meat with no minced meat at all, solely beef or veal, or a mixture of beef, veal, and lamb *döner* began to be marketed as new varieties of *döner kebap* under such names as *efendi döner, oba döner, bey döner, tosun döner, döner light, tava döneri*, and so forth. Other new varieties of *döner* were made by simply adding feta cheese, fried eggplant, or pieces of french fries to the *döner kebap*. It is important to note that all these changes were accompanied with price differentiation and price increases with each new variety.

Today, in Berlin, *döner* or *kebap* serve as generic terms for all fast-food types prepared in *pide*, such as vegetarian *döner*, zucchini *döner*, chicken *döner*, or turkey *döner*. The most recent example of these new products is the Korean *döner* offered primarily to Koreans. *Pide* is filled with some pieces of meat (not *döner* meat) and cooked soy sprouts topped with Korean hot sauce. It is noteworthy that in all these new forms offered as different types of *döner, pide*, rather than the *döner* meat, is the only common ingredient, and all have the quality of being a meal in themselves. These new varieties, however, with the exception of chicken *döner*, are not yet widespread.

The most important change taking place in the marketing of *döner* is at the symbolic level, however. Both *döner* producers and *Imbiss* owners are trying to give *döner kebap* a new image with a different field of connotations. Although *döner* was becoming almost a generic name for fast food served in *pide* in a fashion similar to *döner kebap*, and new varieties of *döner* made their way to the fast-food market in Berlin, another type of practice gained momentum. Today, more and more Turkish *döner Imbiss* stands offer their regular, ordinary *döner kebap* under names such as "McKebap," "Keb'up," "Mac's Döner," "Mister Kebap," "McKing," "Dönerburger," and so forth. But the *döner kebap* offered under these names are not actually different from ordinary *kebap*. There are no alterations, either to the *döner* meat or to the garnishings, and it is important not to confuse this development with the previously mentioned product differentiation.[10] Although the Turkish owners of these *Imbiss* stands do not speak English (most speak some German), all the names they choose for their products are in English. In all these names, except "McKing," either *döner* or *kebap* is used in combination with an English word or suffix.

McKebap *Imbiss* chain has five stores (two of them in the former East Berlin), all called "McKebap." The allusion of this name is clearly to McDonald's. The other chain, also with five stores (two of them in the Eastern section of the city), is called "Keb'up." The Keb'up chain is more ambitious than the McKebap chain, however. The staff working in each branch dress in white T-shirts with red aprons and red caps, with Keb'up prints all over their clothes. Keb'up stores offer three types of *döner*: mini *döner*, *döner*, and big *döner*. All are wrapped in Keb'up-imprinted paper pockets. Again, the model of presentation and the labeling of their products is clearly the fast-food chains of McDonald's or Burger King. In fact, McDonald's and its place in German society influence the major *döner*-producing firms and the owners of *Imbiss* chains considerably in their attempt to transform the image and the place of *döner* in German society. I will return to this point later in this chapter.

Mister Kebap, on the other hand, is an *Imbiss* chain of 22 *Imbiss* stands in the former East Berlin. Each *Imbiss* has the emblem of Mister Kebap that appears between Coca-Cola stickers (see Figure 8.1). The script "Mister Kebap" takes the form of a crescent and apparently alludes to the Turkish flag. The owner also explained the emblem in this way: According to him, the Turkishness of the food is symbolized by the crescent.

Again, everything on this logo, including the name of the company (although it is based in Berlin and operates only in Germany), is written in English. Neither symbolically nor linguistically is there any reference to Germany. This absence is noteworthy. When I asked the owner of the

Figure 8.1. The Logo of *Mister Kebap*

Mister Kebap chain why he chose a name particularly in English, given that he was established in Germany, he answered:

> You know, here in Germany, everything American has a better value. How can I say—they have high esteem. That is the reason, for example, why some friends [he refers to other *Imbiss* owners] chose names like McDöner or McKebap. Now there is this phenomena McDonald's. I think they wanted to imitate it [McDonald's]. So we thought ours should also be international. We combined English with something from us. We said, "Let's take one from you and one from us." (Informant interview)

The Symbolic Field of *Döner Kebap*

In our contemporary world, identities and belongingnesses are more and more asserted by lifestyles, which in turn are encoded in the images of consumer goods that act as markers (Featherstone, 1987). Thus, material objects are more than ever a pivot around which social identities are constructed and asserted (Miller, 1987). In this context, goods associated with a particular lifestyle easily become a social arena for the social positioning struggle of various groups, as well as an arena in which belongingness is formulated and asserted. Thus, the analysis of the way the meanings and images of goods are manipulated and transformed is important to explore the processes by which identities and social relations are constituted.

To understand the factors behind Turkish migrants' attempts to redefine their image and place in the society by manipulating the image of *döner* in Berlin, one must examine the web of meanings and social relations in which *döner kebap* is embedded in Berlin and, for that matter, in German society. In Germany and Berlin, *döner kebap* is strongly associated with Turks. It became the traditional ethnic food of Turks.[11] In this way, it symbolizes Turks and things thought to be Turkish. This strong association, almost an identity, is observable at different levels in a wide spectrum of practices ranging from children's books to official international evenings.[12]

Döner, by means of its strong association with an ethnic group in Germany, found its way into the folklorism of multiculturalist policies. It is commonly used to refer to the multicultural quality of Germany (see "Das Image des Döner-Kebab," 1989) and of Berlin. The name of the widely announced youth get-together organized for Turkish and German youth in Berlin in 1987, "Disco *döner*," is only one example of how *döner* is used to refer to Turks in Germany within the context of multiculturalism.

Because of this association, *döner* became integrated into the discourse on the *Ausländerfrage* (the question of foreigners) in Germany. *Kein döner ohne Ausländer!* (No *döner* without the foreigners!), *Kein döner ohne Türken!* (No *döner* without Turks!), and *Kein döner ohne Wir!* (No *döner* without us!) were the banners of the biggest proforeigners demonstrations of the 1980s in Berlin. Given the fact that *Ausländer* and *Turks* were almost synonymous at that time, again a direct association between *döner* and Turks was manifest. This association reached such dimensions that a young German man, asked to comment on the attacks on the foreigners and the increasing enmity against the foreigners on television in 1991 (after the brutal attacks raged by the Neo-Nazis in the autumn of 1991), answered, a little surprised, as if his opinion on this subject was very obvious, by saying "I have nothing to do with these, I am not against the foreigners, I eat my *döner*." It is noteworthy that although the attacks were not against Turks but against other foreigner groups in the former GDR, he voiced his opinion by means of his relationship to *döner*. Thus, *döner*, because of the strong association it acquired with Turks and consequently with foreigners, functions as an arena in which hostilities against and solidarity with Turks and foreigners are asserted.

This association between Turks and *döner kebap* in Germany is manifest at different levels in the society. A 1992 article titled "Kebap Kapitalisten" (the *Kebap* Capitalists) in *Die Zeit Magazine* on successful Turkish businesspersons in Germany illustrates this. Despite its title, the article is about successful Turkish businesspersons in Germany. Ironically, none of the Turkish business owners portrayed in the article has or had anything to do with the *döner* business, but all are active in areas different from *döner*-related ones. The *kebap* in the title is simply used to substitute for the adjective *Turkish*. Sometimes *kebap* is used instead of *the Orient* and *Islam*. An example is the title of a symposium organized by the Evangelische Akademie Iselohn in November 1993 in Iserlohn—*Kebab oder west-östlicher Diwan* (*Kebab* or West-East Divan [Council]). Nevertheless, none of the topics on the program had anything to do with *kebap* but dealt with issues related to Islam and Orient-Europe relations.[13]

German Turks in the *döner* trade would prefer to be rid of the previously mentioned association of *döner kebap* with Turkishness, although in the past their strategy was to accentuate the Turkishness or exoticness of their product.[14] Now they prefer to distract their customers' attention from their ethnicity. In adopting new names for *döner*, Turkish *döner Imbiss* owners try to pluck *döner* from its articulation and rearticulate it with a different set of connotations. They seek to use language and the image of modern technologies to dissociate *döner* from the web of connotations in which it is embedded. It is not simply a matter of adopting new names for their products and the *Imbiss* stands—it is also a matter of changing marketing, presentation, and the image. Today in Berlin, more and more Turkish *Imbiss* stands seek to downplay their previous folkloric and oriental Turkish atmosphere in their new decorations.

In 1992 a new *döner Imbiss* (called Efendi) was opened at the site of an old Turkish *döner Imbiss*, Topkapi, in downtown Berlin. The modern decoration of the former with no allusion to Turkey and Turkishness at all is in stark contrast with the heavy oriental atmosphere displayed by Topkapi, although the owner remained the same. When asked for the reasons behind this drastic change, he said:

> Before, there was a place called "Topkapi" here. A place with our [Turkish] atmosphere. But I thought, in the midst of Europe, on Ku'damm I want to realize something close to McDonald's. I want to show that Turks are also capable of setting up good business and running it. The problem is to change the atmosphere, to offer a Turkish specialty without our

atmosphere, to present it in a modern way. I want *döner* to go further. We changed it. Believe it, even the nature of customers changed. (Informant interview)

It is clear that the adoption of American names is part of the new marketing strategies of the *döner Imbiss* stands.[15] McDonald's, representing the highest level of modern Western technology, plays an important role in orienting their endeavor to renew the image of *döner* and to give it a character in which the hold of Turkishness has partly evaporated. The tendency is to dislocate *döner kebap* from the particular set of connotations woven into German society and to present it within a context in which its ethnic and folkloric associations are downplayed but never totally eroded. From this point, the transformations of *döner kebap* manifest the new ways of articulation and negotiation between the local and the global.

It would be misleading to suggest that Turkish *Imbiss* owners' most important motive for imitating McDonald's is that they want to appeal to a wider public, including people who are not attracted by exoticness. Turkish *Imbiss* owners' desire to become upscale might seem to contradict their efforts to model themselves after McDonald's. This is a contradiction, however, only when it is assumed that McDonald's signifies the same thing to everyone in different parts of the world. Although McDonald's caters to a broad public and is not considered prestigious in North America, German Turks have a different image of McDonald's. They identify McDonald's as high technology, good business, and something advanced, clean, and efficient. As the owner of Mister Kebap expressed it, it represents something American that is of great value.

Marketing Strategies of
Döner Kebap and Social Mobility

The confusing thing in *döner kebap*'s story in the German fast-food market is that a new strategy for promotion and image came in the beginning of the 1990s, at a time when *döner kebap* was selling better than ever before. There was no apparent need for an image renewal. The market for *döner* grew significantly through the reunification of Germany; *döner kebap*, as a cheap and exotic fast-food meal in itself, had something to offer to the former East Germans. Ironically, Turkish *Imbiss* owners started to downplay the ethnic connotations of *döner kebap* when the demand for exotic and ethnic food was increasing. Thus, it is not possible to explore the dynamics of this change from within a framework that takes into account only the market forces. *Döner kebap's* story has to be placed into a broader context of German Turks' social exclusion and quest for social mobility in Germany.

THE SOCIAL SPACE GERMAN TURKS OCCUPY IN GERMAN SOCIETY

The social space German Turks occupy in German society has some anomalies. Social space refers to the space of social positions, as defined by objective social structures that shape the subjects' social beings (Bourdieu, 1990). In this view the position of a given agent is identified on the basis of his or her position in different fields and on his or her various types of capital, namely, economic, cultural, social, and symbolic (Bourdieu, 1985). Economic capital refers to all goods that are immediately and directly convertible into money (Bourdieu, 1986). By cultural capital, the ensemble of embodied dispositions such as learnable skills is understood. This usually refers to educational qualifications. Social capital is composed of resources on the basis of connections and group membership (Bourdieu, 1977). Symbolic capital is simply the "form which is assumed by different forms of capital when they are perceived and recognized as legitimate" (Bourdieu, 1990, p. 128). The structure of social space is given by the volume and composition of the overall capital the individual has (Bourdieu, 1974). Moreover, these four forms of capital are, under certain conditions, convertible into one another. Thus, within this framework, social mobility not only refers to changes in the volume of capital but also covers changes in the distribution of total capital among the various types (Bourdieu, 1974).

A focus on the social space German Turks occupy in German society discloses that in terms of economic capital, there are no significant differences between Turkish and German workers. Moreover, there is an increasing trend toward stratification among German Turks, and the growing number of Turkish firms and employees indicates an upward economic mobility achieved by some German Turks (Blaschke & Ersöz, 1992; Şen, 1993).

Although German Turks have a clear deficit in cultural capital in comparison to Germans, their educational qualifications are gradually increasing, and they have started to occupy different positions in respect to this dimension. With regard to distinct forms of capital, however, they have a deficiency in symbolic capital. The distinctive quality of symbolic capital is that "while the other forms of capital have an independent objectification, be it as money, titles or behavioral attitudes and dispositions," this form of capital "only exists in the eyes of the others" (Joppke, 1986, p. 60). Thus, symbolic capital is nothing more than economic or cultural capital that is acknowledged and recognized (Bourdieu, 1990).

The derogatory jokes about Turks, the increasing antipathy toward foreigners, and the attacks and insults directed toward Turks all indicate that German Turks have a very negative image in German society. Their social recognition is deficient, and German Turks are aware that this lack of social recognition negates the success they have achieved in different areas such as business and education. Other types of capital that they manage to acquire lose their value because of this deficiency.

In short, the social space German Turks occupy in German society is characterized by a deficiency in symbolic capital. Although the volumes of economic and cultural capital vary among the stratified German Turks in Germany, this deficit in symbolic capital affects all of them. For those German Turks who have moved up economically, especially for Turkish businesspeople in Germany, this discrepancy between their economic and symbolic capital is more drastic, and it hinders their full *social* mobility.

This anomaly is the consequence of the social exclusion German Turks face in Germany. Turkish businesspeople and those in the *döner* business who compose their majority are particularly affected. In the beginning, *döner* trade was not simply a way of earning a living in Germany but one of the most important ways of becoming self-employed, of becoming one's own boss. It symbolized a break from being a worker in Germany. In that sense, *döner* trade, which functioned as a symbol of economic and consequently social success for German Turks, was a prestigious line of business in their eyes in the late 1970s and 1980s. It was a symbol of their economic integration. Nevertheless, the lack of social recognition and the discrepancy between their upward economic and social mobility became more apparent when they started to increase their economic capital significantly, especially after the fall of the Berlin Wall. Because of *döner kebap*'s aforementioned strong association with Turkishness and Turks' negative image in Germany, this group of German Turks suffered from lack of social recognition as businesspeople per se. Their reluctance to exploit Turkishness and exoticness of *döner* in its marketing can be evaluated in this context of social exclusion and the anomalies of their social space in Germany.

The change in German Turks' marketing strategy of *döner* in Germany is part of German Turks' efforts to rework the connotations of *döner kebap* to make *döner* and, consequently, themselves, more respectable. Changes in *döner kebap*, especially those regarding its image, are part of Turkish migrants' efforts and desires to cut across national boundaries to create a new local identification. As such, it can be seen as a part of "new ways of articulating the particularistic and the universalistic aspect of identity" (Hall, 1992, p. 304). Thus, what is taking place around *döner* is symptomatic of the production of Turkish migrants' new identities in Germany and of their desired place and image in German society.

In all the changes *döner kebap* is going through in Germany, different efforts and strategies to open *döner*'s way up in society are evident. After having been established among the general lay public, *döner* is attempting to become upwardly mobile. *Döner* producers and *döner Imbiss* owners agree that *döner* does not have the place in society it deserves, and for that matter, it has a fair way to go. "First of all, its price should go up," says a manager, immediately adding that its form should be altered so that it could be mass produced. Most important, according to him, *pide* and the salad should be eliminated from *döner kebap*. A bun should substitute for the *pide* and a leaf of lettuce or a pickle should replace the rich and colorful salad in *döner kebap*. "The consumers, their taste and habits are changing," he says:

> Slim-line, diet, freshness, minimality [*öz* in Turkish], etc. These are important. The taste of the meat is more prominent in a sandwich bun. Everything is more aesthetical. Then *döner* would be attractive to other tastes. High society German will also eat it. Someone from the upper class will also eat it. (Informant interview)

It is ironic that what made *döner* attractive among the mass public, namely, the filling quality of *pide* and the combination of different sorts of salad, are seen by the Turkish businesspeople to be the very factors hindering *döner*'s upward mobility in society. Now, targeting a different group of consumers in German society, Turkish businesspeople seek to incorporate *döner* into the consumption patterns and discourses of different social groups.

In this endeavor, there are also Turkish *Imbiss* owners who prefer to dissociate themselves from *döner kebap* completely in their effort to become upscale in the food and catering sector. Those German Turks who used to be in the *döner* trade and owned *Imbiss* chains and who are now moving gradually into the restaurant business catering Italian food belong to this category.[16]

Döner, by having played an important role in the economic success biography of several Turkish business owners in Germany, contributed to their economic empowerment there. Faced with social exclusion, such German Turks employ certain strategies to convert their economic capital into symbolic capital to achieve the social mobility they desire. Thus, the changes in the marketing strategy of *döner kebap* and German Turks' efforts to refashion its set of ethnic connotations are part of German Turks' social positioning struggle in Germany. For this reason, their efforts to move up in German society depend not only on their ability to transform *döner* to fit to the taste of the social groups targeted or on its success in renewing its image but also on the power relations of Turkish migrants embedded in German society.

Notes

1. In the former West Berlin municipalities, the percentage of Turkish *döner Imbiss* stands, grocery stores, and restaurants offering *döner kebap* as fast food in all Turkish stores ranges between 56.3% and 83.3%. Of 129 Turkish stores in Kreuzberg, 75 offer *döner kebap* (Zentrum für Entwicklungsländer-Forschung, 1990).

2. There are commercials of *döner* producers or wholesale meat retailers on Turkish cable TV in Turkish. These target Turkish *Imbiss* owners. In the European editions of Turkish newspapers there were always and still are *döner* producers' advertisements targeting *Imbiss* owners, but all of these are in Turkish and do not address German consumers.

3. In Berlin, the first serious *döner kebap* advertisements (in German) appeared in subway stations in 1992.

4. All data about the introduction and development of *döner* and about its consumption in Germany and in Berlin are based on the interviews I conducted with owners and managers of *döner*-producing firms and *Imbiss* stands during January and February 1992 and September 1993.

5. *Pide* is not the only type of Turkish bread produced and consumed by German Turks. There is also a Turkish loaf of bread. It is noteworthy that the former type enjoys the status of bread in Germany, whereas in Turkish cities this term is reserved for the latter.

6. This is one of *döner*'s major advantages over Gyros produced and marketed by Greek migrants in Germany. The latter contain pork.

7. In fact, on the basis of a regulation enacted in 1989, to use *döner* meat from the previous day in *döner kebap* is prohibited. Fines could be charged in such cases.

8. Of course, *döner*, as a fast food with a considerable meat content, is not in line with the vegetarian nutrition discourses. Nevertheless, its exoticness and low-fat content still have something to offer to those young Germans and students who are relatively health and price conscious.

9. According to this regulation, for example, no binding substances and chemicals are allowed, and the rate of minced meat cannot be higher than 60%. (For a detailed definition of the ingredients of *döner kebap*, see *Berliner Verkehrsauffassung für das Fleischerzeugnis*, 1989.)

10. In the *Imbiss* stands offering new varieties of *döner kebap*, there is a sign of *döner kebap* somewhere on the shop window, but the real emphasis is on the adopted new names. These names are printed on the aprons of the workers, on the napkins, and on the waxed paper pockets for *döner*.

11. In Germany, Istanbul has the reputation as the homeland of *döner*. A recent notice in a Turkish newspaper illustrated this connection: According to the newspaper, two officials in Berlin were sent to court on charges of insulting foreigners. In the receipt of the parking ticket sent to a Turk, these officials are accused of altering the place of birth of this person (Istanbul) to "*döner* town" ("Iki Alman," 1993).

12. See, for example, R. Meier (1982).

13. I am thankful to Lale Yalcin-Heckmann for bringing this document to my attention.

14. Since the late 1980s, German Turks have worked with considerable effort against the reduction of their image to *döner kebap* (see "Mehr als Bauchtanz und Döner," 1993; "Weg vom Döner-Kebab," 1987).

15. Although this practice of adopting American names is mostly observable in the *döner* business, it is not limited to this area. This is becoming a general trend in the catering businesses run by Turks. The catering company called "Pic-nic" run by two German Turks, which offers "pic-nic *döner kebap*" and "pic-nic fried chicken" ("Pic-nic," 1994), is a striking example of such companies.

16. *Döner Imbiss* owners are now opening pizzerias, especially in the former GDR. Pizzeria owners give the following reasons for their decision: low production costs and high profit margins of Italian food in comparison to *döner* and Turkish food; the unsaturated market for Italian food in the former GDR and the former East Germans' eagerness to adopt West German lifestyles; the increasing hostility against foreigners, especially Turks and Turkish business places in the former GDR; and last but not least, the prestige involved in running a "proper" restaurant.

References

Berliner Verkehrsauffassung für das Fleischerzeugnis. (1989). Döner Kebap. Senatsverwaltung für Gesundheit, Ges. IV, C3.

Blaschke, J., & Ersöz, A. (1992). *Bitte sehr! Buyurun: Türkische unternehmer in Berlin* [Come in, please: Turkish entrepreneurs in Berlin]. Berlin: Edition Parabolis.

Bourdieu, P. (1974). *Distinction: A social critique of the judgement of taste*. Malbourne, UK: Routledge & Kegan Paul.

Bourdieu, P. (1977). *Outline of a theory of practice*. Cambridge, UK: Cambridge University Press.

Bourdieu, P. (1985). The social space and the genesis of groups. *Theory and Society, 14*, 723-724.

Bourdieu, P. (1986). The forms of capital. In J. G. Richardson (Ed.), *Handbook of theory and research for the sociology of education* (pp. 241-258). New York: Greenwood.

Bourdieu, P. (1990). Social space and symbolic power. In P. Bourdieu (Ed.), *In other words: Essays towards a reflexive sociology* (pp. 123-139). Cambridge, UK: Polity.

Castles, S., Heather, B., & Wallace, T. (1984). *Here for good: Western Europe's new ethnic minorities*. London: Pluto.

Das Image des Döner Kebabs ins Rotieren Gekommen [*Döner kebap*'s image is changing]. (1989, February 15). *Tageszeitung*, p. 26.

Die Bohnen-Bulette [The bean-balls]. (1994, May). *Zitty*, pp. 18-22.

Döner auf Berliner Art [Berlin-style *döner*]. (1992, January 15). *Der Tagesspiegel*, p. 10.

Döner Kebap: Ende unserer Curry Wurst? [*Döner kebap*: The end of our *Curry Wurst?*]. (1982, August 4). *Bild Berlin*, press archive.

Döner Kebap macht der Curry Wurst immer mehr Konkurrenz [*Döner kebap* creates more competition for *Curry Wurst*]. (1989, October 30). *Berliner Morgen Post*, p. 10.

Douglas, M., & Isherwood, B. (1979). *The world of goods*. New York: Basic Books.

Duden: Rechtschreibung der deutschen Sprache [German dictionary] (19th ed.). (1991). Leipzig, Germany: Dudenverlag.

Featherstone, M. (1987). Life style and consumer culture. *Theory, Culture & Society, 4,* 55-70.

Hall, S. (1992). The question of cultural identity. In S. Hall, D. Held, & T. McGrew, (Eds.), *Modernity and its futures* (pp. 274-316). Cambridge, UK: Polity.

Iki Alman görevli Mahkemede [Two German officials are in court: They changed Istanbul's name to Dönertown]. (1993, April 2). *Hürriyet*, p. 1.

Joppke, C. (1986). The cultural dimension of class formation and class struggle: On the social theory of P. Bourdieu. *Berkeley Journal of Sociology, 31,* 53-78.

Kebap Kapitalisten [The *kebap* capitalists]. (1992, August 28). *Die Zeit*, pp. 14-18.

Mehr als Bauchtanz und Döner: Ein Verein will deutscher und türkische Kunst und Kultur nähebringen [More than belly dancing and *döner:* An association will bring German and Turkish art and culture together]. (1993, October 23). *Der Tagesspiegel*, p. 13.

Meier, R. (1982). *Achmed und Stefan*. Düsseldorf, Germany: Schwann Verlag.

Miller, D. (1987). *Material culture and mass consumption*. Oxford, UK: Basil Blackwell.

Mintz, S. (1985). *Sweetness and power*. New York: Elisabeth Sifton Books.

Pic-nic [Advertisement]. (1994, May 31). *Hüurriyet*, p. 16.

Redhouse Turkish-English Dictionary. (1984). Istanbul: Redhouse Yayinevi.

Şen, F. (1988). *The Turkish enterprises in the Federal Republic of Germany* (Report). Berlin: Türkei Zentrum.

Şen, F. (1993). 1961 bis 1993: Eine kurze Geschichte der Türken in Deutschland [1961 to 1993: A short history of Turks in Germany]. In C. Leggewie & Z. Senocak, (Eds.), *Deutsche Türken—Türk Almanlar*. Hamburg, Germany: Rowohlt.

Statistisches Bundesamt, Die Ausländerbeauftragte des Senats [Federal Statistics Office, The Commission for Foreigners]. (1991). *Türkische Berliner* [Berlin Turks]. Berlin: Verwaltungsdruckerei.

Statistisches Landesamt, Die Ausländerbeauftragte des Senats [State (Provincial) Statistics Office, The Commission for Foreigners]. (1991). *Türkische Berliner* [Berlin Turks]. Berlin: Verwaltungsdruckerei.

Weg vom Döner-Kebab und Bauchtanz-Image [Away from *döner kebap* and belly dance image]. (1987, April 14). *Volksblatt Berlin*, p. 11.

Wildt, M. (in press). *Plurality of taste: Food consumption in West Germany during the 1950s*. Bremen, Germany: Edition Con.

Zentrum für Entwicklungsländer-Forschung [Center for Developing Countries Research]. (1990). *Die Raumliche Ausbreitung Türkischer Wirtschaftsaktivitäten in Berlin (West): Dichte der türkischen Wohnbevölkerung, Gesamtzahl der Türkischen Läden, Prozentualer Anteil der einzelnen Branchen* [Spatial distribution of the economic activities of Turks in West Berlin: Density of Turkish population, total number of Turkish shops, percent division of different branches]. Berlin: Free University.

Zentrum für Türkeistudien. (1992). *Konsumgewohnheiten und wirtschaftliche Situation der Türkischen Bevölkerunf in der Bundesrepublik Deutschland* [Consumption patterns and the economic situation of Turkish population in Germany]. Unpublished manuscript, Zentrum fü Türkeistudien, Essen, Germany.

9

Blurred Borders: Local and Global Consumer Culture in Northern Ireland

THOMAS M. WILSON

During the last year, few results of the initial stages of the completion of the European Community's (EC) single internal market have captured the attention of both the media and the EC's people. Until recently, *1992* (the target date for the completion of the single European market) symbolized the EC's drive toward a market without barriers to the free movement of people, goods, capital, and information, a goal that is meant to have serious and long-lasting effects on the everyday lives of all Europeans—not just those in the EC's 15 member states. The single market is a process, however, and in 1995 a great deal remains to be done to complete a true common market.

Perhaps the most immediate and most recognized impact of *1992* is in the world of marketing and consumption. The ironic title of a *New York Times* article perhaps best sums up the relatively undramatic advent of a "New Europe": "Barriers Fade for European Shoppers" (Stevenson, 1992, p. E2).[1] A whimper rather than a bang heralded a new

AUTHOR'S NOTE: I gratefully acknowledge the financial support of the National Endowment for the Humanities, the Wenner-Gren Foundation for Anthropological Research, the British Council, and the Queen's University of Belfast. I acknowledge with thanks the critical comments of the editors and two anonymous readers.

EC-Europe, in which market forces are supposed to achieve further European economic and political integration and perhaps even political union. Sound effects notwithstanding, this new economic order frees more than 340 million consumers from most customs and excise taxes. Perhaps the 1992 project has not yet brought lower prices for consumer goods throughout the EC, although a number of production and service costs have been reduced, and perhaps in these recessionary times the majority of EC consumers find it all but impossible to avail themselves of bargains in other countries. But as a result of the single market, a number of shopping arenas have become much more important than they were previously, and some have taken on more international and interethnic significance. Among these are the shopping zones that help to define the EC's borderlands.

Some of the key features of border cultures—aspects of the cultural landscapes of international borders that seem so familiar to travelers but that often symbolize the differences of a cultural Other—are commercial relations. Although transfrontier political systems have been receiving increasing scholarly attention (see, for example, Anderson, 1982), the same has not been true of transfrontier cultural systems (Donnan & Wilson, 1994). One of the least studied and understood aspects of such systems and the relations that bind and divide populations on both sides of borders is consumption. It is also ironic that among the most recognizable and predictable features of cross-border commerce and consumption is shopping, a behavior that is second only to tourism for its importance in the daily lives of the citizens and residents of modern nation-states.

The transparency of shopping behavior across international borders may be misleading. Cross-border shopping involves regularized patterns of behavior that entail complex negotiations of language and other cultural symbols (such as advertisements and road signs); the movement of many people; the transfer of a great deal of capital; and the myriad economic, political, social, and cultural ramifications of attracting, servicing, and satisfying a large number of customers and clients (most of whom may not share a common heritage, race, ethnicity, nationality, or religion with the marketer or shopkeeper). International shopping is one of the many problematical areas for the social science of economic and political integration throughout the world, most notably in such areas as the EC, the North American Free Trade Area, and the new states of the former Soviet empire.

This chapter explores some of the issues of marketing and consumption at a contested border in Western Europe. It seeks to examine a few of the contradictions inherent in the processes of economic and political integration in the EC, especially between and among ethnic and national minorities in Ireland, some of whom may resist the integrating forces of the free market as much as they have the bullet and bomb of the state and the terrorists. For over 70 years, shopping has been one of the key factors in maintaining communication across barriers of nationalism and sectarianism at the Irish border. The economic roller coaster of the 1992 project, as it has been experienced at the border, has not been the shoppers' "liberation" that has been noted in other EC countries since 1993. On the contrary, the forces of economic integration, at the very least in the forms of tax and price harmonization, have diminished cross-border shopping across much of the Irish border (Wilson, 1993b). In doing so, the EC and its "Europe without frontiers" have removed one of the stimuli to cross-border and cross-national interaction and experience. The cultural barriers to cross-border communication in Ireland are strong. If the attractions are removed, then the cultural constructions of the Other will have one less experiential component. This is sure to lead to a strengthening of notions of ethnic and national difference, and its effects on a wide range of cultural identities—such as villager, county person, Irish, British, Catholic, Protestant, European—may become some of the most important problems for policymakers and scholars in the New Europe of the 21st century.

Let me end this introduction on a cautionary note. Shopping often does not seem like much, in the contexts of elite culture and of many domains of popular culture or in comparison with other areas of modern life. Nonetheless, it is a cornerstone of everyday life in the modern world. It involves a great deal of people's time, social energy, and capital as they sort out images and information, work to buy, travel to shop, consume, and negotiate the multitude of meanings about what they own and use in an extended self (Belk, 1988). This is as true of the Irish border people as it is of anyone. In this case, however, shopping for bargains across an international frontier may mean entering a war zone. Risking one's life for a bargain is an indication of the importance of shopping, at least for some products and at some times, in local culture. It is this importance—and some of the changes that the culture of consumption has undergone during the last few years—that are of concern in this chapter.

Consumer Culture

Consumer culture in all of its forms and at every level of sociocultural integration, including local cultures of consumption, has become an element in the constructions of our postindustrial and postmodern worlds. Consumer cultures are part of a process of creating an inter-dependent service society on a global scale, in which the technology of communication is helping many of the societies, nations, and cultures of the world break their bonds to their pasts, short-lived as they may have been in an epoch of *modernité*. One of the major impediments to this global culture, however, is the nation-state, which has been threat-ened since World War II by competing global hegemonies:

> In the postwar world, the nation-state was clearly obsolete, along with nationalism and all its rituals. In its place arose the new cultural imperial-isms of Soviet communism, American capitalism, and struggling to find a place between them, a new Europeanism. Here lay the hope of eroding the state and transcending the nation. (Smith, 1990, p. 172)

A manifestation of this Europeanism is the EC's internal market, which is another step in the creation of a continental political econ-omy in which cultural imperialism from the top down does not neces-sarily obliterate people's attachments to ethnic and national symbols, values, and histories. The Europe of the EC, like America, has sought unity through diversity, in which a pan-European global political-commercial culture might coexist with surviving ethnic and national cultural allegiances (Featherstone, 1991; Smith, 1990).

The EC processes of integration may not, in effect, be globalizing at all. Rather, they may be creating a European citizenry whose ethno-national allegiances are suppressed and/or co-opted by the social and cultural imperatives of postindustrialism on a continental scale (Schlesinger, 1987; Smith, 1990). Forces of European integration can re-sult in the strengthening of cultural differences between the very peo-ple who are the intended beneficiaries of increased economic and political interdependence (Wilson, 1993a). The globalization of cul-tures, through the creation of consumer societies, for example, will threaten the maintenance of continental-wide social systems, such as the United States and the EC, that are based on the balancing of national culture—that is, the construction of nation-state symbolic attachments determined and disseminated from above—and local ethnonational cultures, which to some of their members predate the creation of their states (e.g., Native Americans, Gaelic culture(s), and the Basques). The images of culture that are beamed throughout Europe and carried in person by business travelers and tourists may do as much to blur the definitions of the New Europe, which the EC is attempting to construct, as might the pressures emanating from its constituent nation-states, which are attempting to privilege their notions of national culture in an evolving continental system.

In the midst of these competing notions of cultural identity in Europe, in which the imagined community of the nation (Anderson, 1991) is increasingly pitted against the imagined community of the EC supranation, there creeps a third imagining, that of a common global culture of walking and talking consumers—real people. In fact, the everyday lives of Europeans are often lost in the cultural wars of state and suprastate making and maintenance. As Smith (1990) has concluded, "the main thrust of 'late capitalism' and/or 'postindustrialism' analyses is away from the small-scale community and towards a world of cultural imperialism, based on economic, state and communication technology institutions" (pp. 175-176). The EC, in its efforts to create a true internal market, is also helping to recreate consumer culture on the local and global levels. The changes that are resulting at the local level of the border in Ireland may be blurring both the distinctions between competing notions of consumer culture and the goals of the *1992* project. Anthropology has much to offer in the identification and comparative analysis of "the positive forms of consumption as a process" (Miller, 1987, p. 18). In the following sections I seek to identify some patterns of local consumption that produce local culture, aspects of which inform definitions of ethnicity and nation.

It is not my intention in this chapter to engage in any theoretical, classificatory, or methodological debate on the definitions of ethnicity and nation. In the Northern Ireland context, and I suggest perhaps in many places worldwide, it is more useful to look at contested and overlapping notions of ethnic and national identity. I suggest this precisely because the notions of ethnicity and nation are so mercurial in Northern Ireland, irrespective of the stubborn manner in which all people there identify themselves as members of majorities and minorities. In Northern Ireland, as elsewhere, " 'ethnicity' is a term that only makes sense in a context of relativities, of processes of identification, and that nevertheless aspires to concrete and positive status both as an attribute and as an analytical 'concept' " (Chapman, McDonald, & Tonkin, 1989, p. 16). In Northern Ireland, each side of the political divide sees itself as a "community of culture," that is, its members are united with each other and separated from the others by the possession of that culture (Smith, 1981, p. 13). Most definitions of nation encompass this notion of cultural identity, as, for example, in Smith's (1991) conclusion that a nation is "a named human population sharing an historic territory, common myths and historical memories, a mass, public culture, a common economy and common legal rights and duties for all members" (p. 14). In the Northern Irish context, however, the essential link of "nation" to common "state" structures excludes those nationalists who contend that mass public culture, legal rights and duties, and the economy are all British. *Their* nation is south of the border. As such, they are the ethnic and national minority in a "foreign" state.

Definition of ethnicity and nation are not matters of academic debate in the everyday lives of Northern Ireland's people. On the contrary, they are the basis of widespread "national" political movements. From an outsider's viewpoint, Protestants in Northern Ireland are part of dominant British life and are supporters of the British state, but they are not part of the British nation (which may not exist at all) or of the English nation. As a result, they are members of a minority group, an ethnic group, within the United Kingdom. Their overlapping identities (with concentric loyalties, such as those of the Scots as described by Smout, 1994) of Protestant, loyalist, unionist, and British make them British nationalists. They are thus, to some extent, opposed to becoming part of an Irish nation-state, in which they would be a very small and powerless minority, and are also confused about their future role in the British state. The nationalist community in Northern Ireland, on the other hand, aspires to the (re)unification of the Irish nation in an Irish Republic that incorporates the six counties of Northern Ireland. Although nominally nationalist, many Catholics and many Republicans also recognize their minority, regional, Northern Irish identity within Ireland and are aware that they share aspects of local identity, culture, and even ethnicity with their neighbors in Northern Ireland who may be part of different traditions. As Todd (1989) has concluded:

> Northern nationalists see themselves as struggling on behalf of the Irish nation for the right of national self determination: the nature and goals of the Irish nation are internally contested, but that such a nation exists is agreed by all. Unionists do not agree what nation, if any, they are struggling for—a British nation, an Ulster Protestant nation, a Northern Irish nation? Nor is it clear that any of these identities is itself a clear national identity. (p. 125)

The Blurring of Nation and State

After 6 years of war, rebellion, mutiny, and political crises in both Ireland and the rest of the British Isles, the Irish Free State was established in 1922. Within the year, the legal constitutional status of what was already a political fact was also established—six of the nine counties of Ireland's northern province, Ulster, were to remain a part of the (new) United Kingdom of Great Britain and Northern Ireland (as the new Irish political entity, sometimes called a *province*, was henceforth known). Although Northern Ireland set itself apart from the rest of Ireland (i.e., the 26 counties of the Free State), the majority of its people did not see themselves as separating or dividing anything. They were remaining loyal to the British Crown by maintaining political and economic union. In their eyes, the rest of the Irish, who were renouncing their Britishness, were the separatists. Thus, by 1923 an "international" border existed in Ireland where none had before. Since that date, the causes and effects of the partition of Ireland, as well as the essential definitions of *nation, ethnic group*, and *state* in Ireland have been contested throughout the British Isles. This has resulted in 70 years of misery and bloodshed, the most recent round of which erupted in 1969. Although the 1994 cease-fire provides some hope, the hostilities remain. The war is considered by some to be a civil war between Irish people, a war of national liberation against an imperial state by others, and a conflict of criminal terrorism and the basest sectarianism and racism by others. It is now entering its second quarter century. In Northern Ireland this war is known as "the Troubles." (For controversial historical overviews of these events, see Lee, 1989.)

Although, with little modification, the treaty-imposed land border between the Irish Free State (now the Republic of Ireland) and Northern Ireland followed existing county borders and approximated the traditional, if not mythic, provincial "border" of Ulster, the newly designated border was immediately controversial. (See Whyte, 1991, for an excellent analysis of the controversies surrounding the origins and the results of the creation of this border.) This controversy has become the stuff of nation building and mythmaking, if for no other reason than it created, or, perhaps stated more accurately, it reified an unequal, if not racist, society in Northern Ireland. One thing is clear: the "traditional" province of Ulster was divided, largely according to the wishes of the unionist majority in six of Ulster's nine counties, thereby relinquishing three mainly nationalist, republican, and Catholic counties to the new Free State. This, in effect, created a province in which two thirds of its people were Protestant (i.e., most were Church of Ireland [Anglican] and Presbyterian) and one third were Catholic. The sociopolitical system thus created was based on sectarianism, in which the Protestant majority (most of whom were loyalist and unionist) established itself as the political leaders of the province. The Catholic minority, who would have been a majority in Northern Ireland if all nine counties had been kept together, experienced this sectarian leadership as "mastery" and with a no less sectarian reaction.

A sociopolitical history of the province from the 1920s to today is beyond the scope of this chapter. Suffice it to say that contrary to much of the sound-bite journalism that informs the production of global images of Northern Ireland throughout the world today, the war that is now raging is much more complex than the perception that it simply involves Catholics and Protestants killing each other because of ancient tribal hatreds. The bloodshed may indeed be reduced to the simplest of levels—by academics, journalists, and the people who are its perpetrators and victims—but this violence is experienced in a multitude of ways, with a multiplicity of meanings. The people of Northern Ireland, from all cultural traditions, share a common culture because of their life experiences in the province. Some of this common culture is racist, sectarian, and murderous. Some of it is generous, loving, and respectful. Much of it is a complex morass of political and religious symbolic actions that define the identities of the Northern Irish people who belong to the many national and ethnic groups who populate a province that— to an American audience conditioned to CNN images—looks like a lot of white Christians murdering each other because of outdated notions that the Irish hate the English and want their freedom.

All political behavior and events in Northern Ireland are multivocal symbolic acts. This may seem to be patently obvious. After all, every political act is symbolically charged. But in Northern Ireland, as is crystal clear to its people, the symbolism of any political act is extremely complicated and is received in varying ways, depending on whether the audience is unionist, loyalist, Protestant, and British or republican, nationalist, Catholic, and Irish. To the majority of outsiders, these symbolic categories may appear to be largely synonymous and equally matched and paired. The reality in Northern Ireland is much more complicated.

Not all Northern Ireland Protestants are unionists (a political ideology committing people to the maintenance of the province's political role as an integral part of the United Kingdom), nor are all Protestants loyalists. The loyalist is a more difficult social status to define than unionist because it reflects past family and community traditions and ties, and it connotes rather than denotes a Britishness, in which one is loyal to the Crown, the United Kingdom, and/or (simply) the British way of life. Many people I have interviewed during the last few years[2] have suggested that loyalists are principally loyal to the Northern Ireland Protestant way of life, which many loyalists often mistakenly believe is similar, if not the same, to the British (read English) way of life. Many, if not most, unionists are loyalists, and vice versa, but this relationship is not a necessary one. Many unionists do not act out of blind or traditional loyalism, as some of their detractors suggest. They want to sustain political ties to the United Kingdom because they hope for a better Northern Ireland. Without this tie, for example, within a "Europe of the Regions," which some nationalists seek (see, e.g., Hume, 1988), they believe the province will suffer. Many loyalists, on the other hand, do not belong to or agree with the activities of the unionist political parties, yet they are in sympathy with their aims. Thus, loyalism and unionism are both political traditions and ideologies among Protestants. I have not yet met a Catholic unionist or a Catholic loyalist, but Northern Ireland people have told me that they exist. In the maze of political-cultural life that is Northern Ireland, I do not doubt it. (See Donnan & McFarlane, 1986; Jenkins, 1986, for the clearest anthropological introductions to the cultures of Northern Ireland during the Troubles.)

Notions of nationalism and ethnicity are important for everyone in Northern Ireland and are just as complicated and overlapping as their political ideologies. Unionists and loyalists are clearly seen by most people, including themselves, to be British. This is a statement of origins—they are among the original "British" people (for a review of the complications of the historical constructions of Northern Ireland Protestant culture, see Buckley, 1989)—and one of intent—they will stay part of "Britain" (i.e., the United Kingdom and English-British culture). The notion of nationhood, however, is much more problematic to Northern Ireland Protestants than the simple ascription of "British." Protestants recognize and valorize their distinct culture as Northern Ireland Protestants. They know that although they may be British, they are also a separate people with a clearly defined history. For most, this means that they descend from the groups of people who were settled, or "planted," in Northern Ireland as a result of waves of forced migration from elsewhere in the British Isles. Most of these ancestors arrived in Ireland after the 15th century from Scotland and England, and the vast majority of them were Protestants. A small minority of Northern Irish people, however, apparently think that they descend from the original inhabitants of Ireland, who departed its shores in prehistory to settle and populate Scotland and then returned, as Scots, in the 17th century. This belief functions as a way of awarding "Ulsterman" (an appellation connoting Protestant radicalism) proprietary rights to the island and denying origin myths to the Catholic, republican nation (which is itself a historical invention; for a discussion of the constructions of Ulster history, see Buckley, 1989).

The recognition and projection of distinct culture is a two-edged sword for Protestants. Because most seemingly want to retain both the union and their Britishness, which represent their state and nation respectively, their Ulster Protestant character has made them a regional or ethnic culture within Britain. Very few Ulstermen (Catholics eschew this title in favor of "Irishmen" and are also denied it by many Northern Ireland Protestants) want to see a separate Ulster nation-state. Thus, Protestants are increasingly realizing their ethnic minority status within the United Kingdom and their national minority status in Ireland taken as a whole (see Todd, 1987, 1989, 1990, for an illuminating analysis of the contradictions in Northern Ireland political culture).

Most Catholics in Northern Ireland, on the other hand, see themselves as part of the Irish nation, which, in "the South" (i.e., the Republic of Ireland) at least, has already achieved its "nationhood" (i.e., statehood and state hegemony). Those nationalists who pursue violence to end Northern Ireland's role in the United Kingdom are often called republicans. This is a misnomer in a number of cases because many members of the branches or factions in the armed republican movement (the largest of which is the Irish Republican Army, or IRA) espouse the creation of a socialist republic. If unification is achieved, and there is a 32-county state, these republicans may still wage war against that state's capitalist structures. Not all Northern Ireland Catholics are republicans, however, nor are they all nationalists (i.e., those who seek the reunification of the Irish nation and state). There are many nationalists, in fact, who publicly oppose the methods and the goals of the republicans. But it is very difficult for Catholics, raised in a tradition of victimization, to avoid adopting the political title given to them within Northern Irish culture. They are the "nationalist community," but this title obscures the many divisions and disputes that exist among all of Northern Ireland's minority peoples—just as titles such as Protestant and unionist obscure the many cleavages among its majority peoples. In this environment of traditional and renewed violence and hatred, there are many factors that militate against regularized, informal, and mutually satisfying relationships, both between Catholics and Protestants in the province and between Northern Ireland people and those of the Republic. Nonetheless, some sets of relations do transcend ethnic, national, and sectarian barriers, and some of these are in the realms of work and leisure, within cultures of production and consumption. One arena in which this has occurred is at the border between Northern Ireland and the Republic.

Border Shopping

The creation of the land border between the two Irelands did much more than create a symbolic battleground for contesting nations. It physically and legally separated people and their communities. At some points the border literally divided farms in half and even ran through the middle of buildings. Today this sometimes has its lighter side. I have heard of a man who put his farm's diesel fuel tank astride the border, with taps at both ends so that he could smuggle cheap fuel from either side of the border, depending on which had cheaper prices. Overall, however, the borderline divided kin, friends, and business relations. In the northwest of Ireland, the entire county of Donegal was made part of the Free State, creating an international boundary between it and its urban center, Derry—the second largest city in Northern Ireland. At the eastern end of the border, the frontier created a series of legal and economic barriers between the twin towns of Newry, in the North, and Dundalk, in the Free State. Although separated by 12 miles, neither of these towns had the infrastructure in the 1920s to suddenly become regional urban centers. Nonetheless, this was exactly what they were forced to do, as each became its country's last urban area on the road to either Dublin or Belfast. Furthermore, the border brought such obstacles to free movement and commerce as different currencies, customs regulations, immigration laws, and government standards in areas of industrial production, consumer relations, censorship, and health. Newry and Dundalk were made to turn away from each other and from many of the people in their surrounding rural areas, who had relied on their local town as a commercial center. Dundalk is only 4 miles away from the nearest point of Northern Ireland, but the people there were henceforth inclined to go to Newry for much of their business. Likewise, the Cooley peninsula north of Dundalk remained in southern Ireland, although its inhabitants clearly have better roads to Newry, 6 miles away. Nevertheless, their sociopolitical lives were turned around and made part of Dundalk, 12 miles distant.

Over the last three generations, however, the border in this eastern region has become an opportunity as well as an obstacle. Although the border appears to outsiders to be a barrier to communication and relationships, to many border people it is a conduit for the maintenance of a regional border culture. As I have reviewed elsewhere (Wilson, 1993a), borderers have sustained long and deep relations with kin and friends across the divide despite the obstacles involved. They have achieved this through church-related organizations, religious observances, sporting occasions and clubs, and socializing in pubs and discos. Although there have been very few political ties across the border in the past, except in illegal terrorist activities, cross-border activities by local and national governments are now encouraged by the EC. Border people have also sustained many economic relationships across the border. All locals know smugglers or know about ways to smuggle. I have met very few people who admit to being a smuggler, yet millions of pounds of goods are annually smuggled each way across the border. But one of the most important, and least dramatic, ways that people from both sides of the border have consistently kept in contact despite many ethnic and national differences has been through cross-border shopping. This may not be surprising to those who know about getting a bargain elsewhere in Europe or America, for example, across the Danish border in Germany, the French border in Spain, or the Canadian one in the United States. But for 25 years, this shopping has taken place in the middle of a war.

After partition, the relations between the people of the rural and urban areas of Newry and Dundalk both diverged and converged. A great deal of these relations were commercial. The people of this border region adapted in ways that allowed them to live and work together, regardless of the machinations of statesmen and irrespective of their own nationalist and sectarian beliefs, traditions, and prejudices. Thus, throughout the Economic War of the 1920s, World War II (in which Éire, as the Free State was then known, was neutral), the postwar recessions, and the cold war, Newry and Dundalk learned not only to tolerate the border but to define themselves according to it.

By the 1970s, local residents had become used to the bipolarity of their lives. Certain goods were cheaper on either side of the border, so consumers grew accustomed to traveling for bargains. For example, Northerners came south during World War II for fresh farm produce, whereas Southerners crossed the border for the manufactured goods of Britain and the United States. Many local families have told me tales of going to shops on the other side of the border for cheap "product x." The product might have been butter, onions, lamb, tires, or petrol. This consumer culture developed rapidly and continued to evolve until both countries joined the EC in 1973, when the traditions of cross-border shopping and smuggling were elevated to a different plane in which the supranational forces of a common market, especially in the guise of the EC's Common Agricultural Policy, intensified the commercial arena. Although the EC seemed to promise the contradictory goals of harmonization of sales and excise taxes, market integration, and member state independence and sovereignty, in practice the economic divergence within the EC between the United Kingdom and the Republic was pronounced and immediate. In 1979, Ireland joined the European Monetary System but the United Kingdom remained outside. This resulted in the split between their currencies as Ireland went off the sterling standard, which, in turn, made prices at the Irish border diverge considerably.

The 1980s saw a local cultural adaptation (i.e., cross-border shopping for lower priced goods) mushroom into a national phenomenon among the people of the South. Because of lower value-added tax on a variety of products—most notably liquor, beer, wine, cigarettes, toys, electrical appliances, and petrol—thousands of Southern consumers flocked to Northern Ireland border communities each year. Busloads of shoppers arrived in Newry and its surrounding villages, some of them after 7 hours on the road. One local likened them to "locusts" as they spread out to make their purchases and, after a few hours of frenzied activity, flew back to their hired coaches with full shopping bags. A sociologist from Limerick reminisced that when he was younger, his mother would return from these chartered bus excursions to Northern Ireland with huge tubs of what started out as frozen butter, purchased at a volume and a price unavailable in the Republic, and obviously worth the risk of meltdown.

The Troubles may have been a consideration but were certainly no deterrent to this "Golden Horde" of Irish shoppers. Prices were up to a third cheaper on the Northern side of the border, Irish customs agents were overworked, there were many unpatrolled border crossings, and, for many people on the Southern side of the border, there was easier access to Northern Irish villages and towns. In fact, at the height of cross-border shopping in the mid-1980s, villages literally sprang up on the northern side. At the road point closest to Dundalk, a shop and petrol station hived off to become five shops, two petrol stations, and a post box—a satellite village just 2 miles away from its own core village. The new village was there to service consumers from the South.

This wave of shoppers became an economic and diplomatic problem for the Republic and a severe threat to the livelihood of merchants on the Southern side of the border. Most petrol stations in and around Dundalk closed in the 1980s as a result of the loss of customers, who were responding to border road sign calls to "fill up at Northern prices!" Electrical shops and liquor stores could barely keep their doors open, whereas pubs relied on traditional clientele, safety, and the fear of drunk driving as their selling points (Northern pubs had cheaper drinks but were favorite targets for bombers and gunmen). Dundalk's merchants were going under, and they demanded that their national government protect them. They wanted a "level playing field," that is, an equal chance to compete with Northern shopkeepers.

The Irish government was well aware of the problem. The EC's common market in the 1980s was anything but a free market for consumers and governments alike. By 1986 the Irish state was losing up to £300 million a year to the North in the value of consumers' purchases and was suffering £20 million a year in lost taxes (Fitzgerald, Quinn, Whelan, & Williams, 1988). Very few Northerners, in turn, shopped south of the border. To make matters worse, Ireland was experiencing increasing prices, rising unemployment, and the threat of reduced EC structural funds, which were, in the final analysis, keeping the Irish economy healthy.

Thus, in 1987 the Irish government risked breaking EC law by establishing stringent limits on shoppers' cross-border purchases, which touched off a controversy that did not end until the beginning of the internal market in 1993. (For a detailed view of the Irish government's actions and their effects at the Irish border, see Wilson, 1993b.) These new laws, in combination with an increase in British taxes and a higher U.K. inflation rate, had the desired effect for the Irish government (but certainly not for the consumers on both sides of the border). By 1992 prices had equalized at the border. Nevertheless, throughout the time of my field research there, Southerners continually went north for petrol, spirits, wine, beer, and cigarettes. They just did not come from as far away. Border consumer culture, in fact, had returned to "normal," that is, the patterns before EC membership.

Nevertheless, this return to cultural forms of the recent past tended to obscure some essential transformations in border life. Newry and Dundalk had grown in very similar ways in the 1980s and 1990s. Each town had a population approaching 30,000 and unemployment rates estimated at from 25% to 35%. The industrial infrastructure of each town had deteriorated as the industries that had made the towns famous closed. Newry relied increasingly on British state subsidies, whereas Dundalk depended on Irish state grants. In a country among the poorest in the EC, however, those "state" funds were often from Brussels. Each of the towns had developed reputations, both locally and nationally, as rough, violent, and republican. Both towns' populations are principally Catholic, and there is a great deal of popular support and sentiment for the IRA in each. Consequently, the few Protestant enclaves in and around Newry have taken on another sort of frontier mentality in that they perceive they are surrounded by "the enemy." This is ironic, because it is exactly this sort of ideology that pervades most Catholic communities in Northern Ireland. They, too, feel threatened on all sides.

Newry is a violent town because of the ongoing war. The violence is experienced in many ways, from arguments in pubs to 500-pound bombs. Army foot and motorized patrols are a constant presence. Yet they and the police cannot seem to stop a determined enemy. During 1992 to 1994, for example, mortar rounds have been fired at Newry's town center, police cars have been attacked by rockets near the shopping district, and snipers have stalked the security forces in the surrounding hills.

Helicopters constantly patrol the border. British army checkpoints dot the roads into the province. Some of these roads are blown up by the security forces to prevent their use by terrorists. Electronic surveillance towers videotape all cars entering and leaving Northern Ireland. To get to Newry on the main road from Dundalk, one must pass through a state-of-the-art permanent border checkpoint, complete with a complex of high-tech electronics and low-tech army grunts, who ask for drivers' identifications and who have the power to strip down any person and vehicle they suspect. And still the shoppers come.

In the run-up to the 1992 deadline for a common market, the differences in cross-border prices in everything except alcohol, cigarettes, and petrol were so small that the number of shoppers from the South had fallen drastically. To many merchants in Newry, this was a portent of things to come in the single market. After all, the harmonization and integration of the two economies might be beneficial to their respective states but promised to be detrimental to the local Newry economy, which had depended for almost 20 years on the strong cross-border trade. The 1992 project promised to put an end to customs stops at the border, which would threaten the jobs of almost 200 people who worked as government and private customs agents in the Newry-Dundalk area. In a single market, the heavy lorry traffic would no longer have cause to stop in either town on their way to and from Northern Irish ports (which are the most heavily used container ports in Ireland). In 1992 many businesses on both sides of the border geared up for a slow start to the new year.

The falloff in Southern consumers in Newry was not without its silver lining, however. Many Newry people had long been fed up with the noise, pollution, traffic, parking problems, and crowded stores. Common religion, ethnicity, and political values may be factors of cultural convergence and for some the basis for radical political action, but for many Newry people they were not sufficient reasons to accept a diminished quality of life. In short, the influx of shoppers had become an irritant to some Newry people.

Anthropologists, among others, have for years analyzed some essential contradictions in Northern Irish culture, not the least of which is that two communities who seem to have so much in common, who have lived together for years in relative peace, have now entered into a bitter war, with overtones of a battle to the death. In some communities in Northern Ireland, both before and since the Troubles returned, Catholics and Protestants have seemed to understand and tolerate each other. In others, however, daily life has become one of survival, in a zero-sum game with the Others. As I outlined above, one could explain both the violence and the tolerance by reference to notions of religion, ethnicity, culture, and nationality. One conclusion that might be drawn is that Protestants and Catholics in Northern Ireland do not get along with each other in terms of the most important aspects of their lives, that is, their definitions of their cultural identities. Protestants view religion as central to their identities, whereas Catholics see culture as the most important element in theirs (Elliott, 1993a, 1993b). Nevertheless, for hundreds of years both groups have lived and worked together in mixed communities. A solution to the problems of nation and religion in Northern Ireland is distant, as are solutions to parallel wars of ethnonationalism in Yugoslavia, Transcaucasia, and Southeast Asia. (See Whyte, 1991, for an overview of ethnographic studies in Northern Ireland; see also Harris, 1972; Leyton, 1975; and Sluka, 1989, as good examples of the range of interpretations of Northern Irish society by ethnographers.)

The state of consumer culture in Newry also offers a parallel. I do not imply that bloodshed would result if shopping queues are too long at the supermarket, but I do suggest that Newry residents get along with Southerners because they agree with each other on the important aspects of identity, namely, religion, culture, and ethnicity. There are, however, many aspects of community life that they do not share with Southerners but have in common with Northern Protestants because of shared experiences *of* community *in* Northern Ireland. Simply put, people from the Republic are different from Northern Irish people in a number of locally recognized, somewhat unimportant, but nevertheless noticeable ways. Dress, dialect, education, and sense of humor are among the stereotypes I hear most often on both sides of the border. I do not want to overstate this, but it shows that on the most human of levels—that of with whom do we want to live and with whom do we not want to live—there is no simple match between the people of like ethnicities who live across an international divide from each other. At any rate, the EC's 1992 project seemed to promise an end to the pull factor of cheaper prices in Northern Ireland, that is, until the crisis in the EC currency market in autumn 1992.

European Harmony?

By mid-1992 Dundalk merchants had begun to breathe sighs of relief. The price for most commodities had equalized between the United Kingdom and the Republic. The Irish government had announced new industrial schemes intended to revitalize the town's economy. The expected layoffs in the customs clearance business were still at least half a year away (and even as recently as late 1992, many people on both sides of the border professed ignorance regarding the 1992 project and its consequences in their lives). Overall, business, in the form of shoppers, was improving.

This had the opposite effect in Newry. Shops were feeling the loss of cross-border customers. Since 1987, when the Irish government moved to control the spending of day-trippers (Wilson, 1993b), Newry's economy had to adapt to the changes in border consumer patterns. This is not to say that Southerners no longer traveled in search of value and bargains. Few did so from great distances, however. The bus extravaganzas were a thing of the past. On weekends in March 1992, fully a third of parked cars in Newry's central car parks were registered in the South (count on the basis of my own random sampling). Most of these cars from the Republic came from border counties. Parking attendants later in the year estimated that the numbers had fallen to a trickle of less than 10% of the total number of parked cars in town center. My observations support these estimates. In the summer of 1992, Newry people began to miss the steady influx of cross-border shoppers. In September, however, the pattern of border consumption changed once again because of developments at the national and supranational levels.

The United Kingdom was forced to withdraw from the Exchange Rate Mechanism of the European Monetary System in September 1992. To protect it the British government devalued its currency. In just a few weeks, as a consequence, the pound's value dropped by over 10%. At the border, where in August the pound had been worth 1.07 Irish punts, the currency value flip-flopped. The punt was worth 1.07 pounds. This immediately brought the shoppers back, many of whom jumped at the chance to spend punts at face value (e.g., petrol stations displayed signs such as "Irish pounds, one for one").

Newry merchants had been developing a marketing strategy before this new development that served them well in the months that followed. Although wholesale prices did not begin to rise very quickly, it was inevitable that they would because of the United Kingdom's high import levels. From September, Newry merchants wanted Southerners' cash, and they wanted it fast. Their competition was not merchants in the South, however, who once again were handicapped because the prices they could charge were 20% higher than in Northern Ireland. Irish banks, on the other hand, began offering extremely high interest rates to draw in the capital to finance their currency speculation on world markets. Newry retailers expected that their prices would have to rise because of the projected higher costs, so they intensified their marketing on both sides of the border. The success of this strategy among Southern shoppers is exemplified by Newry's shopping center.

THE BUTTERCRANE

Newry's modern shopping center, the Buttercrane, opened in 1988. It was, in the words of its present general manager, a "child of the cross-border boom."[3] Since its start it has become the prime retail area in the town. Most of the nationally famous retail outlets (the "high street" names) in Newry have their local branches in the Buttercrane. It is easy to see why. It has a modern design and includes 38 shops, with 195,000 square feet of retail space and parking places for 530 cars on a total site of 7.5 acres just beside the Newry canal, south of town center (putting it closer to the border than its competition in the town high street).

The Buttercrane site was picked to take advantage of two consumer trends. Lower prices, product variety, brand-name quality, and retailer recognition were designed to draw the shopper across the border. The local and provincial marketing of the center was also intended to draw Northern Ireland shoppers from as far away as Belfast (35 miles). To achieve this, the Buttercrane projected a number of images. For the family-oriented shoppers, the center adopted a "Big Bird"-type logo, which is now recognizable throughout the province. The Buttercrane also projected an image of high street quality, namely, that of British national chain stores with high recognition value (such as Boot's chemists, Clark's shoes, and Burton's suits), and advertised the accessibility and facility of a free car park at the center's door. Also, all the shops were under one roof, which is no small draw in a country in which it rains two days out of every three.

Newry is one of the biggest retail centers in Northern Ireland (after Belfast, Derry, and Lisburn). This is because of the large population in its catchment area, which includes the cross-border counties. It is also because many people in the North have discretionary capital. This may be surprising given the Troubles and Northern Ireland's economic peripherality. A number of factors account for this among Newry's working and middle classes. Northern Ireland has the lowest housing costs in the British Isles. Most people in the province are in service employment, and most of them are employed by the state. Because of the Troubles and because there is no solution in sight, there is no reason to think that the government will reduce its workforce in the foreseeable future. This job security helps to encourage a "work to spend" or "work to enjoy" ethos in the province. Newry's local economy is also made wealthier through the smuggling of a wide range of farm goods, petrol, diesel fuel, spirits, beer, and electrical goods. This "black economy" produces a great deal of discretionary income in the form of cash, a good proportion of which is injected into the local economy.

Although the shopping center missed the cross-border boom, over the years it has developed a steady trade with customers in the South. This is due in part to its marketing strategy on local and national radio and television, which is aimed at the "housewife" audience. Television ads run, complete with the Big Bird logo, during the news hours, soap opera slots, and wrestling programs (the Buttercrane's manager assured me that the wrestling-slot ads were certain to reach the provinces' housewives). These strategies work. In 1989 a Buttercrane survey of customers showed that 25% of them live more than 10 miles away, whereas 50% live less than 5 miles away.[4]

Southern shoppers made up a large proportion of the Buttercrane customers from the start. As prices began to converge, however, their numbers dwindled. In the first quarter of 1992, cross-border trade at the center was only 8% of total business. After the September devaluation, however, Southern customers returned, swelling their share of the Buttercrane's total business in the last quarter of 1992 to 25%. This mini-boom did not last. First quarter business in 1993 dropped, especially after the Irish punt was also devalued. Today, Southerners continue to use Newry's shopping center, especially on holidays such as St. Patrick's day, which is a national holiday in the South, where all shops are closed. On St. Patrick's day, 1993, there was a queue of cars 2 miles long crossing the border into Newry. Such injections notwithstanding, the Buttercrane, like all merchants in the Newry area, can no longer rely on Republic shoppers for a major share of their business. The border may be more open because of the EC, but if international economic integration seeks to level off prices, then there will be little incentive for people in the South of Ireland to journey northward into a province fraught with violence, where the real borders are those of nationality and religion. The sociocultural consequences of this are the subject of the next section.

Local Identity and Consumption

In Northern Ireland, commercial relations tend to minimize the outward signs of ethnic conflict. Commercial relations reinforce rules of behavior that establish patterns of cooperation, coexistence, and social distance among Catholics and Protestants. Social scientists have explored the essential contradictions in Northern Irish society. These contradictions have parallels in most modern societies. All Protestants and Catholics demonstrate remarkable degrees of tolerance and cooperation in the public domains of work and leisure. Some of this is clearly because of the fear of trouble. This public tolerance of the Other may also be a reflection of a phenomenon in Northern Ireland that has been recognized by a number of ethnographers and other social scientists: In the private domains of family, church, and community, Catholics and Protestants also believe in tolerance and respect. (For a comprehensive review of these ethnographic viewpoints, see Donnan & McFarlane, 1986.) On the surface, this appears to be a predictable if not a commonsense relationship. The contradiction is, of course, that Protestants and Catholics also distrust, fear, hate, and oppose the Other in both the public and private domains. Sectarian politics, church leaders' pronouncements (one famous Belfast churchman refers to the Pope as the "anti-Christ"), and discriminatory hiring are but a few of the established patterns of ethnic and religious conflict. There is great pressure brought to bear by families and communities against mixed marriages, that is, between a Catholic and a Protestant. Regardless of expressed beliefs in tolerance, Protestants and Catholics will live with each other in very few communities in the province. Sectarian ghettos have divided cities into battlegrounds. One often knows the ethnic allegiance of an area by the national flags, wall paintings, and painted curbstones (red, white, and blue, the colors of the Union Jack; or orange, white, and green, the colors of the Irish Tricolor). On interpersonal levels, Catholics and Protestants often get along easily. At group and community levels, mistrust and antagonism, fueled by at least 25 years of violence and perceived by some to be the product of as many as 800 years of domination and resistance, are often the principles behind most social relations.

Contact and communication between the peoples of Northern Ireland and the Republic are also diverging in the public and private domains (in ways that are in need of much more scholarly attention). At the level of political ideology, many people in the Republic support the notion of a united Ireland. Fewer, however, either are committed to achieving unification or are willing to commit the resources necessary to seek solutions to the problem. The actions of the Irish government during the last quarter century might be interpreted as testament to the ambivalence of Irish national leaders to the North and "its" (not "our") problems. Many Northern Republicans today look to the Dublin government for leadership and support but are dismayed at recent Irish agreements with the British government that suggest that peace is attainable if unionists are also granted the right to self-determination. Unionists, on the other hand, see the recent Downing Street Declaration as a sellout to Republicans.

At personal levels, Southerners and Northerners often interact with each other across the border, in such activities as church and sports. But most of Ireland's people are remarkably tied to the place and idea of their community. For 70 years there have been two states on the island. This may not be a long time in the history of nations or states, but it can be a long time in terms of diverging cultural identities. As one historian in Belfast remarked to me:

> We Irish debate notions of the nation all the time, as if we never change. Just look at West and East Germany and the problems of unification there. The West Germans were surprised to discover that the East Germans have become different. And they were only separated for 45 years.[5]

In this chapter I am suggesting that the people of Northern Ireland and the Republic have also become different after 70 years of divergent state, national, and ethnic relations. The people on both sides of the border recognize this but are unsure of how different they have become and how important these differences are. One way in which they have kept in touch, through face-to-face relations, was in cross-border shopping.

I do not suggest that shoppers from the Republic are crossing the border in places such as Newry to intentionally improve relations between people on either side of the border. In fact, whenever I interview Southerners regarding their motives for shopping in Northern Ireland, the overwhelming response is that they do so for the economics, namely, the variety, quality, and low cost of goods. Their evidence usually centers on their fear of violence and random acts of terrorism. Many phrase it as "why else would we go into the middle of a war, if it weren't for the prices?" I also do not intend to imply that many Southerners have no other reasons for traveling into Northern Ireland. As mentioned previously, business relations, sports, religious activities, and tourism are some of the pull factors that encourage cross-border traffic. But among the people of the Republic's borderlands and for many others further south whom I have interviewed, the principal factor that influenced their cross-border movement, especially on day trips, was shopping.

Many shoppers express their mixed motives, however. Southerners are nominally interested in a united Ireland, and they feel tremendous sympathy for everyone, regardless of their religion and politics, who suffers personally because of the Troubles. Ireland's radio, television, and print news cover all Northern Ireland events as if they were local or national news. This gives events in the North an immediacy and relevance that is often lost on people in Great Britain and North America. Nevertheless, few shoppers go across the borderline to express solidarity with their Northern counterparts or to keep in touch in any special, cultural, or political sense. Day trips are undoubtedly recreational days, "out of the house" and away from other familiar settings (away from the usual village or town shops, for example). Such trips are also testament to a borderland's stubbornness that the war will not be allowed to upset everyday life. But if prices were equal and product availability were comparable, Southern shoppers would probably stay away.

A chapter such as this runs the risk of overstating the positive effects of shopping relations. After all, the media, sports, and religion also play parts in maintaining direct contacts among the people of Ireland, as well as building images that help all groups construct views of the others. But shopping is one of the few elective aspects of the public domain of border life and is perhaps the last elective aspect of cross-border relations that involves large numbers of people in purely commercial, low-key, face-to-face interaction. I do not wish to make a case for these ephemeral relationships as anything more than what I suggest; it is certain that they will never be a solution to the Troubles. But without the experience of the Other that such moments bring, can there ever be a solution? The people of the Republic seldom journey to Northern Ireland. Without shopping as an incentive, they will do less of it. This is sure to have consequences in the construction of ethnic, sectarian, and national stereotypes in both Irelands.

Conclusion

Cultural divergence of the sort I witness at the Irish border may be expected and predictable in an era of strong nation-states, but European nation-states are under the dual attack of EC supranation building from above and the globalization of culture through the communications media and multinational corporations. The EC's 1992 project is supposed to facilitate communication and understanding, primarily in and through commerce but also in just about every aspect of consumers' lives. The processes of price and tax harmonization and the move toward economic union and a common European currency may not have the EC's desired effects in the lives of certain communities, or even member nations. At the Irish border, consumer culture has fostered ties in the face of ethnic and national prejudices, values, and war. These ties are in danger of being cut.

The study of consumer culture at both the local and the global levels can help explore the blurred borders that exist in the construction of a postmodern world and in its social science. The EC's efforts to achieve "unity through diversity," through the creation of a 15-state consumer culture from the top down, may also be creating diversity as a reaction to the imposed unity. The 1992 project is intended to create a Europe without borders, yet in Northern Ireland it may be aiding processes of cultural divergence and alienation. The EC seeks to fashion the conditions under which new EC cultures of consumption, marketing, and other commercial relations can take hold. But at the Irish border, culture does not necessarily follow structure. Economic convergence cannot succeed if it overlooks "the vital role of common historical experiences and memories in shaping identity and culture" (Smith, 1990, p. 180). The shifting world in which all Europeans live is landscaped with dynamic populations of tourists, migrants, refugees, and, in many border areas, shoppers. These "ethnoscapes" (Appadurai, 1990, p. 297) permanently blur the borders between nations and states in Europe and elsewhere and make difficult attempts to construct the imagined communities of local, national, and international cultures.

At a global level, consumer culture is a force for cultural integration and homogenization. In its local manifestations, however, as lived and perceived in everyday lives, it can also divide by mitigating the processes of creating a common *ethnie,* that is, a set of symbols, myths, and traditions that form a basis for common cultural identity (Featherstone, 1991; Smith, 1990). Local consumer patterns at the Irish border have been disrupted by international forces aimed at, among other things, homogenizing and globalizing consumers' lives in the EC. Forces such as these are having an impact on people whose cultural identities are threatened by state and EC building, regionalism, ethnic conflict, and the divisive trends of world postmodern culture. Local consumer culture at the Irish border—cross-border shopping and smuggling that mediated cultural, ethnic, religious, and national conflict in the everyday lives of diverse groups—is at odds with global consumer culture to the extent that global forces ignore or exclude the realities of cultural identity in the lives of consumers.

Border cultural landscapes in Europe and beyond have always mediated between national cultures. Their inherent transnationalism accommodated the contradictions of ethnic groups and nations. Scholars of global culture may well be advised to view them as "third cultures" (Gessner & Schade, 1990, p. 259; see also Featherstone, 1991)—flash points at which the mismatches between and among cultural identities and the forces of global economic and cultural integration occur. Irish and British national identities in Northern Ireland do not depend on notions of local or global consumer culture for any part of their essential definition, but these common cultures can help shape the future of these identities. Nevertheless, consumer culture in Northern Ireland, like so many other aspects of Irish culture, is a contested boundary between ethnic and national communities. Perhaps it is inevitable that the border between local and global cultures and between Europeans' everyday experiences and the structures of the EC will become blurred in an era in which the nation-state can no longer contain ethnic conflict.

Notes

1. Copyright © 1992 by The New York Times Company. Reprinted by permission.

2. I have been conducting intermittent ethnographic field research at the Irish border since 1991.

3. My interview with Peter Murray, March 16, 1993.

4. The Buttercrane's surveys were based on customer interviews, a survey of car registrations, and the amount of Irish currency taken in at the center's tills.

5. My interview with Tony Canavan, August 19, 1993.

References

Anderson, B. (1991). *Imagined communities*. London: Verso.

Anderson, M. (1982). The political problems of frontier regions. *West European Politics*, 5(4), 1-17.

Appadurai, A. (1990). Disjuncture and difference in the global cultural economy. *Theory, Culture & Society, 7*, 295-310.

Belk, R. W. (1988). Possessions and the extended self. *Journal of Consumer Research, 15*, 139-168.

Buckley, A. (1989). "We're trying to find our identity": Uses of history among Ulster Protestants. In E. Tonkin, M. McDonald, & M. Chapman (Eds.), *History and ethnicity* (pp. 183-197). London: Routledge.

Chapman, M., McDonald, M., & Tonkin, E. (1989). Introduction. In E. Tonkin, M. McDonald, & M. Chapman (Eds.), *History and ethnicity* (pp. 1-21). London: Routledge.

Donnan, H., & McFarlane, G. (1986). Social anthropology and the sectarian divide in Northern Ireland. In R. Jenkins, H. Donnan, & G. McFarlane (Eds.), *The sectarian divide in Northern Ireland today* (pp. 23-37). London: Royal Anthropological Institute.

Donnan, H., & Wilson, T. M. (Eds.). (1994). *Border approaches: Anthropological perspectives on frontiers*. Lanham, MD: University Press of America.

Elliott, M. (1993a, August 16). Facing home truths. *Belfast Telegraph*, p. 10.

Elliott, M. (1993b, August 17). How little they know about us. *Belfast Telegraph*, p. 10.

Featherstone, M. (1991). *Consumer culture & postmodernism*. London: Sage.

Fitzgerald, J. D., Quinn, T. P., Whelan, B. J., & Williams, J. A. (1988). *An analysis of cross-border shopping*. Dublin: ESRI.

Gessner, V., & Schade, A. (1990). Conflicts of culture in cross-border legal relations: The conception of a research topic in the sociology of law. *Theory, Culture & Society, 7*, 253-277.

Harris, R. (1972). *Prejudice and tolerance in Ulster*. Manchester, UK: Manchester University Press.

Hume, J. (1988). Europe of the regions. In R. Kearney (Ed.), *Across the frontiers: Ireland in the 1990s* (pp. 45-57). Dublin: Wolfhound.

Jenkins, R. (1986). Northern Ireland: In what sense "religions" in conflict? In R. Jenkins, H. Donnan, & G. McFarlane (Eds.), *The sectarian divide in Northern Ireland today* (pp. 1-21). London: Royal Anthropological Institute.

Lee, J. J. (1989). *Ireland 1912-1985, politics and society*. Cambridge, UK: Cambridge University Press.

Leyton, E. (1975). *The one blood: Kinship and class in an Irish village*. St. John's, Newfoundland: Memorial University.

Miller, D. (1987). *Material culture and mass consumption*. Oxford, UK: Basil Blackwell.

Schlesinger, P. (1987). On national identity: Some conceptions and misconceptions criticised. *Social Science Information, 26*(2), 219-244.

Sluka, J. (1989). *Hearts, minds, fish, and water*. New Haven, CT: JAI.

Smith, A. (1981). *The ethnic revival*. Cambridge, UK: Cambridge University Press.

Smith, A. (1990). Towards a global culture? *Theory, Culture & Society, 7*, 171-191.

Smith, A. (1991). *National identity*. London: Penguin.

Smout, T. C. (1994). Perspectives on the Scottish identity. *Scottish Affairs, 6*, 101-113.

Stevenson, R. W. (1992, January 10). Barriers fade for European shoppers. *New York Times*, p. E2.

Todd, J. (1987). Two traditions in unionist political culture. *Irish Political Studies, 2,* 1-26.
Todd, J. (1989). Conflicting ideologies. *Revue Française de Civilisation Britannique, 5,* 117-129.
Todd, J. (1990). Northern Irish nationalist political culture. *Irish Political Studies, 5,* 31-44.
Whyte, J. (1991). *Interpreting Northern Ireland.* Oxford, UK: Clarendon.
Wilson, T. M. (1993a). Frontiers go but boundaries remain: The Irish border as a cultural divide. In T. M. Wilson & M. E. Smith (Eds.), *Cultural change and the new Europe: Perspectives on the European Community* (pp. 167-187). Boulder, CO: Westview.
Wilson, T. M. (1993b). Consumer culture and European integration at the Northern Irish border. In W. F. van Raaij & G. J. Bamossy (Eds.), *European advances in consumer research* (Vol. 1, pp. 293-299). Provo, UT: Association for Consumer Research.

10

Marketing Developing Society Crafts:
A Framework for Analysis and Change

KUNAL BASU

In a world of growing economic hegemony marked with the emergence of mass cultures, the drive toward cultural homogenization seems relentless. Beyond the functional thrust for standardization dictated by global commerce, the fundamental tenets of consumption and its relationship with culture are being reexamined. Increasingly, global criteria are seen as replacing local perspectives, resurrecting old debates on "who produces and for whom," on individuality versus universality in perception and preference, on appropriation and reappropriation, and eventually, on modernity and tradition. Whether the discourse is located within general theories of culture or political ideology or contextualized for a given people, the issues invariably encompass both material conditions for creation and transaction of goods and their appreciation in host and foreign cultures.

A particularly salient domain—aesthetics—may be viewed as a sensitive crucible that provides a locus for the study of cultural transformation. Clearly, the social history of the arts serves to illuminate the

AUTHOR'S NOTE: I am grateful to Russell W. Belk, Annamma Joy, Samuel J. Noumoff, the editors, and two anonymous reviewers for helpful comments.

dialectics of change that involve individuals and entities driven by respective production and consumption goals. This chapter will examine a specific genre of aesthetic products—traditional crafts from developing nations—from the dual perspectives of creation and consumption of culture. To the extent that developing society crafts are related to the cultural identity of their creators and, as an industry, support economic survival, a marketing analysis is likely to enhance the understanding of the key flows, that is, the transactions that act as the crucial vehicles for change. In the following section, a premise for the study of crafts will be presented on the basis of developmental and culture-related considerations, leading to an enunciation of specific study objectives.

Crafts: Economic
and Cultural Considerations

Production and marketing of traditional crafts are viewed in many developing nations as providing dual benefits of generating employment and foreign exchange earnings. Despite their extremely decentralized nature, which evades accurate measurement of output and employment, regional analyses routinely report artisans as constituting the second largest sector of rural employment after agriculture and as often associated with a higher household income (Jain, 1986). Full-time craft employment in Asia alone is estimated to be over 20 million (Pye, 1988) and is believed to be of special relevance to women, who constitute the majority in specific craft categories, for example, batik workers in Java (Joseph, 1988). In recent years, craft exports have grown faster than overall trade earnings for a number of developing countries. India, for example, has increased its international sales by 30%, Thailand by 38%, and Kenya by 25% per year for most of the past decade (Pye, 1988). International trade statistics for the Organization for Economic Cooperation and Development (OECD) countries, which dominate world import of crafts, indicate that developing countries account for 37%, or 15 billion dollars annually (Kathuria, 1986).

Besides its substantial economic scope, production of traditional crafts is believed to provide cultural continuity, to revive ethnic identity, and to strengthen local cultural institutions in developing societies (Stephen, 1991). It is argued that under the threat of economic and cultural integration that tends to turn indigenous communities into pale imitations of the masses of larger societies, practical and decorative crafts often provide the community's symbolic external boundaries reinforcing shared beliefs, customs, and values. The special economic relationship thus serves as recognition of cultural diversity, ensuring a value beyond its contribution to subsistence (Graburn, 1969).

Despite its attractiveness, craft ventures in most developing countries seem to be confronted with fundamental challenges. As such, locally produced handicrafts are often in competition with imported manufactured products. As rural incomes rise, cheaper, mass-produced goods are often chosen over traditional items,[1] and eventually the process of development itself, which enhances awareness of and access to organized production systems, leads to the disappearance of rural crafts industries (Cable & Weston, 1982). Examples include substitution of handloom and hand-printed textiles by machine-printed fabric, brass and bell-metal utensils by aluminum, and hand-knotted carpets by machine-made floor coverings. Although declining local demand often turns artisans toward other audiences, external or export requirements tend to induce considerable strain on the traditional production system—from determining where artisans should live and work to the symbolism and aesthetics associated with the products themselves. Export-led growth, although credited with survival of several crafts communities in developing countries (particularly in the context of tourism-driven revival of certain disappearing art and craft traditions; Belk, 1992; Belk & Costa, 1992), has nevertheless been critiqued because of a cultural subversion of sorts. Design and technical changes influenced by consuming publics of the external, dominant world have allegedly led to a genre of tourist or airport arts, in which the original symbolic content is reduced to conform to popular notions or stereotypes regarding minority groups—an ethnokitsch that is more a part of the worldview of dominant societies than that of the artisans themselves (Forster, 1964; Greenwood, 1977; Leong, 1989). The acculturation in turn may be responsible for the destruction of the very authenticity that formed the basis for its most genuine appreciation in external cultures.

As noted by several authors (Aziz, 1980; Stephen, 1991), the viability of crafts as an economic venture in the long run and also their cultural survival rest largely on the marketing system responsible for guiding the transaction of traditional goods in an increasingly accessible, secularized, and monetized global marketplace. The global transaction is seen as increasingly substituting the traditional exchange of indigenous crafts as gifts, with corresponding depersonalization in terms of their essential cultural meanings (Gregory, 1982). An entire tradition of research in cultural anthropology and folklore has examined indigenous production modes and forms and the dynamic aspects of change (Graburn, 1976). Consequently, a rich store of primary ethnographic and secondary macroeconomic data is available on several societies. International organizations (such as the International Trade Centre, Geneva) and national forums have also researched critical aspects of production and trade. Although market considerations have been salient in most of the above, the absence of a marketing perspective tends to limit analysis to aspects of the phenomenon, for example, the organization of production, export agents, and so forth, without comprehensive assessment of processes, agents, and structures within the major flows of the industry. The latter clearly is crucial in moving from a descriptive approach to a strategic orientation. The objective then is to explore the mutual interrelationships, to ask whether or not cultural identity will remain compatible with the chosen paths of development, and to assess whether or not demands for efficiency succeed in accommodating distinct indigenous expressions. The following sections include a specification of the domain of inquiry, that is, definitions of crafts and description of three constituent sectors—consumers, creators, and intermediaries. Last, a descriptive framework of marketing transactions is presented that allows identification of specific characteristics of the industry, with directions for change.

Crafts:
Definitional Issues

Besides the need for conceptual distinction, definitional clarity is critical for facilitating transactions within craft industries. Although most importing nations have preferential trade terms for crafts, there exists a wide variety in definitions, creating complex and confusing certification requirements for exporters in developing countries. The United Nations Council for Trade and Development's (UNCTAD) tariff classification characterizes crafts as those products that embody artistic features typical of the producing region and, further, requires that such be imparted by the manual part of the process, as opposed to machine-created components (Benjamin, 1981; Kathuria, 1986; UNCTAD, 1979). (The cited example in Kathuria, 1986, is hand embroidery in which the production of textile and apparel is achieved through machinery.) Some countries such as Canada and Australia further constrain the use of machine-produced raw materials and powered tools except under very limited conditions (Keesing, 1982). No specific definition, however, is applied in the European Economic Community (Commission of the European Communities, 1984). Besides the issue of trade regulations, there appears to be substantial variance across developing countries in terms of which products are deemed suitable for inclusion within the domestic crafts sector and hence qualified to receive special assistance (e.g., production and/or marketing subsidies). In Nepal, for example, crafts are undifferentiated from and included within other cottage industries (e.g., distilleries or detergent producers) on the basis of the value of the fixed assets of the enterprise, regardless of the nature of the product (Upadhyay & Sharma, 1988). In the Philippines, different agencies use different definitions: The Chamber of Handicrafts Industries prefers manual dexterity and indigenous materials as the twin criteria, excluding rattan products, whereas the Central Bank includes the latter in its classification (Pye, 1988). Broadly surveyed, most legal definitions seem to encompass varying subsets of three aspects: aesthetic representation symbolic of the producing culture, predominance of manual value addition in processing (with *handmade* signifying potentially more primitive and, hence, authentic creative forms), and small group or community-based organization for production.

By contrast, in academic literatures, the definition of crafts is often sought in relation to that for the arts. Becker (1978), for example, differentiated the two in terms of work organization, work ideology, and varying emphasis on standards of utility, virtuoso skill, and beauty. Crafts are viewed as products created to serve utilitarian needs of a customer, with emphasis on acquisition of specialized skill (such as that of a potter) and without serious consideration for beauty ("he contents himself that the pipe he installs carries water, the bookcase he builds is sturdy and fits in the space he measured for it," Becker, 1978, p. 866). Distinctions, however, are drawn with an "artist-craftsman-with more ambitious goals and ideologies" (p. 866), that is, one who is free from the employer-employee relationship and more closely resembles an artist. Hirschman (1983) has followed the above categorization in defining art as more abstract, subjectively experienced, nonutilitarian, unique, and holistic when compared to products generally (see also Hirschman & Wallendorf, 1982; Semenik, 1987). Viewed in conjunction with the above distinction, crafts may then be considered to embody either the obverse or lower proportions of these properties.

Although the range of crafts variously labeled as "folk," "primitive," "tribal," or "Third World" clearly include both craftlike as well as artlike qualities as described previously, the problem of categorization is compounded by the notion that aesthetic products may be "art by destination," that is, intended by their producers to be art per se, or "art by metamorphosis," the case when products serving various goals in one society are transferred to another and labeled as art (Maquet, 1971; cited in Graburn, 1976, p. 3). The latter may exemplify certain craft exports from developing nations, such as hand-knotted carpets—an alien utilitarian product that is vested with complex meanings in the Western world—or Mayan pottery that has no utilitarian appeal to urban-industrial consumers and is useless except as decorative objects. This transformation is also evident in the decontextualization that typically accompanies the display of ritual objects in ethnographic as well as art museums in the West (Ames, 1992). The utility-based distinction and resulting definitions of arts and crafts, however, have been critiqued as elitist, emerging in the high civilization of the postindustrial age without parallels in ancient societies (Graburn, 1976). Varadarajan (1991), for instance, claimed that scriptures such as the *Aitareya Brahmana* (900 to 700 B.C.) do not differentiate between art and craft, stating that aesthetic products (*silpa*) must reflect skill and be endowed with *chhanda*, that is, rhythm, balance, proportion, and harmony.

What characterizes crafts from developing societies, then, appears to be their aesthetic manifestation of regional culture with varying degrees of utility association in production and/or ultimate usage. This is common to the first of the three criteria invoked in the many policy-related characterizations described earlier and may constitute a parsimonious definition. Inherent is the recognition of diversity, in terms of both consumer perception (i.e., segments) and motivations of artisans. The simultaneous consideration of creators and consumers also allows focus on both production and consumption cultures with opportunities for contextual analysis of issues such as transformation, revival, or appropriation. If cultural preservation is the goal, analysis of authentic cultural representation could serve as the cornerstone to policy. To the extent that preservation of certain production organizations is the objective (as with several developing societies striving to support income-generating activities of indigenous communities), a varied scheme for trade or domestic policy may be needed. It may be advantageous, then, to move toward multiple categories of crafts themselves, each embodying varying combinations of human-machine involvement in processing (e.g., handmade batik, compared with machine-printed cloth using batik motifs) and small group-factory organizations of production. The "cultural representation" aspect would provide overall discrimination with respect to other products, that is, act as the outer boundary.[2] Definitional issues such as these illuminate the complexity of consumption, production, and transaction modalities that characterize crafts industries and are reviewed in the following sections.

Consumers and the Craft Product

Crafts and their consumers have been discussed under various organizational schemes, reflecting several disciplinary goals. In addition to chronological treatments by art historians, classifications have been based on the content of craft products, such as their degree of use of traditional or modern aspects of style, materials, and processes. (Graburn, 1976, for example, has proposed seven categories reflecting degrees of acculturation in craft products.) Classifications have also been based on consumers (domestic or export consumption; Subramanian & Cavusgil, 1991). Both approaches draw implicitly on analysis of the consumer-craft relationship in describing the existence of different markets for crafts.

In the absence of a direct appraisal of consumers' desires with respect to acquisition of craft objects and respective craft product implications, however, the assessment of variety in crafts appears to be somewhat sporadic. Tracing such desires to the nature of craft products may provide a simultaneous classification that bridges the perspectives of both creators and consumers and facilitates an inner dialogue in the industry. Also, it is important to ensure that such schemata not be ahistoric because the consumer-craft relationship has demonstrated both evolutionary and revivalist trends. I suggest five conceptually distinct categories of consumer desires—craft as trophy, knowledge, self-identity, status, and memory, each associated with a subset of nine craft product aspects: traditional portrayal, exoticism, compatibility with external usage contexts, relative age, material value, simplicity, singularity, portability, and affordability—that may influence the nature as well as transaction modalities of specific craft products. These reflect intuitive categories on the basis of a variety of ethnographic, historical, and economic analysis of transactions and suggest dominant consumption patterns without necessary mutual exclusion.

CRAFT AS TROPHY

Early examples of crafts outside their regional domains of creation and usage may be traced to imperial collections (Bascom, 1973). Although trade on items of perceived value such as gold, ivory, spices, silk, and so forth was predominant, crafts were not systematically collected. Colonial officers, after they had overcome their revulsion toward conquered societies, sometimes returned with souvenirs that found their way into private homes of European nobility (Claerhout, 1965). The Austrian imperial collection, for example, began with the voyages of Captain Cook, the dukes of Burgundy were known for their African collection in the early 1600s, and the London and Cambridge museums had Polynesian and Melanesian specimens (Gerbrands, 1957). Indeed, as described by Thomas (1991), the artifacts of non-Western people were known over a long period as "curiosities," and the creators of such—the indigenous peoples—were in fact "absent from the transactions which ostensibly constituted their engagement with the civilized world" (p. 183). Either obtained as gifts or plundered from shrines, these crafts probably reflected unacculturated traditional forms, symbols, or utilities. With the exception of precious gems or metals, there were hardly any bases for preference, and their ownership excluded appreciation of cultural or aesthetic meaning.

Although the desire for crafts exclusively as trophies, or symbolic of conquest, is uncharacteristic of present-day consumption, aspects of such are manifest from time to time in relation to pilfering of idols, ritual accessories, and so forth, in relatively inaccessible terrains (e.g., sub-Himalayan nations) or where internal strife has led to laxity in preservation (such as in Mayanmar or Cambodia). Admittedly, this is largely abetted by the need for antiquity, although their function as trophies (objects of material value) to the adventurous traveler remains plausible and has been documented on occasion (Maurer & Zeigler, 1988). The latter raises a parallel with modern-day tourism and the needs of certain segments of tourists to enshrine personal triumphs and voyages through acquisition of crafts (Gordon, 1986). This, though, is often related to the building of tangible memory traces and will be discussed in the section on "Craft as Memory."

CRAFT AS KNOWLEDGE

By the end of the 16th century, the importance of crafts emerged in European states possessing colonies as a means of understanding the subject peoples and creating an awareness and interest in them at home to foster trade. This coincided with the founding of ethnographic museums and the systematic study of other cultures. The focus on knowledge as a tool for exercise of power over conquered societies led to methodical study of the means and relationships of production and to the task of determining what Tylor (1871) described as the relation of the mental condition of savages to that of civilized man. Crafts, along with other aspects of material culture, provided "scientific" evidence of skill development among exotic peoples. In the absence of aesthetic appreciation, ethnological sections were usually separated from other collections in European museums and focused on harpoons, axes, oars, arrows, and the like (Goldwater, 1967). As Defert (1982) described, however, the "discovered people" (p. 13) were not submitted to an analysis of their internal coherence but studied within the methodologies of chronology and inventory that had meaning only for diplomatic, commercial, and religious strategies of domination.

In postcolonial Western societies, acquisition and display of developing society artifacts are subjected to cultural reconstructions that often exhibit "the dominance of a set of historically determined Euro-centered ways of seeing and imagining" (Lavine, 1991, p. 83). As claimed by Vogel (1991), representations of traditional artifacts are not politically neutral, and "the meanings we give to the objects visiting in our homes and museums are not those that inspired their creators" (p. 192). Thus, the craft object undergoes cultural dislocation, is recontextualized and reinterpreted, is emphasized selectively (Leong, 1989), and in the end serves to act as a document in confirmation of largely Western cultural and political theories. The Western desire for cultural documentation of the colonies also probably heralded the duplication of ritual and functional crafts for purposes of export and, in terms of craft product implications, an interest in realism or faithful naturalistic representations. The latter may also have followed from an attempt to depict the native as distinctly as possible from Western traits and value systems. Thus, portraits of village life and everyday utility items were favored over objects vested with nonmaterial meanings (Boyer, 1976). Although craft for knowledge, as a basis for cultural demarcation and interpretation of other societies, continues to permeate museum displays (Kirschenblatt-Gimblett, 1991), the need for global awareness in certain lifestyle segments in modern societies seems to contribute toward a desire for traditional items of everyday use from developing societies and justifies their continued presence in craft markets (Bouchard, 1981).

CRAFT AS SELF-IDENTITY

The role of crafts in providing a sense of identity and cultural discrimination has been historically pervasive. In addition to control of the colonized world, anthropological, biological, linguistic, racial, historical, and artifactual studies strengthened what Edward Said (1979) has termed "the idea of Europe, a collective notion identifying 'us' Europeans as against all 'those' non-Europeans" (p. 7). Crafts, as well as other aspects of material culture, helped define the "reason," "clarity," "directness," and "nobility" of the Occident as opposed to the "imprecision," "gullibility," "infantilism," and "emotion-proneness" of the Orient among other subject races (Cromer, 1913/1969; cited in Said, 1979, pp. 38, 40). Exemplifications in crafts focused on the most hideous specimens to testify to the strangeness and inhumanity of their customs (usually cult objects; von Siebold, 1843). These attempts at cultural demarcation also led to the examination of crafts from both aesthetic and symbolic perspectives. Relying on Darwinian theories, forms of art were seen as reflective of natural evolution—of intelligence (Haddon, 1895). "Primitive" art was viewed as conventionalized and simplified representations of natural objects, that is, the lowest form. Yet the very "savage-child" boundary in defining aesthetic identity in colonial societies formed the basis for some of the most influential cultural movements in Europe, particularly romanticism (in the late 18th and early 19th centuries), which sought an identity different from the artificial and complicated and embraced the simplicity and naturalness of subject peoples and their aesthetic modes of expression (Gauguin, 1931; Lovejoy, 1923). The influence of primitive or aboriginal crafts on several schools of art (postimpressionism, German expressionism, and fauvism) and artists has been well documented (Goldwater, 1967). These artists may be credited with ushering in a more complex relationship involving crafts from developing societies and their Western consumers—a relationship on the basis of vesting these objects with personal, symbolic meanings.

After World War II, the market for developing society crafts witnessed an unprecedented surge, and American and European buyers were sent into Asia, Africa, Oceania, and Latin America with large orders. This was also the beginning of a larger market for crafts beyond museums and private collections of the elite. The use of products generally as crucibles of symbolic meaning and vehicles for expressing identity has been prevalent in past eras. (See Belk, 1988a, for a review of the notion of self in relation to possessions.) Nevertheless, postindustrial societies appear to have elevated the role of material possessions in the determination of self-image (Belk, 1985). Furthermore, in the case of aesthetic objects, facets of consumption and symbolism relating to multisensory, fantasy, and emotive aspects (i.e., hedonistic) seem to dominate over those that are utility related (Hirschman & Holbrook, 1982). Undoubtedly idiosyncratic, such symbolic extensions in the case of craft products, however, may be construed in terms of certain key trends.

A major trend, ontologically similar to the early romantic perspective, is the revival of traditionality (in consumption mores) as an antithesis to the complex relationships of modern civilizations. Alienation between meaning and conditions of life or livelihood appears to give rise to "Modern Man losing his attachments to the workbench, the neighborhood, the town, the family, which he once called 'his own' but, at the same time, developing an interest in the 'real life' of others" (MacCannell, 1976, p. 91). Crafts and artisans appear to be outside of industrial time, "working like spiders, weaving to perfection" (p. 69). The consumption of traditional craft objects that provide a simple identification with chastity, purity, even poverty, allows the consumer to symbolically transgress the existing borders of his or her society. Often, functional objects from developing societies are desired for what they are, without adaptations for style or usage context, such as the *mola* dress of the Cuna Indians (Salvador, 1976). On occasion, the need for traditional and naturalistic depiction acts as a market signal leading to new genres—the application of indigenous styles and skills for creation of nonindigenous products, such as the *amate* bark-paper paintings of Xalitla, Mexico, which depict village nativity or historical scenes.

A second trend, commonly summarized as exoticism, draws from the continued interest in seeking differences in intellectual and artistic traditions as a way of establishing both personal and social identity (Csikszentmihalyi & Rochberg-Halton, 1981). Bourdieu (1984) claimed that such a manifestation of novelty (i.e., through aesthetic objects) serves to establish social distance. Although natural depictions from foreign cultures, as previously mentioned, may adequately serve such a purpose even without the antecedent motive of traditionalism, a common manifestation may be found in the search for exotic objects. Such objects, in the context of crafts, are often construed in terms of grotesqueness and gigantism. As described by Stewart (1984), "the spectacle of the grotesque involves a distancing of the object and a corresponding 'aesthetization' of it" (p. 107); the object is viewed as a "freak of nature," an aberration that "normalizes" the viewer. It appears to invoke wonder while avoiding contaminations—"Stand back, ladies and gentlemen, what you are about to see will shock and amaze you" (p. 108). Desire for exaggeration, distortion, or "something larger than life" tends to reinforce the excitement for the unknown and the untamed, the awe or terror, and creates the distinction from routine environments. Although certain crafts from developing countries (such as the Naga statuettes from India and Mayanmar or those from the Melanesian islands) seem to satisfy such canons of taste for exotic novelties in their original form, others have undergone mutations as a function of such a requirement. Probably the most notable of these are the *shetani,* or spirit forms developed by the Makonde people of Mozambique and Tanzania in the last 20 years, a departure from the *bindamu* carvings of purely African naturalistic forms (Körn, 1974).

It is important to recognize that the search for distinction via exotica is not limited to decorative objects but manifests in common usage items as well. Besides the adoption of traditional utility items in modern life (such as wicker baskets, straw bags, terra cotta planters, etc.), designers have sought distinction through "ethnic implants" in styles, motifs, colors, and materials. Thus, crafts without moorings in cultures of their origin have come to coexist with other displaced things and people. A particularly noteworthy example cited by Gupte (1988) involves the use of brocaded *saris,* a traditional attire for women in India, as shower curtains. Such divergence between the symbolism associated with creators and consumers has opened the door for a broader range of experimentation involving crafts from developing countries and the desire for compatibility with external usage contexts. Nevertheless, it has also raised complex definitional issues with respect to their status as cultural objects (Appadurai, 1990).

CRAFT AS STATUS

Although symbolic display is close to the notion of self-identity, and status may constitute a dimension of the latter, a separate discussion here may be useful in understanding how requirements of social power and authority might manifest in the desire for specific craft aspects. As Veblen (1899) pointed out, besides contributing to a complex set of meanings and gratification of beauty, aesthetic objects may be "coveted as valuable possessions, and their exclusive enjoyment gratifies the possessor's sense of pecuniary superiority" (p. 96).[3] Crafts, then, may be seen as providing the "evidence of wealth, it becomes honorific, and failure to consume becomes a mark of inferiority and demerit" (p. 64). In fact, Veblen went further in claiming that handcrafted items allow better opportunities for status discrimination because they are largely nonutilitarian and more expensive than comparable machine-made products. According to Brooks (1981), this "veneration of the archaic" (p. 22) is believed to foster "competitive display" (p. 19) and emulation in craft markets hierarchically structured with a small elite of dealers, investors, and connoisseurs who act as opinion leaders and manage the shifting secrets of quality.

The need for achieving status through possession of crafts probably underlies the demand for authenticity as a key determinant of quality. Spooner (1986) defined authenticity as "a conceptualization of elusive, inadequately defined, other cultural, socially ordered genuineness" (p. 225). Inherent are the twin issues of objective attributes and the social mechanisms for the negotiation of authenticity. Probably the key material determinants are assessment of antiquity, perceived conformity with traditional designs, handcrafting (as opposed to machine-produced clone commodities with easy replaceability), material value, and the degree of singularity—that is, specification of origin, for example—to a tribe and, in the extreme case, to a specific creator.

Although relative age remains the dominant criterion for rare craft objects and constitutes a basis for auction house and gallery-based dealerships, at the level of creation it has led to the fairly widespread phenomenon of "staged authenticity" (MacCannell, 1976, p. 91), or faking.[4] Several crafts have seen the emergence of dating techniques such as dipping ceramic pottery in mineral mixers, wooden carvings into termite molds (Carpenter, 1971; Crowley, 1970), and special treatment of paper for traditional paintings (Maduro, 1976). In terms of design, there has been a revival of traditional patterns and even adoption of such from other producing cultures. An example is the use of traditional Persian designs in contemporary carpet production in India and Pakistan (Cable & Weston, 1982). Emphasis on valuable raw materials has in some cases led to the substitution of traditional ingredients such as common wood with ebony and mahogany in certain genres of African carvings and to the use of ivory or bone implants (Segy, 1989). Last, the attribution of authenticity to specific creators and regions has led to the emergence of "branding," the practice of adding signatures to craft products. Thus, from "nameweavers" to labeled carvings, traditionally anonymous crafts are resingularized, taking on much of the characteristics of contemporary art (Price, 1989, p. 56).

As described by Spooner (1986), in addition to material evidence, the perception of authenticity is also largely determined through the reconstruction of the context of origin of the craft product. Here, the lore associated with the object is viewed as equally important. The historical information regarding producers, merchants, and processes of transaction constitutes a rich framework within which the craft object is valued. Thus, Bukhara carpets are appreciated for the lore encompassing the ancient central Asian city as a trading post, with myriad period-related associations. Clearly, the role of craft dealers and information is critical in the maintenance of authenticity and the structuring of price-based differentiation within a number of craft categories.

CRAFT AS MEMORY

Since World War II, growth in international tourism has led to an unprecedented rise in the consumption of crafts as souvenirs or memory markers. Indeed, the interdependence is manifest in much of contemporary destination marketing (Aznam, 1992). Although it may be inappropriate to characterize all craft acquisitions made by tourists as guided by the need to perpetuate memory of travel, the latter may co-exist with other motives across various segments. An example may be purchase of crafts as evidence of "having been," to establish social identity or to demonstrate status-congruent discretionary leisure activities in addition to building self-relevant tangible memory traces (Kelly, 1992). The sense of past is integral to identity, and as Belk (1988a) explained, "Possessions are a convenient means of storing the memories and feelings that attach our sense of past. A souvenir may make tangible some otherwise intangible travel experience" (p. 148).

Furthermore, specific types of possessions related to places, such as handicrafts, may be more attractive because they may be perceived as vested with protracted human and cultural involvement (Wallendorf & Belk, 1987). As Hirschman and Holbrook (1982) described, aesthetic objects such as crafts are capable of generating internal, multisensory images of two types. First, these might trigger "historic imagery"—those images associated with actual events—and allow enjoyment through evocation. Second, "fantasy imagery" may result through constructions and enhance appreciation of the past (p. 92). Crafts, then, may act as personal trophies, as discussed previously, and be valued for their ability to serve as evocative cues.

Ben-Amos (1973) has described such memory cues as "a minimal system which must make meanings as accessible as possible across visual boundary lines" (cited in Graburn, 1976, p. 17). Although more complex cues (i.e., crafts with substantial symbolism) might well serve the need for memory, these may be more related to self-definitional motives of knowledge for distant cultures or of achieving distinction in social life. At its primary level, memory-supporting crafts, then, act as visual cross-cultural codes or signs and embody the requirement of simplicity or ease of understanding. The nexus between travel and acquisition also leads to functional requirements within certain tourist segments, such as portability and affordability. The emphasis on crafts as an everyday reminder imparts utilitarian requirements, whether or not such was intended in a given craft product in its producing culture. A large number of tourists with the above requirements imposes a macrolevel challenge on crafts: the ability to create high volumes.

Desire for simple understanding may have led to a conformity in developing society crafts to popular notions or stereotypes associated with indigenous cultures (Graburn, 1976). To the extent that members of dominant cultures recognize ethnicity as a set of overt features (such as skin color, traditional occupations, natural habitat, etc.), such are reflected in souvenir choices. Examples include statuettes demonstrating hunting prowess, dolls in native costumes, or in the extreme, dyeing light-colored wooden souvenirs to match the skin colors of their producers (Seiler-Baldinger, 1985). There is a trend toward traditional naturalism here as well because portraiture serves the goal of simplistic identification.

Miniaturization for many varieties of crafts may follow from the requirement of portability. In addition, reduction in size and decorative complexity also affords the creators the opportunity to reduce cost as well as increase the volume of production. The perceived scope of large markets may in addition lead to a revival of traditional craft themes (Belk, 1992) and, in specific contexts, to the substitution of traditional materials where these require substantial processing time (e.g., use of chemical dyes in place of vegetable extracts for Yagua and Ticuna hammocks of Colombia and Peru; Seiler-Baldinger, 1985). Skill-demanding crafts may even be abandoned for those that are easily made and require less time and resources. The utility-related aspect of consumption also leads to designed adaptations described earlier, that is, transformation of purpose and meaning between producing and consuming societies.

The aforementioned classification, relying on five sets of consumer desires vis-à-vis crafts, each associated with a subset of nine craft product aspects, is not premised on exclusive membership, similar to most social categorization schemes (Lingle, Altom, & Medin, 1984): (a) Consumers may well display multiple desires and craft aspects associated with each of these; (b) a specific craft may appeal to different desires, necessitating variety in form and transaction; (c) a particular craft aspect (e.g., traditional portrayals) may satisfy diverse desires; and (d) desires historically dominant in given periods may recur and assume similar connotations at a given time (e.g., reemergence of craft as personal trophy aided by modern-day tourism). Useful from the point of view of creators of a given craft is to identify the range of relevant desires and their respective implications (in terms of craft product aspects) to determine appropriate conditions for creation and delivery. The latter undoubtedly would necessitate focus on communications and transaction mechanisms in addition to the design, process, and organization of craft production.

The Organization
of Craft Production

Production systems for crafts have received attention in relation to macroeconomic indices such as national employment and income; division of labor; and production inputs such as raw materials, skills, credit, design, technology, and delivery aspects. Although material conditions for craft creation appear undoubtedly to facilitate or inhibit capabilities to serve a variety of consumption desires and related craft product aspects, these have not received systematic analysis. Neither has there been an analysis of traditional forms of creation compared to more innovative cultural patterns. In the following sections, four different entrepreneurship forms—household, cooperative, subcontracting, and factory—are described with a view toward tracing the relationships between consumption and production sectors.

HOUSEHOLDS:
THE SPECIALIST/MASTER ARTISAN

Historically, the craft production system consisted of rural households in which the creators were required to meet a traditional and known demand. The ritual or utility aspects were manifest in designs associated with specific craft families or master artisans and transmitted in tribal or genealogical terms. Craft workers were generally born into craft families and learned their skills through observation and the socialization process. Raw materials were largely collected from the natural environment or bartered through rural exchange modalities. In the absence of institutional facilities, family savings or loans from local intermediaries provided the necessary credit. Value addition through manual processes constituted the majority of craft products and coexisted with certain innovative indigenous technologies (such as locally developed looms for weaving; Spooner, 1986).

Although the evolution of craft markets (especially for exports) has led to a shift from household organization forms, such forms still constitute a majority in most developing countries (Kathuria, Miralao, & Joseph, 1988). The key advantages of this mode are the ability to create craft objects that embody traditional designs, exotic innovations, and the relatively high degree of singularity of these creations. The social location of artisan households makes them best suited to reflect relatively less acculturated forms in their crafts because many continue to serve both local and external audiences. Even when the external orientation is economically dominant, artisan households are likely to be resistant to changes in the essential symbolism characterizing a craft product because of a perceived relationship between the quality of their work and their community status as experts (Hughes, 1981). Despite their loyalty to tradition, these master artisans are often also the best innovators, capable of infusing personal imagery and symbolism into traditional forms through their superior skills (Silver, 1981). It is probably best to view such artisans as "artist-craftsmen" (Becker, 1978, p. 866; see previous discussion in section titled "Crafts: Definitional Issues") who lead the dynamic tradition of indigenous crafts. As Price (1989) has described, there is "a delicate interaction between individual creativity and the dictates of tradition" (p. 58), and a traditional artisan may act as both the curator and the agent of change. To the extent that exoticism is associated with departure from realism and infusion of imagination, "the primitive artist moves from naturalism to abstraction without embarrassment" (Newton, 1981, p. 53). The individualism associated with certain artisans or craft families also renders their work singular—identifiable to external audiences.

The innovations described, however, are usually distinct from the reductionism inherent in the need for simplicity. Although certain traditional items may indeed provide a simple identification of culture, a deliberate simplification is often equated with trivialization. Also, the typical lack of access to distribution does not predispose artisan households toward producing large numbers of small (portable) and inexpensive items, even though their traditional repertoire often includes such examples. Lack of interaction with external consumers also reduces the opportunity to adapt local crafts to suit external usage contexts. In the past, artisans working in households had access to valuable raw materials such as rare wood, ivory, and precious metals because these were viewed essential in the creation of certain ritual objects and were often made available by the community. Current restrictions on trade (such as on import of silk in the Philippines and logging permits in regions of Africa), however, along with the impoverished status of most rural artisans, preclude the use of valuable materials.

The household mode of organization, then, has the potential for serving knowledge and self-identity desires through creation of both traditional and uniquely exotic crafts. Lack of exposure to consumers in external cultures, however, renders adaptation of crafts for alien contexts (a potential aspect of self-identity) problematic. Individualism may, in addition, serve status requirements. The latter may be enhanced if valuable raw materials are made available and if specialized intermediaries ensure antiquity through long-term buying strategies. Although these organizations are also capable of producing simple, portable, and inexpensive crafts (such as those serving a desire for memory), lack of organized distribution usually places them in a competitively weaker position compared with urban-based organized production systems.

COOPERATIVES

Although informal cooperation among rural artisans and development of collective genres of crafts have many historic examples (Brody, 1976) with parallels to the guild system, production cooperatives reflect a more recent development often supported by domestic craft policy (Kathuria et al., 1988). Although retaining many of the features of household production, the cooperatives are seen essentially as providing greater control to artisans with respect to the creation process (e.g., access to institutional credit, bulk buying of raw materials, use of technology, and a larger pool of trainers and trainees), enhanced leverage in negotiating with intermediaries (e.g., through determination of a standard price and capability toward carrying inventory), and market exposure through collectively owned retail outlets and shared costs of transportation.

Clearly, a variety of cooperative forms has been implemented on the basis of modalities for division of labor, resource sharing, and management responsibilities. Two broad categories—organization by product and by process—are characteristic of the above and pertain to the discussion of serving segments of consumption desires and their related craft aspects. The first of these is similar to individual household-based creation and allows for distinctive expressions. This arrangement may also allow similar service capabilities with respect to consumption desires, with the additional advantage of ensuring larger volumes. Potentially threatening is the rivalry among artisan families to establish quality standards in the context of a region (Taimni, 1981). The organization by process, which typically involves community workshops, shared equipment, and division of a product by components (Hakemulder & Last, 1980), seems to have been less successful because of both a reluctance among participants to share skills and a lack of local management expertise (Gormsen, 1985).[5] In principle, such cooperatives seem to possess advantage in creating large volumes of crafts, especially those that are relatively small (portable) and shorn of individual innovation and complexity. Efficient management of resources could also allow for low-cost production and render these products fairly affordable. The congregation of artisans has the added opportunity for maximizing contact with external consumer experts, such as designers, and for adapting local crafts (through changes in specific stages of creation) to match consumption contexts.

Cooperatives, in general, afford the creation of larger volumes of craft production than do household organizations. Although cooperative organization by products has essentially similar service capabilities as individual artisan families, cooperative organization by process offers the opportunity for adaptations, that is, serving the desire for self-identity through grafting of "ethnic" craft features to a variety of consumption items in external cultures. In addition, these cooperatives can target the memory segment with affordable crafts that are both simple and portable.

SUBCONTRACTING

In many developing society cultures, subcontracting or the "putting out" form of organization acts as a specialized cooperative system with either horizontal (between products) or vertical (between processes) division of labor among rural households. The entrepreneur maintains the flow of raw materials and finance—supplying inputs (such as a craft product at a certain stage of creation) to the outworkers, collecting the finished goods, and settling payments. In many regions in which subcontracting (especially by process) is well entrenched, artisans rarely deal with each other financially or even physically. Thus, silk weaving in Thailand, which involves eight different steps, is performed in eight different households (Mead, 1981) in a way that Mies (1980) described as akin to "an invisible assembly line where each is assigned only to make a component part of the whole which she never saw let alone would ever use herself" (cited in Cable & Weston, 1982, p. 18).

Advantages of the subcontracting system are its flexibility in serving both large volumes and diverse varieties of crafts. Although for the entrepreneur the ability to draw from a large pool of skilled artisans without incurring fixed overhead is attractive, the autonomy of the artisan is also somewhat assured. Nevertheless, the complex task of coordination among units, often geographically dispersed, and of maintenance of quality introduces a degree of standardization in the craft products, with consequent emphasis on process-based rather than product-based organization. Thus, relatively simple representations and easily transportable items are preferred over those that require complex manifestations of individual creation. Because many of the entrepreneurs in developing countries also act as exporters, these standardized forms are often influenced by designers external to the rural producing communities. As Teske (1986) described, such contacts often "impose outside aesthetic criteria upon traditional artists, to introduce standards of quality control designed to produce commercial sameness, and to undermine the confidence of folk artists and craftsmen in their ability to judge what is good and beautiful" (p. 80). Memory-serving crafts, those that are simple, portable, and affordable by virtue of volume production, are hence facilitated by this system. Also, the prevalence of creation-to-design enhances the scope of adaptation to external usage contexts, that is, those that seek embellishment of a wide range of products (utilitarian, fashion, etc.) with "ethnic" themes. The shift in focus from the individual artisan or craft family, however, potentially excludes the subcontracting organization from creating idiosyncratic items of tradition or products marked with innovation.

THE CRAFTS FACTORY

Increasing demand for large volumes of craft objects serving specific consumption motives described earlier has led to the transformation of craft workers in several developing countries from community-based artisans integrated with agricultural life to urban-based wage laborers (Jain, 1986). The change is increasingly evident for crafts that have received sustained appreciation in the West, such as carpets from India and Pakistan, batik textiles from Java, and rattan furniture from the

Philippines. In the latter, large corporations employ hundreds of workers with significant foreign participation in marketing, product design, and capital investment (Upadhyoy, 1973). Such factory organizations also tend to rely on training of workers outside hereditary skill acquisition in rural craft families and to use technology to enhance speed and to ensure standardized specifications of their products. Raw material supplies are usually negotiated with large contractors, often aided by government subsidies (Aguilar & Miralao, 1984) and at times ensured through backward integration (examples include ownership of rattan-producing farms by furniture manufacturing companies in the Philippines).

Although separation of craft workers from the entire creative process endows factory-produced crafts with much of the same characteristics as the process-based subcontracting arrangement, the superior resources of factory organizations (in terms of market information and quality delivery capability) allow a broader range of crafts than subcontractors. Thus, in addition to serving large orders for relatively simple and inexpensive items, they have made inroads into crafts as self-identity and status, supporting higher value product markets as well, particularly in fashion, furniture, and home accessories. Adaptation to usage contexts also allow these craft products, within a range of traditional styles, to provide high material value (e.g., use of expensive materials such as silk, special quality wood, rare gems for jewelry, and certain varieties of stone) and to target more affluent segments in Western markets. Attempts to singularize such high value-added crafts occur through branding, and designer labels are becoming more common. The identification, though, is more complex than that involving a rural artisan and includes aesthetic inputs (i.e., from designers) that draw inspiration from external cultures as well. To quote one such designer with her own namebranded line, "Just a touch of color, a delicately drawn, clean outline, gemstones perfectly interspersed—these things can transform ancient artisanship into high-fashion jewelry for the American woman, or into furnishings for her home" (Gupte, 1988, p. 30). Clearly, although suited for crafts that serve the desire for memory, status, and aspects of self-identity, the factory organization shares the disadvantage associated with process-based subcontracting and cooperative arrangements that exclude idiosyncratic traditional expressions and innovative creations of master artisans functioning within autonomous rural households.

Although each of the four organizational forms is more or less prevalent in most craft industries in developing countries, often competing with each other for end-use consumers or intermediaries, the national focus on foreign exchange earnings through exports is exerting an influence toward greater organization on the traditionally unorganized production system (Jain, 1986). The transition is claimed to receive momentum from national governments in developing nations that favor large factories over rural households through provision of scarce raw materials, subsidies in training, investment credits, and marketing support (Jain, Krishnamurthy, & Tripathi, 1985). Critics, on the other hand, have pointed out that reliance on limited production organizations would reduce a developing society's capacity for serving diverse consumption desires vis-à-vis crafts and potentially jeopardize an attractive dimension of the industry—the provision of rural employment. Besides creators and consumers, the transition is also likely to affect the vast network of intermediaries and redefine their roles in the craft industry.

Intermediaries in Craft Industries

The network of entrepreneurs and institutions that interfaces between creators and consumers is diverse and is viewed as indispensable in terms of economic sustenance of the industry. Indeed, there are examples of craft households selling directly to consumers (i.e., tourists) and cooperatives operating retail outlets; however, their contribution is relatively minor compared with the major flows in craft products (Harrison, 1979). Even in the case of cooperatives, such as those for batik in Java, inability to establish linkage with go-betweens often precludes market access (Joseph, 1988). Traditionally, intermediaries have provided coordination and created enabling conditions for the creation of crafts and, similar to the organizations of production, have witnessed transition in form and relationships. In many developing countries, new patterns of intermediaries have emerged with innovations in terms of both organizational form and functional activities. The following sections describe five generic categories, identifying specific characteristics and their relationships with particular production organizations and consumer segments.

BUYING AGENTS

The dispersed location of craft families and rural cooperatives has traditionally led to itinerant agents providing the necessary functions of coordination, market access, credit, and at times, supply of raw materials, coexisting with local artisan-patron relationships. Typically, the buying agent is specialized, in terms of either crafts from a region or a specific craft category (such as agents in the Teotihuacán Valley dealing in a variety of ceramics; Charlton, 1976). The restricted range of crafts limits their outward interactions to larger merchant exporters who are urban based and possess export know-how. Buying agents are increasingly attracted to importers who seek to bypass larger intermediaries for cost savings, but their limited inventory precludes them from competing with the more powerful merchants.

By virtue of their intimate contact with craft families and regions, the agents are well placed to locate traditional forms, especially innovative artisans, and antique works. They are also often responsible for discovering novel genres that subsequently receive attention from commercial and government initiatives. Low volumes, limited variety, and inability to provide design inputs, however, have largely excluded them from playing an independent role in the larger markets serving consumers' desire for crafts as memory and in segments that desire specially adapted craft products.

MERCHANT EXPORTERS

The complex requirements of exporting, such as dealing with foreign importers and retailers, transportation and packaging, design inputs, and knowledge of regulations, have led to the emergence of merchant traders in many developing countries. The resources of merchant exporters, who are usually based in urban centers, allow them to carry substantial inventory, to meet delivery schedules, and to evince power in negotiating with importers and retailers. Although buying agents contribute to their varied stock, merchant exporters tend to rely heavily on subcontracting arrangements—usually commissioning products to meet designed specifications—and provide quality checks. Depending on the volume of stock they need, at times they buy directly from factories, using their excess capacities.

As a group, the merchant exporters serve the entire range of craft desires, although complex exporting arrangements usually predispose them toward dealing in large orders of relatively simple, low-breakage, portable crafts that are adapted to the usage contexts of Western consumers. Specialization within this group also allows for high value-added crafts directed toward boutiques or fashion outlets. As pointed out by Hughes (1981), museum quality or rare craft objects are seldom

carried, although some merchant exporters have undertaken the duplication of traditional objects through cooperatives and by subcontracting and, in addition, may act as key information sources leading to their
acquisition.

MANUFACTURER EXPORTERS

As described earlier, the sustained appreciation of certain craft varieties in the West and the growth in tourism and memory-serving crafts
have led to substantial volume requirements. The latter has provided
the impetus for greater control over the chain of creation to ensure both
quality and delivery. The manufacturer exporters tend to inspire confidence among importers and retailers and display substantial power
in negotiations. Although they are committed to their factories, they are
also led by large orders to engage in subcontracting arrangements.
These arrangements form the basis for horizontal channel conflict
(Stern & Gorman, 1969) with merchant exporters who typically have a
stronger association with the subcontracting outworkers (Kathuria
et al., 1988). In dealing with both import wholesalers and retailers with
known demand for large volumes, they also contribute to vertical rivalry between the two and are able to extract higher margins than what
would be warranted through exclusive arrangements.

In creating-to-design, the manufacturers have the greatest advantage
in serving segments that seek specially adapted products. In transform-
ing the production organization from rural to urban and from specialist
artisan to wage laborer, however, the capacity to serve traditional craft
requirements is considerably reduced. The inflexibility in terms of
variety also leads toward specialization within particular categories
and reduces access to knowledge and certain identity-based segments.
Such specialization may occur at either the low or high end of the
value-added continuum. Certain manufacturers may focus on low cost,
simple (memory-serving) crafts, whereas others with considerable
overhead are predisposed toward more expensive goods, often involving materials of high value (usually designer fashion, furniture, and
home furnishing products), and serve the status-seeking markets.

IMPORTERS

Paralleling merchant exporters in developing countries, the wholesale importing organizations usually carry a wide range of craft products and inventory to supply diverse retailers, from boutiques and

specialty stores to department chains. With direct access to market information, they often provide extensive design support to merchants and manufacturers in developing countries and assume the risk of new craft ventures. Usually their margins are higher at early stages of the cycle and tend to decline with acceptance of the craft and subsequent competition from retailers who attempt to buy directly from local intermediaries. Among external commercial organizations, they are the most knowledgeable and devote substantial attention to both purchasing and marketing. In terms of serving consumer segments, they usually carry a broad portfolio, although the emphasis on designed adaptation and on the standardized crafts necessary to serve large volumes limits their access to traditional specialties.

RETAILERS

Drawing largely from import wholesalers, some retailers, especially those who require large volumes of standard lines, sometimes buy directly from local merchants and manufacturers to reduce intermediary margins. Because fashion and gift sections tend to rely on novelties, however, direct buying is relatively uncommon. Their relative lack of knowledge also leads them to greater reliance on importers, through whom design requirements are usually communicated.

Highly adapted fashion and home-use products continue to form the basis for most purchases, although specialty craft shops and boutiques aim at serving the knowledge, identity, and status segments through specialized importers, local merchants, and even knowledgeable buying agents. Marketing cooperatives (such as nongovernmental organizations) with cultural interests in the developing world often bypass large intermediaries and support craft-producing cooperatives or undertake purchasing visits to developing countries.

Although the preceding discussion reflects the generic categories of intermediaries, these may be construed more broadly in many nations. For example, intermediaries may include taxi and trishaw drivers and tour guides who act as intermediaries by bringing tourists to artisan households, cooperatives, or local retailers (generally for a commission).

Contrary to attempts to singularize the crafts industry and impose a definition-bound reductionism for policy purposes, this discussion of consumers, creators, and intermediaries shows a range of diversity, recognition of which underlies the success of rendering it effective and satisfying to its constituent sectors. The continuing interaction between consuming and producing societies provides for its evolutionary nature, and marketing innovations are likely to direct its future course. Although there appear to be both complementary and contradictory forces at play, understanding the key flows is critical in identifying strategic opportunities and longer-term potential.

A Marketing Framework

Marketing crafts and aesthetic products in general has been a subject of critical inquiry, viewed especially from the perspective of adapting the creative process to serve customer preferences. Walle (1986), for example, claimed:

> The main danger of modern marketing is that the marketing concept consciously directs attention towards the customer. Since the "folk" are seemingly "production people," it is easy—too easy—to forget their needs and wants and, instead, to focus attention toward clients (those who will buy the goods if the proper "marketing mix" is adopted). (p. 100)

Presumably, the needs of the producers (i.e., traditional artisans) refer to their own cultural and symbolic aspirations, which are rendered incidental as traditional artisans are reduced to the role of technicians creating to satisfy an externally designed craft requirement (Teske, 1986). Similarly, Hirschman (1983) has proposed that the marketing concept is inapplicable for aesthetic products because the creative process reflects personal values and social norms rather than considerations of consumer preference (see also Searles, 1980; Woods, 1987). The order of primacy between *artistic needs* and *consumer needs* is believed to contribute to either a product or a market orientation. Holbrook and Zirlin (1985) have proposed to accommodate both by suggesting that nonprofit organizations (e.g., museums) are better served by an artist-oriented product ideology, whereas those committed to profits could successfully ascribe to consumer-driven operations. This perspective, however, raises questions with respect to the relative scale of the two modes. Because museum acquisitions are meager compared with retailing and purchase of crafts, museum buying alone would allow survival of only a small number of highly specialized and acclaimed artist-craftspersons, leaving the vast majority of creators and intermediaries to serve the consumer-profit sector.

Viewed historically, aesthetic creations seem to have been related to patrons or clients (such as the monarchy, clergy, landlords, etc.; Hauser, 1951), and marketing the craft product was integral to the artisan's rationale for survival (Joyce, 1986). As pointed out by Johnson (1986), "in the day-to-day scheme of events, selling is the craftperson's most important form of recognition" (p. 87). Indeed, the economic opportunity afforded by a craft industry creates conditions for continued pursuit in most developing countries. The challenge, then, is to foster multiple marketing flows that allow coexistence of a variety of consumption desires and production organizations (with their respective motivations). Rather than choosing between consumer-driven adapted craft production and self-driven traditional expressions, the marketing task is to help match particular crafts with market segments most likely to appreciate them (Holbrook, 1980). The debate between market and product orientations is not particularly moot if the industry as a whole adopts the marketing concept of seeking and strengthening complementarities, as long as the constituent sectors are free to create or consume items of their choice. A master artisan, hence, could very well pursue his or her imagination or symbolic standards of a community without adapting, and such could contribute to his or her economic well-being if marketing systems were in place to make available these creations to knowledge- or identity-motivated craft consumers. Intermediaries who are generally more integrated into the transaction system than rural artisans may be better positioned to adopt the marketing concept and support both the indigenous (artist-driven) and relatively acculturated (consumer-driven) forms of crafts within the profit-generating sector itself. As pointed out by Pye (1988), the variety of craft desires has led to expanded potentials for different forms with substantial returns associated with both simple and complex craft objects. Three major flows of crafts, on the basis of particular configurations of consumption desires/craft aspect requirements, intermediaries, and production organizations, are shown in Figure 10.1. The following sections identifying the nature of transactions of these three flows, with suggestions for enhancing marketing effectiveness for each.

THE FLOW OF INDIGENOUS CRAFTS

A significant flow within the craft industry involves the satisfaction of craft as knowledge and self-identity desires through objects that embody traditional themes, as well as exotic innovations by master artisans. As described earlier, craft families and rural cooperatives organized on the product basis are best suited to create such objects. Local buying agents usually provide the necessary credit and raw materials. Importers and retailers who focus on specialty products acquire these

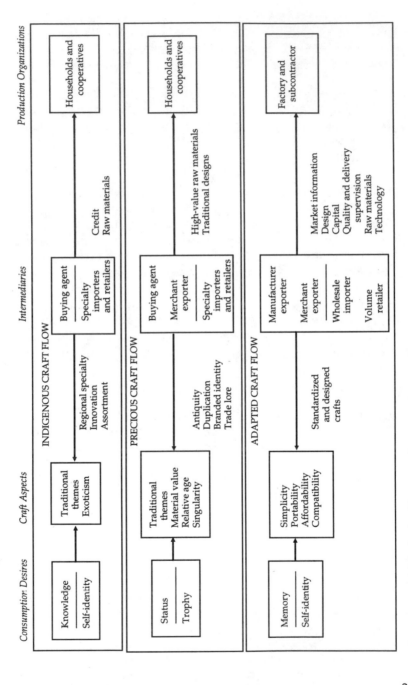

Figure 10.1. A Marketing Framework

284

objects from the agents and make them available to consumers in external cultures. As a group, these crafts probably reflect the most unacculturated forms and seem to contain all three definitional elements—cultural symbolism, manual value addition, and production in small groups.

Evidently, museums as well as individual consumers with the aforementioned craft desires are likely to constitute the target segment. As Belk (1988a) described, collecting has become a significant activity and often acts as a vehicle for creating one's extended self, in addition to filling gaps in one's sense of thoroughness regarding unfamiliar cultures. The requisite marketing mix would involve positioning these crafts in terms of the desired benefits and rooting these in specific cultural contexts. Providing an assortment either within a particular region/specific category or across genres is likely to serve the desire for in-depth understanding or variety. Presumably, price-quality differentials would characterize submarkets within the overall segment, with perceived value determined on the basis of factors such as the relative inaccessibility of a region and its craft products, adherence to known traits of tradition, and the aesthetic assessment of innovations. The credibility of promotional messages, as well as that of the retail outlets, is likely to determine how traditional or artistic these crafts are perceived to be. Craft shows, demonstrations by artisans, and reviews in the media are likely to be viewed as effective promotional vehicles; specialty stores, such as museum shops and boutiques, would also allow the consistent portrayal of these items as aesthetic and traditional expressions of cultural value. Thus, besides judicious procurement, substantial efforts are necessary in terms of positioning these crafts to the consumers (museum curators and individual consumers defined along appropriate segmentation variables) by rendering accessible their cultural meanings and conditions of origin.

THE FLOW OF PRECIOUS CRAFTS

Precious crafts represent the economic high end of the craft market, serving desires for status and trophy through their associated aspects. Although intermediaries and production organizations similar to those for indigenous crafts provide the necessary supply functions, the nature of transactions are somewhat different, given the high material value of the items. A key distinction is the role played by merchant exporters, who, either independently or through their network of buying agents, provide the expensive raw materials to households and cooperatives, reintroduce original designs when artisans possess skills but have lost touch with traditional forms through acculturation, and assume ownership of the completed products, thereby freeing the artisans and agents from the responsibility of carrying expensive inventory. These merchants provide specialty importers and retailers with region or genre identification through historic lores of creation, ownership, and trade. Precious crafts also seem to satisfy the most rigorous definition of crafts, although the transposition of producing regions and historical genres sometimes leads to rivalry among developing nations seeking tariff concessions (such as those for Persian carpets produced in the Indian subcontinent).

Antiquity and material value are critical both in the positioning of crafts within this flow and in each of the mix decision elements. Auction house sales, catalogs, galleries, and special shows (often by appointment only with a dealer) provide the venue for purchase and serve as market signals heralding the availability and desirability of these craft items. Promotion is also heavily dependent on re-creation of the sociocultural context of creation and the interpretation of genuineness (such as published commentaries on antique carpets by experts in trade journals). Often, the pedigree of an object is determined by its history of ownership, the prices paid at each transfer, and the exhibits and publications in which it has appeared (Price, 1989). Clearly, determination of price depends on comparative assessment of these within specific genres and is influenced by experts or connoisseurs in the field. Duplications, of course, allow for a wider range of prices, provided these can be endowed with region- or culture-specific identities.

THE FLOW OF ADAPTED CRAFTS

Adapted crafts arguably represent the most dominant flow within the industry, a flow based on response to requirements of large volume. The emergence of craft factories and widespread subcontracting and the pivotal role of manufacturer/merchant exporters, wholesalers, and volume retailers in importing societies are attributed to the necessity for bulk. As a group, these crafts embody varying levels of aesthetic and symbolic aspects of the producing region. There is greater reliance on large-scale production and use of technologies, however, as opposed to manual value addition. As a consequence, they pose certain complications in terms of their classification as cultural goods and may indeed warrant a separate treatment for purposes of trade or domestic policy.

Two distinct markets coexist within adapted crafts distinguished by the served needs, inputs into the creation process, and the choice of marketing mix. The first involves serving the desire for memory through simple, portable, and affordable objects. Although largely associated with tourism, these products are also sold directly in importing societies and may be related to self-expressive needs as well—as day-to-day objects and as distinctive gift items. The marketing process, initiated by wholesalers and retailers, usually follows the standard paradigm: selection of crafts most likely to appeal to consumer segments, their adaptation for maximum compatibility, test marketing followed by refinements, suitable packaging, and a combination of "push" and "pull" strategies for promotion and distribution. The chosen marketing mix also reflects mass-merchandising features, with emphasis on distinctiveness and utility; intensive distribution through department stores or home-furnishing outlets; and awareness campaigns often tied to seasonality, tourism, or country themes (such as joint promotion of Southeast Asian crafts and tourism by Western department store chains, travel agents, airlines, and respective tourism departments before the winter holiday season). The price range is usually restricted, given the notion that neither tourists nor consumers of gifts or of minor daily objects are likely to view these in complex symbolic terms or as status objects.

A second stream of adaptation pertains to high-value items of fashion or home furniture, where compatibility of usage coexists with the requirement of distinctive self-expression. Designer items with "ethnic" embellishments, although demanding of volume (and hence, having similar supply inputs and conditions as the first market for adapted crafts), share features of the indigenous craft flow, especially in the creation of distinctive culture-based images (e.g., designer fashions with an "African theme" in motifs or fabric). Their promotion and distribution tend to be more exclusive than the mass-marketed variety and reflect price premiums associated with specifically branded identity.

At the level of the consumer, coexistence of these multiple flows affords the manifestation of diverse craft desires, as well as the option of "graduating" from one flow to another as a function of learning and increased exposure. As described by Belk, Wallendorf, Sherry, Holbrook, and Roberts (1988), collections often are initiated by gifts or other unintended acquisitions, although it is important to note that not all consumers may be collectors. Over time, self-identity or knowledge motives may come to encompass an individual's world of crafts, leading to a shift from adapted crafts to indigenous crafts or even to precious crafts. At the level of the industry, multiple flows ensure cultural

preservation as well as economic survival for communities in developing societies. Although the dominance of one, say adapted crafts, to the
exclusion of others could eventually lead to unlearning traditional
skills and failure to create unique products to compete in international
markets, spurning volume requirements could also lead to economic
deprivation of factory and subcontracting workers and reduce the attractiveness of the industry to domestic policymakers. The necessary
balance undoubtedly calls for sensitive facilitation, recognizing the
unique character of each of the marketing flows and their constituents.

Facilitating Change in Craft Industries

For the most part, governments in developing countries are in favor
of supporting domestic craft ventures through a range of policies. Local
and international nongovernmental organizations have also participated quite actively in this sector, in which facilitations are conceived
in terms of infrastructure building, production inputs, and marketing
support. Unfortunately, in the absence of systematic analysis of requirements to facilitate specific craft flows, most policy initiatives tend
to view such requirements as similar across different types of crafts.
Deficiencies in critical inputs and redundancies consequently characterize many craft assistance programs. Furthermore, craft policies tend
to be conceived at the central levels without reference to cultural preservation policies (if any) and without assessment of local vagaries
(Taimni, 1981) and invariably run into implementation problems.
Short-term demands for export earnings, in addition, tend to emphasize support for particular flows (usually urban-based factories) with
neglect of the remaining crafts. It seems necessary, then, to move from
a general, centrally administered, short-term orientation to one that is
based on specific requirements and is managed locally within a long-
term plan encompassing the entire domestic industry of a developing
country. Table 10.1 relates the long-term needs of the three marketing
flows to specific aspects of change programs on the basis of characteristics of creators, intermediaries, and consumers discussed earlier.

DEVELOPMENT OF INFRASTRUCTURE

Organized production systems such as cooperatives are viewed in
many developing societies as potentially increasing the volume of creation in a region, as well as enhancing the bargaining power of artisans

TABLE 10.1 Program for Change in Craft Industries

Key Marketing Flows	Suggested Requirements		
	Infrastructure	Production Inputs	Market Support
Indigenous Craft Flow	• Cooperative organization • Land and equipment acquisition • Management training • Transportation to buying centers • Information dissemination system	• Design advice from experts • Raw materials	• Organized exposure to buying agents and merchant exporters • Packaging expertise • Promotion of overall craft profile
Precious Craft Flow	• Cooperative organization • Land and equipment acquisition • Management training • Transportation to buying centers • Information dissemination system	• Design advice from experts • Rare and expensive raw materials • Regional awards • Preservation and cultural documentation	• Market encounter between merchant exporters and specialty importers/retailers • Encouraging auction house submissions • Catalogs and information service
Adapted Craft Flow	• Transportation and container arrangements • Warehousing facilities • Telecommunications • Simplification of export requirements • Joint ventures	• Skill training • Indigenous technologies • Quality inspection • Market information	• Trade fairs, exhibitions, on-site demonstrations • Promotion of overall craft profile • Marketing management training • Export handling assistance

with respect to buying agents. Consequently, assistance in the form of land and equipment acquisition and transportation arrangements is usually emphasized. Rural outworkers and volunteers are also engaged in organizing the craft families and setting up acceptable modalities for cooperation. Unfortunately, the failure of many such cooperative ventures has been traced to the lack of experience and expertise in general administration (such as proper accounting procedures, determination of a profit sharing formula, and leadership) and demand assessment that would allow for maintenance of adequate inventory (Gormsen, 1985). In addition, poor communication between administrative centers and rural artisans and cooperatives often leads to missed opportunities[6] (procurement camps, delivery schedules for raw materials, etc.). For indigenous and precious craft flows, building effective communications and training a pool of local management talent would enhance production and marketing efficiencies.

By contrast, the adapted crafts flow, characterized by the movement of large volumes, requires different forms of infrastructural support. In this case, efficient transportation from rural to urban centers; adequate warehousing, shipping, and container arrangements; simplification of legal and administrative requirements; and enhanced access to modern telecommunications would facilitate export operations. Creation of an institutional base with responsibility for the above could serve both planning and coordination functions between governmental and nongovernmental programs. For many developing countries, however, the organization itself of such institutions with defined agendas appears to be a greater challenge (Aziz, 1980). Recognition of mutual strengths in public and private organization could lead to effective joint venture arrangements. Change agents could facilitate these by identifying partners with relative strengths in given areas and by participating in negotiations.

PRODUCTION INPUTS

Given the success requirement of traditional themes in indigenous crafts, design assistance appears to be a critical input. This is probably most relevant in areas in which artisans have lost touch with original ritualistic and utilitarian forms through acculturation, although retaining the skills for creation of the same. Folklorists, cultural anthropologists, and museum curators could play a vital role in the process of revival and rejuvenation. Several developing countries have undertaken to establish research centers that draw artisans and culturalists to facilitate the process of revival and relearning. Documentation, recreation of traditional tools, and discussion on historical, religious, and mythological themes are believed to help further a reappropriation that goes beyond the mere reproduction of older craft pieces (Varadarajan, 1991). With respect to other production inputs, although the transaction of raw materials is not inherently problematic, providing cheaper access to these may help artisans in overcoming historic indebtedness to intermediaries and may allow a greater latitude for experimentation (Harrison, 1979).

For precious crafts, however, raw material supplies may be more critical because of their high costs and/or their unavailability in local contexts and may require preferential buying schemes for artisans and cooperatives. Revival of traditionality through design support continues to be important, as does encouragement for innovations. Conducting regional competitions could provide incentive for the latter, and as Stromberg (1976) has described, tying awards to preferential purchase has the potential for sustaining individual creativity. Because precious crafts are also negotiated on the basis of cultural and trade lores, documentation and dissemination of the same to market intermediaries would constitute an important facet of change activities. Preservation for future sale, inculcated in policy terms, would serve the need for antiquity and keep alive the supply of antique objects, deflecting the urge toward pilfering them from their natural habitats.

Although formal skill training is largely unnecessary for households and rural cooperatives serving the indigenous and precious flows in craft objects, it constitutes a critical element for craft factories that serve the needs for adapted crafts. Craft factories in most developing countries draw human resources from the pool of urban poor and migrant farm workers who are unversed in traditional skills. In addition, available technological resources need to be adapted to serve the requirements of mass production with assurance of quality standards. To the extent the latter are specified by designers (both local and foreign), the monitoring of market information and its input into the production process remain critical from a systemic perspective as well as in actual processing terms.

MARKET SUPPORT

Facilitating market encounters is critical, although their nature varies depending on the specific craft flow. For indigenous crafts, organized exposure of artisans and cooperatives to buying agents and merchant exporters would enhance the awareness of the range of available products and increase the potential for introduction of new genres. A critical but often overlooked aspect is the development of packaging that ensures transportation free of physical damage and that enhances appropriate demonstration and use. Both creators and intermediaries stand to benefit from packaging innovation, the lack of which at times is blamed for recalcitrance among quality-conscious importers.

To the extent that the overall craft profile of a developing country invokes awareness and interest among consumers, promotion serves as the key element of "pull," or creating receptivity in external consumer segments. A range of partnership arrangements may be used to promote the craft profile, including national campaigns, cosponsorship with wholesalers, and provision of promotional materials (e.g., brochures) to specialized retail establishments.

Although similar market encounters appear to be necessary for precious crafts, facilitating access to auction houses and their catalogs could locate these crafts among the international repertoire of valuable artifacts. Large merchant exporters could be encouraged to participate in art shows and be provided with necessary financial resources and documentation attesting to authenticity of their submissions.

Market support for adapted crafts usually involves organization of trade fairs, on-site demonstrations by artisans, and promotion of a country's overall craft profile through various partnership arrangements. The provision of marketing skills, especially in exporting, is the key in identifying segmental preferences, selection of distribution partners, and formulation of mix ingredients.

Conclusion and Future Directions

The value of a descriptive framework lies in its ability to locate specific events within the complexity of the overall phenomenon and in suggesting a set of contingencies most relevant to their manifestation. In addition, a framework judiciously applied may indicate directions for change and suggest areas that warrant detailed investigation. The need for an organizing principle is most evident in the crafts industries of developing countries, especially in terms of the marketing flows toward external audiences. The diversity in creation, intermediary roles, and consumption desires often leads to piecemeal analysis or undue reductionism to suit short-term policy requirements. The framework suggested in this chapter may provide a starting point in relating constituents, transactions, and strategies and may serve as an inductive basis for richer theory building and empirical research.

As shown in this chapter's discussions, marketing research is crucial both in delineating specific relationships (e.g., between a consumption desire and aspects of a craft product) and in determining the impact of specific marketing programs (e.g., the creation of craft awareness in foreign markets through trade fairs and increasing the effectiveness of market encounters in extending the line of crafts carried by importers). Description of the transactions in the specified flows also highlights the effectiveness of different research methodologies. Although naturalistic inquiry may be well suited to determine expectations and requirements of rural artisans, more structured tools could complement these in studying relatively organized groups or individuals among the intermediaries and consuming segments.

It is critical to recognize that the analysis of marketing processes for crafts is inseparably linked to the issue of cultural identity of the indigenous peoples in the developing world. As Hinsley (1991) described, the danger lies in the glorification of the exchange values of these artifacts as exotic commodities, deprived of their contextual associations as an integral part of a culture. Success, therefore, from a conventional marketing point of view, may serve short-run economic ends while disrupting an ongoing heritage unless sensitive practices are in place that reinforce both cultural and economic bases for perpetuation of these traditions.

Notes

1. Although on occasions such a substitution is guided by functionally superior modern goods, at times even inferior products may be chosen for their apparent perception of modernity (Belk, 1988b).

2. The demarcation may serve to exclude other small-scale and manually produced products (such as Western-style work boots and light industrial components) from the category of crafts, that is, those that do not serve cultural preservation goals.

3. For a contemporary account on the trade of luxury goods, see "The Luxury-Goods Trade" (1992-1993).

4. The notion of "staged authenticity" was originally applied (MacCannell, 1976, p. 91) in the context of performing arts.

5. Although it is difficult to generalize across large numbers of craft cooperatives throughout many developing countries, the literature appears to document more negative experiences than those that are viewed as successful.

6. A survey of rural Malaysian artisans (Pye, 1988), for example, showed that about 75% of them were unaware of a special subsidy program for raw materials instituted by the government during the previous few years.

References

Aguilar, F., & Miralao, V. (1984). *Rattan furniture manufacturing in Metro Cebu: A case study of an export industry* (Paper Series No. 7 [mimeo]). Manila, Philippines: Ramon Magsaysay Award Foundation.

Ames, M. (1992). *Cannibal tours and glass boxes.* Vancouver, Canada: University of British Columbia Press.

Appadurai, A. (1990). Disjuncture and difference in the global cultural economy. *Theory, Culture & Society, 7,* 295-310.

Aziz, A. (1980). *Rural artisans: Development strategies and employment.* Bangalore, India: Institute of Social and Economic Change.

Aznam, S. (1992). Tourism: Growth from Asian markets. *Far Eastern Economic Review, 2,* 54-55.

Bascom, W. (1973). *African art in cultural perspective: An introduction.* New York: North.

Becker, H. S. (1978). Arts and crafts. *American Journal of Sociology, 83*(4), 862-889.

Belk, R. W. (1985). Materialism: Trait aspects of living in the material world. *Journal of Consumer Research, 12,* 265-280.

Belk, R. W. (1988a). Possessions and the extended self. *Journal of Consumer Research, 15,* 139-168.

Belk, R. W. (1988b). Third world consumer culture. In E. Kumcu & A. F. Fırat (Eds.), *Marketing and development: Towards broader dimensions* (pp. 103-127). Greenwich, CT: JAI.

Belk, R. W. (1992). Third world tourism: Panacea or poison? The case of Nepal. *Journal of International Consumer Marketing, 5*(2), 27-68.

Belk, R. W., & Costa, J. A. (1992). A critical assessment of international tourism. In K. Bothra & R. R. Dholakia (Eds.), *Proceedings of the Third International Conference on Marketing and Development* (pp. 371-382). Kingston: University of Rhode Island.

Belk, R. W., Wallendorf, M., Sherry, J., Holbrook, M., & Roberts, S. (1988). Collectors and collecting. In M. Houston (Ed.), *Advances in consumer research* (Vol. 15, pp. 548-553). Provo, UT: Association for Consumer Research.

Ben-Amos, P. (1973). *Pidgin languages and tourist arts.* Paper prepared for the Advanced Seminar in Contemporary Developments in Folk Art, School of American Research, Santa Fe, New Mexico. (Manuscript copy on file at Temple University, Philadelphia)

Benjamin, M. (1981). The promotion of handicraft exports. *The Courier, 68,* 58-59.

Bouchard, D. (1981). Promoting utilitarian handicrafts. *The Courier, 68,* 60-62.

Bourdieu, P. (1984). *Distinction: A social critique of the judgment of taste.* Boston: Harvard University Press.

Boyer, R. M. (1976). Gourd decoration in Highland Peru. In N. H. H. Graburn (Ed.), *Ethnic and tourist arts* (pp. 183-196). Berkeley: University of California Press.

Brody, J. J. (1976). The creative consumer: Survival, revival and invention in Southwest Indian arts. In N. H. H. Graburn (Ed.), *Ethnic and tourist arts* (pp. 30-84). Berkeley: University of California Press.

Brooks, J. (1981). *Showing off in America: From conspicuous consumption to parody display.* Boston: Little, Brown.

Cable, V., & Weston, A. (1982). *The role of handicrafts exports: Problems and prospects based on Indian experience* (Working Paper No. 10). Overseas Development Institute.

Carpenter, E. C. (1971, January 28). *Do you have the same thing in green? or, Eskimos in New Guinea.* Paper presented at the Shell program on the Canadian North, Scarborough, Ontario, Canada.

Charlton, T. H. (1976). Modern ceramics in the Teotihuacán Valley. In N. H. H. Graburn (Ed.), *Ethnic and tourist arts* (pp. 137-148). Berkeley: University of California Press.

Claerhout, G. A. (1965). The concept of primitive applied to art. *Current Anthropology, 6,* 432-438.

Commission of the European Communities, Directorate-General for Information. (1984, April). *The European Community and India* (No. 73/84). Commission of the European Communities.

Cromer, L. (1969). *Political and literary essays, 1908-1913.* Freeport, NY: Books for Libraries Press. (Original work published 1913)

Crowley, D. J. (1970). The contemporary-traditional art market in Africa. *African Arts, 4*(1), 43-49, 80.

Csikszentmihalyi, M., & Rochberg-Halton, E. (1981). *The meaning of things: Domestic symbols and the self.* Chicago: University of Chicago Press.

Defert, D. (1982). The collection of the world: Accounts of voyages from the sixteenth to the eighteenth centuries. *Dialectical Anthropology, 7,* 11-20.

Forster, J. (1964). The sociological consequences of tourism. *International Journal of Comparative Sociology, 5,* 217-227.

Gauguin, P. (1931). *The intimate journals of Paul Gauguin.* London: Heinemann.

Gerbrands, A. A. (1957). *Art as an element of culture: Especially in Negro-Africa.* Leiden, the Netherlands: E. J. Brill.

Goldwater, R. (1967). *Primitivism in modern art.* New York: Vintage.

Gordon, B. (1986). The souvenir: Messenger of the extraordinary. *Journal of Popular Culture, 20*(3), 135-146.

Gormsen, J. (1985). Mexican arts and crafts for tourism and exportation. In E. Gormsen (Ed.), *The impact of tourism on regional development and cultural change.* Mainz, Germany: Geographisches Institut der Johannes Gutenberg-Universität.

Graburn, N. H. H. (1969). Art and acculturative processes. *International Social Science Journal, 21,* 457-468.

Graburn, N. H. H. (1976). The arts of the fourth world. In N. H. H. Graburn (Ed.), *Ethnic and tourist arts* (pp. 1-32). Berkeley: University of California Press.

Greenwood, D. J. (1977). Culture by the pound: An anthropological perspective on tourism as cultural commoditization. In V. L. Smith (Ed.), *Hosts and guests: The anthropology of tourism* (pp. 129-138). Philadelphia: University of Pennsylvania Press.

Gregory, C. A. (1982). *Gifts and commodities.* New York: Academic Press.

Gupte, P. (1988). Indian designer promotes mass sales of artifacts. *Asian Finance, 15,* 29-31.

Haddon, A. (1895). *Evolution in art.* London: W. Scott.

Hakemulder, R., & Last, J. (1980). *Potters: A study of two villages in Ethiopia.* Addis Ababa, Ethiopia: United Nations Economic Commission for Africa.

Harrison, P. (1979). The fruits of rural industry. *New Scientist, 83*(1169), 584-587.

Hauser, A. (1951). *The social history of art.* New York: Vintage.

Hinsley, C. M. (1991). The world as marketplace: Commodification of the exotic at the world's Columbian Exposition. In I. Karp & S. D. Lavine (Ed.), *Exhibiting cultures: The poetics and politics of museum display* (pp. 344-365). Washington, DC: Smithsonian Institution Press.

Hirschman, E. C. (1983). Aesthetics, ideologies and the limits of the marketing concept. *Journal of Marketing, 47,* 45-55.

Hirschman, E. C., & Holbrook, M. B. (1982). Hedonic consumption: Emerging concepts, methods and propositions. *Journal of Marketing, 46*(3), 92-101.

Hirschman, E. C., & Wallendorf, M. (1982). Characteristics of the cultural continuum. *Journal of Retailing, 58,* 5-21.

Holbrook, M. B. (1980).Some preliminary notes on research in consumer esthetics. In J. C. Olson (Ed.), *Advances in consumer research* (Vol. 7, pp. 104-108). Provo, UT: Association for Consumer Research.

Holbrook, M. B., & Zirlin, R. B. (1985). Artistic creation, artworks and aesthetic appreciation: Some philosophical contributions to nonprofit marketing. In R. W. Belk (Ed.), *Advances in nonprofit marketing* (Vol. 1, pp. 1-54). Greenwich, CT: JAI.

Hughes, J. (1981). Village craftsmanship versus mass production. *The Courier, 68,* 66-68.

Jain, L. C. (1986). A heritage to keep: The handicrafts industry, 1955-85. *Economic and Political Weekly, 21*(20), 873-887.

Jain, L. C., Krishnamurthy, B. V., & Tripathi, P. M. (1985). *Grass without roots: Rural development under government auspices.* New Delhi: Sage.

Johnson, G. (1986). Commentary. *New York Folklore, 12*(1-2), 85-87.

Joseph, R. (1988). Women's role in the Indonesian batik industry: Some implications of occupational segmentation in crafts. In S. Kathuria, V. Miralao, & R. Joseph (Eds.), *Artisan industries in Asia: Four case studies* (pp. 71-89). Ottawa, Canada: International Development Research Centre.

Joyce, R. O. (1986). Marketing folk art. *New York Folklore, 12*(1-2), 43-47.

Kathuria, S. (1986). Handicraft exports: An Indian case study. *Economic and Political Weekly, 21*(40), 1743-1755.

Kathuria, S., Miralao, V., & Joseph, R. (Eds.). (1988). *Artisan industries in Asia: Four case studies.* Ottawa, Canada: International Development Research Centre.

Keesing, D. (1982). *Exporting manufactured consumer goods from developing to developed economies* [Draft]. New York: World Bank.

Kelly, R. F. (1992). Vesting objects and experiences with symbolic meaning. In L. McAlister & M. L. Rothschild (Eds.), *Advances in consumer research* (Vol. 20, pp. 232-234). Provo, UT: Association for Consumer Research.

Kirschenblatt-Gimblett, B. (1991). Objects of ethnography. In I. Karp & S. D. Lavine (Eds.), *Exhibiting cultures: The poetics and politics of museum display* (pp. 386-443). Washington, DC: Smithsonian Institution Press.

Körn, J. (1974). *Modern Makonde art.* London: Hamlyn.

Lavine, S. D. (1991). Art museums, national identity and the status of minority cultures: The case of Hispanic art in the United States. In I. Karp & S. D. Lavine (Eds.), *Exhibiting cultures: The poetics and politics of museum display* (pp. 79-87). Washington, DC: Smithsonian Institution Press.

Leong, W. T. (1989). Culture and the state: Manufacturing traditions for tourism. *Critical Studies in Mass Communication, 6*(4), 355-375.

Lingle, J. H., Altom, M. W., & Medin, D. L. (1984). Of cabbages and kings: Assessing the extendibility of natural object concept models to social things. In R. S. Wyer & T. K. Srull (Eds.), *Handbook of social cognition* (Vol. 1, pp. 71-117). Hillsdale, NJ: Lawrence Erlbaum.

Lovejoy, A. O. (1923). The supposed primitivism of Rousseau's discourse on inequality. *Modern Philosophy, 21,* 165-186.

The luxury-goods trade: Upmarket philosophy. (1992, December 26—1993, January 8). *The Economist,* pp. 95-98.

MacCannell, D. (1976). *The tourist: A new theory of the leisure class.* New York: Schocken.

Maduro, R. (1976). The Brahmin painters of Nathdwara. In N.H.H. Graburn (Ed.), *Ethnic and tourist arts* (pp. 227-244). Berkeley: University of California Press.

Maquet, J. (1971). *Introduction to aesthetic anthropology.* Reading, MA: Addison-Wesley.

Maurer, J. L., & Zeigler, A. (1988). Tourism and Indonesian cultural minorities. In P. Rossel (Ed.), *Tourism: Manufacturing the exotic* (pp. 65-92). Copenhagen: International Work Group for Indigenous Affairs.

Mead, D. C. (1981). *Subcontracting in rural areas of Thailand* (Research Paper No. 5). Bangkok, Thailand: Kasetsart University, Centre for Applied Economics Research.

Mies, M. (1980). *Housewives produce for the world market: The lace makers of Harsapar.* ILO World Employment Program Research.

Newton, D. (1981). *The art of Africa, the Pacific Islands and the Americas.* New York: Metropolitan Museum of Art.

Price, S. (1989). *Primitive art in civilized places.* Chicago: University of Chicago Press.

Pye, E. A. (1988). *Artisans in economic development: Evidence from Asia*. Ottawa, Canada: International Development Research Centre.

Said, E. (1979). *Orientalism*. New York: Vintage.

Salvador, M. L. (1976). The clothing arts of the Cuna of San Blas. In N. H. H. Graburn (Ed.), *Ethnic and tourist arts* (pp. 165-182). Berkeley: University of California Press.

Searles, D. P. (1980). Marketing principles and the arts. In M. P. Mokwa, W. M. Dawson, & E. A. Prieve (Eds.), *Marketing the arts* (pp. 65-69). New York: Praeger.

Segy, L. (1989). *African sculpture speaks*. New York: Da Capo.

Seiler-Baldinger, A. (1985). Some impact of tourism on traditional Yagua and Ticuna culture. In E. Gormsen (Ed.), *The impact of tourism on regional development and cultural change* (pp. 78-91). Mainz, Germany: Geographisches Institut der Johannes Gutenberg-Universität.

Semenik, R. J. (1987). State of the art of arts marketing. In R. W. Belk (Ed.), *Advances in nonprofit marketing* (Vol. 2, pp. 99-124). Greenwich, CT: JAI.

Silver, H. R. (1981). Calculating risks: The socioeconomic foundations of aesthetic motivation. *Ethnology, 20*, 101-114.

Spooner, B. (1986). Weavers and dealers: The authenticity of an Oriental carpet. In A. Appadurai (Ed.), *The social life of things* (pp. 195-234). New York: Cambridge University Press.

Stephen, L. (1991). Culture as a resource: Four cases of self-managed indigenous craft production in Latin America. *Economic Development and Cultural Change, 40*(1), 101-130.

Stern, L. W., & Gorman, R. H. (1969). Conflict in distribution channels: An exploration. In L. Stern (Ed.), *Distribution channels: Behavioral dimensions* (pp. 156-175). Boston: Houghton Mifflin.

Stewart, S. (1984). *On longing: Narratives of the miniature, the gigantic, the souvenir, the collection*. Baltimore, MD: Johns Hopkins University Press.

Stromberg, G. (1976). The amate bark-paper paintings of Xalitla. In N. H. H. Graburn (Ed.), *Ethnic and tourist arts* (pp. 149-162). Berkeley: University of California Press.

Subramanian, T. S. R., & Cavusgil, S. T. (1991). *Handicrafts: Developing export potential*. Geneva, Switzerland: International Trade Centre Monographs.

Taimni, K. K. (1981). Employment generation through handicraft cooperatives: The Indian experience. *International Labor Review, 120*(4), 505-517.

Teske, R. T. (1986). Crafts assistance programs and traditional crafts. *New York Folklore, 12*(1-2), 75-83.

Thomas, N. (1991). *Entangled objects: Exchange, material culture, and colonialism in the Pacific*. Boston: Harvard University Press.

Tylor, E. (1871). *Primitive culture: Researches into the development of mythology, philosophy, religion, language, art and custom*. London: John Murray.

United Nations Council for Trade and Development (UNCTAD). (1979). *Handbook on handicrafts: Preferential treatment for handmade goods* (UNCTAD/TAP/24-6). Author.

Upadhyay, K., & Sharma, S. (1988). Evidence from Nepal. In E. A. Pye (Ed.), *Artisans in economic development: Evidence from Asia* (pp. 32-43). Ottawa, Canada: International Development Research Centre.

Upadhyoy, M. N. (1973). *Economics of handicrafts industry*. New Delhi: S. Chand.

Varadarajan, L. (1991). Indian crafts: Towards a definition. In C. Margabandku, K. S. Ramachandran, A. P. Sagar, & D. K. Sinha (Eds.), *Indian archeological heritage* (Vol. 2, pp. 645-649). New Delhi: Agam Kala Prakashan.

Veblen, T. (1899). *The theory of the leisure class*. New York: New Library Edition.

Vogel, S. (1991). Always true to the object, in our fashion. In I. Karp & S. D. Lavine (Eds.), *Exhibiting cultures: The poetics and politics of museum display* (pp. 191-204). Washington, DC: Smithsonian Institution Press.

von Siebold, P. F. (1843). *Lettre sur l'utilité des musées ethnographiques et sur l'importance de leur création dans les Étas Européens qui possèdent des colonies* [A letter on the utility of ethnographic museums and on the importance of their creation in those European states who possess colonies]. Paris: Librairie de l'Institut.

Walle, A. (1986). Mitigating marketing: A window of opportunity for applied folklorists. *New York Folklore, 12*(1-2), 91-112.

Wallendorf, M., & Belk, R. W. (1987). *Deep meaning in possessions* [Video]. Cambridge, MA: Marketing Science Institute.

Woods, W. A. (1987). Classical aesthetics and arousal theory: Implications for fine arts marketing. In R. W. Belk (Ed.), *Advances in nonprofit marketing* (Vol. 2, pp. 203-239). Greenwich, CT: JAI.

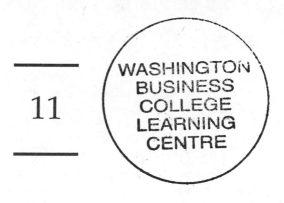

WASHINGTON
BUSINESS
COLLEGE
LEARNING
CENTRE

11

Culture and the Marketing of Culture:
The Museum Retail Context

JANEEN ARNOLD COSTA

GARY J. BAMOSSY

The marketing and sale of culture is characteristic of certain forms of tourism. Yet this marketing does not occur in the same way in all instances. The cultural background of the country in which the organization is found influences various aspects of the marketing process, including the attitude of the organization toward consumers, clients, and constituents; toward the product to be marketed and sold; indeed, toward marketing itself. In this chapter, we address this issue of the way in which culture affects the marketing of culture in the specific context of museum gift shops, bookstores, and catalogs.

Quest for Authenticity

Tourism often involves an avaricious attitude toward the consumption of services, goods, and experiences (Dunbar, 1977; Rossel, 1988). The actual acquisition of objects representative of the experience may be seen in the purchase and consumption of souvenirs, which are used

299

in various ways: "Tourists use their souvenirs to reminisce, differentiate the self from or integrate with others, bolster feelings of confidence, express creativity, and enhance aesthetic pleasure" (Littrell et al., 1994, p. 3; see also Gordon, 1986; Littrell, 1990; Littrell, Anderson, & Brown, 1993; MacCannell, 1976).

Littrell et al. (1994) suggested that "souvenirs hold strong symbolic value as tangible evidence of the travel experience and of having found the 'authentic' " (p. 3). The quest for authenticity involves a search for the "real," for what seems true to the experience and to actuality. In souvenirs, the tourist may seek either an "authentic" object or something that "authenticates" (validates, legitimates) the touristic experience. Thus, the souvenir may take a number of forms and need not be an object originally produced for another purpose and of historical or archaeological significance, as we might assume if an object is referred to as authentic. Rather, souvenirs in the context of authenticity and authentication can include photographs and postcards, arts and crafts produced for tourists, reproductions and replications, and innovatively altered yet "culturally representative" objects, as well as "original" artifacts.

THE MUSEUM PERSPECTIVE

In the context of museum visitation, the search for authenticity takes on a particular characteristic as it pertains to the purchase of souvenirs. Here, the tourist seeks an object, print, or other reproduction that somehow validates the museum visit and/or replicates the museum artifact in an "authentic" way:

> The museum may possess beautiful and charming paintings, prints, or objects that appeal to visitors who are looking for souvenirs. Thus postcards, slides, notepaper, Christmas cards, and the like are developed and then attractively framed [as are] reproduction prints and authentically reproduced objects and jewelry. Some museums with collections of furnishings even start reproduction programs and license manufacturers to produce authentic copies of furniture, ceramics, silver, pewter, glass, fabrics, wallpaper, and other materials. The museum sales desk and merchandising program is more than a source of revenue. It is an extension of the museum collection outside its walls, a form of interpretation. And it is a kind of taste-making, with strict canons of authenticity and appropriateness. No miniature Indian canoes with the name of the town on the side, but tasteful objects treasured in the museum and suitable for modern living. (Alexander, 1979, p. 207)

The desire for authenticity flows in *both* directions in the museum context. It is not only the consumers, the purchasers of the opportunity to view the museum exhibits and/or the museum souvenirs, who are concerned with the authentic. Perhaps with a greater depth of concern, as well as with what may be seen as a professional responsibility or even a moral obligation, are the museum curators, managers, and staff, who also concern themselves with authenticity.

For the museum personnel, the focus on authenticity is part of the entire professional process. In the determination of the originality and authenticity of a proposed acquisition, in the research of provenance, in the design of an appropriate exhibit, in proper procedure in deaccessioning, and in the sale of museum reproductions as souvenirs, museums are constantly concerned with the issue of authenticity. According to Horne (1992), this concern might well be characterized as "cultish":

> To the people who run heritage sites and museums, there has been a quite different consideration: it has been the cult of authenticity, in which when a thing becomes a part of our "heritage" it enters the realm of extraordinary purity in which, in an age of meretriciousness, it becomes authentic— the real thing. (pp. 101-102)

It seems appropriate to frame museums' focus on authenticity in religious terms, given this cultlike concern with authenticity *and* the sacralization of the object, an issue to which we will return presently.

Thus, in all aspects of museum association with the object, the concern with authenticity is manifest. The preoccupation can become so paramount that some museums choose to exhibit objects independent of *any* contextualization, thereby allowing the focus to remain on the object, to allow the object to "speak for itself," in a sense. Because a museum's "principal moral drives" are "authenticity and scholarship," there consequently may be a deliberate attempt to avoid any distortion of that authenticity, because "trying to arrange these things so they might attract the curiosity of visitors could be seen as a betrayal of their 'objectivity,' and an affront to reality" (Horne, 1992, p. 129).

This possible distortion of the authentic, here feared to result from even the mere *arrangement* of the objects and their exposure to the "tourist gaze" in museum exhibits (Urry, 1990), is even more an issue in the context of museum souvenirs. Again, the concern arises for a number of reasons. Because museums have an obligation to "be on guard against forgeries and fakes" (Alexander, 1979, p. 127), they must exercise appropriate caution in the reproduction of any museum artifact, lest such reproduction be mistaken for "the real thing." Further-

more, museums must monitor the reproduction to ensure that the reproduced object faithfully represents the object that has been copied,
again without being so similar to the original that a mistake in actual
identity might take place. It is also typical for museums to be concerned
with the presentation of and potential use for the reproduction, with
the objects and its marketing designed to ensure "appropriate" use by
its purchasers.

THE OBJECT: CONTROL, OWNERSHIP, AND KNOWLEDGE

With respect to the marketing of reproduced objects, museum professionals are acutely aware of the possible "distortion" to the object
"caused" by the consumer. Because they cannot *ensure* that the reproduced object will be appropriately appreciated and used by the consumer, museum personnel may manifest their concerns about the lack
of control over the consumer in a number of ways. A common strategy
by which to address this lack of control over the consumer is again to
focus on the object itself: Scrutiny of the quality of the reproduction and
of the production process, providing educational material and information with the reproduction, and "proper" contextualization of the
object in promotional efforts are all part of this strategy.

Although these measures may seem almost antithetical to the exhibit
approach advocating isolation of the object in its presentation, the critical difference lies in the assumed level of knowledge of the consumer,
as well as in the museum's ability to control the domain in which the
object is consumed. In exhibit space, the object remains in the control of
the museum. Museum personnel carefully guard the object, monitor
the light and humidity used in the display, and actively discourage any
inappropriate behavior with respect to the object. The museum continues to own the object, to preserve and protect it, and to vouch for its
authenticity. Knowledge concerning the object is almost implicit in the
object itself, and the museum is the owner and arbiter of *both* the object
and the knowledge concerning it.

The visitor to the museum who consumes visually may or may not
already possess knowledge about the object. Those museums that believe the object should speak for itself and be viewed in isolation may
not even take steps to educate this visual consumer. It is not uncommon
in art or archaeology museums, for example, to see objects identified
only by a number. Museums may provide a separate guidebook to the
numbers, or a visitor may be forced to rely on a docent to obtain further
information about the object. In this approach, the museum may see

itself as *protecting* the authentic objects from the ignorant consumer: "Museums pride themselves on being the last refuge for the 'real thing,' the 'authentic object' " (Ames, 1992, pp. 158-159).

As guardian of the sanctity of the object and its meaning, museums further sacralize the object, both from their perspective and from the perspective of the consumer:

> Authenticity can provide a secular epiphany of meaning equal to a super-natural revelation. . . . Faith in authenticity may cast a radiance of value and scarcity that hallows the object-in-itself. A museum can become a collection of isolated objects, each sacred because it is authentic, and, because of their authenticity, offering a unique reality. (Horne, 1992, p. 45)

Whether a museum chooses to provide full contextualization of the displayed object through educational materials, dioramas, and so on or, conversely, to display the objects in isolation, it is assumed that the museum is the proprietor of knowledge about the object. A hierarchy of knowledge and of ownership of the object is maintained, placing the knowledgeable museum personnel at one end of a continuum and the uneducated viewer at the other. At its extreme, this hierarchy becomes a setting for antagonism, even subconscious (or not) discrimination, by which the museum maintains its superordinate level in the knowledge hierarchy.

"EDUCATING" THE CONSUMER

In the retail/souvenir context, and with reference to the aforementioned strategies for maintaining control over the object, museums again take steps to ensure that the meaning of the object is not misappropriated and the object is not misused. Here, however, the museum *cannot* guard the object and its meaning once the reproduction is removed from museum premises. Nevertheless, museums take steps to control the use of the object. In some instances, this concern for appropriate use can even culminate in a disdain for the visitor/tourist who seeks to acquire a museum-reproduced object. Perhaps at the other end of the range of possible behaviors through which a museum attempts to maintain its control over the object in a retail context is the strategy that seeks to educate the consumer and to democratize knowledge through the sale and consumption of museum reproductions.

Even in this situation, in which education and democratization are sought, the focus on the object and on maintaining its authenticity remains. The concern with authenticity becomes *part* of the marketing strategy, however, integrated into the design, reproduction, promotion, and sales efforts. As with the fully contextualized display of museum objects, the objects for sale are also fully contextualized. Here, the museum personnel exercise control over the objects and guard against possible misuse through a democratization of knowledge and ownership of the reproduced object, rather than through class- and knowledge-based exclusive access to the object.

CULTURE AND THE MUSEUM

We suggest here that the museum's *national culture of origin* markedly influences the orientation toward the consumer, both in the exhibit process and in the retail context, although only the latter will be explored in this chapter. This orientation is, furthermore, embedded in an overall orientation toward retail marketing of museum products and toward the object itself. It may be most appropriate to consider the orientation in a holistic way, in fact, whereby the various aspects of attitudes toward the object, the consumer, education and knowledge, and commerce/retailing as an activity; the experience of the museum personnel; the perceived mission of the museum; and the national culture of origin are all considered in an integrated fashion.

Figure 11.1 is a graphic representation of this integrated set of attitudes and influences, in which national culture of origin is represented by the outer, all-encompassing ring. The next level, perceived mission of the museum, recognizes that there will be variance in attitudes toward education and so forth *within* countries, even though national culture of origin ultimately shapes the retail orientation. The attitudes toward education and knowledge as they relate to art objects similarly affect the attitudes toward retailing, marketing, and, ultimately, the customer.

Part of a national culture's influence on the attitude toward museum display and retail is based on historical development of museums and of museum functions within the nation in question. Thus, museums in various European nations, particularly in France and Great Britain, developed their collections through the expansion of empire. The museums became an expression and manifestation of the imperial enterprise, reinforcing both the imperial expansionism and the growing national awareness of the center of the empire, the nation itself: "As part of newly forming public cultures, museums were naturally among the places that defined, and then guarded, the body of national knowledge and the national past. In the most powerful nations, muse-

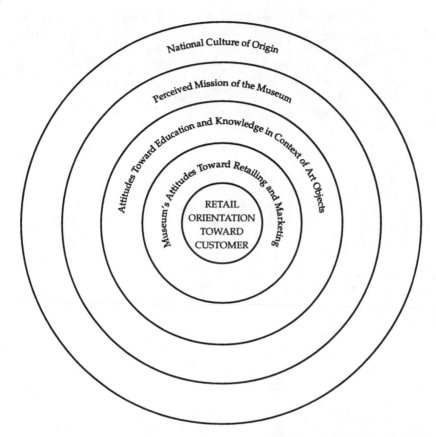

Figure 11.1. Influence of National Culture on Retail Orientation Toward Customer

ums became grandiose declarations of imperial power" (Horne, 1992, p. 123).

The Louvre in France and the British National Museum in London are clear examples of conquest-based collections that also became the focus of French and British national identity. Other European nations such as Greece and the Netherlands, however, saw themselves as victims of empire. In the latter case, the Rijksmuseum was founded in Holland as a response to French acquisitiveness (Alexander, 1979). Greek response to British imperial collecting enterprises is manifest in the ongoing effort to recover the Elgin marbles of the Parthenon, for example.

National culture and historical development as they affect museum function and orientation are similarly apparent in the case of American museums. In the United States, a country founded in diversity and based on democracy in education and opportunity, museums were established, and continue to function, as centers for education and *public* enlightenment (Alexander, 1979). This orientation was clear in the original charters of the Metropolitan Museum of Art in New York and of the Boston Museum of Fine Arts, both established in 1870 in the newly industrializing country, for example. In the United States today, museums continue to function as a social instrument (Alexander, 1979). The American historical and cultural backgrounds affect the overall orientation of the museum toward the objects and toward its multiple audiences. Our research suggests this orientation is further manifest in retail marketing strategies, not only in America but in Europe as well.

A final issue of concern here may also, in fact, be related to historical and cultural experience. As indicated previously, the Rijksmuseum was founded as a protective response to the culture-acquiring French (Alexander, 1979). Much of the tourism literature and the on-the-ground experience of host countries today suggest that tourism *also* can be a culture-acquiring, even culture-destroying activity (see, e.g., Belk, 1993; Belk & Costa, in press; Bendix, 1989; Canan & Hennessy, 1989; Greenwood, 1989; Nash, 1989). Given the historical experience of the Dutch with the French and the extant skepticism about tourism, discussed further in an upcoming section, might we not expect a Dutch museum orientation toward the culture consumer to be somewhat protective of the objects and, perhaps, slightly (or even overtly and strongly) suspicious and antagonistic toward the tourist? Such an attitude is, in fact, manifest in our preliminary empirical research on Dutch museums.

Similarly, the American nation, although founded in diversity and in an effort to avoid discrimination in European countries, itself became a culture-conquering and material-acquisitive society. Would we then not expect the orientation of museums in such a society to be demonstrative of conquest of the object, both in acquisition by the museum and by the consumer of culture? Would we not also expect that guaranteeing equality of access to the object—democratization of access and acquisition—would also be part of the museum orientation in the United States? In addition, the United States is a country in which virtually all efforts to legally create revenues are acceptable. Under such conditions, we would expect that commercial support for organizations, even artistic or cultural institutions such as museums, would be deemed desirable and appropriate. Again, our research suggests that these are, in fact, attitudes and orientations that are manifest in American museums.

CONSUMERS AND CLIENTS

It is apparently a fact of museum life that economic and political trends demand that museums become more consumer—and people— focused (Ames, 1992). In the context of exhibit strategy, this is evident in the emphasis on interactive exhibiting, increased contextualization and education, and the expanded use of multiple media in the exhibit environment (Smithsonian, 1984). The economic trends in which cultural institutions such as museums find themselves in need of increased cash flow and a greater amount of non-state-provided funds in general mean that museums must turn more and more to such strategies as retailing. Thus, the need for consumer focus moves beyond the exhibit context and may become even more critical in the retail environment. Therefore, the consumers of culture must be visually and experientially motivated in the context of visiting the museum and viewing its displays, thereby possibly increasing the frequency of visits, with a consequent rise in revenue from entrance fees. The consumers of culture also must be fruitfully motivated to further support the museum economy through the purchase of souvenirs. In this situation, it behooves the museum to become focused on the needs and desires of the retail consumer, albeit in the context of maintaining focus on authenticity and on the object itself.

The museum manager and the museum retail manager thus have multiple audiences and multiple goals (see Figure 11.2) that may at times, depending on the overall social and national cultural environment, seem antithetical, even antagonistic, toward one another. With respect to the curators, the board of directors, other museums, and any other academic-, scholarship-, or class-based audience, the manager must focus on the sanctity, authenticity, and protection of the object. On the other hand, with respect to the lay public on whom the museum must increasingly rely for economic and political support, the manager must pursue, at least to some extent, a policy of democratization of education, knowledge, and access to the object while still maintaining control over its authenticity.

In Figure 11.2, we portray the complex multiple audiences and goals to which museum personnel must respond. As related to Figure 11.1, the perceived mission of the museum can take a variety of forms and emphases, illustrated in Figure 11.2 in the multiple goals box, from

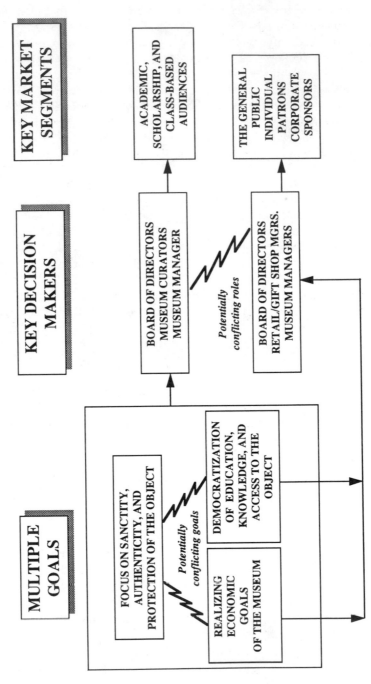

Figure 11.2. Multiple Goals and Multiple Market Segments

which an arrow is drawn directly to the board of directors/museum curators/museum managers box. The argument is that the varied goals of a museum should all contribute to the museum's mission, however defined, despite the fact that some goals may appear to conflict. Also, the other goals (economic and democratization) are not only under the decision-making control of the board of directors/museum curators/ museum managers but also under the control-decision processes of the retail/gift shop managers. These two groups of key decision makers overlap in terms of personnel but may still have potentially conflicting roles to sort through in their efforts to serve key market segments and to reach their multiple goals.

The Interview Data

On the basis of our experience and background, we began with the assumption that, despite similar organizational challenges, museums in different countries might assess and address those challenges in different ways. Thus, we postulated that national culture might affect museum orientations and strategies. To explore this assumption further, we began our study with interviews at museums in the Netherlands, France, and the United States. Using the data derived from nationally important museums, the interviews on which we will report here were conducted at the Van Gogh Museum and the Rijksmuseum in the Netherlands, the Louvre in France, and the New York Metropolitan Museum of Art in the United States.

The museum personnel responsible for the retail operation in each museum were interviewed, with interviews lasting approximately 2 hours. In each case, the interviews were conducted primarily in the manager's native language, with the occasional use of a translator in certain situations. Although these interviews were intended as preliminary, the insights derived from the interviews were sufficiently important to be reported as preliminary research results. On the basis of the understanding gained in these interviews, additional data are being gathered using a survey approach. The following information is derived from our fieldnotes on the interviews.

THE OBJECT FOR SALE

Each of the museums in which interviews were conducted has one or more bookstores/gift shops. The amount of space and number of objects sold vary greatly, with the Dutch museums having relatively small shops with a limited product selection and both the Louvre and the Metropolitan Museum of Art in New York having substantially larger shops and selections. This disparity reflects different attitudes toward the reproduced object, toward the consumer/tourist, indeed toward retailing or "commerce" in the museum environment itself. Although our data are limited at this point, we suggest that the totality of these attitudes can best be understood in the context of the national cultures in which these organizations are found. Again, please refer to Figure 11.1 with respect to these attitudes and national culture.

The Louvre

The Louvre in Paris is arguably the most important museum in the world, with a collection based on the Napoleonic French imperial expansion. This eclectic but magnificent collection is further made available to the consumer in the products offered for sale in the Louvre gift shops. The product assortment includes 18,000 different titles of books, which represent 50% of sales; 400 jewelry pieces; 400 molded sculptures, which are available in bronze, plaster, and synthetic materials; 16,000 images used for chalcographic prints (although only 2,000 sell well); 6,000 images of other types; and 4,000 gift items. Product groups also include clothing, videos and slides, postcards in an entirely separate but connected section of the store, and a children's section that involves education about the arts as well as toys.

The museum gift shop personnel of the Louvre advocate a specific philosophy toward the object to be sold. The mandate of the Louvre gift shop is to represent the museum collection, so the number of non-collection-based products in the line is very limited. In addition, the vast majority of the products are *direct copies* from the Louvre's collection; there are very few of the "museum adaptations" found in some other museums' gift selections. Another effect of this policy is that, except for a special gift shop, books, and a few objects, there is only limited drawing on the collections of museums other than the Louvre. This again is at variance with certain other museum gift shops. Nevertheless, the Louvre's retail manager sees the gift shop as the "window" on the world's great museums, so the Louvre carries a selection of important collection pieces, as well as the catalogs of other museums. The manager claims that the Louvre is the only museum gift shop in the world to carry other museums' catalogs; he sees this as a function of the "world's most important museum."

Because of their reputation and their standing, Louvre museum personnel adopt policies of protection of both the museum objects and the Louvre name itself. Some visitors to the museum are interested in purchasing an object that *authenticates the visit* rather than replicates an authentic museum object. For the purposes of serving such customers, the gift shop offers quality products with the name Louvre inscribed on them. It is also typical for the Louvre to avoid combining the Louvre brand with other brand names, unless the object to be dual-branded seems appropriate and the other brand is prestigious. So, for example, the gift shop sells Parker pens with the brand name Louvre on the side. Dual-branding occurs also in the offering of Hermes silk scarves with the Louvre name on them. The manager explained that this was natural and appropriate, because both Parker and Hermes are well-respected, elite products and names.

Museum visitors often seek other types of products to serve the function of authenticating the visit. In this situation, the museum must again protect the objects in the collection. Although the gift shop offers T-shirts for sell, for example, only the Louvre name is printed on them; none of the artwork from the museum is reproduced on a T-shirt. Cultural differences concerning appropriate use of reproductions are illustrated in this example, however: The Louvre does reproduce art work on French telephone company calling cards for corporate sales. To us, as interviewers, this seemed to be a gross commercialization of the image of Mona Lisa, the example presented to us. The manager assured us, however, that this was a perfectly appropriate use for reproduced art.

The Louvre gift shops have a consumer-friendly atmosphere, with a few exceptions. The shops are well designed for traffic flow, and the objects are generally quite accessible to the inquisitive consumer. Sales personnel are attentive and speak numerous foreign languages. Separate spaces are designed to accommodate the various types of products; each product group has a manager. The books are located on the ground floor and are divided into separately managed sections on the history of art, discovering art, the collections of museum(s), and individual artists; many titles are available in three or more languages. Also on the first floor is the postcard section of the store, which has separate cash registers and is divided from the rest of the shop by a large window, allowing easy access and providing a distinct space for what is obviously a quite different shopping activity than that present in the rest of the shop. A post office is located nearby, providing access to postal service for those patrons wishing to mail their postcards immediately. On the second floor, the video and slide section of the gift shop is visually motivating. The slides are displayed in a lit box, so that all slides are visible on a rotating basis. The videos are available in several languages. A video monitor is set up on the counter, and a copy of available videos is constantly running. The product manager of the second floor indicated that customers like to touch the products they are going to buy, particularly in the jewelry and clothing areas. The sculptures are displayed primarily in glass cases that can be viewed from at least two sides, so that a relatively full view of the object to be purchased is available. A separate area is also being designed for jewelry, which, according to the manager, is a high value-added product that requires a different type of space and merchandising than they currently have. He plans an area with large display cases and comfortable chairs to accommodate customers wishing to try on pieces of jewelry. The chalcographic print area includes Macintosh and hypercard technology, which can be used by clients to search through the inventory for themselves. The primary exception to the consumer-oriented atmosphere is the signage, all of which is in French. The manager indicated that he had run into great difficulty getting any signage whatsoever, much less in languages other than French.

The detached children's shop is the area in which the noncollection-based products were most evident, primarily as toys. The manager seemed very proud of this part of the gift shop, saying it is unique and performs an important service. In addition to books that educate children (and adults) about art, there are books about natural science, history, and so forth, not all of which can be related directly to the collection. Exceptions to this include books such as those on the history of Egyptian civilization, which has a direct connection to the collection. Books in other languages are separated from the rest of the selection and are labeled as books for foreigners. This part of the shop is particularly consumer friendly; an island rack in the shape of a boat dominates the central section of the shop, with products at each end and along the sides, as well as stools for children to sit on while they play with the displayed products.

The Dutch Museums:
The Rijksmuseum and the Van Gogh Museum

In comparison with the Louvre, the Dutch museums we visited had very limited product selections and did not manifest consumer-friendly orientations. The majority of products in both the Rijksmuseum and the Van Gogh Museum are print reproductions of paintings in the collection and books about works of art. Museum adaptations and other types of products are notably few.

In both museums, postcards are the largest selling item. In the Rijksmuseum, it is naturally the most famous paintings that command the greatest attention from visitors—and sell the most postcards; these include Rembrandt's *Nightwatch*, Vermeer's *Kitchen Maid*, other Vermeer landscapes, Rembrandt's *Jewish Bride*, and paintings with wind- and water mills. Guidebooks, published in several European languages and in Japanese, are the next best-selling products in the Rijksmuseum, followed by poster-sized reproductions of the paintings.

A few other items, including spoons and nonart merchandise, are offered on a very limited basis. The Rijksmuseum manager spoke about them with an air of distaste. When asked to describe the product selection, in fact, the manager said there were virtually no nonart products, although our later perusal of the shop itself revealed decks of cards, coasters, jewelry, dishes, and a Rijksmuseum spoon. There was even a bottle of "Night Watch Perfume" on display in the enclosed glass case. Except for the spoon, none of these was mentioned in the manager's description of the products offered.

In consultation with fashion experts and by relying on her own perceptions of what is Dutch and should be associated with the museum, the manager had supervised the museum production of a Hermes scarf with a tulip motif. This scarf was displayed in the gift shop, as was a T-shirt with artists' signatures on it, which she indicated sold well and was not a problem in terms of presentation of art. As in the Louvre, no T-shirts with artwork are offered.

The Rijksmuseum gift shop area is relatively small and dark. Postcards line lit shelves along the walls at each end of a long, dimly lit hall. Posters hang in racks for viewing; some canvas reproductions are available. The slides are displayed in backlit windows in little alcoves next to the sales counters. The slides are hard to reach, and the space is cramped, so only one person at a time can comfortably view the slides. Some books are displayed in a glass case opposite the slides, whereas other books are directly in front of the sales counters. Except for the catalogs, all books are encased in glass and cannot be handled. The books are almost exclusively Rijksmuseum productions, and the selection is very limited. Although the manager mentioned that it would be appropriate to eventually have samples of books that customers could scan before buying, this consumer convenience is not yet available. The manager indicated that no marketing research is conducted, and product development is based on intuition and past experience only.

There seems to be a clear "inside-outside" perspective in the Rijksmuseum bookstore/gift shop relative to the museum, even though the bookstore/gift shop is located on the first floor of the museum (but away from any of the collections). The integrity of the art in the collection is critical; commercialization through the sale of reproductions is approached with caution, even disdain. The art/objects/ collection as "inside" can thus be opposed to the customers/tourists/ bookstore/commercial activities as "outside."

In the Van Gogh Museum, similarly, commercialization of the product is to be avoided. There are no T-shirts with van Gogh images on them, although the shop sells T-shirts with the stylized signature of "Vincent" (van Gogh) written on them. There were no displays of this type of product in the shop. Instead, a small stack of shirts (two to three) was at the end of one long display case, as though put there as an afterthought. Any interested customer was obliged to pick up the shirt and look at it on his or her own. T-shirts with van Gogh artwork on them were for sale from third-party vendors outside the museum during the van Gogh centennial celebration in 1991; the museum personnel we interviewed clearly felt this was an abomination of sorts. A popular T-shirt had Japanese writing on it, but this was apparently popular with all nationalities, not just with the Japanese.

Again, the integrity of the art is carefully guarded. The personnel are proud of their postcards, which are excellent reproductions and are priced lower than those in other museums in which Van Gogh Museum personnel conduct comparison shopping. The Van Gogh managers seemed pleased that they could say they were fully aware of what other museums offer. Van Gogh's flower pieces are the best-selling postcards—the sunflowers and the irises, especially. The next best-selling type of artwork is landscapes. In addition, the shop sells books about van Gogh, about artists who influenced him, and about the artistic schools of his time. Good-selling products are calendars and agenda books, which the museum produces specially each year with different van Gogh reproductions.

The Van Gogh Museum gift shop, although still small, is better lit and more accessible to the consumer than is the Rijksmuseum shop. Here the postcards are displayed on shelves on the wall to the left as the visitor enters. Books are exhibited horizontally along the window across the back of the bookstore, with unwrapped samples of each book available on top of each stack; customers can peruse the books conveniently and at their leisure. The book islands jut into the center of the shop, ending in circular, turning racks with more, smaller books (and samples) on them. The shop offers books that the museum itself produces, as well as virtually any other book about van Gogh that has been deemed to be good by the museum, regardless of publisher. Of the 210 paintings in the museum, 140 are available in reproduction; posters are displayed along the wall behind the counter, opposite the postcards. On the fourth wall, customers may look through additional posters displayed on poster racks. Two cash registers and counters mark the exit.

The Van Gogh Museum, although more consumer oriented than the Rijksmuseum, still presents a cautious attitude toward the consumer and toward reproduction of its objects. The museum reproduces what sells: Salespersons monitor customer requests and pass them along. The museum's books are available in several languages, and postcard captions are written in four languages, all on the same card. The museum receives requests for lists of their products from other museums and from wholesalers and retailers. The museum follows a passive marketing strategy, by which it responds to these requests but has no sales force of its own. The Van Gogh gift shop monitors sales via computerized data from the cash registers. In addition, the shop conducts some market research, including collecting information on foreign visitors.

The Metropolitan Museum of Art

In clear contrast to the Dutch museums, and more in line with what is offered by the Louvre, the Metropolitan Museum of Art in New York City has a vast product selection and is very consumer oriented. A pamphlet concerning the Metropolitan's reproduction activities indicates that "through printed texts, printed pictures, and three-dimensional copies of art objects the Metropolitan has long led the way among American museums in making its collections known, understood, and appreciated by diverse audiences" (Kellerman, 1981, p. 5). These three-dimensional copies take a variety of forms; the Metropolitan offers books, prints, jewelry, sculptures, scarves, rugs, stained glass, ceramics, glass, calendars, coasters, toys, and so on.

The main gift shop in the Metropolitan is located to the right in the entry hall and is accessible without paying the entrance fee to the museum (in contrast to the Louvre, Rijksmuseum, and Van Gogh Museum). This main shop occupies 12,500 square feet and is attractive, well lit, and inviting to the consumer. Space and opportunity for browsing are adequate. Knowledgeable salespersons provide information and service at each of the numerous sales counters. Samples of books and other objects for the consumer to handle before purchase are found throughout the shop. The Metropolitan also has smaller satellite kiosks located throughout the museum to serve the customer interested in buying products related to special exhibits or to certain galleries. The Metropolitan operates off-premises gift shops in several locations in the United States and abroad as well. In addition, nearly 20 million mail-order gift catalogs are sent to interested purchasers throughout the year. In effect, the commercial activity of the Metropolitan is sophisticated and broad.

The objects that are available are both actual copies and adaptations from the collections of the Metropolitan *and* from other museums from which the Metropolitan has obtained permission to sell reproductions and adaptations. It is impossible to describe here all of the objects available for sale. The shop's most important source of revenue is the sale of jewelry; jewelry counters dominate the sales space. As with all of the objects sold, the museum provides a small placard with the jewelry piece, describing its provenance and function. A customer may thus purchase a pair of reproduced Egyptian earrings from circa 1800 B.C., a Greek necklace from the Hellenistic period, or a pin based on a Chinese wine vessel from the sixth century B.C., each accompanied by a placard providing the relevant information.

As indicated, not all objects for sale are direct copies but are, instead, adaptations from objects in the Metropolitan's collection or from the collections of other museums or individuals. For example, a pin and earrings are adapted from "the floral border of a 17th century Mughal manuscript album that once belonged to Shah Jahan, builder of the Taj Mahal"; silver and copper-plated business card cases are "based on an illustration from a page of Arabian ornaments in *The Grammar of Ornament*, by Owen Jones, published in London in 1863"; and the "Venus Earrings" are "adapted from earrings—one a white pearl, the other black—in *Venus Before the Mirrors*, by Peter Paul Rubens" (The Metropolitan Museum of Art, 1994, pp. 49, 30, 43, respectively). Such adaptations are particularly difficult, requiring special attention to detail in the reproduction process and in providing information to the consumer about the appropriate use of the object. Issues relative to authenticity will be addressed in greater detail below. The retail manager suggested that the adapted art object was by far the most difficult type of object to sell in an appropriate manner. Still, each of the objects, whether direct reproductions or adaptations of other objects, requires careful monitoring in the reproduction process.

The museum has its own reproduction studio, in which master molds are made and in which some final finishing of the product, including patination, occurs. The majority of the objects (approximately 90%), however, are reproduced by independent companies and artists and are then subject to scrutiny and approval by the museum itself. Strict canons for quality control are maintained at all times, on the basis of the "need for control" over the reproduced object (Kellerman, 1981, p. 42).

The Metropolitan provides copies of art objects and of visit-validating souvenirs in numerous forms. The visitor may purchase a bag with the name of the museum on its side, for example, and the numerous calendars, cards, and so on also include the brand name of the Metropolitan for prestige and identification. The gift shops also offer guidebooks to New York City and other souvenirs as a service to their customers.

AUDIENCES FOR THE AUTHENTIC

The museum personnel interviewed all indicated concern with authenticity and protection of the object. Most often, this guardianship function is housed in and dictated by the curators of various parts of the collections. When the managers we interviewed mentioned problems or questions about authenticity, they invariably referred to the curators as the proprietors of knowledge and as the ultimate decision makers in questions about the appropriateness of a reproduction or adaptation.

In the Louvre, for example, most of the products are direct copies of items in the Louvre's collections, and curator approval is not required. Nevertheless, curator approval *is* required for anything that is innovative and/or involves a combination of collection objects. After 3 years of effort, for instance, the manager was finally nearing approval of a "Louvre Perfume." Because the product was not a strict replication, it required approval from the curators, and the manager indicated that it needed to be consistent with the image of the Louvre itself. The perfume bottle for women was derived from the Marie Antoinette period, whereas the fragrance for men would be sold in a bottle based on the Napoleonic era. Despite the fact that the bottles themselves are accurate replications, their use for the perfume required special approval. The manager indicated that the perfume itself was mixed by experts. The product box displayed the museum logo and again required approval as consistent with the Louvre's image. In further indication of protection of the Louvre's name and products, the manager pointed out that the curators would not allow the perfume to be sold in duty-free shops and the like but would approve it for sale in "better" perfume stores. Recall the aforementioned instance concerning the Parker pens and Hermes scarves, similarly approved for use by the curators because of the prestige of the Parker and Hermes brands. Even questions about whether or not a book is a good selection for the bookstore are referred to curators, because all books sold must be "scientifically accurate." Again, the curators are the ultimate arbiters in the product-line strategy.

The curators of the Louvre meet each Tuesday. The manager presents possible products to them at these meetings. According to the manager, the curator-commercial relationship requires "soft diplomacy"; he commented that the overall view of the curators and of museum staff is that "commercial activities are bad, although the money generated is good." The manager himself seemed quite comfortable with this need to protect the object and to guarantee its authenticity and appropriate use in a commercial sense. His only real frustration seemed related to the signage for the shops; the signs were small and in French only.

In the Dutch museums, concern with authenticity is paramount, and curator control is strict. No artwork is represented on T-shirts or other "inappropriate" venues, for example, and reproductions of artwork are strictly controlled. The manager at the Rijksmuseum commented specifically, for instance, that the aforementioned T-shirt with artists' signatures on it presented no difficulties because there was no attempt to actually reproduce art on the T-shirt. The Van Gogh Museum similarly avoids the production of T-shirts with van Gogh artwork on them, although T-shirts with the printed signature of the artist are allowed. The museum personnel at the Van Gogh and at the Rijksmuseum were very clear in their philosophy that commercialization of the product should be avoided. Again, decisions are made by the curators, even with respect to direct reproductions of artwork. So, for example, the Rijksmuseum curator who specializes in a particular collection is consulted before a series of reproductions can be printed or produced.

At the Metropolitan Museum, authenticity is, again, a major concern, Here, however, the concern for the authentic is mitigated by the need to raise funds *and* by the desire to democratize access to the objects. This means for the sale of objects that extra care must be taken in the reproductive process and in the marketing of the objects themselves to ensure authenticity to the extent possible. In his efforts to authentically reproduce objects, the manager of the retail operation seeks out specialized firms and artists capable of producing the objects using appropriate techniques. For example, to reproduce "a small selection of colonial and Federal silver from the collections of the American Wing," the Metropolitan licensed the Gorham Company, silversmiths located in Providence, Rhode Island, as the exclusive producer of this type of copy for

the museum (Kellerman, 1981, p. 35). Attention to detail in reproduction has led to the manager's "studying both advanced and time-
honored duplicating techniques and searching for lost or forgotten
methods of manufacture" (Kellerman, 1981, p. 32). Specific techniques
in blown and pressed glass, silver, ceramics, and the lost-wax process
for bronze sculptures are examples. To differentiate the copies from the
original artifacts, the identifying mark of the Metropolitan Museum is
placed clearly on each object. Curators' approval is required for each
object to be duplicated or adapted.

In addition to curators, each museum's board of directors or similar
organization influences handling of the reproduced object and concern
for authenticity. In both the French and Dutch museums, this organization carefully monitors all commercial activities to avoid overcommer-
cialization of the product. For example, the Louvre manager indicated
that although he would like to advertise the gift shop's products, such
a commercial activity would be deemed inappropriate. The association
of 34 French museums, the Réunion, does publish a catalog that shows
the products that all the museums in the Réunion offer for sale to organizations and corporate customers. Although the catalog is profes-
sionally produced, it is very simple and is quite unlike the catalogs
produced by major American museums such as the Metropolitan Museum, the Boston Museum of Fine Arts, and the Smithsonian. The manager again implied that a Louvre catalog similar to those produced by
these American museums would be inappropriate. The Louvre does
not engage in direct mail marketing, although they respond to customer requests for copies of specific works of art.

Another example of the control of the Louvre's board over commercial activities is the aforementioned signage directing visitors to the
Louvre gift shop area. As previously indicated, all signs are in French
only and are quite small and unobtrusive. The manager indicated that
he had asked for larger signs to route customers upstairs, but his re-
quest was defeated at the board level. Finally, a discrete sign in French
indicating that the shop included a boutique and was not just a book-
shop was placed at the entrance to the shop area.

The gift shop in the Rijksmuseum is part of the Stichting Rijksmuseum
(Rijksmuseum Foundation) and employs 10 full-time salespersons. The
store manager is also the director of the foundation, which handles all
of the museum's copyright sales, any aspects relating to film location
work, and so forth. In her role as director of the foundation and gift
shop manager, our interviewee expressed disdain for any activity that
might be seen as overly commercial. The manager indicated that
when the director of the museum wore a T-shirt with Rembrandt's

famous *Nightwatch* on a popular Dutch talk show to publicize a special exhibit at the museum, quite a stir was created among a number of museum personnel and patrons who considered it entirely inappropriate.

The foundation of the Van Gogh Museum is also directly responsible for managing the gift shop, as well as for reproducing works and granting permission for reproduction, although the copyrights actually expired 50 years after Vincent van Gogh's death. At the Van Gogh Museum, as at the Rijksmuseum and the Louvre, the foundation is actually separate from the museum itself and provides funds to the museum. It was expressed clearly in all three European museums in which interviews were conducted that commercialism is inappropriate in direct association with the museum, and separate foundations or boards are required.

Although commercialism is bad, nevertheless the funds derived from the commerce are good and are very important to the museums' continued functioning. In the Rijksmuseum, for example, all store revenues go to the foundation, which supplies roughly 67% of the museum's acquisition budget. The Dutch government supplies the remaining 33%. In January 1995, the museum became independent of government support, thereby increasing the importance of the foundation as a source of revenue. Similarly, in the Van Gogh Museum, money earned in the gift shop is used to support acquisitions by the museum. The contribution of the gift shop is significant. As of January 1993, the gift shop at the Louvre became independent and now pays 7% of its revenues to the Louvre as rent; the Louvre uses these funds in whatever way it chooses. The gift shop is still nonprofit, however, and, as a member of the Réunion, redistributes revenues among its members. The Réunion also produces books and handles copyright arrangements.

At the Metropolitan Museum, the board of trustees also maintains strict control over commercial activities. As suggested earlier, the attitude is much more procommercial, although the concern for authenticity is maintained. Although consistently involved in ascertaining and monitoring the quality of reproductions and the appropriateness of various objects for sale, the board also sees itself as responsible for *providing access* to the collections through the sale of objects. The Metropolitan's 1870 Charter mandated "popular education," and the original trustees of the museum interpreted this to include reaching a "vast and diverse public" through publishing and commercial activities (Kellerman, 1981, p. 3). Thus, in the guise of education, commercial activities are condoned but carefully monitored.

As with the other museums in our interview sample, the Metropolitan Museum relies heavily on revenues generated from the gift shop and related activities. Directly addressing the question of whether or not "commercialism . . . is out of place in such an institution as the Metropolitan," the chair of the board indicated in 1981 that, in fact, the commercial activities serve the Metropolitan appropriately through education and through the provision of sorely needed funds to meet even "basic operating expenses" (Kellerman, 1981, pp. 3-4). Each year the contributions of the gift shop and mail-order catalog operations to the operating funds of the museum are substantial.

The third type of audience for the authentic, beyond the curators and the major directing organizations of the museums, is the visitor. The museum managers were aware of national differences in their customers' orientations toward the objects for sale and toward the collections in general. Of the roughly 1 million visitors to the Rijksmuseum per year, 85% are foreign tourists, the greatest number of which are Americans, followed by French, Italians, Spanish, and Japanese. The manager clearly expressed her opinion that most visitors have a very low level of art appreciation. This is particularly the case with the Americans, she said, who only come to see the "famous clock" (Rembrandt's *Nightwatch*) and then leave.

Although the Rijksmuseum gift shop manager is aware of segmentation as a strategy and discussed it in relation to gender, she does not see a great deal of difference in the buying behavior of particular nationalities. Her only comments in this context were that Italians are very interested in buying books and that the Dutch do not seem interested in spending money on "culture" in any way. As with the Rijksmuseum, the managers at the Van Gogh Museum see their clientele as largely uneducated with respect to art. It is common for customers to ask for reproductions of van Gogh's famous painting *Starry Night*, which the museum does not own. Only 10% of the Van Gogh's customers are Dutch, and, as with the Rijksmuseum, the comment was made that the Dutch themselves do not spend a lot on culture. Although the Van Gogh managers estimate that about 34% of museum visitors buy something in the shop, they commented that both Japanese and Italians buy a lot; the latter are particularly interested in books.

One in 20 visitors to the Louvre makes purchases in the gift shop. The manager sees this as a very low level of purchase activity and attributes it to many visitors arriving as part of bus tours with limited schedules. He also suggested that the lack of signs contributes to poor awareness. The Louvre manager was quite aware of national differences in buying orientations. For example, he indicated that there is very strong interest from Japanese consumers, on the basis of the prestige of the product and "brand name" of the Louvre. Although they are probably only 1% of the visitors, the Japanese are the biggest spenders. Echoing the impressions of our Dutch managers, the Louvre manager indicated that Italians are big book buyers. On the other hand, he said that Americans "don't read"—they prefer to purchase jewelry and videos. Unlike the Dutch museums in which it was estimated that only 10% of the customers are Dutch, 33% of the Louvre's customers are French.

The Louvre manager expressed his opinion that foreigners are often buying the museum itself, indicating they visited the Louvre, when they purchase products from the gift shops. It is his role and the role of the gift shop to be "guardians of the image" of the Louvre, and, by extension, of the image of France itself, he said. The manager went on to explain that the Louvre is the center of Paris, and Paris is the center of France, so, of course, they are selling France and French culture in the Louvre gift shops.

From the perspective of the Metropolitan Museum, as alluded to earlier, the customer has a right to knowledge about, even quasi ownership of, the actual object, accomplished through the copying and sale of reproduced museum objects. Thus, the retail operations provide an important venue for the democratization of art and education.

ORGANIZATIONAL CULTURE AND
NATIONAL CULTURE OF EMPLOYEES

Beyond the aspects of culture and organization as they affect the retailing activities of the museums in our sample, organizational culture, the national culture of the employees, and the individual personalities and experiences of the retail personnel and managers affect the ways in which the gift shops are operated. In the Netherlands, the negative attitude toward commercialism permeates the organization, sometimes to the dismay of the retail managers. For example, the manager of the Rijksmuseum indicated she felt that the gift shop was quite provincial in terms of scope and operation. In fact, she was somewhat apologetic about the shop, saying that it was small, given the size of the Rijksmuseum, and that we would find it to be "amateurish." She further expressed dismay and surprise that plans for developing the "museum square" connecting the Rijksmuseum, the Van Gogh Museum, and the Stedelijk Municipal Museum in Amsterdam did not include plans for a gift shop that would consolidate offerings from all three museums.

The negative attitude toward commercialism in the museum context, apparent in the limited product selection, the merchandising, and the layout of the shop, is again evident in the training and attitude of the Rijksmuseum sales personnel. Salespersons receive no formal training in retailing other than how to manage the cash register. They are given guidebooks to familiarize themselves with the museum's collection; language skills are more important than any background or strong interest in art per se. The sales personnel are primarily students, housewives, and others who want to work part-time.

The marketing strategy of the Rijksmuseum is also limited in scope and perspective. Sales are tracked by computer and by feedback from the sales staff. If an item sells, it is reordered. No criteria of "successful sales" levels exist, and the manager suggested that whatever they offer tends to sell because of "impulse purchases" as a result of merely visiting the museum. As indicated earlier, the Rijksmuseum offers reprints to some of the better art houses in the city, but it is the retailers who contact the foundation, rather than vice versa. No direct mail catalogs are produced, and the single attempt at a direct mail campaign to sell the museums replications failed and was not attempted again. Again, the manager was more procommercial than the overall organization; she indicated that the mailing probably failed because the catalog had a "purchase at buyer's risk" warning, with a policy of no refunds. The manager also indicated that she felt it would be appropriate to have some sort of educational function performed by the bookstore/gift shop beyond that currently provided. She seemed uncertain how that would occur, however; she mentioned that the education department of the museum itself has had limited impact in implementing its programs.

The Rijksmuseum is also relatively unconcerned about or reactive to competition. For example, many other bookstores in the city sell postcards of objects in the museum's collection, but the manager does not particularly view these bookstores as competitors. She even reorders postcard inventory by consolidating her order with that of the kiosk that sells postcards in the square across the street from the museum; she sells to the kiosk at a discount. Like the Rijksmuseum, the Van Gogh Museum and its personnel similarly reflect a basic negative attitude toward the commercialization of art. They avoid any great attention to retail activities, and they focus very clearly on accurate and appropriate replications of van Gogh's art. The marketing strategy, like that of the Rijksmuseum, is passive and limited. They typically reorder the products that sell well in the shop, although they mentioned one instance in which a particularly popular product was not reordered; they seemed unsure why that was the case. Although the layout of the shop and the product displays are more consumer friendly than are those of the Rijksmuseum, the Van Gogh Museum is still very cautious in its approach to commercialism. Nevertheless, they are aware of their competitors' (other museums) activities, they are price conscious, and they pay attention to the detail of the product.

The retail training of the Louvre's shop manager was quite apparent. He is a sophisticated merchandiser and marketer with an extensive background in department stores. He presents an image of prestige and knowledge. The Louvre manager has a detailed marketing plan, a well-developed strategy, and an expressed ambition for shop growth. For example, the manager plans to take over a space that is currently operated by another organization and involves the marketing of products from other museums. He described the merchandising and marketing activities of this area as "terrible" and indicated the organization had no clear concept of who they were and what they were trying to sell.

The Louvre manager is aware of the needs of the consumer and responds fully to them. This awareness is manifest in virtually all aspects of the layout and orientation of the gift shop. The manager is also excited about the prospect of more commercial space and better access for visitors, which will be made available through the planned multistory underground parking structure at the Louvre, providing parking for private vehicles and for buses. Still, in comparison with the Metropolitan Museum, the retail activities, particularly direct mail marketing efforts, are less developed. The strategy of the Louvre is clearly in line with a cautious attitude toward commercialism and with the expressed opinion of the manager that he and his personnel and shops are "guardians of the image" of the Louvre, of its art, and of France itself.

The orientation of the personnel of the Metropolitan Museum of Art in New York City is, in comparison with the other museums in our sample, procommercial and procustomer. The retail space is large, well lit, well designed, and attentive to detail and to the customer's needs. The product selection is vast, varied, and consistently high in quality. In addition, the direct mail activity is very extensive and meets the needs of distant consumers. The funds derived from these commercial activities are extremely important for the operation of the museum itself. Management has an extensive history both in retailing and in museum directorship. All of this orientation is consistent with the national culture of the employees and with the organizational culture in general; both cultures emphasize democratization of knowledge and of access to the object.

Still, consistent with the museum functions of scholarship and protection, the Metropolitan retail environment is constantly monitored by
its various publics. Justification for the extensive commercial activities
is apparently needed on a regular basis. A further manifestation of its
protective role is found in the attention to quality and detail in the reproduction process itself. Thus, the protection of the object is *part of* the
marketing strategy, rather than perceived as *antithetical* to it.

Conclusion

Our preliminary research has provided evidence of the powerful impact of national culture on the "marketing of culture," specifically in
the museum retail context. Of course, we expect, and numerous studies
have shown, that national culture affects many types of organizations
and marketing and is not unique to the museum environment. This
national cultural effect is of particular interest in the context of museums and the marketing of culture, however, because the objects that are
sold become the focus of cultural identity, perhaps of cultural protec-
tionism, and the transfer of ownership may even become an issue of
cultural clash.

Inherent in the focus on authenticity in the national museum context,
then, are preservation and protection of the culture embedded in the
object. This "culture" often takes the form of what has been referred to
as "culture with a big C"—culture in the sense of high art, for example.
Our research indicates that not only is it culture associated with enrich-
ment and gentility, however, that becomes an integral part of the object
and its meaning. Rather, the attitude toward the object, perhaps even
the object itself, becomes imbued with the national culture of the museum in which the object is found. The treatment of the object, including its reproduction and sale in a retail context, is similarly affected by
the national culture of the organization.

National culture affects the goals and mission of the museum, as well
as the overall system of attitudes toward the object, toward retailing,
and toward the consumer. Our contrasting samples of Dutch, French,
and American museums indicate marked cultural differences in goals
and attitudes, despite similar organizational challenges. The Dutch
museums are clearly the most conservative in their orientation to public consumption of the object, with a markedly cautious attitude toward
commercial activities and toward the retail consumer. At the other extreme lies the Metropolitan Museum of Art in New York City, in which

sale of the retail object is found to be part of the museum mission to educate and democratize access to the museum's collection and to art in general. The Louvre occupies an attitudinal space between the Dutch and American examples. Although less developed and complex than the retail activities of the Metropolitan, the Louvre's commercial orientation is, nevertheless, sophisticated, albeit within the context of a conservative attitude toward retail efforts and sale of the object.

In this chapter, we had originally questioned whether or not variation in cultural attitudes toward museum marketing of the object could be found to be explicable in the larger historical and cultural context of the societies in question. We believe our research results indicate these original questions were warranted. The American museum attitude is democratically and publicly oriented, with a favorable orientation toward commercial activities, profit within a nonprofit setting, and material acquisitiveness. All of this is consistent with the American culture in general, founded on democratic principles, with an open attitude toward capitalistic enterprise and an emphasis on materialism. The Dutch museums might seem to be an enigma within the overall context of Dutch attitudes toward commerce, which are historically well developed and contribute to Dutch success in the global economy of today. Placed within a historical framework, however, the enigmatic aspects of the Rijksmuseum and Van Gogh Museum management are no longer puzzling. The Rijksmuseum was established for the protection of Dutch art objects and national culture; van Gogh's art is seen as a national treasure. Given the imperial quest for art objects, clearly evident in the collections of the Louvre, the British National Museum, and the Hermitage in St. Petersburg, for example, concern with the object and a cautious, even negative attitude toward tourists who are imperial in their own ways seem appropriate in the Dutch museum context. Finally, the Louvre management's attitude toward their own collections and toward retail activities exemplifies French nationalism, even ethnocentrism. Tourists "obviously" would like to own something that reminds them of their visit to "the world's greatest museum," center of Paris and of France, in the French perspective. Still, the objects must be protected, particularly from those who would not understand their value, so organizational control of the commercial activities is paramount. As we place our data in these larger cultural contexts, the orientations become understandable, even predictable.

Museums face organizational challenges involving multiple goals and multiple market segments, within and between which conflict may occur. Within the goals and mission of the museum, for example, the focus on sanctity, authenticity, and protection of the object may potentially conflict with realizing the economic goals of the museum and/or democratization of education, knowledge, and access to the object. This potential conflict is more likely to become a reality when the economic goals of the museum are threatened or achieve greater emphasis as a result of funding difficulties. Economic challenges are increasingly apparent in the worldwide museum context today, given reduced state funding. Conflict between goals is also more likely to occur when, as in the case of the Metropolitan, democratization is a clear goal of the museum, but focus on authenticity, sanctity, and protection must be maintained.

In any case, it is the responsibility of key decision makers in the organization, including the board of directors, curators, managers, and retail/gift shop managers, to direct the organization in maintaining its mission and achieving its goals. The responsibilities of these decision makers can again become conflictual when the key market segments of the organization are considered. When the market focus is on academic-, scholarship-, and class-based audiences, responsibility for decisions lies with the directors, curators, and general managers. When the general public, individual patrons, and corporate sponsors are also important target markets, however, the retail/gift shop managers are also critical to the decision-making processes, and the roles and orientations of the various key decision makers may conflict with one another.

The interview data clearly indicate national cultural differences in the museum retail context. The results warrant further research, and we have developed a survey instrument to gather data from larger national samples in four countries—the Netherlands, France, the United States, and Italy. The latter was added as a result of subsequent research in Italy that indicated further cultural differences and orientations toward marketing of the museum object exist and should be explored. We might expect such differences to be manifest in all cultures studied, with an eventual conclusion that cultural contextualization is imperative in the study of museum retail marketing throughout the world.

References

Alexander, E. P. (1979). *Museums in motion: An introduction to the history and functions of museums.* Nashville, TN: American Association for State and Local History.

Ames, M. M. (1992). *Cannibal tours and glass boxes: The anthropology of museums.* Vancouver, Canada: University of British Columbia Press.

Belk, R. W. (1993). Third world tourism: Panacea or poison? The case of Nepal. *Journal of International Consumer Marketing, 5*(2), 27-68.

Belk, R. W., & Costa, J. A. (in press). International tourism: An assessment and overview. *Journal of Macromarketing.*

Bendix, R. (1989). Tourism and cultural displays: Inventing traditions for whom? *Journal of American Folklore, 102*, 131-146.

Canan, P., & Hennessy, M. (1989). The growth machine, tourism, and the selling of culture. *Sociological Perspectives, 32*(2), 227-243.

Dunbar, S. (1977, Spring-Summer). Why travel? *Landscape*, pp. 45-47.

Gordon, B. (1986). The souvenir: Messenger of the extraordinary. *Journal of Popular Culture, 20*(3), 135-146.

Greenwood, D. J. (1989). Culture by the pound: An anthropological perspective on tourism as cultural commoditization. In V. L. Smith (Ed.), *Hosts and guests: The anthropology of tourism* (2nd ed., pp. 171-186). Philadelphia: University of Pennsylvania Press.

Horne, D. (1992). *The intelligent tourist.* McMahons Point, NSW, Australia: Margaret Gee.

Kellerman, R. M. (1981). *The publications and reproductions program of the Metropolitan Museum of Art: A brief history.* New York: The Metropolitan Museum of Art.

Littrell, M. A. (1990). Symbolic significance of textile crafts for tourists. *Annals of Tourism Research, 17*(2), 228-245.

Littrell, M. A., Anderson, L., & Brown, P. J. (1993). What makes a craft souvenir authentic? *Annals of Tourism Research, 20*(1), 197-215.

Littrell, M. A., Balzerman, S., Kean, R., Gahring, S., Neimeyer, S., Reilly, R., Stout, J. (1994). Souvenirs and tourism styles. *Journal of Travel Research, 23*(1), 3-11.

MacCannell, D. (1976). *The tourist: A new theory of the leisure class.* New York: Schocken.

The Metropolitan Museum of Art. (1994). *Holiday Gifts 1994.* New York: Author.

Nash, D. (1989). Tourism as a form of imperialism. In V. L. Smith (Ed.), *Hosts and guests: The anthropology of tourism* (2nd ed., pp. 37-52). Philadelphia: University of Pennsylvania Press.

Rossel, P. (1988). Tourism and cultural minorities: Double marginalization and survival strategies. In P. Rossel (Ed.), *Tourism: Manufacturing the exotic* (Document 61, pp. 1-20). Copenhagen: International Work Group for Indigenous Affairs.

Smithsonian. (1984, December). Workshop on museum exhibit production attended by J. A. Costa, Washington, DC.

Urry, J. (1990). *The tourist gaze.* Newbury Park, CA: Sage.

Index

About the Contributors

Gary J. Bamossy is Professor of Marketing at the Vrije Universiteit and Research Fellow at the Tinbergen Institute (both in Amsterdam). His research activities in the area of cross-cultural consumer behavior have focused on the effects that country-of-origin information has on product evaluation and choice; materialism among expatriates and children; ethnicity, cultural identity, and consumption; and methodological issues in crosscultural research. He is coeditor of *European Advances in Consumer Research* and *Advances in Nonprofit Marketing* and is coauthor of *Principles of Marketing: A Global Perspective.*

Kunal Basu is Associate Professor of the Faculty of Management of McGill University in Montreal and is the Director of its Center for International Management Studies. After graduating in mechanical engineering from Jadavpur University in India and completing a master's degree in the United States, he turned to writing and directing a film, acting on the professional stage, and contributing to literary journals. He returned to academia in the early 1980s and received his doctorate from the University of Florida in consumer behavior. He has published articles on information processing, advertising, brand loyalty, and decision making in *Journal of Consumer Research, Journal of Marketing Research, Journal of Consumer Psychology, Journal of the Academy of Marketing Science,* and *Canadian Journal of Administrative Sciences.* During the past 6 years, he has undertaken development projects, research, and teaching in India, the People's Republic of China, Indonesia, Malaysia, Singapore, Thailand, Pakistan, Cuba, and the Maldives. Focusing on the least privileged in these societies, he has been involved in areas such as women and literacy, agricultural cooperatives, indigenous crafts, and the impact of multinationals (particularly in pharmaceuticals and tourism) on domestic economies, organizations, and cultures.

Russell W. Belk is N. Eldon Tanner Professor in the David Eccles School of Business at the University of Utah, where he has taught since 1979. He received his doctorate from the University of Minnesota in 1972 and has held appointments at the University of Illinois, Temple University, the University of British Columbia, and the University of Craiova, Romania, where he spent 1991-1992 on a Fulbright fellowship. He is past president of the Association for Consumer Research (1986); is a fellow in the American Psychological Association, the Association for Consumer Research, and the Society for Consumer Psychology; is past recipient of the University of Utah Distinguished Research Professorship (1986); and has been an advisory editor for the *Journal of Consumer Research* and an associate editor of the *Journal of Economic Psychology, Marketplace Exchange,* and the *Journal of Visual Sociology.* He has edited the series *Advances in Nonprofit Marketing* and currently edits *Research in Consumer Behavior.* He has also served on the editorial review boards of 15 journals, has written or edited 12 books and monographs, and has published over 180 articles, papers, and videotapes. His research primarily involves the meanings of possessions and materialism. He has given presentations and lectures in various countries including Romania, Hungary, Turkey, India, Australia, France, Hong Kong, Singapore, Costa Rica, Canada, Norway, Finland, England, and the Netherlands. He recently coedited *Consumption in Marketizing Economies* and wrote *Collecting in a Consumer Society.*

Dominique Bouchet is Professor of Marketing at Odense University in Denmark, where he moved after studying business economics, sociology, and international economics in Paris. His main research interests lie in social change, cultural differences, and the cultural dimension in marketing. He teaches courses in cross-cultural marketing, cross-cultural communication, social psychology, and cultural analysis in relation to marketing, marketing and social change, and advertising. He has also taught international economics, sociology, and social psychology. He has served as consultant to and has held courses or talks for more than a hundred corporations, human service agencies, governmental bodies, and educational institutions in such areas as cross-cultural communication, international marketing, consumer behavior, semiotic analysis, social change, human resource development, problem solving, and strategic planning. He lectures comfortably in French, Danish, English, and Spanish.

Ayse S. Caglar is Research Associate in the Department of Social Anthropology, University of Manchester. She has degrees in anthropology and sociology from universities in Canada and in Turkey. Her research interests include cultural anthropology, ethnicity, nationalist ideologies (with special emphasis on Turkey), theories of ideology, material and consumer culture, labor migration to Europe, popular cultures of migrants, and popular culture theories. She has published in several books, including *Dominant National Cultures and Ethnic Identities, Changing Food Habits: Case Studies From Africa, Latin American and Europe,* and *Turkish State, Turkish Society,* and in *Sozialanthropologische Arbeitspapiere* and *Zeitschrift fur Türkeistudien.* She has presented numerous papers at conferences in the Netherlands, Germany, the Czech Republic, Turkey, England, and Canada. She speaks Turkish, English, German, and Ottoman and has reading knowledge of French.

Janeen Arnold Costa is Associate Professor of Marketing at the David Eccles School of Business and Adjunct Associate Professor of Anthropology, University of Utah. She received her doctorate in cultural anthropology from Stanford University in 1983 and undertook a postdoctoral position in marketing at the University of Utah in 1987. Her research focuses on social and cultural dimensions of consumer behavior and marketing, including assessment of the role and influence of culture, gender, class, ethnicity, and cross-cultural marketing, particularly in the context of tourism. She has chaired and edited the proceedings of two conferences on gender and consumer behavior in 1991 and 1993. She edited *Gender Issues and Consumer Behavior* (Sage, 1994) and coedited *Research in Consumer Behavior* (Volume 6). Her research has been published in *Journal of Marketing, Journal of Macromarketing, Contemporary Marketing and Consumer Behavior, Advances in Consumer Research, Research in Consumer Behavior, Advances in Nonprofit Marketing, Anthropological Quarterly, Cultural Change and the New Europe, Journal of*

Modern Greek Studies, and numerous other books and conference proceedings.

A. Fuat Fırat is Professor of Marketing at Arizona State University West. He received his degree in economics (Licencié en Economie) from the Faculty of Economics, Istanbul University, in 1970 and his doctorate in marketing from Northwestern University in 1978. He has held academic positions at Istanbul University, University of Texas at Dallas, University of Maryland, McGill University (Montreal), and Appalachian State University (North Carolina). His research interests cover areas such as macro consumer behavior and macromarketing; postmodern culture, marketing, and the consumer; feminist studies in consumer research; marketing and development; and interorganizational relations. His work has been published in a number of journals, including *International Journal of Research in Marketing, Journal of Macromarketing, Journal of Marketing, Journal of Organizational Change Management,* and *Journal of Economic Psychology,* as well as in several edited books, including *Gender Issues and Consumer Behavior* (Sage, 1994). His article "Consumption Choices at the Macro Level" with coauthor Nikhilesh Dholakia won the *Journal of Macromarketing* Charles Slater award. He has coedited two books, *Philosophical and Radical Thought in Marketing* and *Marketing and Development: Toward Broader Dimensions.* He is also the coeditor of two special issues of the International Journal of Research in Marketing on postmodernism, marketing, and the consumer. He is now chief editor of the new journal *Consumption, Markets and Culture: A Journal of Critical Perspectives.*

Michael Hui is Associate Professor in the Department of Marketing at Concordia University in Montreal. He has degrees in business from Hong Kong, France, and the United Kingdom. His main research interests involve ethnic consumption and the marketing of services. His publications include articles in the *Journal of Consumer Research, Journal of International Consumer Marketing, Long Range Planning,* and the proceedings of the American Marketing Association, the Association of Consumer Research, and Administrative Sciences of Canada.

Annamma Joy is Associate Professor in the Department of Marketing at Concordia University in Montreal. She has degrees in anthropology and business from universities in India and Canada. Her research interests include topics such as culture and consumption, marketing of the arts, ethnicity and marketing, and marketing and development. In addition to authoring a book, *Ethnicity in Canada,* she has published a number of chapters in edited volumes and has presented papers at various marketing conferences. Recently, her articles have appeared in the *Journal of Macromarketing, Journal of Social Behavior and Personality, International Journal of Research in Marketing, Advances in Non-Profit Marketing, Research in Consumer Behavior, Canadian Journal of Administrative Sciences,* and the proceedings of the Association of Consumer Research. She is also the recipient of the Charles Slater Memorial Award given by the *Journal of Macromarketing* in 1991.

Chankon Kim is Associate Professor in the Department of Marketing at Concordia University in Montreal. He has degrees in business from Canada and the United States. His interests are mainly in the areas of family decision making, consumer information acquisition and processing, and cultural influences on marketing dimensions. He has published articles in academic journals including *Canadian Journal of Administrative Sciences, Journal of Economic Psychology, Journal of the Academy of Marketing Science, Journal of Global Marketing,* and *Journal of International Consumer Marketing.* His papers have also appeared in proceedings of various marketing conferences.

Michel Laroche is Professor in the Department of Marketing at Concordia University in Montreal. He has degrees in business from the United States and France. His main research interests are communication, consumer behavior modeling, and research methodology. He is the coauthor of several textbooks on consumer behavior and marketing in Canada. His articles have been published in the *Journal of Consumer Research, Behavioral Science, Canadian Journal of Administrative Sciences, International Journal of Research in Marketing, Journal of Public Policy and Marketing, International Journal of Advertising, International Journal of Bank Marketing, Journal of Psychology, Marketing Intelligence and Planning,* and *Journal of Pharmaceutical Marketing and Management.*

Magda Paun is a faculty member and graduate student in the Department of Management in the Faculty of Economics at the University of Craiova in Romania. Her primary area of specialization is production and operations management. During the 1992-1993 year she was an Alexander Hamilton fellow at the University of Missouri, Kansas City. Prior to her academic appointment at the University of Craiova, she was an economist at Electroputure electrical and locomotive factory in Romania.

Eugeen Roosens is Professor and Head of the Department of Anthropology at the Catholic University of Leuven, Belgium, and Extraordinary Professor at the Université Catholique de Louvain, Louvain-la-Neuve. He was appointed P. P. Rubens Professor for the academic year 1989-1990 at the University of California at Berkeley and has been repeatedly a visiting professor at this institution. He has done extensive fieldwork among the Yaka (Zaire) and in the Huron Nation of Quebec, as well as in Geel, Belgium. Since 1974 he has directed "The Cultural Identity of Ethnic Minorities," a long-term fieldwork project by a team of scholars that operates in several countries. His books include *Creating Ethnicity: The Process of Ethnogenesis* (Sage, 1989) and *Mental Patients in Town Life: Geel—Europe's First Therapeutic Community* (Sage, 1979), a book published in five languages including Japanese.

Alladi Venkatesh is Professor in the Graduate School of Management at the University of California at Irvine. His research interests include gender issues in marketing, the diffusion of information technologies to households, work at home with computers, and cross-cultural and postmodern developments in marketing. His doctoral dissertation at Syracuse University was selected as part of the Landmark Dissertation Series in Women's Studies and was published in 1985. His publications on gender issues and work at home have appeared in journals and books, including *Journal of Consumer Research, Advances in Consumer Research, Journal of Advertising Research, Gender Issues and Consumer Behavior* (Sage, 1994), and *Management Science*. He recently spent 6 months each in India and Denmark studying cross-cultural aspects of consumption and the impact of new technologies on households and consumers. He is an editor of the new journal *Consumption, Markets and Culture: A Journal of Critical Perspectives*.

Thomas M. Wilson is Senior Research Fellow at The Queen's University of Belfast's Institute of European Studies. He is the coeditor of *Border Approaches: Anthropological Perspectives on Frontiers* (1994), *Irish Urban Cultures* (1993), *Cultural Change and the New Europe: Perspectives on the European Community* (1993), and *Ireland From Below: Social Change and Local Communities* (1989). He is also the editor of the State University of New York Press's series on national identities. His current research focuses on border cultures and transfrontier economic cooperation in the European Union.